The La Varenne
COOKING COURSE

Books by Anne Willan

Entertaining
Great Cooks and Their Recipes

BOOKS BY ANNE WILLAN & L'ÉCOLE
DE CUISINE LA VARENNE

La Varenne's Paris Kitchen
French Regional Cooking
The La Varenne Cooking Course

ANNE WILLAN

and l'École de Cuisine La Varenne

The La Varenne
COOKING COURSE

with photographs by JAMES SCHERER and VICTOR WATTS

Edited by Judith Hill

William Morrow and Company, Inc.
New York   1982

*To Jane Grigson, with whom it all began,
to my colleagues, family and friends
whose advice I have so freely borrowed and whose tastes
I have so candidly exposed to public view,
my warmest regards and thanks*

ACKNOWLEDGMENTS

At La Varenne: Research and recipe drafting by Faye Levy;
editorial assistance by Jane Sigal

At *The Observer:* Joy Langridge

At William Morrow: Narcisse Chamberlain

BOOK DESIGN BY SALLIE BALDWIN, ANTLER & BALDWIN, INC.

Library of Congress Cataloging in Publication Data

Willan, Anne.
    The La Varenne cooking course.

    Includes index.
      1. Cookery, French. 2. École de cuisine La Varenne. I. Hill, Judith. II. École de cuisine La Varenne. III. Title.

TX719.W569 1982   641.5944   82-3473
ISBN 0-688-00539-X   AACR2

Printed in the United States of America
First U.S. Edition
1 2 3 4 5 6 7 8 9 10

Contents

THE FRENCH TOUCH

The special French way with foods common to all nations

Introduction

THIS BOOK REFLECTS my own personal experience of French cooking as we teach it at the École de Cuisine La Varenne in Paris. It is a thorough course that can take you from beginner's level to real proficiency, right in your own kitchen. The chefs who teach at La Varenne appreciate that many of their students are just starting out, and they willingly teach the simplest of basics. But that is not to say that they ever relax their standards! You will gain an insight into the way French chefs think about cooking—the importance they place on freshness of ingredients and on technique, their love of color and presentation. You'll work with La Varenne's recipes for cuisine and for pastry and acquire some of the skills that, combined with imagination, have for three hundred years made French cooking the liveliest in the world.

The lessons in this course—there are thirty-five in all—are not progressive in the sense that Lesson 1 is the easiest and Lesson 35 is the hardest. Instead they are grouped by subject with something in each for beginners and for more experienced cooks alike. The challenge comes in combining more and more basic techniques, using them as building blocks. A simple recipe like *sauté de veau à la normande* requires only a knowledge of how to sauté meat and reduce a sauce, whereas a dish such as *profiteroles d'oeufs pochés à la purée de haricots verts* uses four subsidiary preparations: poached eggs, choux pastry, vegetable purée, and tomato sauce. So when you are using this book, look for the shorter, easy recipes in a chapter and then move on to the more complex dishes that require more skill.

At La Varenne we follow exactly the same plan. Students start by learning a few techniques, then more and more are combined in complicated dishes as proficiency develops. The students cluster around the chef and watch everything he does. They work hard and do as they are told, but they are quick to ask questions as well. "Why are the scallops so sweet today?" "Why are artichokes sometimes bitter?" "Is a copper pan really necessary to make a good hollandaise?" "Should a soufflé be cooked in a moderate oven or a very hot one?" "What are the merits of steamed as against boiled vegetables?" At the lunch or dinner that follows the class, we all taste, criticize, praise, and talk about food at length, seriously, as the French themselves do.

We gave the name "La Varenne" to our school in honor of the writer of the first modern French cookbook. In 1651, the Sieur de la Varenne, master cook to the Marquis d'Uxelles, published *Le Cuisinier François*. It began, as French cookbooks still do, with a recipe for basic stock and included a bouquet garni and a white sauce. Our contemporary curriculum is based on classical principles, but we've also tackled regional cooking and *nouvelle cuisine*, *charcuterie*, and chocolate work, not to mention some recipes of the original La Varenne himself.

Since it opened in 1975, the La Varenne cooking school has welcomed students from twenty-three different countries. Chef Fernand Chambrette, the school's director of cuisine, has brought back more than nine tons of butter and five hundred crates of carrots from the market at Rungis; *pâtissier* Albert Jorant has taught puff pastry to more than five thousand students; and chef Claude Vauguet has demonstrated *galantine de poulet* in Venice and *beignets de Camembert* in San Francisco, all in a day's work.

The chefs' expertise and patience have been indispensable to the development of this book. And as you will see, their individual characters have influenced much of my own thinking about food: crusty Chef Chambrette, who loves hearty country dishes, especially the simple stews and braises, but who is also famed for the delicacy of his fine fish dishes; Chef Jorant, the pastry magician—given the simplest of ingredients, he can make anything from the common ladyfinger to a castle of meringue and do both with panache and in record time; and Chef Claude, the youngest of the trio, who combines amazing dexterity and an eye for presentation with an easy humor that seems to need no translation.

We all agree that without the right equipment and the right ingredients it is impossible to cook well. But this book will show that "right" is a flexible term. One of the first things La Varenne students learn is how to improvise with what they have—where corners can be cut (and where they can't). Our recipes describe both hand and mechanized methods, since at the school we use both. Time and labor can be cut, and ingredients can be substituted, too. French chefs are masters at making the most of what they have at hand. Chef Chambrette often exchanges one fish for another, and Chef Claude uses only the vegetables that are in season. The difference between North American and French ingredients, mainly in flour, cream, fish, and cuts of meat, need not stand in your way because in this book all the adjustments have already been made.

Most important of all, THE LA VARENNE COOKING COURSE will give you confidence. We want you to understand methods and techniques and why they work in a particular way. We want to develop basic skills, so that you come to regard recipes not just as blueprints to be followed to the letter but also as sketches, exercises from which you can learn and then go on to create your own personal style.

Huge numbers of books have been written in French about the cooking of France. The following are those we used most often when researching this book.

Ali-Bab. *Gastronomie Pratique.* Paris: 1928. Reprinted 1955. Abridged translation by Elizabeth Benson under title *Encyclopedia of Practical Gastronomy.*

L'Art Culinaire Français. Paris: 1948. Several reprints with translation into English as *The Art of French Cooking.*

Delplanque, A. & S. Cloteaux. *Les Bases de la Charcuterie.* Paris: Editions J. Lanore, no date (c. 1977).

Dictionnaire de l'Académie des Gastronomes, 2 volumes. Paris: Editions Prisma, 1962.

Escoffier, Auguste. *Le Guide Culinaire.* Paris: 1902. Several reprints with translations into English under the title *A Guide to Modern Cookery* and *The Complete Guide to the Art of Modern Cookery.*

———. *Ma Cuisine.* Paris: 1934. Several reprints with translation into English under same title.

Gringoire, Th. & L. Saulnier. *Le Répertoire de la Cuisine.* London: 1914. Several reprints and translations under same title.

Montagné, Prosper. *Larousse Gastronomique.* Paris: 1938. Several reprints (reissued under title *Nouveau Larousse Gastronomique* with translations under title *New Larousse Gastronomique*).

Pellaprat, Henri-Paul. *L'Art Culinaire Moderne.* Paris: 1935. Several reprints, with translations into English under title *Modern French Culinary Art.*

Saint-Ange, Madame. *Le Livre de Cuisine de Madame Saint-Ange.* Paris: 1927. Reprint by Editions Chaix, Grenoble.

Sylvestre, J. & J. Planche. *Les Bases de la Cuisine.* Paris: Jacques Lanore, 1969. Several reprints with translation into English available from same publisher under title *Fundamentals of French Cookery.*

THE BASICS

Throughout this book are basic recipes, each flagged by an ornament above its name. These recipes are the "building blocks" of French cuisine, the essential components from which many recipes are constructed. They appear in the chapters where they are most relevant but are referred to in other chapters as well.

References appear in the lists of ingredients of individual recipes and include the page where you can find the basic recipe *and* the measurements of the ingredients needed for the particular dish. When you turn to the basic recipe, often you will find the ingredients and proportions are the same, but *not* always; in the recipe you are using, the ingredients of the basic recipe may have been adjusted for the special purposes of that dish. For example, a flavoring may be changed, a certain stock may be specified for a sauce, an extra egg yolk may enrich a custard. The *method* of preparation will always be the same.

An important characteristic of the way professionals cook in France made me decide to emphasize the "building blocks" in La Varenne recipes, both of those we use at the school and those that appear in our books: the methods described in basic recipes are second nature to a chef, and he combines the basics in endless ways to prepare classic recipes and to create new ones. Learn the fundamental procedures for these elements that occur over and over again in French cooking, and you will have a thousand dishes at your fingertips.

TECHNIQUES

Sautéing

SAUTER IS one of those tantalizing words that are untranslatable. When faced with the incongruities of "leap the beef" or "jumped potatoes," translators have given up looking for an equivalent, and *sauté* has entered our vocabulary intact. Appropriately so, for sautéing is a very French process, calling for just the right amount of fat, a brisk but even heat in the pan, and the cook's total concentration. The resulting food, whether meat, fish, poultry, or vegetables, should be golden brown and lightly crisp. Sautéed food is never drained on paper towels but should be moist from the cooking fat.

The dish called a sauté is an extension of this method of cooking. A sauté is a kind of quick stew, for which the main ingredient is first sautéed in fat until partly done and then cooked briefly with a bit of wine, stock, cream, tomatoes, water, or a combination of them. Sautés differ from stews not only in their short cooking time but also in that a small quantity of liquid is used. The food steams rather than simmers in the sauce, and this calls for careful handling. Not until the invention (about two hundred years ago) of the closed range with a flat, evenly heated top could the speed of cooking be controlled sufficiently to cook gently in scanty liquid and to produce the essence of juices appropriate to a sauté, rather than the bath of liquid associated with a stew. "Don't drown it in sauce!" is one of the perennial cries of the chefs at La Varenne.

Because of their fast cooking, sautés demand more luxurious ingredients than stews. Small chickens of about 3 pounds (1.5 kg) are ideal, as are duck, rabbit, and pheasant (provided they are young and tender), firm fish like eel or monkfish, and meats such as veal scallops, chops, and kidneys, and the better cuts of pork. Only the expensive cuts of lamb and beef can be used. Most cuts take too long to cook to be suitable for a true sauté.

SAUTÉ DE POULET À L'INDIENNE
Chicken sauté, lightly flavored with curry powder, ginger, and saffron and served with boiled rice

Whatever the meat, it must be cut into medium, even-sized pieces that will cook together at the same speed. Chicken for a sauté is divided in a special way that yields equal pieces (see p. 16). Then the chicken or meat is sautéed in clarified butter, or in butter mixed with oil to raise the scorching point (plain butter burns at too low a temperature). Dark meats should be thoroughly browned, whereas chicken and the lighter meats are usually cooked to a golden hue.

Once the meat for a sauté has been browned, liquid is added. Then comes the garnish. A sauté is one of those splendid dishes in which anything goes. Sometimes the garnish is cooked together with the meat; more often it is sautéed separately and added toward the end of cooking so that the flavors have just time to blend. The choice is almost infinite. The chefs' eyes light up when there is a sauté on the menu because they can use up the leftover bits of this and that from the refrigerator: an onion or two, a few mushrooms, the odd tomato, a sliced zucchini, some diced bacon—even shrimps can be added to the pan.

Of course, there are classic combinations like sauté of chicken chasseur, with mushrooms and shallots in a white wine tomato sauce, or veal chops paysanne, with bacon, baby onions, and diced potatoes. One of my own favorites is a newer dish, a sauté of baby chickens set off with the strong flavors of ginger, onion, and escarole. The sauce for this is simply the unthickened pan juices, but traditional sautés include thickening by sprinkling the meat with flour before browning, or adding kneaded butter (beurre manié) or arrowroot at the end of cooking. The aim is always the same—a light, highly concentrated sauce.

By varying the meat, cooking liquid, or garnish, you can invent an almost infinite number of sauté dishes of your own. The culinary Bible, Escoffier's *Guide Culinaire*, lists sixty-five variations on chicken sauté alone, and these can be applied to other meats. For example, cut the shrimps from sauté de poulet à l'Indienne (p. 19) and substitute veal scallops for the chicken; rabbit would take beautifully to the treatment outlined in the recipe for sauté de poulet à la Castillane (p. 18); and duck, after a thorough sautéing to render its fat, could be used in the sauté de poussins sur son coulis d'oignons et de scarole (p. 18).

Perhaps the most famous chicken sauté of all is à la Marengo, an implausible combination of chicken with tomatoes and mushrooms, garnished with croûtons and fried eggs and embellished with crayfish displayed in their shells "en bellevue." The dish was supposedly thought up by Napoleon's chef on the battlefield of Marengo, using ingredients at hand, but its studied virtuosity smacks to me of a Parisian kitchen. So indeed does that of all sautés. Quick, amusing, versatile, a sauté gives a touch of urban finesse to comfortable country ingredients.

FOR SUCCESSFUL SAUTÉING

1. Choose a pan of the right size so that the meat just fills the pan and each piece touches the bottom.

2. Cook in very hot fat so the surface of the meat is "seized" and forms a crust that retains the juices inside the meat.

3. Use just enough fat so that it circulates freely *under* the food; too much fat will give the effect of deep frying.

4. Discard excess fat (particularly with fatty meats like duck) before adding liquid to the pan.

5. Traditionally, cooking is finished on top of the stove, but less attention is needed if a sauté is put in the steady heat of a moderate oven, 350°F (175°C). However, be sure the handle of your sauté pan will withstand the heat.

6. If a sauté starts to dry out before the meat is cooked, add a little more liquid and cover the pan. If, on the other hand, the meat is cooked before the sauce is properly reduced, transfer the meat to a dish to keep warm and boil the sauce down to the right consistency.

 PREPARING AHEAD

1. Sautés can be made ahead and reheated, though some of their fresh flavor will be lost. Undercook both the meat and garnish slightly.

2. If freezing a sauté, increase the quantity of sauce so that the meat is covered when packed for freezing.

 CUTTING UP POULTRY FOR A SAUTÉ

1. Probing with a sharp knife, find the two pockets of meat, the "oysters," that are in the center of the back, outline them with a semi-circular cut, and scoop them out scraping against the bone with the knife, but don't detach.

2. Slice down between the leg and the body at the leg joint, break the joint by twisting the leg, and cut it from the body, scraping along the bones on the underside to get all the meat including the previously outlined "oysters."

3. Remove the second leg in the same way.

4. On the inside of each leg is a white line of fat. Position the knife on this and cut down to sever each leg in half at the joint.

5. Remove the wing by cutting across the breast down through the wing joint so a small piece of breast is included.

6. Remove the second wing in the same way.

7. Cut off the backbone and ribs with poultry shears or scissors.

8. Finally, sever the breast in half lengthwise.

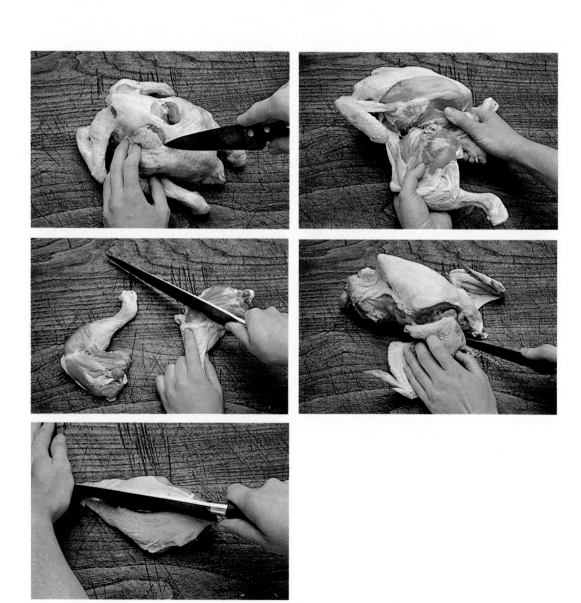

Baby Chicken Sauté with Onion and Escarole
(SAUTÉ DE POUSSINS SUR SON COULIS D'OIGNONS ET DE SCAROLE)

The nouvelle cuisine way with a sauté is to combine unlikely ingredients to achieve a surprisingly delicious effect.

> **four ¾ pound (350 g) baby chickens or 4 Cornish hens**
> **salt and pepper**
> **⅛ teaspoon ground ginger**
> **1 tablespoon oil**
> **3 tablespoons (45 g) butter**
> **4 medium onions, thinly sliced**
> **2 heads escarole**

SERVES 4.

With kitchen scissors remove the backbones from the chickens. Split each bird in two at the breastbone and flatten the halves with the side of a cleaver. Season the chicken with salt, pepper, and ginger.

Heat the oil in a sauté pan over high heat and add the butter. Sauté the chicken until brown, 5–6 minutes. (NOTE: Sauté in 2 batches, or 2 pans, and use more oil and butter if necessary.) Remove the chicken, replace with the onions, and season them with salt and pepper. Reduce the heat and cook slowly, stirring occasionally, until soft but not brown, 7–10 minutes.

Trim the stems of the escarole. Wash the greens and drain well. Cut each head in 4 lengthwise. Add the pieces to the pan, cover, and cook with the onions until softened, about 5 minutes. Return the chicken to the pan, cover, and cook until tender, 20–25 minutes.

Arrange the onions and greens on a platter or on individual plates, top with the chicken, and spoon the pan juices over the meat.

Chicken Sauté à la Castillane
(SAUTÉ DE POULET À LA CASTILLANE)

Two hundred years ago, when this recipe was created, Spanish hams were famous throughout France—hence the title "castillane."

> **1½ tablespoons (20 g) butter**
> **½ pound (250 g) raw lightly smoked ham, cut in small dice**
> **salt and pepper**
> **2½–3 pound (1.25–1.5 kg) chicken, cut in 8 pieces**

2 onions, thinly sliced
½ pound (250 g) mushrooms
½ clove garlic, crushed
1 bouquet garni (p. 118)
3 medium (about 1 pound or 500 g) tomatoes, peeled,
  quartered, and seeded
½ cup (125 ml) chicken stock (p. 115)
1 teaspoon arrowroot, mixed to a paste with 1
  tablespoon of the stock

SERVES 4.

In a sauté pan melt the butter and sauté the ham over medium heat until lightly browned. Season the pieces of chicken and add to the pan, cut side down, starting with the dark meat because it takes longer to cook. When it begins to brown, add the two wing pieces and finally the breast. When all are brown, turn them over and brown on the other side for 2 minutes. Remove the chicken pieces from the pan.

Add the onions, mushrooms, garlic, and bouquet garni to the pan and cook slowly until the onions are soft, 7–10 minutes. Add the tomatoes, return the chicken to the pan, and add the stock. Simmer, covered, until the chicken is tender, 20–25 minutes.

Arrange the chicken and mushrooms on a platter or on individual plates. Whisk the arrowroot into the cooking juices and cook a few moments until the sauce thickens. Taste for seasoning, adjust if necessary, and pour the sauce over the chicken.

Chicken Sauté à l'Indienne
(SAUTÉ DE POULET À L'INDIENNE)

This is not a hot Indian curry at all but rather a chicken sauté lightly flavored with Indian spices.

1½ tablespoons oil
1½ tablespoons (20 g) butter
salt and pepper
2½–3 pound (1.25–1.5 kg) chicken, cut in 8 pieces
1 onion, thinly sliced
1 clove garlic, crushed
1 tablespoon flour
1 teaspoon curry powder, or to taste
¼ teaspoon ground ginger
pinch of cayenne pepper

1 cup (250 ml) chicken stock (p. 115)
pinch of saffron, dissolved in ¼ cup (60 ml) of the
    stock
½ pound (250 g) cooked peeled shrimps

SERVES 4.

In a sauté pan heat the oil over medium heat and add the butter. Season the pieces of chicken and add to the hot fat, cut side down, starting with the dark meat because it takes longer to cook. When it begins to brown, add the two wing pieces and finally the breast. When all are brown, turn them over and brown on the other side for 2 minutes. Remove the chicken pieces from the pan.

In the fat remaining in the pan cook the onion slowly until soft but not brown, 7–10 minutes. Add the garlic, flour, curry powder, ginger, and cayenne and cook gently, stirring, for 2 minutes.

Return the chicken pieces to the pan. Add the stock and saffron, cover, and simmer until the chicken is tender, 20–25 minutes. About 5 minutes before the end of cooking, add the shrimps, stirring to coat them with sauce.

Arrange the chicken and shrimps on a platter or on individual plates. Reduce the sauce, if necessary, to 5–6 tablespoons, taste, and add seasoning if needed. The sauce should be piquant but not overpowering. Spoon it over the chicken.

Plain boiled rice, chutney, and grated fresh coconut make good accompaniments.

Veal Sauté à la Normande
(SAUTÉ DE VEAU À LA NORMANDE)

The combination of Calvados and cream mark this dish as coming from Normandy—the land of apples and rich dairy products.

4 veal chops, 1 inch (2.5 cm) thick
¼ cup (30 g) flour, seasoned with ¼ teaspoon salt and
    ⅛ teaspoon pepper
1 tablespoon oil
1 tablespoon (15 g) butter
2 tablespoons Calvados or applejack
¾ cup (185 ml) white veal or chicken stock (p. 115)
½ cup (125 ml) heavy cream
salt and pepper
1 tablespoon chopped parsley

SERVES 4.

Coat the chops lightly with the seasoned flour. In a sauté pan heat the oil over medium heat and add the butter. Sauté the chops until browned, 2–3 minutes on each side. Off the heat, pour the Calvados over the still warm chops and flame.

Add the stock, cover, and simmer until chops are tender, about 15 minutes. Remove chops and arrange on a platter or on individual plates.

Add the cream and reduce by boiling, if necessary, until the sauce is thick enough to coat a spoon. Taste for seasoning and add salt and pepper if needed. Pour the sauce over the chops, sprinkle with parsley, and serve.

Kidney Sauté with Madeira
(SAUTÉ DE ROGNONS AU MADÈRE)

Crisp fried potatoes are the perfect complement for these.

**3–4 veal kidneys OR 4–6 lamb kidneys, weighing about
   1½ pounds (750 g)
1 tablespoon oil
3 tablespoons (45 g) butter
2 tablespoons (15 g) flour
3 tablespoons Madeira
⅔ cup (160 ml) brown veal stock (p. 117)
1 tablespoon chopped parsley**

SERVES 4.

Skin the kidneys, if necessary, and cut out the cores with kitchen scissors. Cut veal kidneys in thick slices or halve lamb kidneys.

Heat the oil in a sauté pan over medium-high heat and add 1 tablespoon (15 g) of the butter. When the butter foams, put in the kidneys and cook quickly, turning them, until brown on all sides, 2–3 minutes.

Sprinkle the kidneys with the flour and toss to coat. Pour the Madeira over them and flame. Add the stock and bring to a boil, stirring. Simmer until the kidneys are cooked but still pink in the center, 4–5 minutes.

Off the heat, add the remaining 2 tablespoons (30 g) butter in small pieces, shaking the pan so the butter is incorporated. Taste the sauce for seasoning and adjust if necessary.

Transfer the kidneys to a serving platter or to individual plates, pour the sauce over them, sprinkle with parsley, and serve.

DINDE FARCIE AUX MARRONS
The turkey is stuffed with a rich "farce" of ground pork and is garnished with Brussels sprouts and braised chestnuts.

Roasting

ROASTING IS ONE of the first and most basic skills to be learned by an apprentice cook. Nothing appears simpler than to roast a piece of meat, topped with fat and seasoning, either in an oven or on the traditional spit before the fire. But mistakes cannot be camouflaged, and like so many simple processes, roasting can be a false friend.

Of prime importance is the meat, which must be the best both in quality and cut. If in doubt, it is much wiser to braise with liquid than to expose an indifferent piece of meat to the dry, searing heat of true roasting.

Should the meat be boned? Here the chefs at La Varenne and I diverge. I like the bones left *in situ* so the meat juices are retained and there is less shrinkage. The French have a different aim: they like tidy pieces of meat that will cook evenly and slice well and that can be arranged attractively on a platter.

Boning may have gone to the heads of the French cooks, but in trussing and tying meat for roasting, they are unrivaled. First the French trim meat thoroughly, removing sinews and cartilage and cutting away all but a thin layer of outside fat. If the meat has no natural fat, it is often rolled in a sheet of barding fat (thinly sliced pork fat). Sometimes herbs and other seasonings are added, and the meat may be larded (threaded with strips of fat). Pretentious butchers also go in for larding with truffles, pistachios, and other conceits, but there I think they gild the lily—and the bill. Even a layer of barding fat is shunned by some cooks, who claim that it prevents the meat from being sealed by the heat.

Whether boned, tied and barded, or au naturel, the meat or bird is impaled on a spit or set in a roasting pan. The pan must fit the meat—if it is too large, the meat juices will burn on the bottom of the pan during cooking; if too small or too deep, the meat tends to steam.

To improve the flavor of the sauce, you can add a sliced carrot and onion to the pan plus any bones removed from the meat. For both spit and oven roasting, the surface of the meat should be spread with butter, if there's no barding fat, and sprinkled with salt and pepper.

In a modern kitchen, roasting is almost invariably done in the oven. There are purists who insist that the term is inappropriate and that true roasting can only be done on a spit before an open fire. Certainly the effect of oven roasting is not quite the same. But fun though it is, spit roasting often disappoints since heat control is such a problem. It has become an anachronism, nearly as outmoded as the rôtisseur who once roamed city streets with his own spit (turned by a human or sometimes dog-powered treadmill), ready to cook any meat brought to him from the surrounding houses.

There are various theories about what temperature to use for roasting, but I don't think you can beat the French principle of starting at a high heat to sear the meat and then lowering the temperature to finish cooking. An approximate cooking time can be calculated from the type of meat and its weight, but this is a rough guide at best. A chef tests, it always seems to me, by guess and by God. He scrutinizes the meat, pokes it with a finger (the firmer the meat, the more done), and pronounces judgment. A much safer test is to take the inner temperature of the meat. Failing a meat thermometer, a skewer makes a primitive alternative and is, in fact, what a French chef uses when he doesn't quite trust his finger. Insert a skewer into the center of the meat, leave it thirty seconds, and then touch the back of your hand with it. If the skewer is cold, the meat is not done, and if the skewer is warm, the meat is rare. If quite hot, it is pink, and if scalding, the meat is well done.

Last but by no means least comes the sauce, and here I'm united with the French in preferring no thickening and a minimum of additions—the flavor of the meat itself should suffice. The sauce can be made while the meat is "resting," for all roasts should wait for ten to fifteen minutes before being carved so the juices, which retreat to the center during roasting, will redistribute themselves again. One of the more effective demonstrations I've seen at La Varenne was performed by Chef Claude Vauguet. He roasted two pieces of beef to the rare stage, sliced one immediately, and left the other to sit before cutting. The first had an eye of deep pink, but the second was uniformly rosy with only a narrow rim of browned meat.

It was the gastronome Brillat-Savarin who observed *"On devient cuisinier, mais on naît rôtisseur"*—a cook can be made, but a roasting chef is born. In these days of thermostats and meat thermometers, this may seem an exaggeration, but roasting still calls for experience, close attention, and a touch of intuition.

FOR SUCCESSFUL ROASTING

1. Meat for roasting should be at room temperature so the heat will penetrate evenly.

2. Preheat an oven or spit for at least twenty minutes. If cooking is started at too low a heat, the roast is not seared but tends to soften and stew.

3. To prevent stewing in the fat and juices at the bottom of the pan, lift meat or poultry on a rack, or set it on any bones and vegetables that have been added to improve the sauce.

PREPARING AHEAD

1. Meat and poultry can be stuffed up to six hours ahead and kept in the refrigerator, providing the stuffing was completely cold before it was added. Meat stuffings taint a roast more quickly than stuffings made with rice or bread.

2. Except for the brief resting period of ten to fifteen minutes before carving, roast meats should not wait. Rare meats such as lamb and beef are particularly hard to keep hot as they overcook easily; however, pork, chicken, and other meats that are eaten well done can be kept warm for a short time without harm.

3. Leftover roast meat can be stored covered in a cool place (below 60°F or 15°C) for two days; it tends to lose flavor if refrigerated, and it dries out if frozen.

4. Leftover roast meat or poultry is best served at room temperature, perhaps with a piquant mayonnaise or marinated in a vinaigrette seasoned with shallots and capers.

5. Leftover light meats, such as chicken, veal, and pork, can be reheated, particularly in a sauce. Roast red meats do not reheat so well; they must be warmed gently, not boiled, or they will toughen. One suggestion is to cut them in very thin slices, and then to pour over the slices a very hot sauce, perhaps sauce italienne or sauce diable. (NOTE: Never reheat meats then keep them warm. Under these conditions, bacteria develop rapidly.)

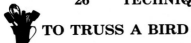

TO TRUSS A BIRD

Trussing not only keeps in any stuffing, it also holds the bird together so a sprawling leg or wing doesn't overcook and the finished roast sits neatly for carving.

1. Set the bird breast up and push the legs well back and down so the ends are sticking straight up into the air. Stick the needle into one leg joint, push it through the bird, and out the other leg joint.

2. Turn the bird over onto its breast and push the needle through both sections of one wing and then into the neck skin, under the backbone of the bird, and out the other side. Now catch the second wing in the same way as the first.

3. Pull the ends of string from the leg and wing firmly together and tie securely.

4. Re-thread the trussing needle and turn the bird breast side up. Tuck the tail into the cavity of the bird.

5. Insert the needle into the end of the drumstick, make a stitch through the skin, which should be overlapped to cover the cavity, and then put the needle through the end of the other drumstick.

6. Turn the bird over and push the needle through the tail.

7. Tie the string ends together.

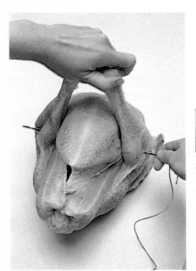

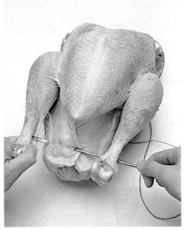
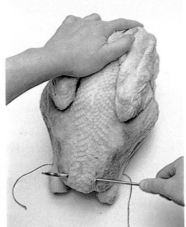

Stuffed Turkey with Chestnuts and Brussels Sprouts
(DINDE FARCIE AUX MARRONS ET AUX CHOUX DE BRUXELLES)

Meat-stuffed turkey with a hearty wintertime garnish of chestnuts and Brussels sprouts makes the perfect centerpiece for a Christmas meal.

6–8 pound (2.75–3.75 kg) turkey
7 tablespoons (110 g) butter
salt and pepper
1½–2 cups (375–500 ml) chicken stock (p. 115)
½ cup (125 ml) white wine
3 pounds (1.5 kg) chestnuts, braised (p. 44) with 2
  tablespoons oil, 2 onions, 2 stalks celery, 4–5 cups
  (500–625 ml) veal, chicken, or turkey stock, salt and
  pepper, and ½ teaspoon allspice
2 pounds (1 kg) Brussels sprouts

For the stuffing:
2 tablespoons (30 g) butter
1 medium onion, finely chopped
1½ pounds (750 g) ground pork
1 turkey liver, chopped
1½ cups (210 g) fresh bread crumbs
2 tablespoons brandy
¼ teaspoon allspice
salt and pepper

trussing needle and string

SERVES 6–8.

For the stuffing: Melt the 2 tablespoons (30 g) butter in a small pan and sauté the onion in it until softened. Combine the onion with the pork, liver, bread crumbs, brandy, and seasonings, beating well with a wooden spoon or your hand to distribute the seasoning. Sauté a small piece, taste for seasoning, and add more if needed.

Fill the turkey with the stuffing and truss. Set the oven at 375°F (190°C). Rub the bird with 4 tablespoons (60 g) of the butter, sprinkle it with salt and pepper, and set it on one side on a rack in a roasting pan. Pour in ½ cup (125 ml) stock, cover the turkey loosely with foil, and roast in the heated oven until the thigh is tender when pierced with a skewer, 2½–3 hours. Turn the turkey from one side to another and then on its back during cooking and baste it often. If the pan gets dry, add more stock. Remove the foil during the last half hour of cooking so the skin browns.

Braise the chestnuts. Trim the Brussels sprouts and cook in boiling salted water until just tender, about 10 minutes. Toss with the remaining butter.

Transfer the turkey to a carving board. Add ½ cup (125 ml) stock and the wine to the roasting pan and deglaze, boiling to reduce well. Taste for seasoning, adjust if necessary, and strain.

Remove the trussing strings from the turkey, surround with the vegetables, and serve. For ease of serving, you can, if you prefer, carve the bird in the kitchen and arrange on a platter with the stuffing, chestnuts, and Brussels sprouts.

Roast Veal Cordon Bleu
(RÔTI DE VEAU CORDON BLEU)

A perfect do-ahead roast, this needs only half an hour in the oven just before serving.

**3½–4 pound (1.75 kg) boneless veal roast, barded and
    tied
salt and pepper
1 onion, sliced
1 carrot, sliced
1 cup (250 ml) white wine
1½ cups (375 ml) white veal (p. 116) or chicken stock
    (p. 115)
mornay sauce (p. 193) made with 2 cups (500 ml)
    medium béchamel sauce, 2 teaspoons Dijon
    mustard, and 2 ounces or about ½ cup (60 g) grated
    cheese
6–8 slices cooked ham
1 ounce or about ¼ cup (30 g) grated Gruyère or
    Parmesan cheese**

SERVES 6–8.

Set the oven at 400°F (200°C). Put the veal in a roasting pan on a rack and sprinkle with salt and pepper. Scatter the onion and carrot slices around the meat. Roast in the hot oven, turning often, until brown, about 30 minutes. Lower the heat to 350°F (175°C), pour ½ cup (125 ml) each of the wine and stock into the pan, and continue roasting until the veal is tender but still slightly pink, 45 minutes to 1 hour longer. Baste the meat often during cooking and add more stock if the roasting pan gets dry. Lift the veal from the pan and let cool. Deglaze the pan with the remaining stock and wine, boiling until well flavored and reduced. Taste the sauce for seasoning, add salt and pepper if needed, and strain.

Make the mornay sauce. When the veal is cool, remove strings and barding fat, and cut it almost all the way through into ⅜-inch (1 cm) slices that are attached at the base. Cut the ham slices to fit the roast and put one in each cut. Press the roast together with your hands and, if necessary, run a skewer lengthwise through the roast to hold it together. The roast and the two sauces can be prepared ahead to this point.

To finish: Allow the veal to come to room temperature if it has been chilled. Heat the oven to 350°F (175°C). Coat the meat with the mornay sauce, preferably on an ovenproof platter. Sprinkle with the grated cheese. Bake the veal in the preheated oven until the sauce is bubbling and brown, 25–30 minutes. Skim the fat from the meat sauce, heat the sauce, and serve separately.

Crown Roast of Pork
(CARRÉ DE PORC EN COURONNE)

A crown roast is always dramatic, and a choice loin of pork deserves this special treatment.

> **rib sections of 2 pork loins, each weighing about 4**
>   **pounds (1.75 kg), made into a crown roast**
> **3–4 tablespoons oil**
> **1 cup (250 ml) white wine**
> **2 cups (500 ml) veal (p. 116) or chicken stock (p. 115)**

For the stuffing:
> **2 onions, finely chopped**
> **2 tablespoons (30 g) butter**
> **¾ pound (350 g) ground pork**
> **¾ pound (350 g) ground veal**
> **½ pound (250 g) cooked ham, chopped**
> **¾ cup (100 g) fresh bread crumbs**
> **1 tablespoon chopped parsley**
> **1 teaspoon thyme**
> **½ teaspoon rosemary**
> **½ teaspoon oregano**
> **2 cloves garlic, finely chopped**
> **salt and pepper**
> **2 eggs, beaten to mix**
>
> ***16–20 paper frills***

SERVES 8–10.

For the stuffing: Cook the onions in the butter until soft but not brown. Cool and combine with the pork, veal, ham, bread crumbs, herbs, and garlic. Add salt and plenty of pepper. Stir in the beaten eggs. Cook a little piece of the stuffing, taste for seasoning, and adjust if necessary.

Heat the oven to 350°F (175°C). Put the pork in a round cake or pie pan. Pile the stuffing in the center and spoon the oil over the meat and stuffing. Roast the pork in the preheated oven until done, 2½–3 hours—a meat thermometer should register 185°F (85°C). Baste the meat and stuffing often during cooking.

Remove the strings from the roast and transfer it to a serving platter. Skim any excess fat from the meat juices, add the wine and stock, and deglaze the pan, boiling until the sauce is well flavored and reduced. Taste for seasoning, adjust if necessary, and strain into a sauceboat. Put a frill on each chop bone. The meat is carved down between the chop bones in wedges, so each chop is accompanied by a slice of the stuffing.

Leg of Lamb Boulangère
(GIGOT D'AGNEAU BOULANGÈRE)

Boulangère means baker's wife. Years ago the bakery often housed the only oven in a French village.

> **5–6 pound (2.25–2.75 kg) leg of lamb**
> **1 clove garlic, cut in slivers**
> **2 teaspoons rosemary**
> **salt and pepper**
> **6 medium (about 3 pounds or 1.5 kg) potatoes, peeled
>   and sliced**
> **6 medium onions, thinly sliced**
> **1–2 cups (250–500 ml) brown veal (p. 117) or beef stock
>   (p. 118)**

SERVES 6–8.

Set the oven at 450°F (230°C). Trim the skin and all but a thin layer of fat from the lamb. Make several incisions in the meat with the point of a knife and insert the garlic slivers. Rub the leg with rosemary and sprinkle with salt and pepper. Put the lamb in a baking dish large enough to hold both it and the potatoes and attractive enough for serving. Sear the meat for 15 minutes, remove from the oven, and lower the heat to 400°F (200°C).

Arrange the potatoes around the meat, layering with the onions and sprinkling each layer with salt and pepper. Return to the oven and continue roasting until the meat is medium rare, 1–1¼ hours longer. Add more stock as needed to keep the potatoes moist.

Serve from the baking dish.

Shell Roast à l'Italienne
(CONTREFILET À L'ITALIENNE)

For an even more luxurious version of this dish, beef fillet could be substituted for the shell roast.

> **3–4 pound (1.5–1.75 kg) shell roast of beef, barded and**
> **tied**
> **salt and pepper**
> **sauce italienne (p. 196) made with 2 teaspoons (10 g)**
> **butter, ¼ onion, 2 ounces (60 g) mushrooms, ½ cup**
> **(125 ml) white wine, 1 cup (250 ml) basic brown**
> **sauce, 1 ounce (30 g) ham, and salt and pepper**
> **¾–1 pound (350–500 g) macaroni shells or other pasta,**
> **cooked and buttered**
> **½ cup (125 ml) white wine**

SERVES 6–8.

Set the oven at 400°F (200°C). Set the meat on a rack in a roasting pan, sprinkle with salt and pepper, and roast in the preheated oven until meat is cooked to the rare stage, 1–1¼ hours.

While the meat is cooking, or earlier if you prefer, make the sauce italienne. Remove the roast from the oven, discard the string and barding fat, allow to rest for 10–15 minutes, and remove to a serving platter. Cook the pasta and reheat the sauce. Remove excess fat from the roasting pan and deglaze with the ½ cup (125 ml) wine, boiling for a moment or two to reduce. Strain into the sauce, taste for seasoning, and adjust if necessary.

Carve about half of the meat in thin slices and arrange them overlapping down one side of the platter with the remaining meat at one end. Arrange the pasta down the other side of the platter. Spoon a little of the sauce over the sliced meat and serve the remaining sauce separately.

Braising and Stewing

IN HIS ADMIRABLE *The Food of France* (1958), Waverley Root points out that the French approach meat cookery quite differently from Americans. To the French, a braise or a *ragoût* (stew), slowly simmered in a rich balanced sauce, are equal, if not superior, to any roast or grill. Ragoûts date back to the Renaissance and were, says Alexandre Dumas, the glory of *ancienne cuisine*. The gluttonous Catherine de Medici is said to have nearly died from overindulgence in a ragoût of cockscombs, kidneys, and artichokes.

Braises and stews call for mature tough meats with plenty of flavor. French animals are deliberately bred, fed, and butchered to provide lean close-textured meat with none of the marbling that gives tenderness to United States beef. The two aims are incompatible, so Americans find French roasts and steaks inferior, and the French think American stews lack body. In France, cooks go for muscular, even gristly, cuts from the shoulder and leg. Gristle may be something of an acquired taste, but given the right low-temperature treatment, it dissolves during cooking to give a flavor and syrupy texture that is highly prized. Calves' and pigs' feet and pork rind may be added for similar effect.

Stewing is a wide term, covering any dish for which the meat (or poultry) is cut in pieces, either browned or not, and cooked slowly in a good deal of liquid. From the French viewpoint, the word loses something in translation, for ragoût has none of the low-budget boardinghouse connotation of stew.

Braising, as it applies to meat, is more narrowly defined: it usually refers to a single, larger piece, that has been browned or at least lightly sautéed and then cooked slowly with a liquid, and a meat braise always uses a *mirepoix*, or mixture of chopped vegetables—carrots, onion, celery—for flavor. Of course, braising is a good method to apply to vegetables on their own, too.

Beef is the favorite meat for ragoûts since stewing suits only the tougher meats. So popular are beef stews that every region has its own version. Provençal *daube*, cooked with olives, tomatoes, and a strip of orange peel until the meat is tender enough to cut with a spoon, has spread nationwide. Éstouffade, derived from *étouffer* meaning to smother, emphasizes the slow cooking involved in dishes like the Gascon *étouffat de Noël*, for which beef is stewed with Armagnac, wine, and shallots. Mutton is another favorite candidate for the stew pot. Pork and veal can be stewed, but the resulting sauce is less aromatic, particularly than that of beef, unless it is pepped up with strong flavors as in our *poivrade*, including wine, vinegar, and lots of pepper.

Although veal, lamb, and innards can be braised to good effect, beef is the top choice for this method. A large piece of beef benefits enormously from the long slow cooking of a braise. Chef Chambrette regularly braised beef overnight in his restaurant. He would bring the pot to a boil before closing time and put it in a very low oven. By the next morning, the meat was so tender that he had to lift it out carefully by hand; if he had used a fork, it would have fallen apart.

For poultry braises and ragoûts, tough old birds that have served their time in the farmyard are needed. This way go the elderly turkeys and chickens. (Geese and ducks are more often preserved in their own fat, though we have a recipe for a stew that makes use of duck legs, which need longer cooking than the breast sections.) Nothing, say the experts with a lewd wink, compares with coq au vin made with an old cock. Battery chickens simply will not do. Braising and stewing are the age-old ways to deal with a tough pheasant that is more than a year or two old and with game. Equally traditional are ragoûts of innards such as kidneys, sweetbreads, and tongue, though one recent revival from the eighteenth century by a three-star chef seems destined for instant oblivion. It consists of a ragoût of cockscombs, wild mushrooms, and truffles served in a cornucopia made from a bread-crumbed and deep-fried sow's ear.

Braises and ragoûts, always favorites in brasseries and bistros as well as at home, are now enjoying a comeback in top restaurants. Each method has its own appeal to the nouvelle cuisine chefs. In their role as self-appointed saviors of regional cooking, they tout the traditional braises essential to country cooking. Ragoûts are

ÉPAULE DE VEAU À LA BOURGEOISE

A boned shoulder of veal, stuffed with ground pork and herbs and braised in wine
and veal stock, garnished here with "turned" vegetables and baby onions

adored even more because, while smacking of the same righteous return to simple good cooking as braises, they are less stereotyped. More or less anything can be added to a ragoût, and you can call it what you please. Already we have ragoûts of seafood and ragoûts of vegetables, and I'm just waiting for the penchant for wild combinations to hit stews—ragoût of beef, crayfish, and passion-fruit juice, anyone?

FOR SUCCESSFUL BRAISING AND STEWING

1. One-third pound (150 g) boneless meat is the usual allowance per person.

2. Meat must be dry before browning, or it will steam rather than color.

3. Pieces of meat should be browned a few at a time; if the pan is too crowded, the temperature of the fat will be lowered and the meat will steam in its own juices.

4. Do not use stock that contains much salt. During cooking it will reduce, becoming saltier and saltier.

5. For extra richness, add pork rind or calves' or pigs' feet to the pan.

6. A stew or a braise can be simmered on top of the stove instead of in the oven. Make sure the lid fits tightly and stir from time to time.

7. Braising and stewing are done at a slow regular simmer; 350°F (185°C) is the temperature usually recommended. If the liquid boils, the meat will dry and shrink.

BRAISING:

8. Do not add too much liquid; the sauce should be flavored with the concentrated essence of the meat and vegetables, not just with wine and stock.

9. Toward the end of cooking when the sauce has reduced, turn and baste the meat often so that it does not dry out.

STEWING:

10. At the beginning of cooking, the liquid should just cover the meat. At the end, the liquid should have reduced but still cover half to two-thirds of the meat. Add extra liquid during cooking if it evaporates too quickly. If the sauce is thin at the end of the cooking time, reduce it by boiling until concentrated.

1. Many think that braises and stews are better when reheated because the sauce mellows with time. They can be kept in the refrigerator for up to three days.

2. When reheating, be careful not to overcook any of the vegetables in the garnish; deliberately undercook them when making the dish ahead.

3. Braised and stewed meats freeze well, particularly when covered in their sauce. Braised meat is also good served at room temperature.

4. Braised vegetables keep well. They can be made two to three days ahead.

Duck Stew with Onions
(RAGOÛT DE CANARD AUX OIGNONS)

For this dish, the duck should be cooked a long time until it is very tender. If you prefer to use a whole duck, quarter it and remove the breast pieces halfway through the cooking time. Return them to heat through shortly before serving.

> **2 tablespoons oil**
> **leg and thigh sections of 2 ducks**
> **salt and pepper**
> **6 large onions, quartered**
> **⅔ cup (160 ml) water**
> **2 tablespoons chopped chives**

SERVES 4.

Set the oven at 450°F (230°C). Heat the oil in a flameproof casserole until very hot. Season the duck sections with salt and pepper and put them in the oil, skin side down. Brown very well over high heat. Remove the duck pieces, put in the onions, and return the duck, arranging the pieces over the onions. Put the casserole back over the heat for another minute and then put it, uncovered, in the hot oven.

When the onions are well browned, in about 15 minutes, remove any excess fat, add the water, and return to the oven. Reduce the heat to 350°F (175°C) and continue cooking until the duck is very tender, 1½–2 hours. If the water evaporates too rapidly, add more. At the end of cooking, the sauce should be thick and dark brown.

Arrange the duck on a platter or on individual plates, pour the sauce and onions over it, and sprinkle with the chives.

Shoulder of Veal Bourgeoise
(ÉPAULE DE VEAU À LA BOURGEOISE)

Bourgeois refers to a garnish of simple ingredients that accompanies braised meats, especially beef, veal, or mutton. For greater elegance, chefs sometimes trim the carrots and potatoes of this vegetable garnish to uniform ovals.

4–5 pound (2 kg) boned shoulder of veal
salt and pepper
1 tablespoon oil
6 tablespoons (95 g) butter
1 onion, chopped
1 carrot, chopped
2 stalks celery, chopped
1 cup (250 ml) white wine
2–3 cups (500–750 ml) white veal (p. 116) or chicken
    stock (p. 115)
2 teaspoons tomato paste
1 clove garlic, crushed
1 bouquet garni (p. 118)
1½ pounds (750 g) baby carrots, or large carrots,
    quartered
1½ pounds (750 g) baby onions, blanched
2 pounds (1 kg) small new potatoes, peeled
¼ cup (30 g) flour

For the stuffing:
    2 tablespoons (30 g) butter
    1 onion, chopped
    ½ cup (70 g) fresh bread crumbs
    ¼ cup (60 ml) white wine
    1 pound (500 g) ground pork
    2 cloves garlic, finely chopped
    1 tablespoon chopped parsley
    1 teaspoon thyme
    ½ teaspoon rosemary
    ½ teaspoon oregano
    salt and pepper
    1 egg, beaten to mix

SERVES 6–8.

For the stuffing: Melt the 2 tablespoons (30 g) butter in a small pan and cook the onion in it until soft but not brown, 7–10 minutes. Let cool. Moisten the bread crumbs with the wine. Mix the pork with the onion, bread crumbs, garlic, herbs, and plenty of salt and pepper. Stir in the beaten egg.

Spread the meat out, cut side up, and sprinkle with salt and pepper. Cover it with the stuffing, roll in a neat cylinder, and tie.

Set the oven at 350°F (175°C). Heat the oil in a large flameproof

casserole, add 2 tablespoons (30 g) of the butter, and when it's hot, brown the meat on all sides. Take it out, add the onion, carrot, and celery, cover, and cook over low heat until the fat is absorbed and the vegetables are slightly soft, 5–7 minutes. Replace the veal, add the wine, 1 cup (250 ml) of the stock, the tomato paste, bouquet garni, and salt and pepper. Cover and bring to a boil. Put the casserole in the hot oven and braise until almost tender, about 1½ hours.

Remove the meat and strain the sauce. Replace the meat, put the carrots around it, pour the sauce over, and add more stock if necessary to cover the carrots. Cover and continue cooking for 20 minutes. Add the onions, potatoes, and enough stock to cover and continue cooking until both vegetables and meat are tender, 20–25 minutes. The dish can be cooked 2–3 days ahead, but the vegetables should be slightly underdone to allow for reheating.

To finish: If necessary, reheat the meat in a 350°F (175°C) oven. Lift out the meat and vegetables and keep warm. Skim any excess fat from the sauce, taste the sauce, and reduce if necessary until well flavored. Mash the remaining butter with the flour until smooth. Whisk enough of this mixture, bit by bit, into the sauce to thicken it slightly. Strain it into a sauceboat and keep hot.

Remove the strings from the meat, cut it in ⅜-inch (1 cm) slices, and arrange them overlapping down the center of a platter. Surround with the vegetables and coat both meat and vegetables with a little of the sauce. Serve the remaining sauce separately.

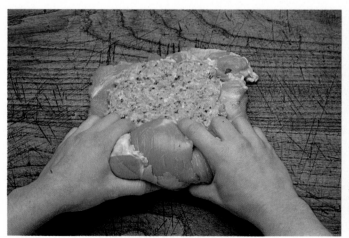

Rolling the boned veal around the stuffing

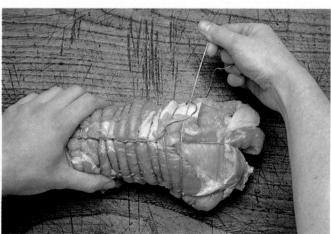

Tying the stuffed veal in a cylinder

Pork Poivrade
(POIVRADE DE PORC)

The term poivrade usually suggests game, and venison could be substituted in this recipe, but pork takes to the treatment admirably. Brussels sprouts purée (p. 394) makes a good accompaniment.

4 pound (2 kg) boneless pork shoulder
3 tablespoons peppercorns
2 carrots
1 large onion, sliced
10 juniper berries
3 cups (750 ml) red wine
¾ cup (185 ml) red wine vinegar
1–1½ cups (250–375 ml) white veal (p. 116) or chicken
 stock (p. 115) or water
2 tablespoons (30 g) butter
⅓ cup (45 g) flour
3 tablespoons red currant jelly
salt
3 tablespoons chopped chives

SERVES 8.

Trim the pork of all fat and sinew and cut it into large chunks. Put the meat, 1 tablespoon of the peppercorns, the carrots, sliced onion, juniper berries, wine, and vinegar into a heavy-bottomed pan. Bring the liquid to a boil and then simmer, uncovered, for 1 hour. Add stock or water as required so the meat is always covered by liquid.

Remove the meat and strain the cooking liquid. Crush the remaining peppercorns. Melt the butter in the pan and add the crushed peppercorns and the flour. Cook slowly until the flour browns. Whisk in the strained cooking liquid and bring to a boil. Reduce the heat, stir in the jelly, and add the pork. Simmer until tender, about 40 minutes longer. Taste for seasoning, add salt if necessary, and serve sprinkled with the chives.

Beef Chasseur
(BOEUF CHASSEUR)

Chasseur, or hunter's style, always indicates the presence of mushrooms, white wine, and tomatoes. Presumably hunters find mushrooms in the forest, and the rest is anybody's guess. Venison is also delicious cooked in this way.

1 tablespoon oil
1 tablespoon (15 g) butter
1½ pound (750 g) lean chuck or round steak, cut in 1½-
inch (4 cm) cubes
1 onion, chopped
1 tablespoon flour
1–1½ cups (250–375 ml) beef stock (p. 118)
½ cup (125 ml) white wine
1 clove garlic, finely chopped
2 shallots, finely chopped
2 teaspoons tomato paste
1 bouquet garni (p. 118)
salt and pepper
½ pound (250 g) mushrooms
1 tablespoon chopped parsley

SERVES 4.

Heat the oil in a heavy-bottomed pan or flameproof casserole over moderately high heat and add the butter. Brown the pieces of beef on all sides, a few at a time. Take them out, add the onion, and sauté over moderate heat until lightly browned, 7–10 minutes. Stir in the flour and cook, stirring, until brown. Let it cool slightly and add ½ cup (125 ml) of the stock, the wine, garlic, shallots, tomato paste, bouquet garni, and salt and pepper. Replace the beef and bring the mixture to a boil. Cover and simmer on top of the stove or cook in a 350°F (175°C) oven until the beef is very tender, 1½–2 hours. Stir from time to time and add more stock if the stew looks dry.

Trim the mushroom stems and quarter the mushrooms if large. Fifteen minutes before the end of cooking, add the mushrooms to the stew, stir, and continue cooking. When the beef and mushrooms are tender, discard the bouquet garni, taste for seasoning, and adjust if necessary. Serve the stew sprinkled with parsley.

Rabbit Stew
(LAPIN EN RAGOÛT)

This stew was recorded by François Pierre de la Varenne, the great seventeenth-century cook after whom École de Cuisine La Varenne is named.

3 pound (1.5 kg) rabbit
4 tablespoons (60 g) butter
¼ cup (30 g) flour, seasoned with salt and pepper
1½ cups (375 ml) veal (p. 116) or chicken stock (p. 115)
2 tablespoons capers
juice of 1 orange or 1 lemon
1 bouquet garni (p. 118)
salt and pepper

SERVES 4.

Cut the front and hind leg sections from the rabbit with a large knife or cleaver. Cut the back into serving pieces and split the leg sections into 2 pieces each. Melt the butter in a heavy-bottomed pan or flameproof casserole and coat the rabbit pieces with the seasoned flour. When the butter is hot, brown the rabbit pieces on all sides over medium heat. Add the stock, the capers, orange or lemon juice, and bouquet garni and bring to a boil. Cover and simmer on top of the stove or cook in a 350°F (175°C) oven until the rabbit is very tender, 45 minutes to 1 hour. Discard the bouquet garni, taste the sauce for seasoning, adjust if necessary, and serve.

Rabbit cut up for a stew

Braised Sweetbreads Demidoff
(RIS DE VEAU BRAISÉS DEMIDOFF)

This rich dish, which in classic cuisine also contains truffles cut in half-moons to match the rest of the garnish, was named for the Russian prince Anatole Demidoff.

1–2 pairs (about 1½ pounds or 750 g) veal sweetbreads
1 slice lemon
salt and pepper
4½ tablespoons (65 g) butter
2 carrots, chopped
2 onions, chopped
⅓ cup (45 g) flour
2 shallots, chopped
1 clove garlic, finely chopped
1 teaspoon tomato paste
1 cup (250 ml) white veal (p. 116) or chicken stock
 (p. 115)
½ cup (125 ml) white wine
1 bouquet garni (p. 118)
1 tablespoon chopped parsley

For the garnish:
4 stalks celery
2 carrots
1 medium onion
1 turnip
¼ pound (125 g) mushrooms
2 tablespoons (30 g) butter
salt and pepper

SERVES 4.

Soak the sweetbreads in cold water for 2–3 hours, changing the water once or twice. Drain, rinse, and put them in a pan with cold water to cover, the slice of lemon, and a little salt. Bring slowly to a boil and simmer 5 minutes. Drain, rinse the sweetbreads, peel them, and remove the ducts. Reserve the trimmings. Press the sweetbreads between 2 plates with a 2-pound (1 kg) weight on top and chill.

For the garnish: Cut the celery in thin slices. Halve the carrots lengthwise, remove the centers, and cut the carrots in thin slices. Quarter the onion and cut in thin slices. Quarter the turnip, trim away the center portion, and cut the remaining turnip in thin slices. Remove the stems from the mushrooms and cut the caps in thin slices. All the vegetables should be in half-moon shapes. Save all the trimmings except those from the turnip.

Heat the oven to 350°F (175°C). Melt 2 tablespoons (30 g) of the butter in a shallow pan. Add the chopped carrots and onions and cook until golden brown. Coat the sweetbreads with ¼ cup (30 g) of the flour and, in the same pan, brown well on both sides. Add the shallots, garlic, tomato paste, stock, wine, bouquet garni, salt and pepper, and the trimmings from the sweetbreads and the vegetable garnish. Bring to a boil, cover, and braise in the preheated oven until the sweetbreads are very tender, 35–45 minutes.

To cook the garnish: Melt the 2 tablespoons (30 g) butter in a heavy-bottomed pan, add the celery, carrots, and onion, and season with salt and pepper. Press a piece of buttered waxed paper on top and cover with the lid. Cook in the heated oven, stirring occasionally, until nearly tender, about 10 minutes. Add the mushrooms and turnip and continue cooking, still stirring occasionally, until all the vegetables are tender, 10–15 minutes longer.

Remove the sweetbreads from the pan and let cool slightly. Strain the cooking liquid into a saucepan and press the vegetables well to extract the juices. Boil the liquid until glossy and well flavored. Mash the remaining butter with the remaining flour until smooth. Over low heat whisk in enough of this mixture, bit by bit, to thicken the sauce.

Cut the sweetbreads in scallops—diagonal slices about ½ inch (1.25 cm) thick. Arrange them on a platter or on individual plates. Add the garnish to the sauce, taste for seasoning, and adjust if necessary. Spoon the sauce and garnish over the sweetbreads and sprinkle with parsley.

**The vegetable garnish cut
in half-moon shapes**

**Slicing the braised
sweetbread into scallops**

Braised Chestnuts
(MARRONS BRAISÉS)

Braised chestnuts are a favorite French accompaniment for goose and turkey.

> 1½ pounds (750 g) chestnuts
> 1 tablespoon oil
> 1 onion, chopped
> 1 stalk celery
> 2–2½ cups (500–625 ml) white veal (p. 116) or chicken
>   stock (p. 115)
> salt and pepper
> ¼ teaspoon allspice

SERVES 4.

To peel the chestnuts, prick the shell of each nut with a knife. Put nuts in a pan of cold water, bring to a boil, and then take from the heat and peel while still hot. Remove both outer and inner skin.

Set the oven at 350°F (175°C). Heat the oil in a large pan and cook the onion until soft but not brown, 7–10 minutes. Add the chestnuts and celery, pour in 2 cups (500 ml) of the stock, and add salt and pepper and allspice. Bring to a boil, cover, and braise in the heated oven until the chestnuts are tender, about 45 minutes. Remove the celery. If all the stock evaporates during cooking, add more. If liquid is left at the end of cooking, remove the lid and boil rapidly on top of the stove to reduce until the chestnuts are coated with a shiny glaze. The chestnuts can be cooked up to 3 days ahead and reheated.

Onions Braised in Wine
(OIGNONS BRAISÉS AU VIN)

Because the recipe can be varied by using red or white wine and stock from any meat, poultry, or game, these braised onions complement many main dishes.

> 4 medium onions
> 1 tablespoon oil
> ¼ cup (60 ml) red or white wine
> ½–1 cup (125–250 ml) stock (p. 112) or water
> salt and pepper

SERVES 4.

Set the oven at 325°F (165°C). Heat the oil in a shallow casserole and put in the onions, root end down. They should fit snugly. Heat until the oil sizzles. Add the wine, bring to a boil, and boil for 1 minute. Add enough stock or water to come halfway up the onions and season well.

Cook, uncovered, in the heated oven until the onions are tender, 1¼–1½ hours. The cooking liquid should be well reduced; if not, remove the onions and boil the liquid on top of the stove until syrupy. The onions can be cooked up to 3 days ahead and reheated.

Broiling
and Grilling

GRILLING IS THE MOST ancient and the most modern cooking technique. If man once knew no way to cook his meat other than holding it over a fire, he has now come full circle and braves smoke once again to prepare his food. Simple as it looks, grilling often proves difficult. It can display the best and worst in food, making the most of tender meat and full-flavored fish but leaving inferior ingredients all too naked and ashamed.

To broil properly, a fierce heat is essential. The rate of cooking, which should always be relatively fast, is controlled by altering the position of the rack, not by lowering the heat. The more robust the meat, the more quickly it should be cooked so that the juices are sealed in; the whole point of broiling is to concentrate flavors inside the food rather than draw them out into a sauce. Beef, game, and lamb must be seared quickly on both sides, at 4–5 inches (10–13 cm) distance from the flame, or about 3 inches (7.5 cm) in the case of an electric broiler, the heat from which is less strong.

If more cooking is needed, the rack is then moved away from the heat to finish cooking. Pork, veal, and chicken are cooked more slowly, further from the heat, but they still need to brown well for flavor. Fish and shellfish are trickiest of all. To prevent them from sticking to the rack, brush well with oil or butter and turn them with a wide metal spatula.

Meat for broiling should be cut in pieces not more than 2 inches (5 cm) thick, and only the most tender cuts, liberally marbled with fat, are suitable. Beef steak is the obvious candidate. Lamb chops are equally good. Lamb steaks cut from a boned leg are an unusual alternative.

Pork chops are fine for broiling, but they need regular basting. Despite its reputation as a fat meat, little fat enriches the lean of modern pork. Poultry suffers from the same problem, and I find broiled or barbecued chicken overrated—unless it has been thoroughly moistened with butter or oil. Veal, fish, and shellfish must be marinated before cooking and then basted during cooking. Fillets of almost any fish can be broiled but best of all are small fish left on the bone for moistness—trout, herring, and small mackeral— and even they are often served drenched in melted butter.

Perhaps most suitable of all are innards, for a touch of charring balances what can be a slightly sickly richness. Liver is good broiled, with a couple of slices of bacon on top to baste it. Brochettes of veal or lamb kidneys, pink in the center and slightly charred on the outside, make a dish that is fit for a king—or a three-star chef.

Careful seasoning adds that extra dimension to broiled meats. They can be marinated beforehand to add flavor and make them tender, the type of marinade and length of time depending on the food. Unless they have already been marinated, all meats benefit from being brushed with butter or oil before broiling, and you can satisfy a creative urge by adding lemon juice, herbs, wine, or garlic.

To salt or not to salt before broiling is a controversial question. Many cookbooks say that salt should never be sprinkled on the surface of raw meat—particularly beef—because it draws out the juices with the result that the meat grays rather than browns. However, when salt is added after cooking it is never absorbed in quite the same way. No harm is done by adding salt before cooking, say the La Varenne chefs, provided it is done at the last minute, and in practice I have found that they are right. Pepper and other dry seasonings pose no such problems.

To America, of course, must go credit for the popularity of the barbecue. The same foods are suitable for grilling out of doors as for indoor broiling, and the same principles for seasoning and cooking apply. The characteristic barbecue flavor is given, not by the coals, but by melted fat, which falls into the coals and flares, singeing the meat. Too much flame is disastrous, and to avoid a raging inferno when the food is put on the grill, the fire must be given time to burn down to a dull gray. Professionals keep two bowls beside the fire, one of sauce for basting and the other of water to extinguish any flames. I've found a squirt gun the best flame douser, and in keeping with the carnival spirit of most barbecues.

Europeans have never taken to outdoor grilling in quite the same way as Americans, their enthusiasm dampened, literally, by their weather. Instead, they are partisan to another offshoot of broiling—panbroiling. Panbroiling means cooking quickly over high heat in a heavy frying pan with little or no fat so that the food is seared very much as it is on a grill. The French use a special pan with a ridged base so that the food can be marked with a diamond pattern, but any heavy pan will do. All meats that can be broiled can also be panbroiled, and it is a particularly good method for cuts that tend to dry out.

There is something indecent about a piece of broiled or grilled meat or fish without an accompaniment. A bunch of watercress is the least of garnishes, with lemon wedges for fish. A cohort of colorful vegetables is acceptable with almost anything, and mushrooms, tomatoes, and onions lend themselves particularly well to grilling. Grilled food can be topped with a generous pat of butter seasoned with herbs or perhaps with anchovy. Or, most interesting of all, it can have a sauce.

Classic meat/sauce combinations are: for beef and lamb—truffle, Madeira, or béarnaise sauces; for pork—diable or Robert (both piquant); for fish—hollandaise or *sauce beurre blanc*. But there are endless unorthodox possibilities. Tartare sauce goes well with grilled chicken, béarnaise is delicious with salmon, and I've had pistachio sauce with chicken, and Roquefort sauce with veal.

Broiling will always have a place in the cooking repertoire as one of the quickest and simplest ways of producing a hot meal. It has a more macabre claim to fame, too: it provided cooks with their patron saint, Saint Laurent, who, poor fellow, was martyred on a grill.

 FOR SUCCESSFUL BROILING AND GRILLING

1. For most meats and fish, allow 5–7 ounces (150–200 g) per person and up to double that for a cut of meat with a large amount of bone, for unboned fish, and also for unboned fowl.

2. So it will cook evenly, leave meat at room temperature for one to one and one half hours before cooking.

3. Before putting any food on the rack, heat a gas or electric broiler for at least five minutes so it is very hot. If using a charcoal grill, light the fire about an hour in advance; the coals should be gray and scarcely glowing when the cooking begins. If the grill is not hot enough, the meat won't sear, and the juices will run into the fire.

4. Do not trim all the fat from the meat. If there is a border of fat around a steak, slash it with a knife to prevent curling.

5. A hot rack prevents food from sticking. To help further, grease the rack.

6. Sear the outside of food as quickly as possible and do not move it until ready to turn because it may stick until a crust has formed.

7. Meats are best handled with an implement like tongs that will not prick them and let juices escape.

8. Serve broiled and grilled food with the side that was cooked first upward; it will usually be the more attractive side.

PREPARING AHEAD

Broiled, grilled, and panbroiled foods must be cooked at the last minute, but they take such a short time that cooking ahead would achieve little.

1. Meat can be trimmed, skewered, and otherwise prepared for cooking a few hours ahead.

2. If the meat is to be marinated, this should of course be done ahead.

3. Accompanying sauces and flavored butters can be made ahead. Most can be made at least one day in advance.

MARINADES

A marinade is a highly flavored liquid in which food is soaked before cooking to give it flavor, prevent it from drying, and to tenderize it slightly.

There are two types of marinade: raw and cooked. Raw marinades such as those for fish or chicken, for which the ingredients are simply mixed together and poured over the food, are used when the food is to be marinated for a short time. They're generally composed of white wine or lemon juice, herbs, pepper, and a slice or two of onion. Cooked marinades, for which the ingredients are simmered until tender, and then completely cooled before pouring over the food, give stronger flavor. They are used with beef and game and usually contain red wine, herbs, and spices such as juniper and peppercorns as well as onion, carrot, garlic, and shallots. All marinades for grilling or broiling must contain a good proportion of oil, especially if used for basting too.

The longer food is left in a marinade, the more flavor it absorbs. In traditional cooking, two to three hours in the refrigerator is usual for fish, six to eight hours for veal and chicken, and about twenty-four hours for lamb. Game and beef can be left for up to three days, by which time the flavor is quite strong. The food should be turned from time to time in the marinade. It will mature twice as fast if left at room temperature rather than in the refrigerator. Before grilling or broiling, drain the food and dry it thoroughly; otherwise it will not brown but will simply stew in excess moisture.

DETERMINING WHEN MEAT IS DONE

Timing depends enormously on the temperature of the broiler or grill so it is impossible to give exact cooking times. Here are the various stages and how to tell by touch when they are reached.

VERY RARE *(bleu):*

The meat is cooked just long enough to sear all the surfaces and offers no resistance when touched. When cut, it is rare to blue inside. For steak and some game.

RARE *(saignant):*

Turn the meat when the blood has just come to the surface and brown the other side. When touched the meat feels soft and spongy. When cut, it is deep pink inside. For steak, game, kidneys, and sometimes lamb.

MEDIUM *(à point):*

Before the meat is turned, drops of blood surface showing that the center of the meat is warm. When pressed with a finger, the meat resists because it is sufficiently cooked to have contracted. When cut, the color is rose-pink inside. For steak, lamb, kidneys, liver, veal, and duck. Some nouvelle cuisine chefs cook fish so that it is still pink next to the bone. Chicken should be medium to well done.

WELL DONE *(bien cuit):*

When touched the meat feels firm. When cut, there is no trace of pink inside. For pork, chicken, fish, and shellfish. Some people insist that red meats should be well done, but this is anathema to any chef.

FLAVORED BUTTERS

Savory butters of various flavors are a favorite accompaniment to grilled meats and fish—and also to boiled or steamed vegetables. The butter can be shaped into a log or rectangle, wrapped in waxed paper, and chilled until firm. Slice it and set a piece on hot food just before serving. Alternatively, drop a spoonful of the soft butter onto hot food just before taking it to the table.

ANCHOVY BUTTER *(beurre d'anchois):*

Soak 4 anchovy fillets in a little milk for 20–30 minutes to remove excess salt. Drain, crush in a mortar with a pestle, and work in 4 tablespoons (60 g) butter and pepper to taste. For fish.

GARLIC BUTTER *(beurre d'aïl):*

Blanch 4 peeled cloves of garlic in boiling water for 5 minutes and drain. Crush them and beat into 4 tablespoons (60 g) creamed butter. Add salt and pepper to taste. For red meats and scampi.

LEMON BUTTER *(beurre de citron):*

Beat the grated zest of a lemon and 1 teaspoon of lemon juice into 4 tablespoons (60 g) creamed butter. Season to taste. For fish and vegetables.

MAÎTRE D'HÔTEL BUTTER *(beurre à la maître d'hôtel):*

Beat 2 teaspoons chopped parsley and 1 teaspoon of lemon juice into 4 tablespoons (60 g) creamed butter. Add salt and pepper as needed. Serve with meat, chicken, fish, and vegetables.

MALTESE BUTTER *(beurre maltais):*

Beat the grated zest of ½ orange, 1 teaspoon of orange juice, and 1 teaspoon of tomato paste into 4 tablespoons (60 g) creamed butter and season to taste. For lamb chops, steaks, fish, and vegetables.

MUSTARD BUTTER *(beurre de moutarde):*

Beat 2–3 teaspoons Dijon mustard into 4 tablespoons (60 g) creamed butter along with salt and pepper. For steaks, fish, and vegetables.

PAPRIKA BUTTER *(beurre de paprika):*

Beat 2 teaspoons paprika, 1 teaspoon tomato paste, and salt to taste into 4 tablespoons (60 g) creamed butter. For veal, chicken, and vegetables.

RAVIGOTE BUTTER *(beurre ravigote):*

Chop together 2 shallots, 1 teaspoon fresh tarragon, 1 teaspoon fresh chervil, 1 teaspoon fresh parsley, and 6–8 spinach leaves. Blanch for 5 minutes in boiling water and then plunge into cold water, drain, and dry on a paper towel. Pound in a mortar with a pestle and work in 4 tablespoons (60 g) butter and salt and pepper to taste. For fish.

SHELLFISH BUTTER *(beurre de crustacés):*

Pound ½ pound (250 g) crushed shellfish shells and trimmings (from crayfish, shrimp, lobster, and so on) and 6 tablespoons (95 g) creamed butter in a mortar with a pestle until smooth. The mixture can also be worked in a food processor. Rub through a very fine sieve or squeeze in cheesecloth to extract the butter. Season with salt and pepper. For fish.

TOMATO BUTTER *(beurre de tomates):*

Beat 1 tablespoon of tomato paste, a crushed clove of garlic (optional), and salt and pepper into 4 tablespoons (60 g) creamed butter. For steak or, without garlic, for fish and vegetables.

Scallop and Shrimp Brochettes
(BROCHETTES DE COQUILLES ST. JACQUES ET DE CREVETTES)

Mussels, lobster tails, pieces of fish fillet, and mushrooms are other possibilities for seafood brochettes. Sauce choron (p. 205), sauce beurre blanc (p. 205), or simply lemon butter (p. 51) could be substituted for the sauce béarnaise.

> 1 pound (500 g) scallops
> 1 pound (500 g) raw peeled shrimps
> béarnaise sauce (p. 204) made with 6 ounces (180 g)
>   butter, 3 tablespoons vinegar, 3 tablespoons white
>   wine, 10 peppercorns, 3 shallots, chopped,
>   1 tablespoon chopped fresh tarragon stems or
>   leaves or tarragon preserved in vinegar, 3 egg
>   yolks, salt and white or cayenne pepper,
>   1 tablespoon chopped chervil or parsley, and 1–2
>   tablespoons chopped tarragon leaves
> ¼ pound (125 g) butter, melted
> pepper

For the marinade:
> 1 cup (250 ml) white wine
> 2 tablespoons oil
> 1 tablespoon chopped tarragon
> 2 teaspoons chopped fresh herbs (thyme, oregano,
>   basil, parsley)

8 skewers

SERVES 4.

For the marinade: Simply combine the wine, oil, and herbs. If there is one, remove the small membrane adhering to the side of each scallop and put the scallops in a bowl (not aluminum). Pour the marinade over them and mix well. Cover and leave to marinate in the refrigerator for at least 2 and, if possible, up to 8 hours.

Removing the membrane from a scallop

To finish: Make the béarnaise sauce. Heat the grill or barbecue and set the rack about 3 inches (7.5 cm) from the heat. Drain the seafood and thread on skewers. Brush generously with melted butter, sprinkle with pepper, and grill until just cooked and still tender, 4–5 minutes. Turn and baste once during cooking. Serve the brochettes and pass the béarnaise sauce separately.

Grilled Chicken with Sauce Diable
(POULET EN CRAPAUDINE, SAUCE DIABLE)

For an even simpler dish, the chicken can be topped with maître d'hôtel or paprika butter rather than sauce diable.

> **sauce diable (p. 197) made with ¼ cup (60 ml) white
> wine, ¼ cup (60 g) wine vinegar, 1 shallot, 1
> teaspoon tomato paste, 1 cup (250 ml) basic brown
> sauce, pinch of cayenne pepper, and salt and
> pepper**
> **two 1½–2 pound (750–1 kg) chickens**
> **salt and pepper**
> **¼ cup (60 ml) oil OR ¼ cup (60 g) butter**
> **1 bunch watercress**

> *4 skewers*

SERVES 4.

Make the sauce. This can be done up to 1 week ahead of time.

Preheat the grill or broiler. Put one of the chickens on a board, breast side down. Cut along one side of the backbone with poultry shears or a heavy knife. Remove the backbone by cutting along its other side. Snip the wishbone in half. Turn the chicken breast side up. With a sharp downward movement of the heel of the hand, press the chicken flat, breaking the breastbone. Skewer the chicken crosswise through both the wings and the legs to hold it flat. Repeat with the other bird. Sprinkle the chickens with salt and pepper and brush with oil or butter.

Preparing the chicken for grilling

Put chickens on the grill or broiler rack, skin side toward the heat, and cook until well browned. Turn and continue cooking until tender, basting often. The total cooking time should be 25–30 minutes, depending on the size of the chickens and the intensity of the heat.

To serve, reheat the sauce if necessary, cut each chicken in half at the breastbone, and garnish with watercress. Top each half chicken with a spoonful of the sauce and serve the rest of the sauce separately.

Grilled Pork Chops with Sauce Robert
(CÔTES DE PORC GRILLÉES, SAUCE ROBERT)

Hearty accompaniments are traditional with pork, mashed or sautéed potatoes being the most popular in France. Besides sauce Robert, the chops could be teamed equally well with sauce diable (p. 197).

sauce Robert (p. 197) made with 2 teaspoons (10 g)
   butter, ¼ onion, ½ cup (125 ml) white wine, 2
   tablespoons wine vinegar, pinch of sugar, 1 cup
   (250 ml) basic brown sauce, 2–3 teaspoons Dijon
   mustard, and salt and pepper
4 thick pork chops
3 tablespoons oil
salt and pepper
1 bunch watercress

SERVES 4.

Make the sauce. This can be done up to 1 week ahead of time.

Heat the broiler or grill. Trim most of the fat from the chops. Brush the chops with oil, season them, and cook until browned on one side. Turn over, brush again with oil and season. Continue cooking until the chops are well done, 25–30 minutes in all—the juices escaping from the meat should be clear rather than pink.

Gently reheat the sauce if necessary, garnish the chops with watercress, and serve the sauce separately.

Scallops of Leg of Lamb with Garlic and Shallot Purées
(ESCALOPES DE GIGOT DE MOUTON AU COULIS D'AIL ET D'ÉCHALOTES)

Lamb is often flavored with garlic, but serving garlic purée with lamb scallops is an exciting new way of combining the two, and purée of shallot adds another note from the onion family.

4–5 pound (2–2.25 kg) leg of lamb, boned
salt and pepper
¼ teaspoon thyme
1 bay leaf, crushed
1 tablespoon oil

For the garlic purée:
   10 heads of garlic, cloves separated and peeled
   3 tablespoons (45 g) butter
   salt and pepper
   2 egg whites

For the shallot purée:
40 shallots
3 tablespoons (45 g) butter
salt and pepper
2 egg whites

SERVES 6–8.

Remove the skin and most of the fat from the lamb and put it skin side down on a cutting board. Using a very sharp knife, cut the meat into ¾-inch (2 cm) slices. Pound to flatten slightly. Put the scallops on a plate and sprinkle with pepper, thyme, crushed bay leaf, and oil. Leave for about an hour to absorb the seasonings and then heat the broiler or grill.

For the garlic purée: Cover the garlic with cold water, bring to a boil, and boil for 5 minutes. Drain thoroughly. Heat the butter, add the garlic, and cook very slowly, stirring frequently, until nearly all the moisture has evaporated, 20–30 minutes. (NOTE: Watch carefully because garlic burns easily.) Work the garlic through a drum sieve, season to taste with salt and pepper, and set aside.

For the shallot purée: Proceed exactly as for the garlic purée.

To finish the purées: About 15 minutes before serving, beat all 4 egg whites until stiff. Bring the garlic and shallot purées to a boil in separate pans and then remove from heat. Add half the beaten egg whites to each purée, whisking vigorously, and return to a boil. Remove from the heat, taste for seasoning, and adjust if necessary. Keep the purées warm in a water bath while cooking the lamb.

Salt the lamb scallops and cook just to the rare stage, 3–4 minutes on each side, and serve with the purées.

Tournedos as Mock Wild Boar
(TOURNEDOS EN SANGLIER)

As the name of this dish suggests, when beef is marinated it develops a flavor remarkably like that of wild boar.

four tournedos, 1½ inch (4 cm) thick
1 onion, sliced
1 carrot, sliced
½ cup (125 ml) vinegar
salt and pepper
2 peppercorns

4 juniper berries
3 tablespoons oil
4 tablespoons (60 g) butter
¼ cup (30 g) flour
1½ cups (375 ml) veal (p. 117) or beef stock (p. 118)
1 tablespoon red currant jelly
3 tablespoons cream
1 bunch watercress

For the marinade:
2 tablespoons oil
1 onion, sliced
1 carrot, sliced
2 shallots, sliced
1 stalk celery, sliced
2 cups (500 ml) red wine
5 peppercorns
5 juniper berries
1 pinch rosemary
1 pinch thyme
2 bay leaves
1 tablespoon vinegar

For the croûtons:
4 slices firm white bread
3 tablespoons oil
3 tablespoons (45 g) butter

SERVES 4.

For the marinade: Heat the oil in a saucepan (not aluminum), add the onion, carrot, shallots, and celery, and cook slowly until soft but not brown, 7–10 minutes. Add the wine, peppercorns, juniper berries, rosemary, thyme, and bay leaves, bring back to a boil, and simmer until the vegetables are tender, about 30 minutes. Leave until cold and add the 1 tablespoon vinegar.

Put the steaks in a deep dish just large enough to hold them and pour the cold marinade over them. Leave in the refrigerator 2–3 days. The longer the meat is marinated, the stronger the gamy flavor. Lift the meat out and pat dry with paper towels.

Put half the onion and half the carrot in a small saucepan with the vinegar, a pinch of salt, the 2 peppercorns, and 4 juniper berries. Bring slowly to a boil, boil until nearly all the liquid has evaporated, and set aside. Heat 2 tablespoons of the oil in another saucepan and add 2 tablespoons (30 g) of the butter. Sauté the remaining half onion and half carrot until lightly browned. Add the flour and cook slowly, stirring constantly until golden brown. Add the marinade, 1 cup (250 ml) of the stock, and a little salt. Bring to a boil, stirring often. Cover and simmer over low heat for 1 hour, stirring occasionally. Add the vegetables cooked in vinegar and the red currant jelly and simmer for 20 minutes longer.

For the croûtons: Cut rounds from the bread just slightly larger than the steaks. Heat the oil, add the butter, and sauté the bread rounds until browned on both sides. Drain on paper towels and keep at room temperature.

To finish: Heat the remaining 1 tablespoon of oil in a sauté pan. Season the steaks with salt and pepper and quickly panbroil to the rare stage, 4–5 minutes on each side. Set the steaks on the croûtons and discard the fat in the pan. Pour the remaining ½ cup (125 ml) stock and cream into the pan and bring to a boil. Strain the marinade mixture into the pan and bring to a boil again. Taste for seasoning and add as needed—pepperiness is characteristic of the sauce. Cut the remaining 2 tablespoons (30 g) of butter into small pieces and, off the heat, add one at a time, shaking the pan or stirring with a whisk to incorporate each piece.

Spoon a little sauce over each steak, garnish with watercress, and serve the remaining sauce separately.

Kidney Brochettes
(BROCHETTES DE ROGNONS)

Matchstick potatoes (p. 66) are the classic accompaniment to grilled kidneys.

**6–8 lamb kidneys OR 4 veal kidneys
mustard sauce (p. 204) made with 1 cup (250 ml)
    hollandaise sauce and 2 teaspoons Dijon mustard
¼ cup (60 g) butter, melted
salt and pepper
1 bunch watercress**

6–8 skewers

SERVES 4.

To prepare the kidneys, peel off any skin and cut away as much of the core as possible with scissors or a small knife. Cut lamb kidneys almost in half horizontally, leaving them joined on one side, and flatten them to form a butterfly shape. Cut veal kidneys almost in half, too, and spread them flat. Secure the kidneys in position with skewers.

Heat the broiler or grill. Make the sauce and keep warm in a water bath.

Brush the kidneys with butter and sprinkle with salt and pepper. Cook, brushing once again with butter, 2–3 minutes a side—they should remain pink in the center.

Remove the skewers, arrange the kidneys on a platter or on individual plates and garnish with watercress. Pass the sauce separately.

Grilled Vegetables
(LÉGUMES GRILLÉS)

For grilling or broiling, it is best to choose fairly large mushrooms and to buy tomatoes that are ripe but not soft. The preferred type of onion to cook by this method is the large mild Spanish onion.

½ pound (250 g) mushrooms
3 tablespoons (45 g) butter
salt and pepper
2 medium tomatoes
¼ teaspoon finely chopped garlic
4 teaspoons dry bread crumbs
2 Spanish onions
1 teaspoon sugar

SERVES 4.

Remove the stems from the mushrooms and fill the cavities with butter, reserving 2 teaspoonful for the tomatoes. Season with salt and pepper.

Halve the tomatoes crosswise and cut out the cores but do not peel. Sprinkle with garlic, salt and pepper, and bread crumbs and dot each half with ½ teaspoon of the butter.

Cut the onions crosswise into thick slices. Sprinkle one side with sugar and salt and pepper.

Heat the grill or broiler and cook the vegetables, seasoned side up, for about 5 minutes.

SOLE COLBERT
Whole boned sole, coated with flour, egg, and bread crumbs, then deep fried and finished with maître d'hôtel butter; photographed on the Normandy coast, not far from where they were caught

Deep Frying

IN FRANCE *friture* has three meanings: the cooking method of deep frying, the deep fat itself, and the food fried in it. The *friteuse* is the pan for deep frying, and in grand kitchens, there is even a *friturier* —a chef solely in charge of deep frying. I would love to claim that with all this attention the French are better at deep frying than anyone else, but alas the reek of deep fat, so evocative of roadside stands and all-night cafés, is as typical of France as anywhere else. No method of cooking is quite so abused as deep frying, and the reasons are not hard to find. Like so much quick cookery, deep frying is not cheap. Good fat or oil is expensive, and there is a strong temptation to continue using it long after it has become scorched and dark. And because it is done at high temperatures, deep frying leaves no margin for error.

The aim of deep frying is to seal food in a crisp coating so all the flavor is captured within. Brillat-Savarin said it should be "surprised." The trouble is that foods are "surprised" at different temperatures and some more easily than others. If food is fried too slowly, it is not sealed and absorbs fat. If the fat is too hot, the food is scorched. The correct temperature for the fat can vary from 350–400°F (175–200°C), and the larger the pieces of food, the lower the heat should be so that the outside does not burn before the inside is cooked. A few foods, notably French fries (see p. 66), are fried twice, once at a lower temperature to cook them through and then at a high temperature to crisp the outside.

If you do much deep frying, it is well worth investing in a deep fryer with thermostatically controlled heat. When using a simple stovetop deep fryer, guesswork can be reduced by the use of a deep-fat thermometer, which should be dipped in hot water, dried, then clipped to the side of the pan so that the bulb of the thermometer does not touch the bottom. But at La Varenne, the chefs still trust mainly to intuition. They might dip in a piece of bread or raw potato and watch the bubbles rise—at 350°F (175°C) the bread simmers, and at 375°F (190°C) the bubbles are brisk. Or they look to see when a haze is rising from the fat—at about 375°F (190°C). (Blue smoke shows the fat is burning and the heat must be lowered *at once*.) Another time-honored test is to throw in a drop of water, which should rebound at once—the army mess hall custom of spitting in deep fat is convenient but less commendable.

By no means can all types of fat be used for deep frying since it must be resistant to high temperatures. Butter burns long before it reaches the temperature required for deep frying. Olive oil is generally considered too strongly flavored. Most popular today are peanut and corn oil since they are bland and do not burn easily. In fact, almost any vegetable or seed oil will do, but they are expensive. The traditional cheaper alternative is beef fat, preferably rendered from the kidney. One advantage is that beef fat can be heated to very high temperatures without burning, so it lasts a long time. It can also be mixed with lard. However, these animal fats give a slight heaviness to anything fried in them, so they are no longer popular.

Most deep fat can be used three to six times, depending on what has been fried in it. In a restaurant, fresh fat is reserved for fried potatoes and delicate fritters. After a few fryings, it is made to do duty with meats or breaded croquettes and then finally demoted to fish, which gives fat an ineradicable flavor. Between each frying, the fat should be strained through cheesecloth or a fine sieve to remove any debris. This is particularly necessary when a bread-crumb coating has been used because the crumbs detach and then burn in and darken the fat. In a busy restaurant, constant straining may be impossible, so it's easy to see why the fat is so often burned.

Given the searing temperature of deep fat, it is not surprising that most foods need to be coated before frying. Flour, egg, and bread crumbs give the greatest protection, and they are used for soft mixtures like croquettes or for foods that are cooked for a relatively long time, like a whole fish. Fritter batter, based on flour and often lightened with beaten egg whites, is good for fruit, vegetables, and some meats, while small pieces of food such as strips of fish or onion rings can simply be coated in flour. One delicious coating is pastry, usually pâte brisée or puff pastry, which is wrapped around food as a turnover (technically known as a *rissole*). Significantly, all these coatings contain starch, and the only foods that can be fried without coating at all, such as potatoes and a few other root vegetables, also have a high carbohydrate content.

Given the right coating, an amazing variety of ingredients can be deep fried. If they have a soft melting texture to contrast with the crisp outside—sweetbreads, brains, eggplant, or creamy croquettes, for example—so much the better. Almost every French province has its own favorite, from the deep-fried mussels of Provence to the rissoles of Saint Flour of Auvergne (turnovers of pâte brisée filled with a mixture of fresh and Cantal cheeses, chives, and chervil bound with egg yolks) to the baby eels of Bordeaux.

Rissoles can be filled with leftover terrine or pâté, and croquettes are the classic repository for bits of cooked ham, chicken, and fish. But they have acquired a bad name because some cooks vainly believe that they can disguise stale food by deep frying. "Don't use the friteuse as a garbage can," warns Favre, author of a ponderous nineteenth-century dictionary of cooking. No less apposite is the Provençal proverb reminding us that, "A fish is born in water, but it should die in oil."

As a method of cooking, deep frying is unusual in providing almost as many desserts as first courses and main dishes. All too many of these fried foods are in eclipse, outmoded by current fashions in diet. *Atteraux*, brochettes of mixed meats and vegetables that are breaded and deep fried, and the first-course mixture of deep-fried meats and vegetables called *friture à l'italienne* are probably no loss. But what about fruit *beignets*, deep-fried fish, and the delicious cheese or mushroom fritters that have almost disappeared from modern French menus? Even choux pastry beignets are hard to find. Together with *pommes dauphine* (potato purée mixed with choux pastry and deep fried), they are almost the only survivors of a more hearty past.

Personally, I can hardly wait for a fried-food renaissance.

FOR SUCCESSFUL DEEP FRYING

1. In deep frying raw foods, the aim is to cook the interior in the same time as it takes to brown the outside. If foods are already cooked, they should only reheat while browning. Therefore, raw foods take slightly longer to cook and should be fried at a lower temperature.

2. Cut food in even-sized pieces so that it all cooks at the same speed.

3. The smaller the pieces, the higher the temperature for cooking the food.

4. Do not try to deep fry anything too large because the outside will

brown before the interior is hot. Normally the largest raw food used is single fish of about ¾ pound (350 g).

5. Coat food thoroughly so that it browns evenly and soft mixtures do not burst through the coating.

6. Do not use a basket for batter-coated foods because they stick to the wires.

7. Food, especially if it has been chilled, lowers the temperature of fat, and the heat should be adjusted.

8. Because of the cooling effect, never fry too much food at once. Deep frying is usually done in several batches.

9. If too much food has been added and it is simmering rather than frying, remove at once and reheat the fat to the right temperature.

10. Unless necessary, do not touch or stir food at the beginning of frying because this can damage a crust that is not yet firm. Often chefs shake the pan to redistribute the food and prevent sticking, but this must be done gently to avoid spilling.

11. Reheat fat to the right temperature before adding another batch.

 **PREPARING AHEAD**

Most foods and coatings can be prepared ahead.

1. Food can be coated in egg and bread crumbs up to six hours ahead and kept uncovered in the refrigerator. This dries the coating so it is crisper when fried. Many bread-crumbed foods, such as croquettes and sole Colbert, can be coated and frozen.

2. Batter can be made ahead and kept overnight in the refrigerator. Food must be dipped in batter just before frying.

3. Food can be tossed in a flour coating one to two hours ahead. Often it is coated again just before frying for extra crispness.

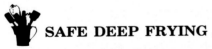 **SAFE DEEP FRYING**

Care must be exercised when deep frying:

1. Check the instructions on the packaging of the fat you buy—not all types of fat are suitable for deep frying.

2. When using a deep fryer, keep the handles of the pan pushed to the inside of the stove so the pan cannot be knocked over.

3. Never fill the pan more than one-third full of fat. This will minimize the risk of overflow or of spilling when the pan is moved.

4. In contact with hot deep fat, water vaporizes so quickly that it explodes—hence the spluttering when any damp food is lowered into a pan of hot fat. Thoroughly dry ingredients for frying and, when adding damp food not coated in batter to hot fat, use a basket so the food can be lifted quickly if the fat threatens to bubble over.

5. Stay by the stove while frying.

6. If you do have a fire, turn out the source of heat. Cover the pan of fat with a lid or baking sheet, or smother the fire with a dry cloth or blanket. Never try to move the pan or to extinguish the fire with water.

FOR SUCCESSFUL CROQUETTES

Croquettes can be made of anything from artichokes to lobster, from rice to whiting. The food is cooked, chopped, and then bound with a rich brown or white sauce. It is rolled into long cork shapes and breaded before being deep fried. Meat or fish croquettes are usually served as a first course, while vegetable croquettes such as potato, chestnut, and lentil are good accompaniments to game and beef.

1. Sauce proportions and proportion of sauce to other ingredients are important. If the sauce is too thin, or if there is too much of it, the croquettes are impossible to shape; if the sauce is too thick, the croquettes are heavy; and if there is too little sauce, they will fall apart.

2. Cool the croquette mixture thoroughly before shaping, preferably overnight. Alternatively, it can be cooled quickly in ice-cube trays in the freezer.

3. Make the croquettes as smooth as possible to avoid cracking during frying.

4. Be generous with the egg and crumbs for coating. During frying this coating acts as a container for the soft filling, and it may burst through any thin patches.

5. Be sure that the fat is hot enough, or the filling will melt before the coating is properly sealed.

6. If a croquette is cooked too long, the filling will boil and burst through the coating.

Fried potatoes: from right to left—mignonette, gaufrette, Pont Neuf, straw, chips, and matchstick

 ## THE PERFECT FRENCH FRIES

Deep fat and potatoes form a natural union. The potatoes can be cut in half a dozen shapes.

STRAW POTATOES *(pommes pailles)*:
The finest possible strips about 3 inches (7.5 cm) long.

MATCHSTICK POTATOES *(pommes frites en allumettes)*:
Julienne strips with a little more body than straw potatoes.

MIGNONNETTE POTATOES *(pommes mignonnettes)*:
¼-inch (6 mm) sticks the same length as straw and matchstick potatoes.

PONT NEUF POTATOES *(pommes pont neuf)*:
½-inch (1.25 cm) sticks about 2½ inches (6 cm) long; so-called because they were sold on the Pont Neuf in Paris.

GAUFRETTE POTATOES *(pommes gaufrettes)*:
Lattice rounds cut with a mandolin slicer.

POTATO CHIPS *(pommes chip)*:
Wafer-thin rounds.

Straw, matchstick, gaufrette potatoes, and chips are fried only once at 375°F (190°C). For best results, soak them for an hour or two in cold water and then dry thoroughly before frying. Gaufrette potatoes and chips can be kept for an hour or two in a warm place, or they can be reheated in the oven.

Pommes mignonnettes and Pont Neuf are fried twice, once at 325°F (165°C) to cook them until soft and just beginning to brown—the time varies from six to twelve minutes depending on the size of the potatoes. Then they are drained. This frying can be done several hours ahead. Just before serving, they are fried at a high heat—around 375°F (190°C)—for one to two minutes until crisp and golden brown, drained well, salted, and served at once.

Mushroom Beignets
(BEIGNETS DE CHAMPIGNONS)

This recipe can be served as a first course at table, or it makes an excellent cocktail hors d'oeuvre.

> ½ pound (250 g) mushrooms
> juice of ½ lemon
> 1 tablespoon (15 g) butter
> nutmeg
> salt and pepper
> choux pastry (p. 225) made with ½ cup (65 g) flour, ½
>   cup (125 ml) liquid from cooking the mushrooms, ¼
>   teaspoon salt, 4 tablespoons (60 g) butter, and 2–3
>   eggs
> deep fat for frying

SERVES 4.

Chop the mushrooms and put them in a saucepan with the lemon juice, butter, nutmeg, salt and pepper, and ½ inch (1.25 cm) water. Cover and cook over high heat until the liquid boils to the top of the pan and the mushrooms are tender, about 5 minutes. Drain, reserving the liquid. Measure the liquid and either reduce it to ½ cup (125 ml) by boiling or add water to bring it to the required amount.

Make the choux pastry with the mushroom liquid. Beat the mushrooms into the dough, taste, and add seasoning if needed—the dough should be quite peppery.

Heat the deep fat to 350°F (175°C). Using 2 teaspoons, drop 1-inch (2.5 cm) balls of dough into the hot fat. Do not fry too many beignets at a time, because they swell. As soon as the last ball is in the fat, increase the heat so the temperature of the fat rises steadily to 375°F (190°C). (NOTE: The beignets should swell gradually. If the fat is too hot at first, the outside of the beignets is sealed too quickly and they cannot swell properly; if it is too cool, the beignets will be soggy.) Fry the beignets until puffed and golden brown, 4–5 minutes. Drain them on paper towels and keep warm in a 350°F (175°C) oven with the door ajar while frying the remaining dough. Serve at once.

Ham Croquettes
(CROQUETTES DE JAMBON)

Use this recipe as a guide to make a variety of meat croquettes. Plain béchamel sauce can be used instead of mornay, and fish or even hard-boiled eggs can be substituted for the meat.

> **mornay sauce (p. 193) made with 1¼ cups (310 ml)
> milk, a slice of onion, a bay leaf, 6 peppercorns, salt
> and pepper, nutmeg, 4 tablespoons (60 g) butter, 4
> tablespoons (30 g) flour, and 1 ounce or about ¼ cup
> (30 g) grated Gruyère cheese
> 2 cups (about ¾ pound or 350 g) finely chopped
> cooked ham
> salt and pepper
> ½ cup (65 g) flour, seasoned with salt and pepper
> 2 eggs, beaten to mix with 1 tablespoon water and 1
> tablespoon oil
> 1 cup (100 g) dry bread crumbs
> deep fat for frying**

MAKES 12–15 CROQUETTES.

Make the mornay sauce and stir in the ham. Taste for seasoning and add as needed. Spread the mixture in a shallow pan and chill until firm. The croquettes can be prepared to this point up to 2 days ahead.

Turn the croquette mixture out onto a lightly floured work surface and roll into a cylinder about 1 inch (2.5 cm) in diameter. Cut it into 3-inch (7.5 cm) pieces and coat each piece first with the seasoned flour, then the egg, and finally with bread crumbs. The croquettes can be kept at this point for up to 6 hours, uncovered.

Heat the deep fat to 375°F (190°C) and fry a few croquettes at a time until golden brown, 2–3 minutes. Drain on paper towels and keep warm in a 350°F (175°C) oven with the door ajar while frying the remaining croquettes. Serve at once.

Rissoles
(RISSOLES)

Serve these small turnovers as a first course; tiny ones are sometimes used to garnish meat dishes.

> **tomato sauce (p. 397) made with 1½ tablespoons (20 g)**
> **butter, ½ onion, 1½ tablespoons flour, 1 cup (250 ml)**
> **stock, 1½ pounds (750 g) fresh or 1 pound (500 g)**
> **canned tomatoes, ½ clove garlic, a bouquet garni (p.**
> **118), ¼ teaspoon sugar, and salt and pepper**
> **pâte brisée (p. 254) made with 2 cups (260 g) flour, ¼**
> **pound (125 g) butter, 2 egg yolks, ¾ teaspoon salt,**
> **and 5–6 tablespoons water**
> **1 egg, beaten to mix with salt**
> **deep fat for frying**

For the filling:
> **¼ pound (125 g) mushrooms**
> **1 tablespoon (15 g) butter**
> **1 shallot, finely chopped**
> **1 tablespoon chopped parsley**
> **salt and pepper**
> **3 ounces (90 g) pork fat, ground**
> **½ pound (250 g) lean pork, ground**

3½–4 inch (9–10 cm) fluted pastry cutter

MAKES 20 RISSOLES.

Make the tomato sauce. It can be made up to 3 days ahead. Make the pâte brisée, wrap, and chill.

For the filling: Chop the mushrooms into very fine pieces. Melt the butter in a frying pan and sauté the shallot until soft but not brown. Add the mushrooms and cook over high heat, stirring occasionally, until all the moisture has evaporated. Off the heat, add the parsley and season to taste. Leave to cool and then mix with the pork fat and lean pork. Sauté a small piece, taste for seasoning, and adjust if necessary.

Roll out the pâte brisée to about ⅛ inch (3 mm) thick and cut in rounds with the fluted cutter. Put a spoonful of filling in the center of each round. Brush beaten egg around the edges, fold the circles in half, and seal. Make sure the filling is tightly enclosed. Set aside to rest ½ hour or refrigerate for up to 24 hours.

Heat the deep fat to 350°F (175°C). Reheat the tomato sauce. Fry the rissoles a few at a time for 7–8 minutes. Remove from the fat and drain well on paper towels. Serve hot with the tomato sauce.

Sole Colbert
(SOLE COLBERT)

Several rich French dishes are named after Colbert—a powerful minister at the court of Louis XIV.

> **maître d'hôtel butter (p. 51) made with 1 tablespoon**
> **chopped parsley, 2 teaspoons lemon juice, ½ cup**
> **(125 g) butter, and salt and pepper**
> **4 whole sole, each weighing ¾–1 pound (350–500 g),**
> **with heads and tails intact**
> **½ cup (65 g) flour, seasoned with salt and pepper**
> **2 eggs, beaten with 1 tablespoon water and 1**
> **tablespoon oil**
> **1 cup (100 g) dry bread crumbs**
> **deep fat for frying**

SERVES 4.

Make the maître d'hôtel butter. This can be done well ahead of time, but be sure to remove it from the refrigerator far enough in advance of the other preparations so that it has softened by the time the fish are done.

Prepare the fish, or have it done at the fish market as follows:

Slit the stomach of each fish and clean. Cut off the fins with scissors and cut the tail into a "V." Grasp the dark top skin of the fish firmly at the tail and rip it off up to the head. Dip your fingers in salt if the skin is very slippery. Scale the white bottom skin but do not remove it.

Working on the skinned side, make a slit down the center and cut the fillets from the bone with smooth strokes of a flexible fish-filleting knife, leaving the fillets attached at the outside edges. Fold the fillets outward to expose the bone and snip the backbone in 2–3 places with scissors. (NOTE: This makes the bone easy to remove after cooking.) Coat the fish with flour, then with egg, and finally with bread crumbs. The sole can be prepared 2–3 hours ahead up to this point and kept, uncovered, in the refrigerator.

Coating the boned
whole sole

Heat the deep fat to 350°F (175°C) and fry the fish, one by one, until golden brown, 6–7 minutes. Be sure the fish are flat and the fillets are folded outward during frying. Drain each fish and plunge the next one into the fat. Pull out the backbone of each fish as it is cooked and keep the fat hot while frying the remaining ones.

Arrange the fish on a platter or on individual plates, spoon or pipe the maître d'hôtel butter into the cavity where the backbone was, and serve.

Potatoes Dauphine
(POMMES DAUPHINE)

In restaurants potatoes Dauphine are often made with leftovers of mashed potatoes and choux pastry, allowing approximately double volume of potatoes to choux dough.

Dropping pommes dauphine into the hot fat

> **choux pastry (p. 225) made with ½ cup (65 g) flour, ½ cup (125 ml) water, ¼ teaspoon salt, 4 tablespoons (60 g) butter, and 2–3 eggs**
> **deep fat for frying**

For the mashed potatoes:
> **1½ pounds (750 g) potatoes**
> **3 tablespoons (45 g) butter**
> **salt and pepper**
> **nutmeg**
> **⅓ cup (80 ml) warm milk**

SERVES 8.

For the mashed potatoes: Peel the potatoes and cut each into 2–3 pieces. Put them in cold salted water to cover, bring to a boil, and then simmer until tender, 15–20 minutes. Drain the potatoes and work them through a potato ricer or a sieve back into the pan. Add the butter, salt, pepper, nutmeg, and milk. Beat the potatoes with a wooden spoon over low heat until they are light and fluffy. The mashed potatoes can be made 4–5 hours ahead and kept, tightly covered, at room temperature.

Make the choux pastry. Beat it into the potatoes. Heat the deep fat to 350°F (175°C). Drop in about half a dozen walnut-sized balls of the potato mixture, shaping them with 2 teaspoons and being sure to allow room for the potatoes to swell. Fry until golden brown, turning them so they brown evenly. Drain on paper towels and keep hot in a 350°F (175°C) oven with the door ajar while frying the remaining potato mixture. (NOTE: To stay crisp while in the oven, the finished pommes dauphine should be spread out so they do not touch each other.)

Fruit Fritters
(BEIGNETS AUX FRUITS)

Beer can be substituted for the milk in this recipe; it makes a light and well-flavored batter. Beignets can also be made with other fruit such as pineapple, apricots, peaches, pears, and plums. The fruit should be peeled and cut into halves or pieces of even size that are not too large.

3 tart apples OR 4 bananas
deep fat for frying
sugar (for sprinkling)
½ cup (150 g) apricot or raspberry jam—optional

For the fritter batter:
1 cup (130 g) flour
1 pinch salt
1 tablespoon sugar
2 eggs, separated
½–⅔ cup (125–160 ml) milk
1 tablespoon melted butter or oil

SERVES 4.

For the fritter batter: Sift the flour with the salt into a bowl, add the sugar, and make a well in the center. Add the egg yolks and ⅓ cup (80 ml) of the milk and stir, gradually drawing in the flour to make a smooth paste. Stir in more milk to make a batter that drops easily from the spoon, though not in a continuous ribbon. Beat it for 5 minutes and then cover and leave for 30 minutes. The grains in the flour will expand, and the batter will thicken. The batter can be made to this point a day ahead and kept, covered, in the refrigerator. To finish it, beat the egg whites until stiff and fold into the batter with the butter or oil.

Heat the deep fat to 375°F (190°C). Warm the jam if serving it as a sauce. Using a fork, dip a piece of fruit into the batter, lift it out, let the excess batter drip off for 2–3 seconds, and drop the fritter gently into the hot fat. Fry the pieces of fruit a few at a time until golden brown, turning them once, and drain on paper towels. Keep warm in a 350°F (175°C) oven with the door ajar while frying the remaining fruit.

Sprinkle the beignets with sugar and serve at once with a little warmed apricot or raspberry jam if you like.

Boiling, Poaching and Steaming

TWO METHODS OF cooking can claim to be prehistoric: grilling and boiling in water. Long before the invention of fireproof cooking pots, man learned to boil water by dropping heated stones into a gourd or wooden container. But it was not until the development of cauldrons that could be placed directly over the fire that the art of cooking in water truly began.

For art it is, despite its apparent simplicity. The liquid may be plain water, salted water, court bouillon flavored with onion, carrots, and herbs, or stock made beforehand with the appropriate bones and vegetables. For sweet dishes, the water can be flavored with sugar and possibly with vanilla, lemon, wine, or spices.

The flavor of the final dish also depends on the temperature at which its cooking began. For instance, if you begin with meat and simple salted water, yet want a rich broth either to serve with the meat or from which to make an accompanying sauce, then meat and water should start cooking together at room temperature so the meat juices are drawn out as the liquid heats. On the other hand, if the flavor of the meat alone is the overriding concern, it should be plunged into boiling water, thereby sealing in its juices and ensuring the best flavor. In this case the broth is thinner.

Each approach has its devotees. Chef Chambrette at La Varenne is a broth man. When he embarks on one of his bouts of dieting, he cooks himself a huge marmite of boiled beef. At lunch he sits down to a great bowl of beef and vegetables liberally soused with broth—excellent eating, though its slimming properties are dubious. Some cooks solve the broth-versus-meat dilemma by cooking the meat so that it is as flavorful as possible, but doing so in stock rather than water so the resultant broth is also tasty.

The speed of cooking in liquid is all-important too. Green vegetables should be plunged into large quantities of boiling salted water and boiled as fast as possible so as to keep their color and flavor, but they are something of an exception. Few foods should actually be cooked with the liquid at a full rolling boil since this tends to disintegrate the outside of the food before the center is cooked. Boiled potatoes, for example, should be simmered, that is, cooked in liquid that is placidly bubbling, as should other root vegetables. The same is true of so-called boiled ham and boiled beef, and pasta cooks perfectly at a simmer, without boiling over.

At the lowest temperature, that for poaching, we enter the domain of grande cuisine. Here the liquid should not actually bubble, but cook at 195–205°F (90–100°C), a temperature signaled by a shivering of the liquid in one area of the pan. Poaching is indicated for delicate foods that break up easily like *quenelles* (meat or fish dumplings), sausages, fruits, and for foods that lose flavor quickly, like fish. Dishes such as poule-au-pot that require several hours' cooking are also often poached rather than simmered as their excellence depends on drawing out flavors during the slowest possible cooking.

To maintain the right speed for poaching requires vigilance, and for some really tricky foods such as *foie gras,* even the chefs like to use a thermometer. I have my own early warning system—my ear. Boiling involves a turbulent churning that instantly flashes danger, if only of an overflowing pot. Simmering is peaceful, a companionable murmur that means all is well. And poaching should make no noise at all.

An alternative to poaching that has recently become popular is steaming. Avant-garde chefs have become steam freaks because of steaming's delicate effects on fish, vegetables, and small cuts of meat. Not for them plain water. They steam over aromatic infusions of vegetables, with the food laid on beds of herbs, sorrel, or even seaweed (a conceit initiated by Michel Guérard and copied by half a dozen famous names).

Blanching, the last direct use of water, usually prepares food for further cooking. As a general rule, the food is put in cold unsalted water, brought slowly to a boil, skimmed, and then simmered a few minutes. Green vegetables, however, are blanched in water that is already boiling. The term *to blanch* is misleading, for as well as whitening, it removes salt and other strong flavors, notably from

PÊCHES POCHÉES
Peaches are one of several fruits that are suitable for poaching in sugar syrup.

POIRES AU VIN ROUGE POIVRÉES
These pears are poached in a syrup flavored with red wine, cinnamon, and black peppercorns—a dessert from the nouvelle cuisine.

bacon; it firms meats like sweetbreads and brains; it sets the brilliant color of green vegetables and herbs, which often do not need further cooking; it loosens the skins of nuts and fruits like almonds and tomatoes; and it rids rice and potatoes of excess starch.

Trust the French to have identified so many nuances in cooking with water. My own English school years of steamed suet puddings and pallid root vegetables boiled to extinction remained so heavily imprinted on my mind that it took fifteen years of French cuisine to eradicate a prejudice against anything to do with water. But at last I *am* convinced of the merits of a pot-au-feu simmered to just the right stage of spoon-soft tenderness and am prepared to admit that a poached chicken can be compared with one that is roasted. Perhaps now I will also learn to appreciate the subtleties of the new cuisine's fish steamed with seaweed and ham on a bed of hay.

 FOR SUCCESSFUL POACHING

MEAT AND POULTRY:

1. Trim off all excess fat.

2. Truss poultry and tie meat in a neat shape to ensure even cooking.

3. For a clearer cooking liquid, meat can be blanched before being poached: put meat in a pan with cold water to cover, bring just to the boil, drain, and refresh under cold running water.

4. Skim frequently during poaching so broth remains clear.

5. For poultry, be particularly careful not to allow the water to boil because the skin may burst or the stuffing leak.

FISH AND SHELLFISH:

1. Always clean small fish through the gills, keeping the slit in the stomach as small as possible so the flesh will not shrink and split during cooking. Large fish that do not have sharp gills, such as salmon, are also best cleaned in this way.

2. Make sure court bouillon or fish stock is cool before adding fish; hot liquid will make the surface of the fish contract, spoiling its appearance and preventing even cooking. Shellfish, however, can be added to hot liquid since they are protected by their shells.

3. Fish and shellfish overcook rapidly; fish becomes soft and tasteless, and shellfish rubbery. Always undercook rather than overcook them.

FRUIT:

1. To keep fresh fruit firm, the poaching syrup should have a higher sugar concentration than the fruit itself.

2. Do not bruise the fruit when peeling.

3. Soak dried fruits in cold water or another liquid before poaching.

PREPARING AHEAD

Preparing ahead really depends on the food in question and how it is to be served, but here are a few general guidelines:

1. Blanching can always be done ahead. The blanched foods should be kept in the refrigerator.

2. Foods for steaming are normally chosen because they cook quickly, so they tend to overcook when reheated. The same is true for small cuts of meat and all fish that are poached.

3. Large cuts of beef and whole poultry can be cooked ahead and reheated in the cooking liquid. Fish to be served cold can be poached ahead, cooled to tepid, skinned, and kept in the poaching liquid.

4. Although their taste is not as fresh as when cooked just before serving, vegetables can be cooked ahead, drained, and then reheated in butter.

FISH POACHER

A fish poacher is a satisfying piece of equipment. Long and narrow, as deep as it is wide, it is shaped so the minimum of liquid is needed to cover the fish. A two-handled rack fits into the base so the fish can be removed easily. The finest material for a fish poacher is copper—also the most expensive; a large poacher can run into hundreds of dollars. Tin-clad aluminum is the workaday alternative in France and fish poachers are also available in stainless steel.

Plenty of substitutes are available, however. An oval casserole will give an attractive curve to a large fish, and a roasting pan will suffice in a pinch. One original makeshift device was the invention of gastronome Brillat-Savarin. Faced with an outsize turbot and no *turbotière* (a diamond-shaped poacher), he ordered the copper laundry boiler to be cleaned—and poured in a court-bouillon mixture. On a wicker tray suspended above it, he placed herbs and the fish. He considered the resulting steamed turbot the best he'd ever cooked.

Green Bean and Tomato Salad
(SALADE AUX HARICOTS VERTS ET AUX TOMATES)

Test the green beans frequently while they are boiling to catch them at the perfect point between raw and overcooked.

**¾ pound (350 g) green beans, cut in 2-inch (5 cm) lengths
4 medium tomatoes
salt
1 tablespoon chopped parsley**

For the dressing:
**1 tablespoon wine vinegar
½ teaspoon Worcestershire sauce
salt and pepper
⅓ cup (80 ml) olive or walnut oil**

SERVES 4.

Cook the green beans in boiling salted water until tender, 10–15 minutes. Drain, refresh with cold water, and drain again thoroughly. Scald the tomatoes for 5 seconds in boiling water. (NOTE: This facilitates peeling.) Peel and core them, halve them horizontally, and squeeze to remove the seeds. Slice them, sprinkle with salt, and leave to drain for 10–15 minutes. Toss in a colander to remove excess liquid.

For the dressing: Whisk the vinegar with the Worcestershire sauce and a little salt until the salt is dissolved. Gradually whisk in the oil so the dressing emulsifies. Taste for seasoning and adjust if necessary.

Carefully mix the beans, tomatoes, and dressing together. The salad should be made at least 1 hour and can be made up to 3 hours ahead; keep it covered in the refrigerator. Sprinkle with chopped parsley just before serving.

Poached Fish
(POISSON POCHÉ)

A whole poached fish is usually served with the head on. Allow ¾–1 pound (350–500 g) fish, depending on the size of the head, per person.

3 quarts (3 L) court bouillon (p. 80), or to cover
about 4-pound (1.75 kg) whole fish (salmon, halibut,
  cod, hake)
hollandaise sauce (p. 201) made with 6 ounces (180 g)
  butter, 3 tablespoons water, 3 egg yolks, salt and
  pepper, and the juice of ½ lemon
2 tablespoons chopped parsley
4 knotted lemons (p. 80)

SERVES 4.

Make the court bouillon and let cool. Wash the fish, cut off the fins, and trim the tail to a "V." To clean the stomach through the gills: Cut a very small slit in the stomach near the tail. Pull out as much of the stomach contents as possible through the gills, carefully cutting out the gills also but leaving in the tiny bit attached to the head. Take out any remaining contents through the stomach slit and then hold the fish under the tap and run cold water in the mouth and out through the stomach until very clean.

Cleaned in this way the fish will look neat after cooking, but if the gills are hard and sharp, make a larger slit in the stomach and clean the fish entirely through this. If the fish has large scales, scrape with the back of a knife to remove them, working from tail to head. However, if the fish has small scales—like those of salmon—leave them on to protect the fish during cooking.

Put the fish in a large pan or a fish poacher. Pour the court bouillon over the fish; it should cover it, and if it doesn't, add more water. Cover the pan and bring the liquid slowly to a boil. Lower the heat and poach until the flesh can be pierced easily with a fork, about 20 minutes. Make the sauce and keep warm in a water bath.

When the fish is cooked, let it cool for a few minutes in the liquid and then lift out on the rack to drain, or drain on paper towels. Skin the fish, leaving the head and tail, and remove the small bones running along the top of the backbone. The fish can be kept warm in a 250°F (120°C) oven for up to 30 minutes.

To serve, set the fish on a platter, garnish with parsley and knotted lemons, pass the sauce separately.

Court Bouillon
(COURT BOUILLON)

Court bouillon can be used not only for poaching fish but also for sweetbreads and brains.

> **1 quart (1 L) water**
> **1 carrot, sliced**
> **1 small onion, sliced**
> **1 bouquet garni (p. 118)**
> **6 peppercorns**
> **1 teaspoon salt**
> **1 cup (250 ml) dry white wine OR ⅓ cup (80 ml) vinegar**
>   **OR ¼ cup (60 ml) lemon juice**

MAKES 1 QUART (1 L) COURT BOUILLON.

Combine all the ingredients in a pan (not aluminum), cover, and bring to a boil. Simmer, uncovered, for 20–30 minutes and strain.

Knotted Lemons

Use these not only to garnish poached fish but any fish preparation and vegetable and veal dishes, too.

1. Cut a thin slice from the top and bottom of the lemon so the two halves will stand up later.
2. Halve the lemon crosswise.
3. Pare a narrow strip of rind from the cut edge, cutting nearly all the way around so the strip hangs free but remains attached to the lemon.
4. Make a simple knot in the rind so it stands out on the edge of the lemon half.

Medley of Steamed Fish with Red Butter Sauce
(MÉLI-MÉLO DE POISSONS À LA VAPEUR AU BEURRE ROUGE)

Although other fish can be substituted in this dish, the color scheme should be preserved: red (mullet), white (brill), and blue (bass).

> **1 quart (1 L) court bouillon (p. 80)**
> **4 red mullet**
> **3 pound (1.5 kg) bass**
> **2 pound (1 kg) brill or other flat white fish**
> **salt and pepper**
> **red butter sauce (p. 206) made with ⅓ cup red wine, 2**
> **shallots, ½ pound (250 g) butter, and salt and pepper**

SERVES 6–8.

Make the court bouillon. Scale, trim, and carefully fillet all the fish, but leave the skin on. (NOTE: The brill fillets can be skinned.) Wipe the red mullet fillets clean but do not wash them or they will lose their color. Wash the pieces of bass and brill.

Sprinkle the fish with salt and pepper and bring the court bouillon to a boil. On a rack or drum sieve or in a steamer above the boiling court bouillon, uncovered, first steam the pieces of bass until barely tender, 5–6 minutes. Remove and keep warm. Next steam the brill fillets 4–5 minutes, and finally cook the red mullet for 3–4 minutes. Or if there is room in the steamer for all the fish, put the bass in first; 1–2 minutes later, add the brill; and a minute after, add the mullet. Make the red butter sauce.

Arrange the fish on a platter or on individual plates, alternating the colors, and serve the sauce separately.

Fish ready to steam in a drum sieve

Chicken in the Pot Henry IV
(POULE-AU-POT HENRI IV)

Poule-au-pot is practically the French national dish, known long before the jovial King Henry IV had his name permanently attached to it by declaring, "Each Sunday I want a chicken in every pot in my kingdom." So popular has it continued to be that Curnonsky, the prince of gastronomes, was led to comment that he thought the seasonings in the stuffing of poule-au-pot must be aphrodisiacs. Originally an old fowl was added to the soup pot with the vegetables, to give more flavor to the soup. Now this richer version including meat is often prepared both at home and in restaurants.

> 3 pounds (1.5 kg) rolled rump roast
> 3 pounds (1.5 kg) short ribs of beef
> 2 pounds (1 kg) veal bones
> 6 quarts (6 L) water
> 12 peppercorns
> 1 bouquet garni (p. 118)
> salt and pepper
> 1 onion, stuck with a clove
> 3–4-pound (1.5–2 kg) chicken or boiling fowl
> 2 pounds (1 kg) beef marrow bones
> 6 carrots, cut in 2-inch (5 cm) lengths
> 6 onions, halved
> 3 medium turnips, cut in quarters
> 6 leeks, halved and cut in 3-inch (7.5 cm) lengths
> 1 cabbage, quartered
> ½ pound (250 g) piece calf's liver—optional
> ½ cup (100 g) rice
> coarse salt, cornichons (sour gherkins), and mustard
>   (for serving with the meat)

For the stuffing:
> 2 tablespoons (30 g) butter
> 1 onion, chopped
> ½ pound (250 g) ground pork
> ½ pound (250 g) bacon, finely chopped
> 1 tablespoon chopped parsley
> ½ cup (70 g) fresh bread crumbs
> ½ teaspoon allspice
> salt and pepper

SERVES 6–8.

Put the roast, the ribs, and the veal bones in a large pan with the water, peppercorns, bouquet garni, and 1 tablespoon of salt. Cut the onion in half and cook it, cut side down, on an electric burner or hold it in a gas flame on a fork until charred and then add it to the pan. (NOTE: This gives color to the broth.) Bring the pot slowly to a boil, allowing at least 20 minutes, skimming often. Simmer and continue skimming until all the thick brown scum has risen, 10–15 minutes. Cover the pot, leaving a small gap for evaporation, and simmer for 2 hours, skimming occasionally.

For the stuffing: Heat the butter in a frying pan and cook the onion in it until soft but not brown, 7–10 minutes. Add the pork and bacon and sauté until the pork is no longer pink. Stir in the parsley, bread crumbs, and seasonings.

Put the stuffing in the bird and truss. Add the bird to the pot after the meat has cooked for 2 hours. Continue simmering until the meat and the bird are tender, 1¼–1½ hours.

Wrap the marrow bones in cheesecloth so the marrow does not fall out during cooking. You can also tie the vegetables in a large piece of cheesecloth so they are easy to lift out. Add marrow bones, vegetables, and liver to the pot and continue simmering until the meat is very tender, ¾–1 hour. Poule-au-pot can be prepared up to 48 hours ahead and kept in the refrigerator. Allow a good 45 minutes for reheating.

Strain some of the broth into a separate pan, bring to a boil, and add the rice. Simmer until just done, 18–20 minutes.

Strain the remaining broth and skim off as much fat as possible. Add the rice and its cooking broth, taste for seasoning, and adjust if necessary. Carve the roast and arrange the slices overlapping down the center of a large platter. Pile the ribs at each end of the platter. Carve the chicken and add it to the platter along with the stuffing, the vegetables, and the marrow bones. The liver, which helps to clear the broth and gives flavor, is not served.

Serve the broth with rice first and then the meats and vegetables along with bowls of coarse salt, *cornichons*, and mustard.

Poached Fruit
(COMPOTE DE FRUITS)

Try any of the suggested fruits or a mixture of them. They should be juicy but firm and not too ripe.

> **1 pound (500 g) fruit (see below)**
> **½ cup (100 g) sugar**
> **2 cups (500 ml) water**
> **1 vanilla bean OR 1 teaspoon vanilla extract**
> **pared zest and juice of 1 lemon**

SERVES 4.

Prepare the fruit as directed below. Combine the sugar, water, vanilla bean (not the extract), and lemon zest and juice in a saucepan and heat until the sugar is dissolved. Bring to a boil and then reduce to a simmer and add the fruit. (NOTE: The fruit should be completely covered by syrup, and large halves or whole fruits, such as pears or peaches, may need to be cooked in 2 batches or in a double quantity of syrup.) Poach until the fruit is just tender; see below.

Let the fruit cool to tepid and then use a slotted spoon to lift it out of the syrup. Boil the syrup until fairly thick and reduced to about 1 cup (250 ml). If using vanilla extract, add it now. Let the syrup cool slightly and strain over the fruit. Serve at room temperature or chilled.

APPLES:

Dessert apples such as Golden Delicious are excellent for poaching, or tart cooking apples can be used. Rub apples with a cut lemon as soon as they are peeled to prevent discoloration. If serving whole, core the apples and poach them for 15–20 minutes, making sure that they are immersed in the syrup. For cut-up apples, halve or quarter them and poach for 8–12 minutes.

APRICOTS:

Cut around the apricots through the indentation, twist them in half, and discard the pits. Poach for 5–8 minutes.

CHERRIES:

Either sweet dark cherries or tart red cherries can be used. Poached tart cherries are often served with meat, poultry, or game. Increase the sugar if they are to be served as dessert. Wash the cherries, discard the stems, and, if you like, remove the pits with a cherry pitter or the point of a vegetable peeler. Poach the cherries for 8–12 minutes.

PEACHES:

Cut around the peaches through the indentation, twist them in half, and discard the pits. If you like, crack a few of the stones and use the kernels to give an almond flavor to the syrup. Poach the peaches for 7–10 minutes. Let them cool to tepid and then peel them. Poached peaches are particularly good with brandy added to the syrup after cooking.

PEARS:

Firm pears should be used for poaching. Rub with a cut lemon as soon as they are peeled to prevent discoloration. If serving whole, core from the bottom and leave the stalk. Poach the pears for 20–25 minutes, making sure that they are immersed in syrup. For cut-up pears, core and halve or quarter them and poach for 5–10 minutes.

PLUMS:

Cut around the plums through the indentation, twist them in half, and discard the pits, or leave them whole. Poach for 8–12 minutes. Poached plums are particularly good served with a sprinkling of cinnamon, or add a cinnamon stick to the poaching syrup.

Peppered Pears in Red Wine
(POIRES AU VIN ROUGE POIVRÉES)

The peppercorns add a surprising note to the flavor of this dessert.

> **4 firm pears**
> **½ cup (100 g) sugar**
> **2 cups (500 ml) red wine**
> **1 strip lemon zest**
> **1 stick cinnamon**
> **1 teaspoon black peppercorns**
> **½ lemon**
> **optional: Chantilly cream (p. 285) made with ½ cup**
>   **(125 ml) cream, ½ tablespoon sugar, and ¼ teaspoon**
>   **vanilla extract**
>
> ***pastry bag with medium star tip***

SERVES 4.

Put the sugar, wine, lemon zest, cinnamon, and peppercorns in a saucepan just large enough to hold the pears and heat until the sugar is dissolved. Bring to a boil and then let cool slightly. Peel the pears, core them from the base leaving the stem, and cut a thin slice from the bottom so they will stand upright for serving. Rub with a cut lemon. Heat the syrup to a simmer, add the fruit, and poach until tender, 20–25 minutes.

Let the pears cool to tepid before removing them from the syrup. Strain the syrup and boil until fairly thick and reduced to about 1 cup (250 ml). Let cool slightly and pour over the pears. The pears can be served at room temperature or chilled. If you wish to serve the pears with the Chantilly cream, pipe a ruff of cream around the stem of each pear.

Boning

"BONE THE MEAT" is an instruction that makes all too many cooks turn hastily to the next recipe. Admittedly, boning is a skill that is rare nowadays—not because it is difficult, but because it takes time. Chefs and suppliers cannot afford to go in for boning unless the results can command a high price, as does a galantine decked in aspic or a boned shoulder of meat stuffed and tied for roasting. On our neighborhood shopping street in Paris, there are three butchers, one of whom displays splendid boned roasts of veal stuffed with pork and pistachios, not to mention larded and barded beef roasts and paupiettes of half a dozen different types. I walk home from school on the other side so as not to be tempted by such expensive luxuries.

Because of rising prices, it is increasingly useful to know yourself how to bone. The best way to start is to look up instructions in a book or two, preferably with illustrations. Study the anatomy of the meat or poultry or fish in front of you and don't hesitate to poke it with your fingers to locate the bones while you work. The aim is to keep the meat in one piece, as neat and intact as possible. While boning, you should cut away gristle, sinews, and excess fat so that in the end you are left with a piece of meat that is all edible. If the meat is simply being boned for chopping, of course, you can work faster since there is no need to keep it in one piece.

The French are great boners of meat, perhaps because boned cuts offer so many possibilities. Meat is rolled and tied in a neat cylinder so that it roasts or braises evenly, as for épaule de veau à la bourgeoise (p. 37). Often it is stuffed before rolling, or at the very least it is sprinkled with salt, pepper, herbs, and perhaps a bit of garlic. A recipe can be transformed simply by using a different stuffing. For instance, lamb can be cooked with the onion and mushroom mixture that is used in the Touraine region, or the bread stuffing with garlic, shallots, and parsley that the Basques prefer for lamb, or a rice stuffing flavored with raisins and pine nuts that quite probably came from Provence, even though it is often called à la grecque. For some cuts, particularly shoulder of lamb or pork, the "melon" idea is possible: the meat is stuffed, sewn up, rolled into a ball, and tied, making segments with the string that look like those of a cantaloupe.

Poultry can be shaped in the same way, but more often the meat and skin are sewn around the stuffing and then trussed so that the bird regains its original shape; the leg and wing bones can be left in to improve appearances. Often the stuffed bird is poached in stock, or it can be baked in an oval terrine. A favorite exercise at La Varenne is the lesson on removing chicken breasts to make suprêmes and then boning the leftover legs to be stuffed and sauced. Two luxury dishes from one relatively inexpensive bird, plus the bones for stock—nothing could appeal more to the economical instincts of the chefs.

As for fish, even its most dedicated fans prefer it without the bones. It can be left whole with a stuffing taking the place of the backbone, in which case it is usually baked in the oven with a moistening of wine and melted butter. Or it can be taken completely off the bone in fillets—the best procedure when serving the fish in a sauce. During cooking, thin fillets tend to curl if they are left flat, so they are often folded in half or in three, or curled like a rollmop herring. Fish bones, like chicken bones, are a bonus for making stock. Meat bones (except those from veal) are not so useful, since they contain less of the gelatin that makes good stock. But never throw them away. Resting on the bottom of the braising or roasting pan, they will always add flavor to the sauce.

Most famous of the French boned dishes are *ballottines* and *galantines*. A *galantine* is made from boned poultry or meat that is stuffed, formed into a symmetrical shape, and then poached in stock. The stock from cooking is almost always clarified for aspic, with which the galantine is then coated, making it one of the favorite dishes for grand buffets. *Ballottines* are similar but are shaped like a bundle (*ballot*) and may be braised and served hot rather than poached and decorated with aspic.

Many elaborate boned dishes have an ancient history, dating from the days when kitchen help was cheap and chefs had time on their hands. A boned stuffed peacock in full plumage was the crowning touch at medieval feasts, carried in procession around the hall by a lady of outstanding beauty and rank. Even more recherché was the *rôti sans pareil* (roast without equal), consisting of a pitted olive wrapped in a boned garden warbler, wrapped in a boned ortolan, and so on through fifteen different birds ending with a bustard. The result must have looked rather like a model of a blimp.

Such an orgy of birds may be out of place today, but a knowledge of how to fillet and skin fish, how to bone poultry and one or two cuts of meat is certainly not. Boning gives a neatly shaped piece of meat that cooks evenly. And with the bones removed, serving is simple. The work is done beforehand in the kitchen rather than when carving at the dining table.

FOR SUCCESSFUL BONING

1. Use a very sharp pointed knife, varying the size with the size of the bones.
2. Keep the knife blade against the bone to avoid cutting into flesh or skin.
3. Use the point of the knife to help locate the bones.
4. Scrape rather than cut the meat from the bones.
5. To help you see what you are doing, pull the flesh away from the bones with your fingers as you work.
6. Work with short sawing or stroking movements of the knife; avoid using force.

PREPARING AHEAD

Boning is generally done as a part of preparations that can be completed ahead of time. All the dishes in this chapter can be prepared, or even cooked, well before serving, with the exception, of course, of the fish dishes.

HOW TO BONE AND SKIN FISH

There are two main types of fish: flat and round. Flatfish, such as sole, turbot, and plaice, are easier to bone because the bones lie flat, with the rib bones fanning out horizontally from the central spine. They usually have four fillets, two lying above the backbone and two underneath (some fish such as bream and John Dory have only two fillets). In round fish, such as salmon, trout, whiting, and hake, the backbone lies vertically rather than horizontally, and there is one fillet on each side.

A fish cannot be completely boned without being divided into its component fillets, though the backbone can be removed, leaving the head and tail. Boning, therefore, almost always includes filleting as well. If possible, use a special fish-filleting knife, which has a very thin flexible blade. Start by cutting off the fins, but do not bother to gut the fish; nor is there normally any need to scale the fish because the skin is usually removed after filleting. Wash the fillets under cold running water before cooking.

TO FILLET A FLATFISH:

1. Cut to the bone just behind the head.
2. Slit from head to tail along the spine, through to the bone.
3. Keeping the knife almost flat, slip it between the flesh and the rib bones. Cut away the fillet, using a stroking motion and keeping the knife in contact with the bones.
4. When the fillet is detached, you will come to a line of small bones on the border of the fish. Free the fillet by cutting along this line of bones.
5. Turn the fish around and slip the knife under the flesh of the second fillet and remove it in the same way. Turn the fish over and remove the other two fillets in the same way.

TO FILLET A ROUND FISH:

1. Cut down to the backbone just behind the fish head.
2. Holding the knife horizontally, slit the skin from head to tail.
3. Holding the knife flat on the backbone, cut the flesh from above the bone, using a stroking motion and keeping the knife in contact with the bone.
4. When the fillet is detached, cut carefully along the abdominal cavity of the fish to free it completely.
5. Cut under the bone with the same smooth motion to release the second fillet.
6. Turn the fish over and cut behind the head, freeing the fillet entirely.
7. If the fillets contain small bones near the center, remove them with tweezers.

TO SKIN FISH FILLETS:

The skin of sole is pulled off before filleting the fish. For other fish, use this method:

1. Place the fillet skin side down, tail end toward you.

2. Make a small cut at the tail end to separate the skin from the flesh.

3. Grasp the skin with the fingers of one hand, dipping your fingers in salt if they slip or using a cloth to help hold the skin.

4. Hold the knife between the skin and the flesh with the edge against the skin and the blade almost parallel to it. Work away from you with a sawing motion, at the same time pulling the skin toward you with your other hand.

 HOW TO BONE A BIRD

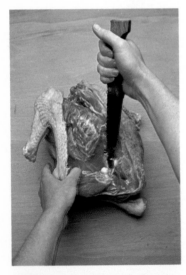

All birds are boned in the same way. Sometimes they are partially boned, leaving the leg and wing bones to add shape when stuffing is added—this is usual for small birds and for chaudfroids. For a galantine or ballottine, the bird is boned completely. For boning, choose a bird with the skin intact so it can be kept whole to use for wrapping.

TO BONE A BIRD PARTIALLY:

1. Cut off the wing tip and middle section leaving the largest wing bone.

2. With the breast of the bird down, slit the skin along the backbone from neck to tail.

3. Cut and scrape the flesh and skin away from the carcass, working evenly with short sharp strokes of the knife. After each stroke, carefully ease the flesh and skin away from the carcass with the fingers of your other hand.

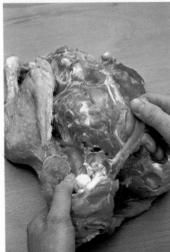

4. Cut the flesh from the sabre-shaped bone near the wing. Cut through the joint and remove. When you reach the ball and socket joints connecting the wing and thigh bones to the carcass, sever them; the wing and thigh are thus separated from the carcass but are still attached to the skin.

5. Using longer strokes of the knife, continue cutting the breast meat away from the bone until the ridge of the breastbone, where skin and bones meet, is reached.

6. Turn the bird around and repeat on the other side. When the skin and meat have been freed from the carcass on both sides of the bird, they will remain attached to the carcass only along the breastbone.

7. Pull gently to remove the breastbone and the carcass from the flesh. Be careful because the skin here is easily torn. The bird is now partially boned.

TO BONE A BIRD COMPLETELY:

8. Holding the end of a wing bone in one hand, cut through the tendons and scrape the meat from the bone. Pull out the bone, using the knife to free it.

9. Holding the end of a leg bone, cut through the tendons attaching the flesh to the bone. Use the knife to scrape the meat from the bone, pushing the meat away from the end of the bone as if sharpening a pencil. Cut free from the skin.

10. Repeat on the other side. The completely boned bird will be flat, with most of the skin lined with meat.

HOW TO BONE MEAT

Here a shoulder, which has an especially complicated bone structure, is used to exemplify the process of boning. A shoulder has three bones: the flat blade bone and two round bones. The blade bone forms a line with the first round (center) bone, which fits into the second (arm) bone at approximately a right angle. As with any piece of meat, there are left and right shoulders.

1. Pull any skin from the shoulder, using a cloth to hold it and cutting it away with a knife where necessary.

2. Trim off most of the fat, leaving only just enough to keep the meat moist.

3. With the fat side of the shoulder on the board, make a slit in the broad end of the meat (opposite the arm bone). You should be able to find a flat rectangular bone with the point of your knife.

4. Scrape this blade bone with your knife until it is completely visible.

5. Cut through the joint and strip out the blade bone by grasping the joint end and pulling it sharply up and toward you.

6. Now turn the shoulder around, take the protruding arm bone in your hand, and scrape downward with short strokes to free the bone from the meat.

7. With the point of the knife, find the joint connecting this bone to the center bone. Cut around the bone at the joint to release it and cut through the joint.

8. The center bone remains, and it is removed in "tunnel" style: cut all the tendons around each end of the bone and carefully scrape the meat from the bone, from the ends toward the center. When the bone is free, pull it out. The shoulder is now completely boned.

  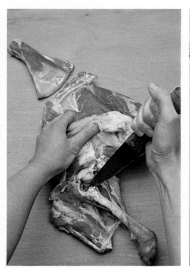 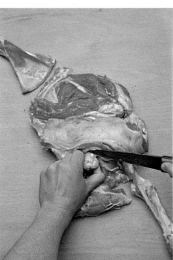

Lemon-Stuffed Trout
(TRUITES FARCIES AU CITRON)

The boning technique in this recipe provides servings that look like whole trout but are infinitely easier to eat.

4 trout, each weighing about ½ pound (250 g)
1 cup (250 ml) white wine
4 tablespoons (60 g) butter
½ teaspoon thyme
salt and pepper
1 tablespoon chopped parsley
4 slices lemon

For the stuffing:
4 tablespoons (60 g) butter
3 shallots OR 1 medium onion, finely chopped
½ cup (70 g) fresh bread crumbs
grated zest from 2 lemons
juice of 1 lemon
6 tablespoons chopped parsley
1 egg, lightly beaten
salt and pepper

SERVES 4.

For the stuffing: Melt the 4 tablespoons (60 g) butter in a small pan and cook the shallots in it until softened. Stir the shallots and butter into the bread crumbs along with the lemon zest, lemon juice, 6 tablespoons parsley, egg, and salt and pepper to taste.

Heat the oven to 350°F (175°C). To prepare the trout, snip off the fins and cut each tail into a "V"; leave the heads intact. Slit the stomach, clean the fish, and wash thoroughly. With a sharp flexible knife, cut along the backbone from just behind the head to the tail and then slip the knife between the bones and the flesh on each side to release the fillets. The 2 fillets should still be attached to the head and tail. Snip the backbone at each end with scissors and pull it out along with the attached fine bones. Sandwich the fillets with the stuffing.

Put the trout in a baking dish and pour the wine over them. Dot with the 4 tablespoons (60 g) butter and sprinkle with thyme and salt and pepper. Bake in the heated oven, basting often, until the flesh can be pierced easily with a fork, 15–20 minutes.

Arrange the trout on a platter or on individual plates, sprinkle with chopped parsley, garnish each fish with a lemon slice, and serve.

Turbot à la Bourguignonne
(TURBOT À LA BOURGUIGNONNE)

Steamed potatoes are the classic accompaniment to this dish. Sole, plaice, flounder, or hake can be substituted for the turbot.

**3 pound (1.5 kg) turbot
fish glaze (p. 118) made with 2 teaspoons (10 g) butter,
    a slice of onion, the bones from the fish, water to
    cover, 5 peppercorns, and a bouquet garni (p. 118)
3 shallots, chopped
1½ cups (375 ml) red wine (preferably Burgundy)
6 tablespoons (95 g) butter
2 tablespoons (15 g) flour
1 tablespoon brandy
salt and pepper
1 tablespoon chopped parsley**

SERVES 4.

Fillet the turbot and use the bones to make the fish glaze. Scatter the shallots in the bottom of a buttered baking dish and lay the fish fillets on top. Pour the wine over the fish and cover with a piece of buttered foil. Leave to marinate for at least 1 hour and up to 3 hours.

Mix 3 tablespoons (45 g) of the butter with the flour until smooth to make beurre manié. Set the oven at 350°F (175°C). Poach the fish in the heated oven until the flesh can be pierced easily with a fork, 12–15 minutes. Drain on paper towels, arrange on a platter or individual serving plates, and keep warm. Strain the cooking liquid into a saucepan, bring to a boil, and whisk in the beurre manié, a little at a time, until the sauce is thick enough to coat the back of the spoon. Add ½ teaspoon of the glaze and the brandy. Remove from the heat, taste for seasoning, and adjust if necessary. Whisk in the remaining butter a bit at a time. Spoon the sauce over the fish, sprinkle with parsley, and serve at once.

Stuffed Chicken Legs Suprême
(CUISSES DE POULET FARCIES, SAUCE SUPRÊME)

This is a good dish to prepare ahead; each element—meat, sauce, and garnish—can be made hours before serving.

4 chicken drumsticks
1 small onion, sliced
½ carrot, sliced
1½ cups (375 ml) chicken stock (p. 115)
1 bouquet garni (p. 118)
salt and pepper
sauce suprême (p. 194) made with the cooking liquid
    from the chicken and the mushrooms, 1½
    tablespoons (20 g) butter, 2 tablespoons (15 g) flour,
    the mushroom stems from the garnish, ¼ cup (60 ml)
    heavy cream, salt and pepper, and 1 tablespoon
    (15 g) butter (to finish)

For the stuffing:
1½ tablespoons (½ ounce or 15 g) chopped cooked ham
1 ounce (30 g) raw veal or chicken
2 ounces (60 g) lean pork
2 ounces (60 g) pork fat
1 egg, beaten to mix
1 tablespoon brandy
nutmeg
salt and pepper
1 canned truffle, with its liquid—optional

For the garnish:
¼ pound (250 g) mushrooms
1 tablespoon (15 g) butter
juice from ¼ lemon
salt and pepper

SERVES 4.

With a small pointed knife, bone the chicken legs following the directions on p. 91. Scrape the bones clean without slitting the meat.

For the stuffing: Work the ham, the veal or chicken, the lean pork, and pork fat twice through the fine plate of a meat grinder. Mix in the egg and brandy and season with nutmeg and plenty of salt and pepper—the mixture should be highly seasoned. Drain the truffle, if included, and cut into 4 thick slices. Reserve these and chop any trimmings. Add the trimmings with the liquid to the stuffing.

Fill the cavities in the legs with stuffing, tuck in the ends to enclose the stuffing, and then tie the chicken into neat parcels. Alternatively wrap each leg in caul fat.

Spread the onion and carrot slices in a saucepan, set the chicken on top, pour in the stock, and add the bouquet garni and a little salt and pepper. Bring just to a boil, lower the heat, cover, and poach until the chicken is tender, 35–45 minutes. Let cool slightly, lift the chicken out of the stock, and remove the strings. Strain the cooking liquid. The chicken can be cooked up to 2 days ahead.

For the garnish: Cut the mushroom stems off level with the caps and reserve the stems for the sauce. Put the mushroom caps in a saucepan with the tablespoon (15 g) butter, squeeze in the lemon juice, and add ½ inch (1.25 cm) water, and salt and pepper. Cover and cook over moderate heat until tender, 5–8 minutes.

Make the sauce, simmering it until it coats the back of a spoon. To finish: Put the chicken legs and mushrooms in the sauce and heat gently.

Arrange the chicken on a platter or on individual plates, spoon enough sauce over the chicken to coat it, top each piece with a slice of truffle, if using, and arrange the mushrooms around the chicken. Serve the remaining sauce separately.

Turkey Ballottine
(BALLOTTINE DE DINDE)

Ballottine is usually served warm as a first course. It makes an admirable main course, however, and since turkeys are normally rather large, this ballottine is more practical for most people to serve as a main dish.

> **8–10 pound (3.75–4.5 kg) turkey**
> **2 tablespoons (30 g) butter**
> **2 onions, chopped**
> **2 carrots, sliced**
> **2 stalks celery, sliced**
> **2 shallots, chopped**
> **1 clove garlic, crushed**
> **1 teaspoon tomato paste**
> **1 cup (250 ml) white wine**
> **3 cups (750 ml) chicken (p. 115) or white veal stock (p. 116)**
> **1 bouquet garni (p. 118)**
> **salt and pepper**
> **Madeira sauce (p. 196) made with 3 cups (750 ml) basic brown sauce (use stock from braising the turkey), ½ cup (125 ml) Madeira, and salt and pepper**

For the mousseline stuffing:
3 pounds (1.5 kg) ground veal
6 egg whites
3 cups (750 ml) heavy cream
½ teaspoon allspice
nutmeg
salt and pepper

SERVES 10–12 AS A MAIN COURSE OR ABOUT 20 AS A FIRST COURSE.

Bone the turkey completely and spread it, skin side down, on a work surface. Reserve the bones.

For the stuffing: Work the veal twice through the fine plate of a grinder. Pound the veal in a mortar with a pestle until smooth and then gradually work in the egg whites; or work the veal with the egg whites a little at a time in a blender or food processor. Put the mixture in a metal bowl over a bowl of ice and gradually work in the cream. Then add allspice and the nutmeg and salt and pepper to taste. (NOTE: Do not season the mousseline until all the egg whites and cream have been added. The salt will stiffen the mixture.)

Pile the stuffing in the center of the boned turkey, sew up the skin, and tie the bird into a neat roll. Set the oven at 350°F (175°C). Melt the butter in a heavy-bottomed casserole and brown the turkey on all sides. Take it out, add the onions, carrots, and celery, cover, and cook over low heat until the butter is absorbed and the vegetables are soft, 5–7 minutes. Lay the turkey on top and add the shallots, garlic, tomato paste, wine, stock, bouquet garni, turkey bones, and salt and pepper. The liquid should come halfway up the ballottine. Cover, bring to a boil, and braise in the heated oven until a skewer inserted in the center of the ballottine for ½ minute is hot to the touch when withdrawn, 1½–2 hours. The ballottine can be made a day ahead and kept, covered, in the refrigerator.

Reheat the ballottine if necessary, allowing ample time for heat to penetrate to the center. Strain the stock, supplement it with more stock or water if needed, and make the Madeira sauce.

Remove the strings from the hot ballottine. Cut the turkey into ½-inch (1.25 cm) slices and arrange them overlapping on a platter with the remaining ballottine at one end. Spoon a little sauce over the meat and serve the rest separately.

Melon-shaped Shoulder of Lamb
(ÉPAULE D'AGNEAU EN MELON)

Any leftover stuffing can be used to fill tomato halves to supplement the garnish of Provençal tomatoes.

> **4–5 pound (1.75–2.25 kg) shoulder of lamb**
> **salt and pepper**
> **1–2 cloves garlic**
> **1 teaspoon rosemary**
> **2 tablespoons oil**
> **1 onion, quartered**
> **1 carrot, quartered**
> **Provençal tomatoes (p. 395) made with 3 tomatoes, salt**
> **and pepper, 3 tablespoons oil, 1 clove garlic, 1**
> **tablespoon parsley, and 2 tablespoons bread crumbs**
> **½ cup (125 ml) white wine**
> **1 cup (250 ml) brown veal (p. 117) or beef stock (p. 118)**

> *For the stuffing:*
> **2 tablespoons oil**
> **1 medium onion, chopped**
> **1 cup (200 g) rice**
> **2 cups (500 ml) water**
> **½ cup (70 g) raisins**
> **salt and pepper**
> **½ cup (75 g) pine nuts**
> **2 tablespoons chopped parsley**
> **2 eggs**

> **trussing needle and string**

SERVES 4–6.

For the stuffing: Heat the oil in a saucepan and cook the onion slowly until soft but not brown, 7–10 minutes. Add the rice and cook, stirring, 5 minutes. Add the water, raisins, and salt and pepper, cover, and bring to a boil. Simmer for 20 minutes. Leave covered 10 minutes, then stir with a fork to separate the grains, and let cool to tepid. Stir in the pine nuts, parsley, and eggs, taste, and add salt and pepper as needed—it should be highly seasoned. Set aside to cool.

Trim the skin and all but a thin layer of fat from the lamb and bone it. Reserve the bones. If necessary enlarge the pocket formed by boning. Season inside the pocket, fill with the cooled stuffing, and sew the openings shut. Bring the sides to the center to form a round cushion shape. Encircle the meat twice with string at right angles like a parcel and tie. Then, with a long piece of string, circle round and round the meat crossing in the center so the string marks segments like those of a melon. The lamb can be stuffed up to 6 hours before cooking, but in this case, the stuffing must be cold before it is put inside the meat. Keep in the refrigerator and allow to return to room temperature before cooking.

About 2 hours before serving, set the oven at 450°F (230°C). Cut the garlic into slivers. Make incisions in the lamb with the point of a knife and insert the pieces of garlic. Sprinkle the meat with rosemary and salt and pepper. Put the oil in a roasting pan, add the lamb bones, onion, and carrot, and put the lamb on top. Sear the lamb in the hot oven until brown, 10–15 minutes. Lower the oven heat to 400°F (200°C) and continue roasting, basting often, until done to the medium stage (see roasting chapter), 1¼–1½ hours. If the pan juices brown too much, add some of the stock. Make the Provençal tomatoes.

When the meat is done, transfer it to a platter, remove the strings, and leave to rest for 15 minutes. While the meat is resting, add the wine to the roasting pan and bring to a boil, stirring to dissolve the browned pan juices. Add the stock and simmer to concentrate the flavor, 5–10 minutes. Strain the sauce into a small saucepan and skim off excess fat. Bring back to a boil, taste for seasoning, and adjust if necessary. Surround the lamb with the tomatoes. Carve the meat in wedges like a melon and serve the sauce separately.

CRÈME CARAMEL
Cooked to perfection in a water bath (bain-marie), a smooth-textured, classic
combination of eggs, sugar, and milk covered with a thin coating of liquid caramel

PETITS POTS DE CRÈME
Another rich custard mixture, also baked in a bain-marie, made in three flavors —
Grand Marnier, caramel, and chocolate

Cooking in a Water Bath

THERE ARE SEVERAL ingenious, if apocryphal, stories to explain that curious name for a water bath—*bain-marie*. One tale traces the bain-marie back to the fourteenth century, when interest in this gentle cooking method coincided with a period of special devotion to the Virgin Mary. Another links it to Miriam (Hebrew for Marie), Moses' sister. Italians attribute their *bagno maria* to Maria de Cleofa, a lady alchemist. More plausible, if more prosaic, is the suggestion that *marie* is a corruption of *mer*—sea.

The origin of its name may be guesswork, but no cook is in doubt about the utility of a water bath. The principle of surrounding a cooking pot with water as protection from the fierce heat of an open fire dates back centuries. In his Renaissance cookbook, *Opera*, Bartolomeo Scappi includes woodcuts of pots with compartments for water at the bottom—the first chafing dishes. Today's water bath consists of a large shallow pan with plenty of room for pots to be set in the water. Many restaurants have a temperature-controlled water bath, like a miniature swimming pool with a grid on the bottom to keep the special tall saucepans (constructed so water cannot splash into them) off the hot base. Often a hot-water tap is installed over the bain-marie so it can be filled easily. At home, almost any pan will do for a water bath, provided it is wide enough to hold the cooking pot or molds and deep enough for a minimum 2 inches (5 cm) of water.

A water bath is used in a professional kitchen for two basic purposes: steady cooking at a low temperature and keeping food hot. Water cannot get hotter than its boiling point of 212°F (100°C), so the temperature of any food set in it is automatically moderated. Nor, since the water produces steam, will the food get dry. A simmering water bath surrounds its contents with a constant, low, moist heat.

A water bath is essential for cooking a variety of dishes: custards, which curdle easily; light soufflé puddings; and pâtés and terrines, for which the heat must penetrate to the center without rendering out the fat or forming a crust on the exterior of the loaf. A water bath is vital for fish and chicken *mousselines*—tricky mixtures of pounded meat, egg white, and cream—and for *pains*—molds of meat, chicken, fish, or vegetables that are set with eggs and, in traditional cooking at least, thickened with béchamel sauce or bread crumbs.

The correct temperature for baking in a water bath varies depending on the nature of the food. For custards, particularly when set in small molds, the water should be scarcely bubbling; a rolling boil indicates that the oven heat, to which the top of the custard is exposed, is too high and the dish may curdle. Mousselines and pains need a medium heat. On the other hand, pâtés and terrines can withstand comparatively strong heat, particularly when the terrine mold is thick; if the water simmers rather than bubbles, they will take a prodigiously long time to cook. Cooking time is estimated from the moment the water starts to simmer, so the water in the bath, with the pan inside it, should be brought to this point before putting it in the oven to cook. Then it is simply a matter of making sure the water continues to simmer and keeping it topped up with hot water.

Cooks use stovetop water baths for a variety of purposes. In a water bath, it is easy to melt chocolate without scorching, to dissolve gelatin without cooking it, or to soften fondant icing without destroying its brilliance. The egg and sugar combination that is the base of génoise cakes and some mousses can be whisked to the ribbon stage over a water bath. Cooked meringue *(meringue cuite)* must be beaten endlessly over hot water, but since the process requires the muscle power of a boxer in good form, this meringue is generally passed over by modern cooks in favor of other types.

Sublime scrambled eggs (and they are one of the most difficult dishes of all) depend on patient stirring in a water bath for half an hour. However, few chefs can find the time, so scrambled eggs rarely appear on restaurant menus. Equally, a chef cannot lose precious minutes making a butter sauce or a hollandaise the safe way—in a water bath. He puts the copper pan over direct heat, and to hell with it.

In a restaurant a water bath on top of the stove is used mainly for keeping things warm. Soups, vegetables, stews, and sauces are prepared and then placed in the hot water to wait until needed. The food dries much less than in the oven and need not be covered.

With a little care even delicate butter sauces keep for a short time without separating, and hollandaise holds for half an hour or more. (For these sauces, the water bath should be warm, nowhere near the boiling point.) At La Varenne, the chefs put dishes that are ready to serve on racks set over the steaming stockpots—a variant of the bain-marie method. Of course, keeping food hot for a long time cannot improve it and often does harm—witness the food from cafeteria steam tables, which are no more than giant water baths.

Used for cooking and in moderation for keeping food warm, a water bath is a boon, as precious to the harassed cook as the gold sought by alchemists—named Maria or otherwise.

FOR SUCCESSFUL COOKING IN A WATER BATH

1. Food to be cooked in a water bath must be generously surrounded by water; otherwise it will cook at the oven temperature rather than at one moderated by the temperature of the water.

2. When cooking in a water bath, the cooking time is counted from the minute the water first comes to a simmer on top of the stove.

3. If a kitchen towel is put in the water bath under the container of food, this insulates it from the base of the bath, thus protecting it from direct heat.

4. Water added to a water bath during cooking must be hot. Cold water will slow the cooking.

PREPARING AHEAD

A water bath is one of the chief aids to early preparation because food can be kept hot at a steady gentle temperature. Advance preparation of dishes that are actually cooked in a water bath varies enormously: from terrines that can, and should, be made up to a week ahead, to warm molds that are served at once. In general, water bath dishes contain eggs. Therefore, they are best served within a day or two of cooking and do not reheat well.

Eggs Viroflay
(OEUFS MOULÉS VIROFLAY)

The name of this first course comes from the town of Viroflay near Paris, which used to be famed for its fine spinach.

> **sauce allemande (p. 194) made with 1 cup (250 ml)
> velouté sauce (p. 193), ¼ cup (2 ounces or 60 ml)
> mushroom stems, 1 egg yolk, a few drops of lemon
> juice, salt and pepper, nutmeg, and 2 tablespoons
> (30 g) butter**
> **½ pound (250 g) spinach**
> **4 eggs**
> **salt and pepper**

For the croûtons:
> **2 tablespoons oil**
> **2 tablespoons (30 g) butter**
> **4 slices firm white bread, cut in ovals slightly larger
> than the molds**

> ***4 oval egg molds or other small molds***

SERVES 4.

Make the sauce allemande. This can be done a day ahead if you like.

For the croûtons: Heat the oil in a frying pan and add the butter. Sauté the slices of bread over moderate heat until golden brown on both sides and drain on paper towels.

Remove the stems from the spinach, wash the leaves well, and blanch them in boiling water for 1 minute. Refresh them with cold water, drain thoroughly, and dry on paper towels, spreading out each leaf individually. Butter the molds generously and line the bottom and sides of each mold with a layer of spinach leaves, overlapping them so there are no gaps and letting the ends hang over the top rim. Heat the oven to 400°F (200°C) and have ready a water bath large enough to hold the molds.

Break an egg into each mold, season it lightly, and fold the spinach leaves over the egg. Put the molds in the water bath, bring to a simmer on top of the stove, cover water bath pan tightly with aluminum foil, and put it in the oven. Cook just until the eggs become firm, 6–8 minutes. Heat the sauce and the croûtons.

Remove the molds from the water bath, leave to rest for 1 minute, and then turn out onto the croûtons. Coat each egg with sauce and serve.

Chicken Liver Ramekins with Light Tomato Sauce
(PAINS DE FOIES DE VOLAILLE
AU COULIS DE TOMATES)

This rich yet light first course is a good example of the finesse of nouvelle cuisine at its best.

¾ cup (185 ml) heavy cream
6 ounces (180 g) chicken livers
2 eggs
1 egg yolk
¼ clove garlic, very finely chopped
nutmeg
salt and pepper

For the light tomato sauce:
1 tablespoon butter
2 shallots, chopped
1 clove garlic, crushed
2 pounds (1 kg) tomatoes
salt and pepper

four ½-cup (125 ml) ramekins

SERVES 4.

For the light tomato sauce: Melt the butter in a saucepan, add the shallots, and cook until soft but not brown. Add the garlic, tomatoes, and some salt and simmer, uncovered, until the tomatoes are very soft, 30–40 minutes. Purée the sauce in a blender or food processor and then strain it back into the pan or, alternatively, work it through a sieve and return to the pan. Reduce, if necessary, until thick enough to coat the back of a spoon, taste for seasoning, and add salt and pepper as needed.

Prepare a water bath, generously butter the ramekins, and set the oven at 350°F (175°C). Bring the cream to a boil. Purée the chicken livers in a blender or food processor with the eggs and extra egg yolk. Transfer the liver mixture to a bowl and add the cream slowly, whisking. Add the garlic and season to taste with nutmeg and salt and pepper. Pour into the ramekins, filling them not more than ¾ full.

Put the ramekins in the water bath, bring to a simmer on top of the stove, and transfer to the heated oven. Bake until a skewer inserted in the center of a ramekin comes out clean, 30–40 minutes. Reheat the sauce if necessary. Remove the ramekins from the oven and leave to rest 1 minute.

Turn the ramekins out onto a platter or individual plates and coat with sauce. Serve the remaining sauce separately.

Turban of Sole
(TURBAN DE SOLE)

Turban of sole, with its delicate flavor and rich butter sauce, amply rewards the work involved.

>1½ pounds (750 g) sole fillets
>red butter sauce (p. 206) made with 4½ tablespoons
>   vinegar, 4½ tablespoons wine, 3 shallots, 6 ounces
>   (180 g) butter, and salt and pepper
>8 cooked shrimps
>1 truffle, cut in 8 slices—optional

For the fish mixture:

>5 tablespoons (80 g) butter
>¾ cup (185 ml) milk
>¾ cup (95 g) flour
>1 pound (500 g) whiting, haddock, or flounder fillets
>2 egg whites, lightly beaten
>1 cup (250 ml) heavy cream
>salt and pepper

>*1½-quart (1.5 L) ring mold*

SERVES 8.

For the fish mixture: In a saucepan melt the butter in the milk and bring just to a boil. Off the heat, add the flour all at once and beat until the mixture is smooth and pulls away from the sides of the pan. Dry over low heat, beating constantly, for 1 minute and then let cool. In a food processor purée the fish with the egg whites and gradually work in the cooled flour mixture. Force the fish through a drum sieve into a bowl and set the bowl in a pan of ice water. Gradually beat in the cream, followed by salt and pepper. Taste for seasoning and adjust if necessary.

Butter the mold, prepare a water bath, and set the oven at 350°F (175°C). Put the sole fillets between sheets of waxed paper and pound with the side of the blade of a heavy knife or cleaver to flatten. Halve each fillet crosswise, cutting diagonally. Line the mold with fillets, broad end to the outside, tapered end hanging into the center. Spoon the fish mixture into the mold, fold the fillets over the top, and cover the mold with buttered foil. The mold can be assembled 3–4 hours ahead and cooked just before serving; keep it in the refrigerator.

Put the fish mold in the water bath and bring to a simmer on top of the stove. Transfer it to the heated oven and cook 35–45 minutes until firm to the touch. Tip the mold sideways to drain off any excess liquid. The mold can be kept, covered and in a warm place, for up to 30 minutes.

Just before serving, make the red butter sauce. If it must be kept warm for a few minutes, keep it in a warm, not simmering, water bath. Put a heated platter over the mold and invert both to turn it out. Wipe away any liquid with paper towels, coat the molded fish with sauce, top with slices of truffle, if using, and arrange the shrimps around the edge. Serve the remaining sauce separately.

Timbales of Four Vegetables
(TIMBALES DE QUATRE LÉGUMES)

Any variety of vegetables in season can be used, but be sure to choose a good combination of colors.

> **½ small cabbage or cauliflower**
> **½ pound (250 g) carrots**
> **1 pound (500 g) spinach**
> **½ pound (250 g) mushrooms**
> **juice of ¼ lemon**
> **2 eggs**
> **salt and pepper**
> **nutmeg**
> **¼ teaspoon thyme**
> **3 tablespoons chopped parsley**

For the sauce:
> **½ ounce (15 g) dried morels, soaked in lukewarm**
> **water for 1 hour**
> **½ stalk celery, sliced**
> **1 tablespoon (15 g) butter**
> **cooking liquid from the mushrooms and carrots**
> **1 egg yolk**
> **¼ cup (60 ml) heavy cream**

> **four ½-cup (125 ml) dariole molds or ramekins**

SERVES 4.

If using cabbage, cut it in thin strips and cook in a large pan of boiling salted water until very tender, 12–15 minutes. If using cauliflower, separate it into flowerets and cook in boiling salted water until it is very tender, 10–15 minutes. Drain thoroughly.

Slice the carrots, put them in a pan with enough salted water to cover, bring to a boil, and cook until very tender, 8–10 minutes. Drain, reserving the cooking liquid.

Remove the stems from the spinach and wash the leaves in several changes of water. Cook in a large pan of boiling salted water until just tender, 2–3 minutes, and drain well.

Put the mushrooms in a saucepan with the lemon juice and 1 inch (2.5 cm) of salted water. Cover the pan, bring to a boil, and cook over high heat until very tender, 8–10 minutes. Drain, reserving the cooking liquid.

After each vegetable is cooked, purée it in a blender or food processor and then work the purée through a drum sieve. Dry each purée in a separate small saucepan over low heat, stirring constantly, until nearly all the liquid has evaporated. Beat the eggs to mix and divide among the purées. Stir the egg into each purée along with seasoning to taste, including nutmeg in the spinach. Add the thyme to the cauliflower and the parsley to the mushrooms.

Generously butter the molds, prepare a water bath, and set the oven at 350°F (175°C). Layer the purées in the buttered molds: first the spinach, second the cabbage or cauliflower, third the mushrooms, and last the carrot. Put in the water bath, bring to a simmer on top of the above, and then transfer to the heated oven. Cook until just set, 10–12 minutes.

After the layer of mushroom purée, the last layer of carrot purée fills the dariole molds.

For the sauce: Drain the morels, rinse, and slice them. Melt the butter in a saucepan, add the sliced morels and celery, and cook slowly, stirring occasionally, until soft but not brown, about 5 minutes. Add the cooking liquid from the carrots and mushrooms, bring to a boil, and simmer until reduced to half its volume, about 10 minutes. Beat the egg yolk and cream together, whisk in a little of the hot sauce, and return the mixture to the remaining sauce. Cook over low heat until slightly thickened, stirring constantly. Taste for seasoning and adjust if necessary.

Turn the timbales out onto a platter or individual plates and spoon the sauce around them.

Crème Caramel
(CRÈME CARAMEL)

The whole eggs in crème caramel bind the mixture, so that it can be turned out without splitting.

For the caramel topping:
>¼ **cup (60 ml) water**
>½ **cup (100 g) sugar**

For the custard:
>**2 cups (500 ml) milk**
>**1 vanilla bean, split lengthwise OR 1½ teaspoons**
>**vanilla extract**
>⅓ **cup (65 g) sugar**
>**2 eggs**
>**2 egg yolks**

1-quart (1 L) soufflé dish or heatproof mold

SERVES 4.

For the caramel topping: Heat the water and sugar until the sugar is dissolved and then boil steadily to a golden brown caramel. Remove from the heat. When the bubbles subside, pour the hot caramel into the mold and immediately turn the mold around to coat the base and sides evenly with caramel.

The custard mold coated with caramel

Prepare a water bath and set the oven at 350°F (175°C). Scald the milk by bringing it to a boil with the vanilla bean, not the extract. Cover and leave to infuse for 10–15 minutes and then add the sugar, stirring until dissolved. Beat the eggs and egg yolks to mix and stir in the hot milk mixture. Allow to cool slightly, add vanilla extract at this point, and strain into the prepared mold.

Set the mold in a water bath and bring to a simmer on top of the stove.

Cook in the heated oven until the custard has just set, 40–50 minutes. Test by inserting a knife near the center—it should come out clean. Take from the water bath and leave to cool. Crème caramel can be made up to 2 days ahead and kept, covered, in the refrigerator. Up to an hour before serving, unmold the dessert by first running a metal spatula around the edge, then putting a platter on top of the mold, and inverting both.

Petits Pots de Crème
(PETITS POTS DE CRÈME)

These are particularly rich and smooth because of the number of egg yolks used. Unlike crème caramel, which contains egg whites as well as yolks, the consistency is too soft for the crème to be turned out of the little pots successfully. They can be made in a variety of flavors. Here we use chocolate, Grand Marnier, and caramel.

> **1 quart (1 L) milk**
> **1 vanilla bean OR 1 teaspoon vanilla extract**
> **12 egg yolks**
> **1 cup (200 g) sugar**
> **3 ounces (90 g) semisweet chocolate**
> **1 tablespoon Grand Marnier**

> *For the caramel flavoring:*
> **2 tablespoons water**
> **3 tablespoons (35 g) sugar**

> **9 individual pots with lids, or small ramekins**

MAKES 9 PETITS POTS DE CRÈME.

Scald the milk by bringing it just to a boil with the vanilla bean, not the extract. Cover and leave to infuse for 10–15 minutes.

For the caramel flavoring: Heat the water and sugar in a small pot until the sugar is dissolved and then boil steadily to a golden brown caramel.

Add vanilla extract to the milk now. When the bubbles in the caramel have subsided, pour in ⅓ cup (80 ml) of the milk. (NOTE: Be careful because the caramel is very hot and may make the milk boil up.) Stir to completely dissolve the caramel in the milk. Beat 4 of the egg yolks with ⅓ cup (65 g) of the sugar until light and slightly thickened. Stir in the caramel-flavored milk and pour this custard into 3 of the little pots.

Melt the chocolate in a water bath, stirring from time to time. Remove from the heat when just melted and allow to cool. Prepare a water bath and set

the oven at 325°F (165°C). Beat the remaining egg yolks and sugar until light and slightly thickened. Stir in the remaining milk, reserving the vanilla bean for future use. Flavor half this custard with the Grand Marnier and pour into 3 of the little pots. Stir the cool but still melted chocolate into the remaining custard and pour into the last 3 pots.

Set the pots in the water bath and cover with lids or foil. Bring the water to a simmer on top of the stove. Transfer to the heated oven and cook until the custard is almost set and a knife inserted in the center comes out clean, 30–40 minutes. Take the custards from the water bath and let cool. They can be made up to 24 hours ahead and kept, covered, in the refrigerator. Allow to return to room temperature before serving.

Making Stocks

CLASSIC FRENCH COOKING can be thought of as the house that Jack built. Basic preparations are used to construct individual dishes. Thus cooking goes on in stages—first make the basic ingredients and then assemble the final dish. One of the most important basics, the most vital parts of the house, is stock. It is no accident that the French word for stock is *fond*—foundation. Without it there would be few French soups, even fewer sauces, and hardly any braises or ragoûts at all.

Stock is not an end in itself; it is always used to make some other dish, or as a basis for classic white or brown sauces. The best stock is based on raw bones, with vegetables such as onion, carrot, and celery added for flavor. Peppercorns are the invariable seasoning (ground pepper turns bitter during long cooking), plus a bouquet garni. Salt, however, is taboo because even a small amount in the original liquid will become dangerously concentrated as the stock is boiled down. It is much wiser, say most chefs, to add salt when the stock is used in the final cooking. For veal stock, optional additions are garlic and a clove or two, and for fish stock, white wine or lemon juice.

Both brown and white stock are made with the same veal bones, sometimes a few beef bones, and vegetables, but for brown stock, the bones and vegetables are very thoroughly browned before adding water. Brown stock should be rich, full-flavored, and concentrated and is used mainly with beef, game, and lamb. White stock, intended for lighter meats, is more delicate, for the flavor of the stock should never overwhelm the other ingredients. Stocks for

chicken and fish are similarly light-colored and should be full-flavored but not strong.

In cooking stock, the prime essential is patience. Classic cookbooks recommend cooking veal stock for ten to twelve hours. Once brought to a boil and skimmed, however, stock can be left untended to simmer at the back of the stove for the remaining time. It must not be allowed to boil hard (my recurring sin), or it will turn cloudy and acquire an unpleasant taste of bone.

During the cooking process, all the flavor should have been extracted from the bones and vegetables, leaving them tasteless. (This is what distinguishes stock from the broth of dishes such as poule-au-pot, which is much lighter because most of the flavor is left in the meat and vegetables.)

As well as flavor, good stock should acquire body from bone marrow, and when chilled it will also set to a jelly. Veal, being a young meat, is prized for making stock since it contains a good deal of gelatin, particularly in the knuckle bones. Beef knuckle bones are next best. Fish bones are also high in gelatin. In the nineteenth century the gelatin that was used to set the elaborate molded desserts so admired by Victorian matrons had the disconcerting name of "fishglue."

At the end of cooking, stock is strained and skimmed of excess fat. The modern trend is then to reduce the stock by boiling it down to half its volume or less. This is partly for convenient storing, but mainly to make easy the "small" sauces that are becoming more and more popular. Most of these are based on pan juices dissolved in stock, and the more concentrated the stock, the less reduction will be needed at the last minute. In fact, thorough reduction of stock is nothing new. Carried to the extreme, it results in meat (or fish) glaze, a syrupy liquid that, once cool, sets like India rubber. Just a teaspoon or two of meat glaze picks up the flavor of stews, and it is a standard ingredient in many classic sauces. Over two hundred years ago, cookbooks suggested cutting meat glaze into dice for taking on journeys—the forerunner of the bouillon cube.

Brown, white, chicken, fish—these are the classic stocks designed for classic dishes. There is also a simple version, household stock, at which chefs tend to turn up their noses because they cannot rely on its effect in a sauce—it never tastes the same twice. But I am a devotee of household stock. It is made with raw vegetable trimmings and leftover bones from raw or cooked meat and poultry. Everything is simmered together in happy abandon, bones and trimmings are thrown in as they accumulate, and the stock is poured off as needed and replenished with more water. At the end of ten days, my pot is usually so full that I have to strain the stock and start again, using this brew as a good starter for the next.

The stock should be boiled each day, and it is best kept in the refrigerator overnight, although I find this unnecessary in cool weather. When we go away, I simply put the whole pot in the freezer. I suppose one could go on thus for years, but my longest vintage lasted about three months before some oversight caused its demise.

Whether you choose classic recipes or my lazybones version, stock is a firm foundation for your own cuisine.

FOR SUCCESSFUL STOCKS

1. Stockpots are usually made of thick aluminum. It is best to use a deep pot so evaporation won't be too rapid. Choose a pot that will be nearly filled by the stock mixture so it will be easy to skim.

2. As the stock is coming to a boil, it should be skimmed often so that it will be clear.

3. Good clear stock ranges in color from beige or straw (for veal and chicken stock) to medium brown (for beef).

4. Before using, it is best to chill stock so that any fat will solidify and can easily be skimmed from the surface. If you don't have enough time to chill it, skim off as much fat as you can with a spoon or ladle and then draw paper towels quickly across the surface to absorb and remove the last drops of fat.

5. If you need brown stock but have only white, a quick brown stock can be made by thoroughly browning chopped onions and carrots in a little fat and simmering them with white stock and a little tomato purée for about thirty minutes. Strain before using.

PREPARING AHEAD

1. Once stock has come to a boil and simmered for at least half an hour, the cooking can be interrupted for a day without harm. Keep the stock in the refrigerator until ready to continue cooking.

2. Meat stock can be kept for several weeks in the refrigerator if it is brought to a boil and boiled for ten minutes every three to four days. Boil fish and chicken stock every two days.

3. Stock can be frozen almost indefinitely. To avoid using too much freezer space, reduce the stock until it is very concentrated and freeze it in ice-cube trays; a few cubes can then be diluted with water and heated as needed.

Fish Stock
(FUMET DE POISSON)

Fish stock is used in fish soups, for poaching fish, and for making sauces served with fish and shellfish. Don't boil the stock or simmer it for longer than twenty minutes, or it will turn bitter.

> **1 tablespoon (15 g) butter**
> **1 medium onion, sliced**
> **1½ pounds (750 g) fish bones, cut in pieces**
> **1 quart (1 L) water**
> **10 peppercorns**
> **1 bouquet garni (p. 118)**
> **1 cup (250 ml) white wine OR juice of ½ lemon—**
> **optional**

MAKES ABOUT 1 QUART (1 L) STOCK.

In a large pot melt the butter and cook the onion slowly until soft but not brown, 7–10 minutes. Add the fish bones, water, peppercorns, bouquet garni, and wine or lemon juice. Bring slowly to a boil, skimming occasionally, and simmer, uncovered, 20 minutes. Strain and cool. Fish stock can be kept for 1 day in the refrigerator or several weeks if it is boiled every other day, or it can be frozen.

Chicken Stock
(FOND DE VOLAILLE)

Chicken stock is used for poultry dishes and sauces and can be substituted for white veal stock in most recipes.

> **2 pounds (1 kg) veal bones, cracked or cut in pieces**
> **3 pounds (1.5 kg) chicken backs and necks OR 3 pound**
> **(1.5 kg) whole chicken**
> **2 onions, quartered**
> **2 carrots, quartered**
> **2 stalks celery, cut in 2-inch (5 cm) pieces**
> **1 large bouquet garni (p. 118)**
> **10 peppercorns**
> **1 unpeeled clove garlic**
> **3–4 quarts (3–4 L) water**

MAKES 2–3 QUARTS (2–3 L) STOCK.

Blanch the veal bones by bringing them to a boil in water to cover and then simmering 5 minutes. Drain and rinse in cold water. Put the bones, the chicken, and the vegetables in a stockpot. Add the bouquet garni, peppercorns, garlic, and enough water to cover well. Bring slowly to a boil, skimming often. Simmer 3–4 hours, skimming occasionally. (NOTE: The whole chicken can be removed when tender, after about 1½ hours, to use in another recipe. If it is left in for the full cooking time, it will give more flavor to the stock, but the chicken meat will not be worth eating.)

Strain the stock, taste, and if the flavor isn't concentrated, boil to reduce. Skim off any fat before using. Store in the refrigerator for up to 4 days or several weeks if it is boiled every few days, or it can be frozen.

White Veal Stock
(FOND BLANC DE VEAU)

White veal stock is used for soups and for light sauces, sautés, stews, and braises. Because of its neutral flavor, it blends with almost any meat or poultry.

> **4–5 pounds (2 kg) veal bones, cracked or cut in pieces**
> **2 onions, quartered**
> **2 carrots quartered**
> **2 stalks celery, cut into 2-inch (5 cm) pieces**
> **1 large bouquet garni (p. 118)**
> **10 peppercorns**
> **1 unpeeled clove garlic**
> **3–4 quarts (3–4 L) water**

MAKES 2–3 QUARTS (2–3 L) STOCK.

Blanch the bones by bringing them to a boil in water to cover and then simmering 5 minutes. Drain and rinse in cold water. Put the bones and vegetables in a stockpot. Add the bouquet garni, peppercorns, garlic, and enough water to cover well. Bring slowly to a boil, skimming often. Simmer 4–5 hours, skimming occasionally; the stock should reduce very slowly.

Strain, taste, and if the flavor isn't strong enough, boil to concentrate it. Skim off any fat before using. The stock can be kept, refrigerated, for up to 4 days or several weeks if it is boiled every few days, or it can be frozen.

Brown Veal Stock
(FOND BRUN DE VEAU)

Brown veal stock is used for making brown sauces and for adding to sautés, stews, and braises of beef, game, or lamb.

>   **4–5 pounds (2 kg) veal bones, cracked or cut in pieces**
>   **2 onions, quartered**
>   **2 carrots, quartered**
>   **2 stalks celery, cut into 2-inch (5 cm) pieces**
>   **1 large bouquet garni (p. 118)**
>   **10 peppercorns**
>   **1 unpeeled clove garlic**
>   **3–4 quarts (3–4 L) water**
>   **1 tablespoon tomato paste**
>   **½ onion (for color)—optional**

MAKES 2–3 QUARTS (2–3 L) STOCK.

Heat the oven to 450°F (230°C). Put the bones in a roasting pan and cook in the hot oven, stirring occasionally, until browned, 30–40 minutes. Add the vegetables and continue roasting until they are brown and the bones are very well colored, 20–30 minutes. Transfer the bones and vegetables to a stockpot, leaving any fat behind. Add the bouquet garni, peppercorns, garlic, enough water to cover generously, and the tomato paste. Bring slowly to a boil, skimming often. Singe the half onion until the cut side is black by holding it on a fork over a flame or putting it directly on an electric burner, or singe it in a small frying pan. Add to the stock. Simmer 4–5 hours, skimming occasionally; the stock should reduce very slowly.

Roasted bones and vegetables
ready for the stockpot

The singed onion

Skimming the stock

Strain the stock, taste, and if the flavor isn't strong enough, boil to concentrate it. Skim off any fat before using. The stock can be kept in the refrigerator for up to 4 days or several weeks if it is boiled every few days, or it can be frozen.

Beef Stock
(FOND DE BOEUF)

Beef stock is used for rich brown sauces and for game dishes. It has a good mellow flavor but less body than a stock made entirely with veal bones.

Make exactly as brown veal stock except in place of the 4–5 pounds (2 kg) veal bones use 2 pounds (1 kg) beef bones and 2 pounds (1 kg) veal bones.

Meat or Fish Glaze
(GLACE DE VIANDE OU DE POISSON)

Meat or fish glaze is used in very small quantities to add body to sauces and ragoûts.

MAKES ABOUT 1 CUP (250 ml) GLAZE.

Boil 3 quarts (3 L) brown veal stock or fish stock until reduced to about 1 cup (250 ml). As it reduces, change to smaller saucepans and lower the heat progressively to avoid scorching. The finished glaze will be dark and syrupy and will set very firmly when cool. It can be kept, refrigerated, for several months.

Bouquet Garni

The classic bouquet garni that is added to all manner of dishes is made of **1 sprig of fresh or dried thyme, 1 bay leaf,** and **10–12 parsley stems.** The size can be adjusted according to whether you're making a sauté for two or gallons of stock. Hold the thyme and bay leaf together, surround them with the parsley stems, wind a piece of string around the bouquet, and tie securely.

Working
with Gelatin

GELATIN IS NOT a fashionable ingredient. The statuesque creams and the towering *pièces montées* held together with gelatin that were so admired in the nineteenth century are the antithesis of the new cooking in which simplicity, albeit a deceptive simplicity, is the leitmotif. But whether or not they follow fashion, modern cooks cannot do without gelatin; with it would disappear far too many molded desserts and, perish the thought for the dedicated caterer, there would be no aspic.

Aspic, the original airtight covering, is the savory jelly that is used to coat meats, poultry, and fish. It is also an essential of molded dishes built in layers such as boeuf à la mode and may be included in savory mousses in preference to plain gelatin.

As far as the cook is concerned, there are two kinds of gelatin: natural gelatin, which is extracted from bones and skin during cooking, and commercial gelatin. The more natural the gelatin that can be used in a dish, the better—it is commercial gelatin that is frowned on as "artificial." However, savory aspics can be more confidently relied upon to stay set in the heat of the average dining room with added commercial gelatin, and without it many molded desserts, especially Bavarian creams and the charlottes based on them, would fall flat.

Natural gelatin is found chiefly in the knuckle bones of young calves. Pigs' feet also yield a good deal of gelatin, as do fish and chicken carcasses, but the content in beef and lamb bones is relatively low. To extract natural gelatin, long slow cooking is needed—up to eight hours for veal bones—and this is usually done as part of the process of making stock. Aspic has the flavor of the bones from which it was extracted. Veal, with its neutral flavor, can be used with most meats and poultry; chicken aspic is usually reserved for chicken, and fish of course strictly for fish.

Commercial gelatin comes as a powder or in sheets. Powdered gelatin should be sprinkled over a small quantity of liquid and left for a few minutes without stirring until it swells to a spongy consistency. This can then be melted and added to a warmish mixture, or it can be added directly to a mixture hot enough to melt it.

Leaf gelatin, generally used in France, should be soaked in cold water for two to three minutes until soft, then drained, squeezed of all water, and melted or added to a warm mixture in the same manner as powdered gelatin. There is really nothing to choose between the two kinds: both are tasteless (almost) and equally easy to use. With either, be sure to stir so the gelatin is thoroughly incorporated and does not form strings or granules. There was an uncomfortable occasion at La Varenne when an inexperienced student, trying to cut corners, added gelatin to a mixture that was too cool. All appeared to be well until lunchtime, when the chef extracted, one by one, the strings from his portion of mousse.

The trickiest part about aspics and molded desserts is knowing how much commerical gelatin to add, for this can vary according to the heat of the day, the quantity of natural gelatin already present, and how long the dish will be left to stand before serving. We've all chewed on rubbery jellies, sweet or savory, that would bounce if dropped, and it is a great temptation to cut gelatin to a minimum. But even more disastrous is a gelatin preparation that will not set. The legendary Chef Carême, writing during the First Empire, recorded his chagrin when a skimpy amount of gelatin failed to maintain the stability of his charlottes and they collapsed in ignominious heaps.

Better to be safe than sorry. If, after trying a recipe, you think it has too much gelatin, reduce the quantity only a little next time. As a general rule, ½ ounce (15 g) of gelatin will set 1 quart (1 L) of liquid to a good consistency. To test a savory aspic that already contains natural gelatin, put a little on a plate in the refrigerator. When set, you can judge how much more gelatin, if any, should be added (see p. 123).

Gelatin sets quite abruptly. When working with aspic, put it in a metal bowl set over ice and stir frequently until it becomes the consistency of oil. This shows it is about to set and is ready for use. Spoon it over food or into a mold, working quickly because it will set within a few minutes.

TRUITES AU VIN BLANC EN GELÉE
Poached trout, decorated with zigzags cut in the skins, glistening in a coating of
aspic made from the cooking liquid

With desserts, too, the gelatin mixture should be stirred fairly constantly over ice as that part of the mixture in direct contact with the chilled bowl will set quickly. As soon as the mixture starts to thicken, fold in any whipped ingredients such as cream or egg whites and spoon the mixture into the mold at once. If a gelatin dessert separates in the mold, the chances are that the cream or egg whites were added too soon, before the gelatin mixture had begun to set.

Though always called "cold," gelatin dishes are best served at room temperature, not chilled. They should be kept in the refrigerator, but be careful of cold air currents; when too cold, aspic and dessert molds will crystallize and your work will be entirely destroyed. For this reason it is risky to use a freezer for quick chilling when working with gelatin. If a dish does completely crystallize, the only way to save it is to melt it and start again.

Gelatin dishes have an enormous advantage when it comes to serving: all the work is done ahead. Molds must be assembled at least a few hours in advance so that the gelatin will set firmly, and twenty-four hours is perfectly acceptable. Meats coated in aspic are sealed from the air and are, in effect, preserved so their keeping time is extended—one reason aspic dishes are so popular with professional chefs. Nor is much last-minute decoration needed. Desserts demand at most a few rosettes of whipped cream, and for aspic preparations, a bunch of watercress is more than ample. With their spectacular shapes and multicolored layers, gelatin dishes make their own show.

 FOR SUCCESSFUL GELATIN DISHES

USING GELATIN:

1. For aspics or gelatin desserts that are served from the dish rather than unmolded, use less gelatin so the texture is less firm.

2. To melt gelatin after softening, put it in a water bath and leave until dissolved, shaking it from time to time. Do not put it over direct heat, because gelatin can stick to the sides of the pan and burn.

3. To speed up setting, put the gelatin mixture in a metal bowl and put the bowl into a pan or bowl of ice water; the mixture must be stirred until it is on the point of setting.

4. When on the point of setting, aspic has the consistency of oil, and creamy mixtures start to thicken. Use them at once.

5. Aspic that has set too soon can be melted over very low but direct heat. For other mixtures, soften a few seconds in a water bath. If they contain egg, they will curdle, and whipped cream will melt, over direct heat.

MAKING ASPIC:

1. When making the original stock, be sure it only simmers; boiling will make it cloudy. The stock must be completely free of all fat; otherwise the aspic will not be clear.

2. To test whether commercial gelatin is needed for making aspic, check the consistency of the stock as follows: Pour a spoonful of stock on a small plate or saucer. Put the plate over ice or in the refrigerator and wait to see how it sets. If it is very liquid, add ½ ounce (15 g) per quart (1 L) of stock. If very set, do not add any. If in between, add ¼ ounce (7 g). If you're not sure, add less gelatin than you think you need and test again.

3. Seasoning becomes less pronounced as food cools, so warm aspic might be slightly overseasoned.

PREPARING AHEAD

Of necessity, gelatin dishes are made ahead, because the gelatin must have time to set.

1. Meat or poultry aspic can be made up to three days before serving (two days before using if making the finished dish a day ahead) and kept in the refrigerator. Fish aspic should be used within twelve hours if the finished dish is to be kept a day. To prepare the aspic for use, melt it over very low heat.

2. Dishes coated or set in aspic and gelatin desserts can be kept in the refrigerator for a day. Gelatin tends to stiffen on standing so use a little less gelatin in a mold that is to be kept for some time.

3. Aspic dishes and gelatin-molded desserts cannot be frozen.

TO MOLD AND TURN OUT ASPICS AND GELATIN DESSERTS

CHOOSING THE MOLD:

1. The taller the mold, the more spectacular the dish will look, but the more likely it is to collapse.

2. The more complicated the design of the mold, the more likely the mixture is to stick.

3. Aspics and plain sweet molds hold up well, but soft creamy mixtures are best set in simple molds that are relatively shallow. In a charlotte, however, ladyfingers help to retain the filling.

MOLDING:

1. For ease of unmolding, first rinse out the mold with water and leave it damp.

2. Chill the mold thoroughly to hasten the setting process.

3. In gelatin molds constructed in layers, the solid ingredients will float to the top if the gelatin mixture does not set completely. However, if the mold is left too long between each addition, the gelatin will set so firmly that the layers will tend to detach from each other when turned out.

TURNING OUT:

1. Lower the mold into a pan of hand-hot water so the water almost reaches the top. Leave it for two or three seconds and lift it out; metal molds conduct heat better than other materials and should be dipped for a shorter time.

2. Tip the mold sideways and gently pull the mixture away from the edge with your fingers, repeating all around the mold; this breaks the air lock and helps prevent sticking.

3. Rinse the serving plate with water so that if the mold does not land in the middle of the plate you can gently push it into place.

4. Set the plate upside down on top of the mold and quickly turn over both together. Give a quick forceful shake sideways and down, and the mold will fall onto the plate.

5. If the mold sticks, give several shakes. If it still sticks, put a hot wet cloth on top of the mold for ten to twenty seconds—this works best with a metal mold. If the mixture continues to stick, dip the mold in warm water again.

6. If the mold does not turn out neatly, don't despair. A little chopped parsley can cover faults in molded aspics, and whipped cream does wonders for desserts.

Eggs in Aspic
(OEUFS EN GELÉE)

The eggs can be poached or mollet. They must, however, be small so they fit into the molds easily.

> **aspic (p. 139) made with 2 cups (500 ml) stock, 1 carrot,**
> **1 leek, 1 stalk celery, 1 tomato, ¼ pound (125 g) beef,**
> **1 egg white, ⅛–¼ ounce (3–7 g) gelatin if needed, 1**
> **tablespoon Madeira or sherry, and salt and pepper**
> **1 truffle OR 2 black olives OR a few leaves fresh**
> **tarragon or chervil**
> **4 small eggs**
> **2 slices cooked ham**
> **1 bunch watercress**

> ***4 oval egg molds or small ramekins***

SERVES 4.

Make the aspic; if using a canned truffle, add the truffle liquid to the stock before clarifying. The aspic can be made up to 2 days ahead. Poach (p. 368) the eggs or boil them to the mollet stage (p. 367) and then keep them in a bowl of cold water. Cut 4 ovals of ham to fit the bases of the molds. Cut the truffle into 4 slices or pit the olives and cut them in half lengthwise. If using tarragon or chervil for decoration, pick a dozen good leaves or sprigs, pour boiling water over them, leave for 1 minute, and then remove and drain on paper towels.

To assemble: Melt the aspic if necessary and pour a ¼-inch (6 mm) layer into each mold. Chill to set. Put a slice of tuffle, a piece of olive, cut side up, or tarragon or chervil on top of the aspic in the middle of each mold. Carefully spoon over just enough aspic to cover the decoration and chill to set. Top this layer with the ham. Drain the eggs and, if using mollet eggs, peel and dry them gently on paper towels. Put one in each mold. Fill the molds ⅔ full of aspic, chill to set, and then fill the molds to the brim with aspic, and chill until firmly set, 1–2 hours. The egg molds can be prepared up to a day ahead and kept in the refrigerator.

After adding the eggs, fill the molds two-thirds full and chill before filling to the brim.

Not more than 2 hours before serving, dip the molds briefly in warm water and turn out. Garnish with watercress.

Chicken Galantine
(GALANTINE DE POULET)

Strips of ham and tongue, pieces of chicken liver, and pistachios make a pattern in each slice of galantine. Together with aspic made from the cooking liquid, they form the decoration for the dish.

4–5 pound (2 kg) chicken
**½-inch (1.25 cm) slice cooked ham, weighing about ⅓
    pound (150 g)**
**½-inch (1.25 cm) slice cooked tongue, weighing about
    ⅓ pound (150 g)**
1 calf's or pig's foot, split
¼ cup (60 ml) sherry or Madeira
**1–1½ quarts (1–1½ L) white veal (p. 116) or chicken
    stock (p. 115)**
**aspic (p. 139) made with 1 quart (1 L) of the stock in
    which the chicken is cooked, 2 carrots, 2 leeks, 2
    stalks celery, 2 tomatoes, ½ pound (250 g) beef, 2 egg
    whites, ⅛–¼ ounce (3–7 g) gelatin if needed, 3
    tablespoons Madeira or sherry, and salt and pepper**

For the stuffing:
½ pound (250 g) ground pork
½ pound (250 g) ground veal
2 tablespoons (30 g) butter
1 onion, chopped
2 ounces (60 g) pistachios
1 teaspoon allspice
1 clove garlic, finely chopped
2 tablespoons sherry or Madeira
½ cup (125 ml) white wine
1 egg, beaten to mix
salt and pepper

trussing needle and string

pastry bag with medium star tip—optional

SERVES 10.

Cook the galantine at least a day ahead. First bone the chicken completely (see p. 90) and save the bones. Remove the flesh from the skin,

GALANTINE DE POULET
A classic presentation: the decorative slices of galantine are coated with aspic and the platter is decorated with chopped aspic and aspic crescents.

being careful to keep the skin in one piece. Cut the breast meat into strips.

To make the stuffing: Work the remaining chicken meat, the pork, and the veal through the fine plate of a grinder. Melt the butter and cook the onion in it until soft but not brown, 7–10 minutes. Blanch the pistachios in boiling water for 1 minute, drain, and peel them. Add to the ground meat the onion, pistachios, allspice, garlic, sherry or Madeira, wine, egg, and plenty of salt and pepper—the mixture should be highly seasoned. Beat with the hand until the stuffing holds together.

Spread the chicken skin, cut side up, on a working surface and fold the leg and wing skin to close the openings. Spread a third of the stuffing mixture on it in a rectangle, leaving 1½-inch (4 cm) border of skin at each end and 3 inches (7.5 cm) along the sides. Lay half the strips of ham, tongue, and chicken breast lengthwise down the stuffing. Add another third of the stuffing, building it up around the strips of meat so they are surrounded. Top with another layer of meat strips and then the last of the stuffing. Shape it to form a neat cylinder and wrap the chicken skin around it. Sew the skin with a trussing needle and string and wrap the roll tightly in a dishcloth. Tie both ends with string to keep the galantine in shape and fasten the center with a large safety pin. (NOTE: Wrap smoothly because any creases in the cloth will make wrinkles in the finished galantine.)

Blanch the calf's or pig's foot by putting it in cold water, bringing the water to a boil, and simmering for 5 minutes. Drain and rinse. Put the galantine in a large pot with the chicken bones, the foot, the ¼ cup (60 ml) sherry or Madeira, and enough stock to cover. Bring to a boil, cover, and simmer until a skewer inserted in the center of the galantine for ½ minute is hot to the touch when withdrawn, 1½–2 hours. Leave to cool to tepid in the cooking liquid and then drain it. Strain the stock and chill both galantine and stock.

Make the aspic (p. 139). To finish the galantine, unwrap it, carefully remove the trussing string, and cut ½–¾ of the roll into ⅜-inch (1 cm) slices. Put the slices and the remaining roll on a rack set over a tray and chill them. Spoon a layer of aspic onto the platter you will use for serving and chill to set. Cool some of the aspic in a bowl of ice water until just on the point of setting. Working quickly, coat the chilled galantine with aspic; excess will fall into the tray. Refrigerate to set and repeat this process 1 or 2 times more to form a smooth layer of aspic over the slices and surrounding the piece of galantine. Pour the remaining aspic into a tray or pan to form a ¼-inch (6 mm) layer.

To assemble the dish: Put the uncut galantine at one end of the platter of set aspic and arrange the slices overlapping down the center. Turn out the tray or pan of aspic onto a sheet of wet waxed paper, cut out triangles or crescents, and arrange them around the edge of the platter. Either chop the remaining aspic and put it around the galantine or scoop the aspic into a pastry bag fitted with a medium star tip and pipe it onto the platter. The galantine can be prepared and decorated up to a day ahead and kept in the refrigerator.

Poached Trout in White Wine Aspic
(TRUITES AU VIN BLANC EN GELÉE)

This dish comes from Alsace, where the Riesling used for poaching the trout gives the aspic a special flavor.

> fish stock (p. 115) made with 1 tablespoon (15 g) butter,
>   1 onion, 1½ pounds (750 g) bones, 2 cups (500 ml)
>   water, 10 peppercorns, a bouquet garni (p. 118), and
>   2 cups (500 ml) Riesling
> 4 trout, each weighing about ½-pound (250 g), with
>   heads on
> 1 lemon
> ½ ounce (15 g) gelatin if needed
> 4 tablespoons chopped parsley
> salt and pepper
> a few drops lemon juice

SERVES 4.

Make the fish stock. If possible, clean the trout through the gills so there are no slits in the stomachs. Trim each tail to a "V" shape. Put the fish in a baking dish and pour the stock over them. Bring almost to a boil, cover, reduce the heat, and poach on top of the stove or in a 350°F (175°C) oven until the flesh is easily pierced, 15–20 minutes. Let the fish cool to tepid in the stock, then drain them on paper towels, and skin them but leave on the head and tail. If you like, leave also a decorative zigzag of skin (wolf's teeth) along the backbone.

Cut the lemon into thin slices. Arrange the trout close together in a deep dish and decorate each with 2–3 lemon slices. Strain a spoonful or two of the cooking liquid onto a saucer and put it in the refrigerator. If it sets well, there is no need to add gelatin. If it does not set firmly, add the gelatin: First sprinkle it over ¼ cup (60 ml) cool stock and leave until spongy, about 5 minutes. Reheat the rest of the stock and add the gelatin, mixing well to melt it.

Reheat the stock to hot and add the parsley. (NOTE: This makes the parsley bright green.) Add salt, pepper, and lemon juice to taste—the liquid should be highly seasoned—and pour it over the trout. They should be completely covered. Refrigerate until set, at least 2 hours. The trout can be prepared a day ahead.

Cold Beef à la Mode
(BOEUF À LA MODE FROID)

This is one of the mainstays of French cooking. Chef Chambrette, La Varenne's head chef, is a typical Frenchman in speaking nostalgically of his mother's beef à la mode—"the best in the world."

4-pound (1.75 kg) round roast of beef
¼ pound (125 g) pork fat, cut in strips
calf's or pig's foot, split
2 cups (500 ml) white wine
2 cups (500 ml) white veal stock (p. 116)
¼ cup (60 ml) cognac
1 onion, stuck with a clove
3 carrots, quartered
1 large bouquet garni (p. 118)
10 peppercorns
salt and pepper

1 pound (500 g) small or medium carrots
1 pound (500 g) baby onions
1 pound (500 g) green beans
1 pound (500 g) turnips
¼ ounce (7 g) gelatin

2-quart (2 L) terrine or other mold

larding needle

SERVES 8.

Braise the beef at least a day ahead. Begin by larding the beef evenly with the pork fat and tying the meat into a compact shape. Blanch the calf's or pig's foot: Put it in cold water, bring to a boil, and simmer for 5 minutes. Drain and rinse. Heat the oven to 325°F (165°C). Put the beef and the foot in a large pot and add the wine, stock, cognac, onion, 3 carrots, bouquet garni, peppercorns, and a little salt to taste. Bring to a boil, cover, and braise in the heated oven until the meat is very tender, 2½–3 hours. Let it cool to tepid, then drain it, and chill. Strain the cooking liquid, pressing the vegetables well to extract their juices, measure the liquid, and augment or reduce it as necessary to make 1 quart (1 L). Chill.

To make the aspic, skim all the fat from the cooking liquid. It should be firmly set, but if not, sprinkle the gelatin over ¼ cup (60 ml) water, let stand until spongy, and then melt it in a water bath. Heat the cooking liquid, add the melted gelatin, taste, and adjust seasoning if necessary—it should be very well seasoned. Both beef and aspic can be prepared up to 2 days ahead and kept in the refrigerator.

"Turn" small carrots with a knife to shape then into 2-inch (5 cm) ovals. Cut and "turn" larger carrots to the same size. Cook them in boiling salted water until tender, 15–20 minutes, and drain. Blanch the baby onions in boiling water to loosen the skins, drain, and peel them. Cook the onions in boiling salted water until tender, 12–15 minutes, and drain. Trim the green beans and cut into equal lengths. Cook in boiling salted water until tender, 8–10 minutes, refresh with cold water, and drain. "Turn" the turnips to shape them into ovals the same size as the carrots. If you must use large ones, cut into quarters before turning. Cook the turnips in boiling salted water until tender, 3–5 minutes, drain, and refresh with cold water. (NOTE: Be sure the vegetables are cooked through because if they are undercooked they will be hard when cool.) Chill the vegetables. They can be cooked a day ahead.

To assemble the dish, first melt the aspic if necessary. Spoon a thin layer into the mold and chill until set. Carve the beef in ½-inch (1.25 cm) slices. Arrange lengthwise rows of half the green beans, turnips, carrots, and baby onions on top of the aspic. Arrange the slices of meat, overlapping, on top of the vegetables. Pour in enough aspic to hold the vegetables and meat in place and chill to set. Top with the rest of the vegetables, fill the mold with the remaining aspic, and refrigerate. The mold can be assembled up to a day ahead and kept in the refrigerator. Not more than 2 hours before serving, dip the mold briefly in warm water and turn out onto a platter.

Ribboned Bavarian Cream
(BAVAROIS RUBANÉ)

The secret of making this spectacular dessert is to be organized. Once the three custard flavors are ready and the cream whipped, assembling it is easy.

¾ ounce (21 g) gelatin
2 ounces (60 g) semisweet chocolate, chopped
custard sauce (p. 306) made with 1½ quarts (1.5 L)
    milk, 1 vanilla bean OR 2 tablespoons vanilla
    extract, 12 egg yolks, and ¾ cup (150 g) sugar
1 tablespoon instant coffee, dissolved in 2 tablespoons
    hot water
1½ cups (375 ml) heavy cream, lightly whipped

For decoration—optional:
Chantilly cream (p. 285) made with ½ cup (125 ml)
    cream, 2 teaspoons sugar, and ¼ teaspoon vanilla
    extract
candied coffee beans or grated chocolate

2½-quart (2.5 L) tall mold

pastry bag with medium star tip—optional

SERVES 8–10.

Sprinkle the gelatin over ½ cup (125 ml) water and leave until spongy, about 5 minutes. Melt the chocolate in a water bath and set aside to cool. Make the custard sauce and strain it into a bowl. Melt the gelatin in a water bath and add it to the hot custard.

Pour equal amounts of the custard into three separate bowls. Stir the dissolved coffee into one bowl and the cool but still soft chocolate into another. Leave the custards until cool and then set the coffee custard in a bowl of ice water and stir until it starts to thicken. Fold in ⅓ of the whipped cream and pour the custard into the mold. Put it in the refrigerator until set.

Stir the vanilla custard also until on the point of setting, fold in half the remaining whipped cream, and pour gently into the mold. (NOTE: The coffee custard must be fairly firmly set, or it will mix with the vanilla.) Refrigerate until set.

Set the bowl of chocolate custard over ice water and stir. When on the point of setting, fold in the remaining whipped cream and pour into the mold. Cover and chill until firmly set, at least 2 hours. The Bavarian cream can be made up to a day ahead.

Not more than 2 hours before serving, dip the mold in warm water and turn it out on a platter. If you like, decorate the base of the dessert with rosettes of Chantilly cream and top them with the coffee beans or grated chocolate. Keep in a cool place or refrigerate until serving.

Strawberry or Raspberry Charlotte
(CHARLOTTE AUX FRAISES OU AUX FRAMBOISES)

Charlottes can be filled with Bavarian cream as well as a mousse as in this recipe. If you do not make your own ladyfingers, buy ones that are not too dry.

> **ladyfingers (p. 279) made with ¾ cup (95 g) flour, a
>   pinch of salt, 4 eggs, ½ cup (100 g) sugar, ½ teaspoon
>   vanilla extract, and powdered sugar**
> **1 pint (250 g) fresh raspberries or strawberries, hulled**
> **¼ ounce (7 g) gelatin**
> **juice of ½ lemon**
> **3 eggs**
> **2 egg yolks**
> **¾ cup (150 g) sugar**
> **1 cup (250 ml) heavy cream, lightly whipped**
> **Chantilly cream (p. 285) made with ½ cup (125 ml)
>   cream, 2 teaspoons sugar, and ¼ teaspoon vanilla
>   extract**
> **1 tablespoon kirsch**
>
> *1½-quart (1.5 L) charlotte mold*
>
> *pastry bag with medium star tip*

SERVES 6–8.

Line the sides and bottom of the mold with ladyfingers, trimming the edges of the ladyfingers so they fit tightly around the sides of the mold and cutting triangular pieces to fit into the bottom like wedges of a pie. Save at least 8 perfect berries for decoration and work the rest through a sieve or purée in a blender and then put through a sieve. Sprinkle the gelatin over the lemon juice and let stand until spongy, about 5 minutes.

Put the eggs, egg yolks, and sugar in a bowl, preferably copper, and beat until mixed. Set the bowl over a pan of hot but not boiling water and beat until the mixture is thick and light and leaves a ribbon trail when the beater is lifted. Remove from the heat.

Melt the softened gelatin in a water bath, beat into the hot egg mixture, and continue beating until cool. Stir in the fruit purée. Set the bowl in a pan or bowl of ice water and chill, stirring occasionally, until the mixture is on the point of setting. Immediately fold in the whipped cream and the kirsch and pour into the lined mold. Cover and chill until firm, at least 2 hours. The charlotte can be made up to 2 days ahead and kept in the refrigerator.

Not more than 2 hours before serving, unmold the charlotte: Trim the ladyfingers, if necessary, so they are level with the top of the filling, set a plate over the mold, and turn both upside down so the charlotte falls out onto the plate. Using the pastry bag and star tip, decorate the base, top, and sides of the charlotte with Chantilly cream, running cream over the cracks between the ladyfingers. Set a few berries in the cream and refrigerate until serving.

THE FRENCH CREATIONS

CONSOMMÉ BRUNOISE, MADRILÈNE, AND JULIENNE
Consommé brunoise (left) is garnished with a tiny dice of vegetables; Consommé madrilène (front) has a tomato garnish; Consommé julienne (right) is garnished with matchstick-thin strips of vegetables.

Consommé

CONSOMMÉ IS the simplest yet most sophisticated of the dishes made from stock. To make consommé, veal, beef, chicken, or, more rarely, game, or fish stock is reduced and then clarified to produce a limpid, sparkling liquid. Its transparency is deceptive since good consommé has punch—a heady aroma and an equally powerful flavor that is neither bland nor salty, thin nor heavy. The balance is not easy to achieve, and consommé is one of the traditional tests of an accomplished chef.

The heyday of consommé was the Belle Époque when after caviar, oysters, or smoked salmon, soup was the standard second course in every ten or twelve course dinner. Escoffier, Montagné, and all the great names vied to produce the finest consommé madrilène, garnished with tomatoes; consommé brunoise, with its garnish of tiny diced vegetables; or the tricky consommé royale, decked with minute shapes of pale golden egg custard.

Regardless of whether the finished dish includes a simple or elaborate garnish—or no garnish at all—the preparation of the consommé itself is always the same. Well-flavored, fat-free stock is brought slowly to a boil while egg whites are whisked in—three whites to one quart (1 L) stock is the standard proportion. As the egg white cooks, it traps the tiny particles that cloud the stock; and as soon as the mixture looks milky, whisking should be stopped so that the whites can rise gradually to the top of the stock in a grubby gray froth that coagulates to form a filter. The consommé is then left to simmer quietly for half an hour or more, percolating constantly up through the filter until it is clean and sparkling.

The problem with egg whites is that while they clarify the liquid they also steal flavor. Reinforcements are therefore added along with them: vegetables such as carrots, leeks, celery, and tomato, all chopped so they yield their flavor in a short cooking time. Meat is also used: beef for all the meat consommés, with chicken as well for chicken consommé, and fish alone for fish consommé. Hence the term *consommé double*, for meat or fish is used twice in the preparation—for making the stock and for clarifying the consommé. All meat *must be free of fat* (for beef, the preferred cut is the tough scrawny shin), and it is chopped or ground so that it cooks quickly. Recently the chefs at La Varenne have been throwing the whole vegetables and chunks of meat into the grinder and turning out a sort of mincemeat that works admirably to flavor the consommé. In addition to adding flavor, red meat helps to clear consommé because blood is a clarifying agent.

The basic clarifying mixture, then, is a combination of egg whites, vegetables, and meat. Other possible flavorings are legion: herbs, celery leaves, mushrooms, and even (says Escoffier) truffles. No matter what they are, from herbs to truffles, these extra ingredients are strained out at the end of simmering.

Opinions are mixed about the use of alcohol. A dash of Madeira or sherry added just before serving is generally acceptable; some chefs add white wine, Madeira, sherry, or a touch of brandy during the clarification. Either way, alcohol should be an embellishment, not a prop. Made from good stock and properly clarified, a consommé stands on its own, and no amount of alcohol will redeem an indifferent result.

Besides clarity and flavor, color is important. A clear tint, light but not pale is most attractive; consommé of meat should be slightly darker than that of chicken or fish. Pinkness can be added during clarification by including plenty of tomatoes, but the only way of darkening a pallid stock is to use food coloring, and this should be avoided if possible. The key to the color of consommé lies in coloring the original stock well.

It is the gelatin content of consommé that gives it a suave texture when hot and sets it when chilled to just the right shivering jelly. Ideally, the original stock should have been made with enough bones to make it set without additional gelatin. However, this is not always the case, and gelatin can be added (about ¼ ounce per quart or 7 g per L) during clarification to ensure that the consommé, hot or cold, comes out just right. On the other hand, too much added gelatin gives a heavy cloying soup, so extra should be added only if necessary.

Although *consommé double* is perfection in itself, garnishing is a matter to consider. Escoffier rang the changes with 136

variations from *consommé aux ailerons* (chicken consommé with stuffed chicken wings and rice) to *consommé Zorilla* (tomato flavored consommé with chick-peas and rice). If you use a garnish that is to be added to the consommé before serving, it is always cooked separately and put in at the last moment so that it cannot cloud the soup. A tablespoon of garnish per serving is sufficient because it must not detract from the clarity of the consommé. Some possibilities are tiny quenelles, crêpes cut in strips, small pasta shapes, or chopped herbs. Other garnishes are served separately and put in the soup at the table, such as tiny choux puffs flavored with cheese. Sautéed croûtons are frowned on because they form an oil slick over the beautiful clear soup.

Consommé no longer occupies the important position on menus that it once did. Young chefs look for more instant appeal, finding the return too low on the care needed for the preparation of a good consommé. This is a pity because consommé meets the requirements for an appetizer better than anything else I could name. It announces the meal to come with clear rich flavor yet without filling—truly whetting the appetite rather than blunting it.

FOR SUCCESSFUL CONSOMMÉ

1. Stock for consommé should be concentrated and well flavored. If its flavor is weak, boil to reduce it before clarifying.

2. The stock must be completely skimmed of all fat. To do this, chill the stock until set and skim the fat from the surface. Then gently heat the stock and remove any remaining fat by quickly drawing strips of paper toweling across the surface. All the equipment used should also be free of grease.

3. Use a pan of stainless steel, tin-lined copper, or enamel. The action of a whisk in an aluminum pan may give an unpleasant flavor and color to the consommé.

4. The number of egg whites needed depends on the stock. If the stock is very cloudy, add another egg white to the suggested amount.

5. Do not pour hot stock directly on the egg whites or they will coagulate too quickly. It is the slow coagulation of the egg whites that produces a clear consommé.

6. So that the globules of egg white will attract all the particles that cloud the stock, they must be thoroughly mixed with it.

7. Once the crust, or filter, begins to form, stop whisking. Make a hole in the egg white filter through which the stock can bubble. Otherwise, the movement of the liquid will break the filter.

8. When straining, use a ladle to take the liquid carefully from the hole in the filter and ladle it into a strainer lined with a wet dish towel. Let the liquid drain through slowly and don't press the solids. Again, if there is a trace of remaining fat, remove it with strips of paper toweling.

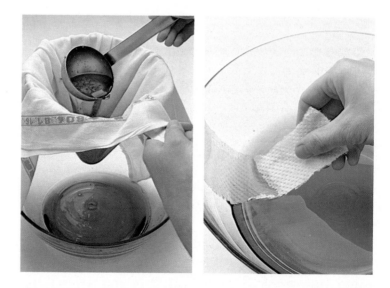

9. If, in spite of all precautions, the liquid running through the strainer is not sparkling clear, pour it through again. If it still isn't clear, repeat the clarification process using an additional egg white; simmer only 5–10 minutes before straining.

10. Egg whites, vegetables, and meat left over after clarification can be added to another batch of simmering stock, which will gain flavor and clarity from the addition.

PREPARING AHEAD

1. The stock for consommé can be made well ahead.

2. Consommé can be made ahead and kept several days in the refrigerator. It will not lose flavor, but it may become slightly cloudy.

3. Consommé can be frozen, but again, it will become less clear.

4. Most garnishes can be prepared in advance. If the consommé is to be hot, reheat the garnish gently in a small amount of consommé just before serving.

Consommé or Aspic
(CONSOMMÉ OU GELÉE)

All consommés based on veal stock, beef stock, or chicken stock are flavored with lean beef. However, a chicken consommé usually contains an equivalent amount of chicken giblets or parts, too. Do not include any chicken skin or fat.

> 1½ quarts (1.5 L) veal (p. 116), beef (p. 118), or chicken
>   stock (p. 115)
> 2 carrots, chopped
> green tops of 2 leeks, chopped
> 2 stalks celery, chopped
> 2 tomatoes, quartered
> ¾ pound (350 g) boneless shin of beef, chopped
> ¾ pound (350 g) chicken giblets or chicken parts,
>   chopped—for chicken consommé
> 3 egg whites, beaten until frothy
> ¼–½ ounce (7–15 g) gelatin—if needed
> 4 tablespoons Madeira or sherry
> salt and pepper

MAKES ABOUT 1 QUART (1 L) CONSOMMÉ.

Skim the fat from the stock, heat the stock in a saucepan, and remove any remaining fat by pulling strips of paper towel across the surface. Let cool.

In a bowl mix the carrots, leeks, celery, tomatoes, chopped beef, chicken, and beaten egg whites. Pour the stock over the vegetables and meat, whisking, and return the mixture to the pan. (NOTE: The stock can be warm but not hot.) Set the pan over moderate heat and bring slowly to a boil, whisking constantly—this should take about 10 minutes.

As soon as the mixture looks milky, stop whisking. Let the filter rise slowly to the top of the pan and then turn down the heat. With a ladle make a small hole in the egg-white filter so the consommé can bubble without breaking the filter.

Let the consommé simmer gently 30–40 minutes to extract the flavor from the vegetables and meat and to give the liquid time to clarify. Depending on the consistency of the stock and the use to which it will be put, you may need to add ¼–½ ounce (7–15 g) gelatin. For aspic (see Chapter 10) the stock must be set fairly firmly, and for consommé it should be lightly gelled. Sprinkle the gelatin, if using, over ½ cup (125 ml) of cold stock and leave 5 minutes, or until spongy. Carefully add the prepared gelatin through the hole in the filter; simmer gently 2–3 minutes to be sure it is dissolved. Add the Madeira or sherry. Taste for seasoning and adjust if necessary.

Put a wet dish towel in a strainer over a clean bowl and ladle the consommé into it. Do not press on vegetables or meat left in the towel. If the consommé running through is not sparkling clear, strain it again through the towel and the filter of egg white deposited in the towel. Leave the consommé to cool. It can be kept, covered and refrigerated, for up to 2 days. Pour a layer of water over the consommé after it has set to prevent the formation of a skin.

If serving the consommé hot, bring it almost to a boil and add any flavorings and garnish just before serving. If serving chilled, stir it with a fork to break it up and then top with any garnish.

Consommé Julienne
(CONSOMMÉ JULIENNE)

Consommé julienne and all the vegetable-garnished consommés that follow make delicious first courses for dieters. They're full-flavored yet low in calories.

1 quart (1 L) veal or beef consommé

For the garnish:
1 small carrot
1 stalk celery
1 small white turnip
white part of 1 leek

SERVES 4.

Make the consommé.

Cut the vegetables into julienne strips. Simmer them in ⅔ cup (160 ml) of the consommé until they are tender, about 5 minutes. The garnish can be cooked up to a day ahead and reheated, if serving hot, when ready to use.

Just before serving, lift the vegetables from their cooking liquid with a slotted spoon and add to the consommé.

Consommé Brunoise
(CONSOMMÉ BRUNOISE)

Brunoise is the name given to the smallest possible dice of vegetables. The tinier the vegetable pieces are, the finer the garnish is considered.

1 quart (1 L) veal or beef consommé

For the brunoise garnish:
1 small carrot
1 stalk celery
1 small white turnip
1 small leek

SERVES 4.

Make the consommé.

Cut the vegetables into julienne strips and then into tiny dice. Simmer the diced vegetables in ⅔ cup (160 ml) of the consommé until they are tender, about 5 minutes. The garnish can be cooked up to a day ahead and reheated, if serving hot, when ready to use.

Just before serving, lift the vegetables from their cooking liquid and add to the consommé.

Consommé Madrilène
(CONSOMMÉ MADRILÈNE)

The French associate tomatoes and pimientos with Spanish cooking, hence the name madrilène which means from Madrid.

1 quart (1 L) chicken consommé
2 tomatoes, quartered

For the garnish:
2 tomatoes, peeled, seeded, and cut in thin strips
1 pimiento, cut in thin strips

SERVES 4.

Make the consommé, adding the extra 2 tomatoes to the basic recipe while clarifying.

Add the garnish to the consommé just before serving.

Consommé Olga
(CONSOMMÉ OLGA)

Even pickles can be used to garnish a consommé, as in this classic combination.

1 quart (1 L) veal or beef consommé
¼ cup (60 ml) port

For the garnish:
1 small carrot
¼ small celeriac
white part of 1 small leek
5 sour gherkin pickles (cornichons)

SERVES 4.

Make the consommé.

Cut the vegetables into julienne strips. Simmer them in ⅔ cup (160 ml) of the consommé until they are tender, about 5 minutes. Cut the gherkins in julienne strips. The garnish can be prepared up to a day ahead and reheated, if serving hot, when ready to use.

Just before serving, lift the vegetables from their cooking liquid and add to the consommé along with the gherkin strips and the port.

Consommé Royale
(CONSOMMÉ ROYALE)

Do not overcook the custard used to garnish this consommé or it will curdle. Consommé royale is served hot.

1 quart (1 L) veal, beef, or chicken consommé
2 tablespoons Madeira or sherry

For the garnish:
> **1 egg**
> **3 egg yolks**
> **salt and pepper**

> **soufflé dish or individual ramekins or custard cups**

> **large plain pastry tip—optional**

SERVES 4.

    Set the oven at 350°F (180°C). Butter the dish, ramekins, or cups and prepare a water bath (see Chapter 8). Whisk together the egg, egg yolks, ⅔ cup (160 ml) of the consommé, and salt and pepper until thoroughly mixed. Taste for seasoning and adjust if necessary. Pour the mixture into the prepared dish, ramekins, or cups to a depth of ⅜ inch (1 cm) and put in the water bath. Bring to a simmer on top of the stove, transfer to the heated oven, and cook until the custard is set, about 20 minutes. Chill the custard; it can be made a day ahead and kept, covered and refrigerated.

    Turn out the chilled custard onto a flat surface and cut it into tiny diamonds or crescents, using the pastry tip to cut the crescents. Add Madeira or sherry and the custard shapes to the hot consommé just before serving.

Consommé aux Cheveux d'Anges
(CONSOMMÉ AUX CHEVEUX D'ANGES)

Cheveux d'anges, which means angel hair, is the very fine noodle used as a garnish in this hot consommé. It is cooked almost as soon as it hits the boiling consommé.

> **1 quart (1 L) veal, beef, or chicken consommé**
> **2 ounces (60 g) vermicelli**

SERVES 4.

    Make the consommé.

    Just before serving, bring the consommé to a boil and add the vermicelli.

RILETTES DE SAUMON (left front)

A good example of nouvelle cuisine. Traditional rillettes are made of slowly baked pork, goose, duck, or rabbit. Only recently have mixtures of similar consistency and richness been made of salmon and other fish.

PÂTÉ DE POISSON LA MARÉE (top)

Green and red peppers and black olives decorate the top of this delicate mousseline of fish layered with strips of salmon. It can be served either hot or cold.

TERRINE DE PORC PAYSANNE (right)

Pistachio nuts and strips of ham add color to a simple country terrine of pork, veal, and chicken livers. Small sour gherkins (cornichons) are the usual accompaniment.

Pâtés and Terrines

PÂTÉS AND TERRINES represent much of the best in French cooking: the combination of a number of flavors to good effect; virtuosity in applying a simple cooking method to a wide variety of different ingredients; and an astonishing range of sophistication, from the sumptuous pâtés of fresh foie gras studded with truffles to rustic terrines that are no more than the Gallic version of a meat loaf. Pâtés and terrines cover almost the whole meal from fish through meat to vegetables, and we only need some wit of the nouvelle cuisine to invent a fruit terrine for the menu to be complete.

Strictly speaking, a pâté is baked in pastry (*pâte*), and a terrine—the word comes from *terre*, earth—is cooked in a special earthenware mold (a terrine), but the definitions have become blurred over the years. In general, finer-textured richer mixtures used to be baked in pastry, so these have become known as pâtés, though the pastry has often disappeared and been replaced by a terrine mold. To distinguish them, true pâtés are often called *pâtés en croûte*. The dough was originally made of flour and water and was not eaten, but nowadays most people tuck into the richer butter or lard-flavored doughs that are used. Traditional terrines are always eaten cold, but pâtés en croûte can be served hot or cold—when eaten hot, the fat content of the forcemeat, usually a fair percentage, is reduced.

Pâtés and terrines probably began as a way of using up bits of the most common meat—pork. Pork is still the favorite ingredient, though veal is much used, and there are also traditional terrines of poultry and game. Whatever the meat, it can be coarsely

145

or finely ground or, even better, very finely chopped by hand. One day, a student at La Varenne was giving Chef Claude a hard time, so Claude put him to chopping the forcemeat for the duck terrine. Chopping does not bruise meat like a grinder, and when, three days later, we compared the hand-chopped terrine with an identical one made with machine-cut meat, the result was a revelation. But the class did not forget the work involved.

The seasoning of a forcemeat is even more important than the texture. Salt and freshly ground pepper are indispensable—our chefs' proportions are 12 grams (2½ teaspoons) of salt and 4 grams (scant teaspoon) of pepper per kilo (2 pounds) of forcemeat, but this can vary depending on the meat used. Spices such as nutmeg, allspice, and cloves lend flavor, as does a spoon or two of brandy or Madeira. Herbs, garlic, onion or shallot finely chopped and sautéed, and green peppercorns are all possible additions. Orange and lemon are great favorites with duck. The only way to test seasoning is by tasting: when all the ingredients are mixed, fry a little of the mixture or bake it in the oven and taste it. The seasonings should balance without one being predominant. Cold food requires more seasoning than hot, and if in doubt, I think too much is better than too little.

There are several tests to tell when a terrine is done, but the simplest is to just lift the lid, touch, and look: if it is firm to the touch and the liquid bubbling at the sides is clear, showing the meat juices are cooked, the terrine is done. If you use a standard terrine mold and seal it with a flour and water paste, you can insert a skewer into the hole in the lid, leave for thirty seconds, and if it's hot when withdrawn, the meat is cooked through. In case you should wonder why commercial terrines retain a pink tinge, this is not due to undercooking, but to the addition of saltpeter, which lengthens their shelf life.

The classic pâtés and terrines are not the end of the story, though, for there are several other members of the terrine family. Rillettes resemble potted meat and are made by cooking chunks of a fat meat, such as pork, goose, or duck, until the meat falls apart. When cool, the meat is pulled apart with forks and mixed with the rendered fat to give a characteristic rough texture. Lately fish rillettes have appeared; they have the same rough texture, but are made differently, being simply mixtures of cooked fish and butter. Salmon, eel, and smoked fish are popular for rillettes.

Fish rillettes are an invention of nouvelle cuisine, and young chefs are vying with each other in the creation of new pâtés and terrines as well, made of fish, not meat. Fish terrines have been thoroughly and successfully explored during the past fifteen years—

terrines of salmon, of sole, of scallops, and other shellfish, often arranged in multicolored layers.

Now fish terrines are rivaled by an even trickier concoction—the terrine of vegetables. This is made by layering a variety of lightly cooked vegetables to produce a gaily striped slice dotted with carrots, peas, green beans, artichokes, and so on. However, vegetables are not as accommodating as meat and fish: they lose flavor easily and render water during cooking. Making a terrine that holds together with vegetables of crisp texture and plenty of flavor is not easy, and quite honestly, even the famed three-star versions can be a trifle insipid. Perhaps there's more hope for a new masterpiece—who's going to invent that fruit terrine?

FOR SUCCESSFUL PÂTÉS AND TERRINES

1. If barding fat is not available to line a terrine mold, use caul fat or pork fat back. Cut the fat back as thin as possible and pound it even thinner.

2. For coarser terrines, the meat can be chopped in a food processor, a grinder, or by hand. For finer pâtés grind the meat twice, and fish pâtés should be worked through a drum sieve as well.

3. If adding ham or bacon to a pâté or terrine, season the forcemeat with less salt than usual.

4. Pâtés and terrines shrink as they cook, so fill the mold completely and pack the forcemeat down well. To keep forcemeat from sticking to your hands, dampen them occasionally.

5. When layering the filling, be sure to place meat strips lengthwise so they are cut crosswise when the terrine is sliced.

6. Press terrines when cool with a weight of at least 2 pounds (1 kg) and leave until very cold.

7. Do not cut a terrine until thoroughly chilled, or it will crumble.

PREPARING AHEAD

1. Pâtés, terrines, and rillettes are intended to be made ahead. Although fish terrines can be eaten warm directly from the oven, they can also be kept, refrigerated, for up to three days before serving. Meat mixtures mellow on keeping; they should be left at least three days and up to a week in a cool place or the refrigerator.

2. Once a meat pâté or terrine is cut open, it should be eaten within two days (one day in the case of fish mixtures). Cover the cut surface with plastic wrap to prevent discoloration.

3. To keep a pâté or terrine even longer, seal it when cold with a generous layer of melted clarified butter or lard. This will double the time it will last.

4. The fat in meat rillettes helps to preserve them by sealing the meat from contact with the air. They can be kept, refrigerated, for several weeks. Fish rillettes should be covered with clarified butter for storage.

5. Terrines can be frozen, but they will be tougher and slightly damp when thawed. The texture of pâtés is spoiled by freezing, but rillettes, because of their high fat content, freeze very well.

TERRINE MOLDS

Terrine molds are believed to have originated in Strasbourg, where a potter had the idea of cooking goose livers in earthenware containers. Now terrine molds come in materials varying from ovenproof porcelain through Pyrex to enameled cast iron. Manufacturers have given full rein to the imaginations of their designers, and terrine molds are ablaze with flowers, fruit, and, a bit more appropriately, vegetables. Some of the most expensive terrines are crowned in traditional style with pottery lids made to resemble birds and animals that designate the contents. The cheapest, made of plain old-fashioned earthenware, probably remain the best.

Molds vary from rectangular loaf shapes to the ovals intended for terrines of boned stuffed poultry. Long narrow terrines are easy to slice. All terrines should have a tight-fitting lid with a hole in it through which you can insert a skewer to test for doneness. If you have no mold, you can improvise with a heavy baking dish and several layers of foil as a lid.

LUTING PASTE

This simple flour-and-water paste is used to seal the traditional terrine mold.

> 1½ cups (200 g) flour
> 1–1¼ cups (250–310 ml) water

Put the flour in a small bowl. Make a well in the center, add 1 cup (250 ml) of the water, and mix with your fingers. Add more water, if needed, to obtain a soft paste just firm enough to shape. (NOTE: Do not beat the mixture, or it will become elastic and may shrink and crack during cooking.)

Turn the paste onto a floured board and roll with your hands into a rope the length of the perimeter of the terrine mold. Put it around the rim and press the lid into it. The paste hardens quickly and prevents steam from escaping.

Fish Pâté la Marée
(PÂTÉ DE POISSON LA MARÉE)

For fish pâtés, the forcemeat is usually a mousseline, that delicate mixture of ground raw fish, egg whites, and cream. If the pâté is served hot, sauce vin blanc makes a perfect accompaniment. If served cold, the pâté can be set off by tomato mayonnaise.

> 1½ pounds (750 g) fillet of pike, halibut, or whiting
> 3 egg whites, lightly beaten
> salt and white pepper
> nutmeg
> 1¼ cups (310 ml) heavy cream
> ½ pound (250 g) salmon fillet

For the decoration—optional:
> ½ green pepper, cored and seeded
> ½ red pepper, cored and seeded
> 1 truffle OR 2 black olives

For the sauce:
> white wine sauce (p. 206) made with 2 shallots, 1
> cup (250 ml) butter, ⅓ cup (80 ml) white wine, 1
> tablespoon heavy cream, juice of ¼ lemon, ½
> teaspoon fish glaze, and salt and pepper

OR

**tomato mayonnaise (p. 370) made with 2 egg yolks,
salt and white pepper, 1–2 tablespoons lemon
juice, ¼ teaspoon mustard, 1½ cups (375 ml) oil,
and 1 tablespoon tomato paste**

1½-quart (1.5 L) terrine mold or loaf pan

SERVES 8.

Purée the white fish fillet in a food processor or work it through the fine plate of a grinder. Pound the purée in a mortar with a pestle until smooth or work it through a drum sieve. Transfer the purée to a metal bowl and set it over a pan or bowl of ice water. With a wooden spoon, beat in the egg whites, about half a white at a time. Season with salt and white pepper and a grating of nutmeg. Add the cream in 3 portions, stirring well after each addition. The mixture should be very thick. Taste—the mixture should be highly seasoned. Refrigerate until ready to use.

Set the oven at 350°F (175°C). Butter the terrine mold or loaf pan, line the base with waxed paper, and butter the paper. Prepare a water bath.

For the decoration: Blanch the peppers in boiling salted water for 1 minute, drain, refresh under cold running water, and drain again. Slice the truffle or cut the flesh from the olives. Make a design with the peppers and truffle or olives in the base of the mold.

Cut the salmon fillet in strips and dry well. Spoon half the mousseline into the mold, pack it well, and arrange the strips of salmon lengthwise on top. Spoon the rest of the mousseline over the fish strips and smooth to an even layer. Cover with waxed paper and the terrine lid, if possible, or if there is no lid, cover with several layers of aluminum foil. The pâté can be prepared ahead and kept, refrigerated, for 2–3 hours.

Set the mold or pan in a water bath, bring the water to a simmer on top of the stove, transfer to the heated oven, and bake until just set, 30–35 minutes. If serving the pâté hot, it can be kept warm in a 300°F (150°C) oven for 15–20 minutes.

For the sauce: Make the white wine sauce or tomato mayonnaise, stirring the tomato paste into the mayonnaise at the end.

Just before serving, run a knife around the edge of the terrine and turn the pâté out onto a platter. If serving the pâté cold, let it cool in the mold or pan. It can be kept, refrigerated, for up to a day but must come to room temperature before serving.

Spoon some of the white wine sauce around each slice as it is served or pass the tomato mayonnaise separately.

Little Fish Pâtés
(PETITS PÂTÉS DE POISSON)

Menon, a mid-eighteenth-century chef, used to prepare these small fish pâtés.
You could update them to nouvelle cuisine by serving them with white butter
sauce (p. 205).

puff pastry (p. 237) made with ½ pound (250 g)
 unsalted butter, 1⅓ cups (175 g) all-purpose flour,
 ⅔ cup (80 g) cake flour, 1 teaspoon salt, 1
 teaspoon lemon juice, ½–¾ cup (125–185 ml) cold water
2 slices firm white bread, with crusts removed
½ pound (250 g) salmon, whiting, pike, haddock, or
 other flavorful fish fillets
salt and pepper
nutmeg
2 shallots, finely chopped
2 tablespoons chopped parsley
1 cup (250 ml) heavy cream
1 egg yolk
1 tablespoon (15 g) butter, softened
1 egg, beaten to mix with salt

eight 3-inch (7.5 cm) tartlet pans

3½- and 4-inch (9 and 10 cm) plain pastry cutters

MAKES 8 PÂTÉS.

Make the puff pastry.

Toast the bread in a 250°F (120°C) oven until dry but not brown. Work
it to crumbs in a food processor or rub it through a sieve.

Chop the fish fillets and mix them with the bread crumbs, salt and
pepper, nutmeg, chopped shallots, and parsley. Purée the mixture in a food
processor or pound in a mortar with a pestle until smooth. Transfer the
mixture to a metal bowl and set in a pan or bowl of ice water. Beat in the
cream in 3 portions. Beat in the egg yolk and butter. Taste for seasoning and
adjust if necessary—it should be highly seasoned. The pâté can be prepared
ahead and kept, refrigerated, for 2–3 hours.

Set the oven at 400°F (200°C). Roll out the chilled pastry approximately ¼ inch (6 mm) thick and stamp out eight 3½-inch (9 cm) and eight 4-
inch (10 cm) rounds. Line the pans with the larger rounds, fill them with the
fish mixture, and moisten the inside edges with beaten egg. Cover with the
smaller rounds and gently press the edges together. Brush the tops with
beaten egg and chill for 15 minutes. Set the pans on a baking sheet and bake in
the heated oven until a skewer inserted in the center of one of the pastries for
half a minute is hot to the touch when withdrawn. Serve as soon as possible.

Salmon Rillettes
(RILLETTES DE SAUMON)

No wonder young chefs have seized on recipes like this one for fish rillettes. They are infinitely quicker and easier to make than terrines and can be kept, sealed under a layer of clarified butter, for up to a week.

½-pound (250 g) piece of salmon, with the bone
fish stock (p. 115) made with 1 tablespoon (15 g)
   butter, 1 onion, the salmon bone, 1 quart (1 L)
   water, 10 peppercorns, a bouquet garni, and 5
   tablespoons white wine
6 ounces (180 g) butter, softened
6 ounces (180 g) smoked salmon
salt and pepper
nutmeg

SERVES 4.

Remove the bone from the salmon and use it to make the fish stock. Poach the salmon in enough fish stock to cover until the flesh can be pierced easily, 5–7 minutes. Leave to cool in the cooking liquid and then remove the salmon from the liquid and discard the skin. Cool thoroughly.

Melt 2 tablespoons (30 g) of butter in a frying pan. Add the smoked salmon and 1 tablespoon of water, cover, and cook until no longer transparent, about 3 minutes. Leave to cool.

Shred the poached and smoked salmon with a fork and mix well. Cream the remaining butter and mix it gradually into the shredded salmon using a fork. Season to taste with salt and pepper and a grating of nutmeg.

Pack the rillettes in individual ramekins or in a pottery dish, cover, and chill thoroughly. Serve with fresh bread or toast.

Hot Veal and Ham Pâté en Croûte
(PÂTÉ CHAUD DE VEAU ET DE
JAMBON EN CROÛTE)

The meat in this pâté should be finely ground. Grind it twice yourself or have the butcher do it for you.

⅓ **pound (150 g) veal scallops**
⅓ **pound (150 g) slice cooked ham**
¼ **pound (125 g) piece bacon**
6 tablespoons white wine
4 tablespoons brandy
2 tablespoons Madeira
salt and pepper
1 pound (500 g) lean ground veal
1 pound (500 g) lean ground pork
¾ **pound (350 g) ground pork fat**
3 ounces (90 g) chicken livers, finely chopped
2 eggs, beaten to mix
1 small can truffles, with their liquid—optional
nutmeg

For the pâté pastry:
1 pound (500 g) flour
½ **pound (250 g) butter OR 3 ounces (90 g) lard and 5
   ounces (150 g) butter**
2 eggs
2 tablespoons oil
2 teaspoons salt
2–3 tablespoons water
1 egg, beaten to mix with salt

¾**–1 inch- (2–2.5 cm) fluted pastry cutter**

SERVES 8–10.

Cut the veal scallops, ham, and bacon into ¼-inch (6 mm) strips, moisten with 2 tablespoons of the wine, 2 tablespoons of the brandy, and the Madeira, add pepper, and mix well. Cover and leave to marinate for 30–45 minutes.

For the pâté pastry: Sift the flour onto a work surface and make a large well in the center. Pound the butter with a rolling pin to soften it slightly. Put the butter or butter and lard mixture, eggs, oil, salt, and water in the well and stir together with the fingertips until partly mixed. Gradually work in the flour, pulling the dough into large crumbs with the fingertips of both hands. If the crumbs are dry, moisten with another tablespoon of water. Press the dough together—it should be soft but not sticky. Now work the dough on a lightly floured surface, pushing it away with the heel of the hand and gathering it up with a dough scraper until it is smooth and pliable. Press the dough into a ball, wrap, and chill 30 minutes.

Mix together the ground veal, lean and fat pork, chicken livers, the remaining 4 tablespoons white wine and 2 tablespoons brandy, eggs, truffles and liquid, if included, nutmeg, and plenty of salt and pepper. Beat with a wooden spoon or your hand until the forcemeat holds together. Cook a piece of the mixture in a frying pan or in the oven, taste, and adjust the seasoning in the remaining forcemeat if necessary.

Roll out the dough and trim to a 14- × 20-inch (35 × 50 cm) rectangle. Divide the forcemeat into 4 portions. Spread one portion lengthwise on the dough in a 4- × 14-inch (10 × 35 cm) strip. Top with a layer of strips of marinated veal, ham, and bacon, using half the veal and ⅓ of the ham and bacon. Cover with another portion of forcemeat and add half the remaining strips of ham and bacon. Cover with another portion of forcemeat and top with the remaining strips of veal, ham, and bacon. Cover with the last portion of ground meat and smooth to make an even layer. Mold the meat with your hands so that the rectangle is compact, tall, and neat.

Cut a square of excess dough from each corner of the pâté pastry and brush the edges of the rectangle with the beaten eggs. Lift one long edge of the dough on top of the filling and fold over the opposite edge to enclose it. Press gently to seal the dough and fold over the ends to make a neat parcel. Roll the parcel over onto a baking sheet so that the seam is underneath. Brush the pâté with beaten egg.

The shaped pâté being wrapped in pastry; the edges of the dough are brushed with beaten egg.

To decorate the pâté, roll out the dough trimmings, cut a long strip, and set it around the edge of the pâté. Decorate the top with any remaining pastry cut in the shapes of leaves or whatever your fancy dictates. Brush the decorations with beaten egg. Make a hole near each end of the pâté so that steam can escape. Chill for 20–30 minutes or up to 3 hours.

To finish: Set the oven at 400°F (200°C). Bake the pâté in the hot oven until the pastry is set and starts to brown, about 15 minutes. Turn the heat down to 350°F (175°C) and continue baking until a skewer inserted in the center of the pâté for half a minute is hot to the touch when withdrawn, about 1 hour. If the pastry browns too much during cooking, cover it loosely with aluminum foil.

Serve the pâté warm or cool. The pâté can be cooked up to 3 days ahead and reheated in a 350°F (175°C) oven.

For cold pâté en croûte:

Increase the amount of pork fat in the forcemeat to 1 pound (500 g) to prevent dryness. The meat should also be more highly seasoned for cold pâté. Chill the cooked pâté well and, if you like, pour cool aspic (see p. 139) through a funnel set in one of the holes. Refrigerate to set.

Duck Terrine with Green Peppercorns
(TERRINE DE CANARD AU POIVRE VERT)

Green peppercorns are preserved in brine. They should be drained thoroughly before using.

4–5 pound (2 kg) duck
3 tablespoons brandy
¾ pound (350 g) lean ground veal
¾ pound (350 g) lean ground pork
½ pound (250 g) ground pork fat
¾ pound (350 g) pork liver, finely chopped—optional
the duck liver, finely chopped
2 cloves garlic, finely chopped
½ teaspoon allspice
¼ teaspoon cloves
3 tablespoons green peppercorns, drained
2 eggs
nutmeg
salt and pepper
luting paste to seal mold (p. 149)

trussing needle and string

2-quart (2 L) oval terrine mold or casserole with lid

Bone the duck completely (see p. 90), leaving the meat attached to the skin. Lay it skin side down on a work surface and sprinkle with 1 tablespoon of the brandy.

Combine the veal, lean pork, pork fat, the livers, and garlic. Stir in the remaining 2 tablespoons brandy, allspice, cloves, green peppercorns, and the eggs and add nutmeg and salt and pepper. Sauté a small piece and taste for seasoning—it should be quite spicy. Adjust the seasoning in the rest of the forcemeat if necessary. Beat the mixture with a wooden spoon or your hand until it holds together. Set the oven at 350°F (175°C) and prepare a water bath.

Pile the forcemeat on top of the duck meat, shape it into a compact oval, and sew the seam together so the forcemeat is completely enclosed. Put the stuffed duck seam side down in the terrine mold or casserole and cover with the lid. Make the luting paste and seal the lid onto the mold.

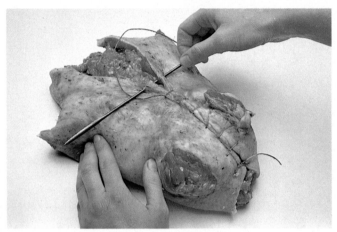

Sewing the duck skin around the forcemeat

Set the terrine in the water bath. Bring the water to a simmer on top of the stove, transfer to the heated oven, and bake until a skewer inserted in the mixture through the hole in the lid for ½ minute is hot to the touch when withdrawn, 1–1½ hours. Cool until tepid, remove the luting paste and lid, and press the terrine with a plate and at least a 2-pound (1 kg) weight until cold. Keep the terrine in the refrigerator for at least 3 days and up to a week to allow the flavor to mellow before serving.

To serve, unmold the terrine, cut part of it in thick slices, and arrange them overlapping on a platter with the uncut piece at one end. Alternatively, serve the terrine directly from the mold.

Pork Terrine Paysanne
(TERRINE DE PORC PAYSANNE)

Nearly every charcuterie in France sells a simple pork terrine such as this one.

1 tablespoon (15 g) butter
1 onion, chopped
1 pound (500 g) lean ground pork
½ pound (250 g) ground pork fat
½ pound (250 g) ground ham
2 eggs, beaten to mix
2 tablespoons sherry or Madeira
salt and pepper
½ cup (75 g) shelled pistachios
½-pound (250 g) slice cooked ham
½ pound (250 g) sliced barding fat or bacon
1 bay leaf
luting paste to seal the mold

1½-quart (1.5 L) terrine or casserole with lid

Melt the butter in a small pan and cook the onion slowly until soft but not brown, 7–10 minutes. Mix the onion with the pork, pork fat, ground ham, eggs, sherry or Madeira, and plenty of salt and pepper. Mix well to combine. Cook a piece of the mixture in a frying pan or in the oven and taste—it should be highly seasoned. Adjust seasoning in the remaining forcemeat if necessary. Add the pistachios and beat the mixture with a wooden spoon or your hand until it holds together.

Cut the slice of ham in ½-inch (1.25 cm) strips. Line the terrine or casserole with the barding fat or bacon, reserving some for the top. Prepare a water bath (Chapter 8) and set the oven at 350°F (175°C).

Spread ⅓ of the forcemeat in the lined terrine and top with half the ham strips and another third of the ground meat. Add the remaining ham strips and cover with the last third of the pork. Lay the reserved barding fat or bacon on top and set a bay leaf in the middle. Make the luting paste and seal the lid onto the terrine.

The layered filling of the terrine will be covered with another piece of barding fat.

Put the terrine in the water bath, bring to a simmer on top of the stove, and transfer to the hot oven. Cook until a skewer inserted through the hole in the lid for ½ minute is hot to the touch when withdrawn, 1¼–1½ hours. Cool until tepid, remove the luting paste and lid, and press the terrine with a plate and a 2-pound (1 kg) weight until cold. Keep the terrine in the refrigerator for at least 3 days or up to a week to allow the flavor to mellow before serving.

To serve, unmold the terrine, cut part of it in thick slices, and arrange them overlapping on a platter with the uncut piece at one end. Alternatively, serve the terrine directly from the mold.

Rabbit Rillettes
(RILLETTES DE LAPIN)

Because the animal is lean, rillettes made entirely of rabbit are not quite traditional; rabbit was often mixed with other meats in country rillettes. Here the needed richness is supplied to the meat by pork fat. Rillettes are served as an hors d'oeuvre or first course, spread on bread or toast.

> **two 3½–4 pound (3.75 kg) rabbits**
> **¾ pound (350 g) pork fat**
> **1½ teaspoons salt**
> **pinch of allspice**
> **1 sprig dried thyme**
> **1 bay leaf**
> **¾ cup (185 ml) water**
> **salt and pepper**
> **nutmeg**

SERVES 4.

Cut the rabbit in pieces (see p. 41) and remove the meat from the bones in as even-sized pieces as possible (see Chapter 7 for information on boning). Cut the pork fat in cubes. Put the rabbit pieces and fat in a heavy-bottomed pot and add the 1½ teaspoons salt, allspice, thyme, bay leaf, and the ¾ cup (185 ml) water. Bring to a boil, cover, and then cook very gently at just below a simmer either on top of the stove or in a 325°F (165°C) oven until all the fat has melted and is clear, 4–5 hours. Add more water if the water evaporates before the pork fat renders enough liquid fat to float the meat.

Lift the pieces of rabbit from the fat with a slotted spoon and put them in a bowl. Discard the bay leaf and thyme. Shred the meat with 2 forks and leave the fat to cool. When it is thickened and nearly set, mix most of it with the meat, reserving about ¼ cup to seal the top, and season with salt and pepper and nutmeg to taste. Melt the reserved fat. Pack the rillettes into a jar or crock and pour a layer of fat over the top to seal. Keep the rillettes in the refrigerator for at least 2 days and up to 2 weeks to allow the flavor to mellow before serving.

The boned rabbit meat is cut into even-size pieces.

After 4 to 5 hours of cooking, the rabbit meat for the rillettes can be shredded with two forks.

Mousses, Mousselines, and Quenelles

MOUSSES, MOUSSELINES, and quenelles are all typically French preparations of a studied refinement that makes the nearest equivalents, such as dumplings, seem a trifle vulgar. Until very recently, their sophistication banished them to grand kitchens, for the work involved in pounding, puréeing, and sieving them was prodigious. I well remember that when I was a student the unfortunates who had incurred the chef's displeasure would be set to pounding fish for quenelles or a mousseline in a mortar with a pestle, while the rest of us kept out of the way. Today, however, flicking the switch of a food processor replaces hours of hand labor. Mousses, mousselines, and quenelles have come of age and play a leading role in modern menus.

In cooking parlance a mousse, meaning literally *foam*, is a light frothy mixture that can be made with almost anything—fish, meat, poultry, vegetables, and fruit. The basic ingredient, which can be raw or cooked, is puréed to the finest possible paste, and then the mixture is lightened, most commonly with cream, sometimes with egg white, and occasionally with both. Beyond this, however, generalizations are very difficult to make. Egg yolks may, or may not, be added for richness. A mousse can be sweet or savory, hot or cold. It can be set with gelatin. It can even be frozen. Many mousses are molded, but unmolded ones, like chocolate mousse, which is

160

always served from the dish, are numerous. Mousselines and quenelles, in fact, can also be loosely described by the more general term *mousse*.

Whereas the definition of a mousse is vague, that of a mousseline is precise. (The noun *mousseline* is not to be confused with the adjective, meaning fluffy, which is applied to some egg sauces and to mousseline potatoes.) Mousselines are based on a purée of meat, fish, or poultry that is bound with egg whites and enriched with cream; unlike mousses, the basic ingredient is always raw when the whites and cream are added. The balance of these three ingredients is delicate, for with too little meat or fish the mousseline is tasteless but with too much it is heavy, with too much egg white the consistency is solid but with too little the mousseline falls apart, and with too much cream the mixture separates during cooking. Many chefs insist on forcing the meat through a sieve after it has been worked in the food processor—a time-consuming step that removes a surprising amount of fiber and results in a noticeably finer texture.

Mousselines collapse more easily than mousses, so they are often cooked in individual molds—bucket-shaped dariole molds are standard, but custard cups or ramekins will do. The mixture can be set in two layers, one white, one pink with tomato or green with spinach. A "surprise" of sautéed mushrooms, a pistachio or two, or strips of whatever meat is the base of the mousseline may be concealed inside. The accompanying sauce (happily for my taste, a sauce is mandatory with mousselines) can provide a further contrast of creamy white, watercress green, or butter gold.

Quenelles are as specific as mousselines. Made also with raw meat or fish purée, egg whites, and cream, quenelles generally have a panade added to bind the mixture. The most basic panade is made with butter and water or milk, into which flour is beaten to make a stiff paste. Simple and cheap, this is the principal ingredient in the ponderous quenelles sold in inexpensive charcuteries. Choux pastry is to be preferred as a binding agent, for its high egg content puffs the mixture during cooking. Best of all is a "frangipane" panade (nothing to do with sweet almond frangipane); it resembles a basic panade but is enriched with egg yolks and nicely maintains the delicate balance between lightness and holding power that is the whole secret of quenelles.

Unlike mousses and mousselines, quenelles are never cooked in a mold, but are poached directly in water or, occasionally, baked in the oven. The mixture is shaped into ovals with two spoons (chefs disdain the quenelle molds touted by kitchen shops) and dropped into simmering stock or salted water, where the paste swells slightly and cooks to a firm but delicate dumpling. Traditionally they are coated with sauce and baked in the oven before serving.

Quenelles are a part of many classic garnishes that are fast disappearing, such as the appropriately rich *financière* combination of quenelles, sweetbreads, mushrooms, truffles, and cocks' kidneys and combs in a brown sauce. However, quenelles are too good to die altogether. Following the fashionable ban on flour, nouvelle cuisine quenelles are often made of mousseline mixture without a panade. And in a typical nouvelle cuisine move, heavier meat mixtures are being replaced by vegetable quenelles such as fennel quenelles with chives in a butter sauce. To avoid curdling the sauce, the quenelles must be set on or coated with the sauce just before serving, giving quite a different effect from the blending of flavors produced when they are baked together.

Mousses, mousselines, and quenelles date a long way back to medieval times, when the cook's aim was to artfully combine and disguise individual flavors by chopping and pounding foods with a heady seasoning of spice. Now the culinary aim is the contrary—to display individual ingredients to the best advantage. That mousses, mousselines, and quenelles have survived such a radical change in taste is proof of their appeal.

 FOR SUCCESSFUL MOUSSES, MOUSSELINES, AND QUENELLES

1. For smoothest texture, particularly of mousselines, push puréed ingredients through a sieve after working in a food processor. Some electric mixers have a sieve attachment.

2. If you do not have a food processor, sieving is much easier if ingredients are first worked through the fine plate of a grinder. Only a few vegetables, such as carrots, can be puréed in a blender because fibers clog the blades.

3. When making mousselines and quenelles, chill and season with salt to stiffen the mixture before adding cream. If the mixture softens considerably when cream is added, chill it again until stiff before continuing.

4. When making a flour-based panade for quenelles, cook it thoroughly to avoid the flavor of raw starch.

5. Test the consistency of a quenelle mixture by poaching or baking a sample.

6. If a quenelle sample does not hold together, beat in another egg white. Alternatively, the mixture can be molded and cooked in a water bath like a mousse.

7. When cooking a mousse or a mousseline in a water bath, cover the mold with foil to prevent the formation of a crust.

8. A molded mousse or mousseline is done when a skewer inserted in the center for half a minute is hot to the touch and dry when withdrawn. A quenelle is done when firm to the touch.

PREPARING AHEAD

1. Most mousses and mousselines can be prepared two to three hours before cooking. Keep them in the refrigerator.

2. Molded mousses and mousselines can be kept hot for a quarter to half an hour in a water bath.

3. When mousses and mousselines are kept warm after unmolding, they often "weep"; dry the platter with paper towels just before adding the sauce and serving.

4. Cooked drained quenelles can be kept in the refrigerator for two to three days and reheated before serving.

5. Freezing is not advisable for mousses and mousselines because the egg whites and cream separate on thawing. Traditional quenelles, however, freeze well due to their flour content. If freezing them in a sauce, it must be thickened with flour and have no egg yolk liaison.

Avocado Mousse
(MOUSSE D'AVOCATS)

This mousse is attractive either molded in a ring or piped into the avocado shells. For an even more luxurious first course or a light main course, serve a seafood salad along with it.

> ¼ ounce (7 g) gelatin
> 4 ripe avocados
> juice of ½ lemon
> ½ cup (125 ml) mayonnaise (p. 351) made with 1 egg
>   yolk, salt and pepper, 2 teaspoons vinegar or lemon
>   juice, ¼ teaspoon mustard, and ¾ cup (185 ml) oil

1 clove garlic, mashed to a paste
salt and pepper
pinch of cayenne pepper
3 tablespoons heavy cream, lightly whipped
1 bunch watercress (for garnish)

5-cup (1.25 L) ring mold OR *pastry bag with medium star tip*

SERVES 6.

Sprinkle the gelatin over ¼ cup (60 ml) cold water and leave until spongy, about 5 minutes. Halve the avocados, scoop out the pulp, mash it, and immediately stir in the lemon juice to prevent discoloration. Save 6 of the avocado skins if using them for serving.

Melt the gelatin in a water bath, stir it into the avocado pulp, and then add the mayonnaise, garlic, salt and pepper, and cayenne pepper. Leave the avocado mixture until cool and then fold in the lightly whipped cream. Taste for seasoning and adjust if necessary—it should be highly seasoned. Pour the mixture into the mold or, alternatively, pipe it into the halved avocado skins. Cover tightly and chill until set, at least 2 hours. The mousse can be kept, refrigerated, up to 12 hours.

Not more than 30 minutes before serving, dip the mold in warm water and turn it out on a platter, or arrange the avocado halves on a platter or on individual plates. Garnish with watercress.

Avocado mousse piped into avocado shells

Trout Mousseline with Watercress
(MOUSSELINE DE TRUITES AU CRESSON)

This delicate mousseline is perfectly set off by a slightly peppery watercress sauce. Be sure to remove all the bones from the trout, especially if you do not plan to work the fish through a sieve after puréeing it.

4 trout, each weighing ½ pound (250 g)
1½ egg whites
salt and pepper
1⅓ cups (330 ml) heavy cream
2 tablespoons (30 g) butter, softened
1 large shallot, finely chopped
½ cup (125 ml) white wine
½ bunch watercress (about 7 ounces or 200 g)

For the watercress butter sauce:
½ bunch watercress (about 7 ounces or 200 g)
5 tablespoons (80 g) butter, softened
1 shallot, finely chopped
⅓ cup (80 ml) dry white wine
⅔ cup (160 ml) heavy cream
salt

four ¾-cup (185 ml) ramekins

SERVES 4.

Fillet the trout and remove the skin (see p. 88). Cut 1 of the fillets crosswise into 8 strips. Purée the remaining fillets in a food processor or work them twice through the fine plate of a grinder. If possible, force the ground fish through a drum sieve. Put the fish in a bowl and set it in a pan or bowl of ice water. With a wooden spoon beat in the egg whites, about half a white at a time. Season with salt and pepper. Add the cream in 3 portions, stirring well after each addition. Refrigerate the mixture until ready to use.

In a frying pan heat the 2 tablespoons (30 g) butter over low heat and cook the shallot in it for about 1 minute. Sprinkle the strips of trout fillet with salt and pepper and add them to the pan. Sauté them over medium heat until they turn white, about 1 minute on each side. Add the ½ cup (125 ml) of the wine and bring to a boil. Remove the strips of trout with a slotted spoon and leave to cool. Reduce the liquid in the pan to 2 tablespoons, strain, pressing on the shallots to extract all the liquid, and set aside to cool.

Prepare the whole bunch of watercress, which will be used for both the mousseline and the sauce, at the same time: Remove and discard the stems. Wash the leafy tops and blanch by putting them in a pan of boiling water and bringing just back to a boil. Drain, refresh under cold running water, squeeze out any excess liquid, and dry on paper towels. Purée in a food processor or chop into the smallest possible pieces.

Set the oven at 375°F (190°C), butter the ramekins generously, and prepare a water bath (see Chapter 8).

Add the cooled cooking liquid from the trout strips to the chilled fish mixture and stir well. Taste for seasoning and add salt or pepper if needed. Combine ½ the watercress purée with ½ the mousseline and adjust seasoning if necessary. Spoon this mixture into the ramekins and flatten to an even layer. Arrange the strips of trout on top, spoon the remaining fish mixture into the ramekins, and smooth the top of each.

Set the ramekins in the water bath, bring the water to a simmer on top of the stove, and cover with foil. Transfer to the heated oven and bake until just set, about 20 minutes.

For the sauce: Add the soft butter to the remaining watercress purée and work it again in the food processor until very smooth. If possible, force it through a drum sieve. Chill. In a small heavy saucepan cook the shallot in the wine until almost dry. Add the cream and bring the mixture to a boil. Continue boiling, whisking occasionally, until the sauce thickens enough to coat the back of a spoon. Just before serving, bring the sauce back to a boil. Remove from the heat and gradually whisk in the cold watercress butter to make a smooth creamy sauce; work sometimes over low heat and sometimes off the heat so the butter softens and it thickens the sauce without melting. Taste for seasoning and add salt if necessary. Strain.

Run a metal spatula around the edge of each mousseline and turn it out onto a plate. Wipe away any excess liquid, spoon the sauce around the mousseline, and serve immediately.

Lime-Flavored Quenelles with Spinach
(QUENELLES AU CITRON VERT AUX ÉPINARDS)

This unusual combination of flavors is nouvelle cuisine in spirit; yet the recipe uses the traditional flour-based panade, enriched with an egg yolk.

**½ pound (250 g) white fish fillets (pike, halibut,
    flounder)
zest of 1 lime, finely chopped
salt and pepper
1 egg
2 egg yolks
5 tablespoons (80 g) butter, softened**

For the panade:
3 tablespoons milk
1½ tablespoons (20 g) butter, melted
5 tablespoons (40 g) flour
salt and pepper
1 egg yolk

For the spinach:
1 pound (500 g) spinach
1 tablespoon (15 g) butter
salt and pepper
nutmeg

For the lime sauce:
juice of 1 lime
salt and pepper
¼ pound (125 g) butter
1 tablespoon chopped parsley

MAKES 12 QUENELLES TO SERVE 6 AS A FIRST COURSE OR 4 AS A MAIN COURSE.

For the panade: In a small saucepan bring the milk just to a boil. Pour the melted butter over the flour, add salt and pepper, and mix well with a wooden spoon. Beat in the egg yolk. Pour the hot milk over the mixture a little at a time, mixing well after each addition. Return the mixture to the saucepan and beat vigorously over low heat for 1–2 minutes until the panade is smooth and pulls away from the sides of the pan to form a ball. Chill. The panade can be kept, refrigerated and covered, for up to 4 days.

Purée the fish fillets in a food processor or work them twice through the fine plate of a grinder. Chill. Blanch the finely chopped lime zest by putting it in a pan of cold water, bringing to a boil, and boiling it 5 minutes. Rinse in cold running water and drain. In an electric mixer beat together the chilled fish and the panade. Add salt and pepper, beat in the egg, then the yolks one at a time, and finally beat in the soft butter a little at a time. If possible, force the mixture through a drum sieve. Stir in the blanched lime zest and chill.

For the spinach: Remove and discard the stems and wash the spinach leaves. Blanch in a large pan of boiling salted water until just tender, 2–3 minutes. Refresh under cold running water, squeeze out the excess moisture, and chop.

Using 2 soup spoons, shape the quenelle mixture into ovals. Bring a sauté pan or shallow saucepan of salted water to a boil and drop half the quenelles into the pan. Lower the heat, poach the quenelles 7 minutes, and then turn them over with a spoon. Continue poaching the quenelles until firm to the touch, 7–10 minutes longer. Lift them out with a slotted spoon and drain on paper towels while cooking the remaining mixture.

For the lime sauce: In a small saucepan boil the lime juice until reduced to about ½ tablespoon. Lower the heat, add salt and pepper, and whisk in the butter in small pieces so that it softens without melting. Stir in the chopped parsley, taste for seasoning, and adjust if necessary.

Heat the butter in a saucepan, add the spinach, and cook, stirring constantly, until most of the excess moisture evaporates, 2–3 minutes. Season to taste with salt and pepper and nutmeg. Spoon onto a serving platter or individual plates. Arrange the quenelles on top, coat them with some of the sauce, and serve immediately. Pass the remaining sauce separately.

Chicken Quenelles with Leeks
(QUENELLES DE VOLAILLE AUX POIREAUX)

Drop shaped quenelles onto a tray or cookie sheet that has been dampened, so they'll slide off easily when you're ready to cook them.

3 pound (1.5 kg) chicken
2 egg yolks
¼ pound (125 g) butter, softened
1 egg white
salt and pepper
nutmeg
⅔ cup (160 ml) heavy cream
3 leeks
1 quart (1 L) chicken stock (p. 115)

For the sauce:
the stock from poaching the quenelles
1½ cups (310 ml) heavy cream
salt and pepper
3 tablespoons (45 g) butter

MAKES 12 QUENELLES TO SERVE 6 AS A FIRST COURSE OR 4 AS A MAIN COURSE.

Bone the chicken completely (see p. 90). Purée the flesh with the yolks and butter in a food processor or work the meat twice through the fine plate of a grinder and then beat in the yolks and butter. If possible force the mixture through a drum sieve. Put the chicken in a bowl and set it in a pan or bowl of ice water. With a wooden spoon beat in the egg white. Season with salt and pepper and nutmeg. Beat in the cream a little at a time. Chill thoroughly before shaping into quenelles.

Cut the leeks into 1½-inch (4 cm) julienne strips. Bring a medium saucepan of salted water to a boil and add the leeks. Boil until just tender, 2–3 minutes, refresh under cold running water, and drain well.

Use 2 soup spoons to shape the quenelle mixture into ovals. In a sauté pan or shallow saucepan bring the stock to a boil. Drop half the quenelles into the pan. Lower the heat and poach the quenelles 7 minutes and then turn them over with a spoon. Continue poaching the quenelles until firm to the touch, 7–10 minutes longer. Lift them out with a slotted spoon and drain on paper towels while cooking the remaining mixture. Keep warm in a 250°F (120°C) oven.

For the sauce: Strain the chicken stock and boil rapidly until reduced to a syrupy glaze. (NOTE: This can be done more quickly in two pans rather than one.) Add the cream and continue to boil until the sauce is thick enough to coat a spoon. Stir in the leeks and heat through. Taste for seasoning and adjust if necessary. Remove from the heat and whisk in the butter a little at a time.

Arrange the quenelles on a platter or on individual plates, spoon the leeks and sauce over them, and serve immediately.

Beat the quenelle mixture thoroughly with a wooden spoon, over a bowl of ice water, and then chill before shaping.

Shape the quenelles with two soup spoons.

Place them on a dampened tray.

Lift the cooked quenelles from the poaching liquid with a slotted spoon.

Ham Mousse with Madeira
(MOUSSE DE JAMBON AU MADÈRE)

Ham is traditionally combined with Madeira, but you might try a velouté sauce (p. 193) flavored with curry rather than the Madeira sauce and substitute another liquid, such as stock or white wine, for the Madeira in the mousse.

½ pound (250 g) ham
2 egg whites
1¼ cups (310 g) heavy cream
¼ cup (60 ml) Madeira
salt and pepper
Madeira sauce (p. 196) made with 1 cup basic brown
    sauce and 3 tablespoons Madeira

3-cup (750 ml) soufflé dish or charlotte mold

SERVES 4–6.

Prepare a water bath (see Chapter 8), butter the mold, and set the oven at 375°F (190°C). Purée the ham in a food processor or work it twice through the fine plate of a grinder. Add the egg whites and work in the food processor again until smooth, or beat in gradually. With the food processor on pour in the cream gradually. Alternatively, set the bowl of ham mixture in a pan or bowl of ice water and beat the cream in gradually. Add the Madeira and season to taste.

Pour the mixture into the mold, set in the water bath, and bring the water to a simmer on top of the stove. Cover with foil and transfer to the hot oven. Bake until just set and a knife inserted in the middle for 30 seconds is hot when removed, about 40 minutes. Meanwhile, make the Madeira sauce, or it can be made ahead and reheated.

Remove the mousse from the oven and let it rest for 5 minutes. Run a metal spatula around the edge of the mold and turn it out onto a platter. Wipe away any excess liquid, spoon a little sauce around the mousse, and serve the rest of the sauce separately.

Frozen Orange-Chocolate Mousse
(MOUSSE AU CHOCOLAT À L'ORANGE GLACÉE)

Remove this mousse from the freezer five to ten minutes ahead of time so the mixture will soften slightly and be easier to serve.

6 ounces (180 g) semisweet chocolate, chopped
½ cup orange juice
4 eggs, separated
1 tablespoon (15 g) butter
1 tablespoon Grand Marnier
½ cup heavy cream, lightly beaten

1-quart (1 L) soufflé dish

SERVES 4.

In a heavy pan heat the chocolate and orange juice gently, stirring, until the chocolate melts. Remove from the heat and beat the egg yolks, one by one, into the hot mixture. Beat in the butter and Grand Marnier.

Beat the egg whites until stiff, add the tepid chocolate mixture, and fold the two together as lightly as possible. Let cool to room temperature and then fold in the whipped cream.

Pour the mousse into the soufflé dish and freeze until firm, at least 2 hours. The mousse can be kept, frozen and covered, for 2–3 weeks.

Soufflés

WHAT IS A SOUFFLÉ? A great many things. Technically speaking, a soufflé is a highly flavored sauce or purée mixed with stiffly whipped egg whites, which expand in a hot oven to give the soufflé its dramatic height. And all soufflés have charisma. It is just about my favorite dish to cook and to serve. The risk involved is amply rewarded by applause, making a soufflé the perfect opening or ending to an outstanding meal.

Tricky it may be, but there is no mystery to the making of a good soufflé. Three points are crucial: preparing the soufflé base, beating the egg whites, and folding the egg whites into the soufflé base so as to retain maximum volume and lightness.

For savory soufflés, the base is usually a béchamel or velouté sauce combined with whatever flavoring is chosen, although unthickened fish or vegetable purées can be used alone. The soufflé base must be well seasoned, and in fact over seasoned, because of the quantity of bland egg whites that will later be folded into it. Egg yolks are nearly always added for richness, but for extra-light diet soufflés, they can be omitted. Most dessert soufflés are based on pastry cream, *crème pâtissière*, again combined with any one of a variety of ingredients.

Best known of the soufflé bases are those flavored with cheese, chocolate, and Grand Marnier, but they are only the beginning of the repertoire. You'll find seafood soufflés in Brittany, chicken soufflés in the region of Bresse, kirsch soufflé in Alsace, and apple soufflé with Calvados in Normandy. A soufflé can be made of lettuce or eggplant; a sweet one might be flavored with candied ginger or even violets. Soufflés are an excellent way to make scanty ingredients go far and can add a touch of elegance to mundane leftovers such as chopped ham or cooked fish. They're absolutely regal with yesterday's lobster or smoked salmon.

SOUFFLÉ AU GRAND MARNIER EN SURPRISE
One of the most celebrated and delicious of the classic French soufflés, flavored with the famous orange liqueur and decorated with segments of orange

SOUFFLÉS AU GINGEMBRE
Most soufflé mixtures can be baked in individual ramekins. This one is flavored with both powdered and candied ginger.

There is now, as with sauces, a crusade for dispensing with flour in soufflé bases. My own favorite non-flour soufflé is one based on lemon, egg yolks, and butter—soufflé chaud au citron, p. 184—and some flourless soufflés based on fruit purée are equally successful. However, most attempts to bind heavy moist ingredients like fish, meat, or vegetables without using flour are doomed to disappoint.

Turning now to the egg whites, one-third to two-thirds more egg whites than yolks should be added to a standard soufflé to ensure lightness; the volume of beaten egg whites should be at least double that of the basic mixture. Egg whites are best beaten in a copper bowl with a balloon whisk. Aluminum or stainless steel bowls are passable alternatives to copper, but volume is lost in glass or pottery bowls because egg whites will not cling to these materials. Nor does an egg beater or electric beater give as good a result as a bicep-building wire balloon whisk—a beater merely sits in the bottom of the bowl and less air is incorporated into the mixture.

When the egg whites have been whisked until stiff, it is vital for the success of a sweet soufflé to "meringue" them: Add a tablespoon of sugar for every three or four egg whites and continue beating for half a minute until the whites are glossy; this makes them much firmer and easier to fold. For savory soufflés, many cooks recommend adding a pinch of salt or cream of tartar just before the end of beating.

Given a good soufflé base, whether savory or sweet, and stiffly whipped whites, the last essential ingredient for success is combining the two as lightly as possible. Heat the base mixture until hot but not scalding to the touch. Off the heat, add about a quarter of the beaten whites and stir lightly but thoroughly; the heat of the mixture will cook the whites so they become firm. Tip the base and egg white combination into the remaining whites, fold gently, and turn the mixture into a buttered soufflé dish.

The chefs at La Varenne never bother using a paper collar to support the rising soufflé, and after working with them for several years, neither do I. When the dish has been thoroughly buttered and the soufflé mixture is appropriately stiff, it rises without any spills.

A hot soufflé, by the way, is not to be confused with the cold version, which is not a true soufflé at all but a creamy mixture that is set in a soufflé dish with a high collar of paper around the outside; when the collar is removed, the mixture looks as if it has risen above the mold like a true soufflé.

Besides the superfluity of a collar for a hot soufflé, another hint I have learned is that a soufflé *can* wait before baking. At La Varenne it is standard practice to keep a soufflé for an hour or two in the refrigerator and bake it at the last moment, and a wait of three or four hours is not uncommon. Although longer waits are not recommended, one memorable day a trainee forgot an endive soufflé and left it in the refrigerator for thirty-six hours. Not wanting to waste it, she stuck it in the oven; it rose without a tremor.

The importance of a particular oven heat is another soufflé myth: a good mixture will rise at almost any temperature. The French like to cook soufflés fast, at 400°F (200°C), so they rise quickly and brown on the outside yet stay soft in the center. In an oven at 350°F (175°C), a soufflé takes longer to cook (the exact time depends on the size and shape of the dish) and will be firm right through—a good method for heavier soufflés such as those based on fish purées. Nor will anything disastrous happen if you open the oven door during baking to turn the soufflé around so that it cooks evenly. But do avoid drafts.

When ready, a soufflé should have risen above the rim of the dish, increasing by half or two-thirds in volume. Shake it gently—if it quakes all over, it is not done; if it just wobbles in the middle, it is done to the French taste.

Set the dish on a plate at once and rush it to the table with a steady hand—it is at this point that a soufflé waits for no one. It should be served with two spoons, tapping the crust lightly to make a wedge-shaped break and scooping down to get some of the soft center along with a section of the firmer outside.

So those are the rules to be followed the first time and then adapted according to experience. And if a soufflé doesn't rise as high as your hopes, don't despair. Even a failed soufflé is edible—if savory, call it a mold; if sweet, dub it a pudding.

Folding the soufflé base into the beaten whites

Level the surface of the mixture in the mold with a spatula.

Make a shallow groove around the edge with a table knife.

Serve the soufflé with two spoons.

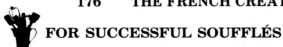

FOR SUCCESSFUL SOUFFLÉS

1. Have everything prepared for baking and serving: Arrange the oven shelf so there is plenty of room for the soufflé to rise without catching on the roof of the oven. Heat the oven. Butter the soufflé dish. If using ramekins, put them on a baking sheet so they can be moved in and out of the oven easily. Have ready your serving tray and spoons.

2. For all soufflés, butter the dish, and especially the rim, generously so the mixture slips easily up the sides. The buttered dish can be coated with bread crumbs for savory soufflés or with sugar for sweet soufflés.

3. To be sure that the soufflé will rise well above the dish, the uncooked mixture should fill the dish or come to at least within ½ inch (1.25 cm) of the rim. Level the surface with a sweep of a metal spatula.

4. If you want the soufflé to form a central "top hat" as it bakes, run a table knife around the edge to make a ½-inch (1.25 cm) groove.

5. Do not bake anything else in the oven at the same time as a soufflé.

6. Never remove a soufflé from the oven during baking.

7. Remember that soufflés that are cooked for a relatively short time in a hot oven will sink more quickly when removed from the oven than those that are cooked more slowly at a lower temperature.

PREPARING AHEAD

"A soufflé should be awaited; it must never wait." Although this has long been considered the golden rule of the soufflé, I would amend the second half to ". . . but once cooked it must never wait." And with preparation done ahead, you needn't keep guests waiting either.

1. The base mixture for most soufflés can be prepared several hours or even a day ahead and kept in the refrigerator.

2. Cover the surface of a soufflé base with a piece of waxed paper or rub with butter to prevent the formation of a skin.

3. Although it is preferable to beat the egg whites and fold them into the base mixture just before baking the soufflé, if beaten until very stiff they can be folded into the base mixture up to two hours ahead. Put the mixture in the soufflé dish and keep refrigerated until ready to bake.

4. A baked soufflé must be served at once. If a five-minute wait is unavoidable, open the oven door and leave the heat on. The outer side of the soufflé will shrivel, but the inner side will stay puffed. After a few minutes in the oven turn the soufflé halfway around so that the fallen side faces the heat. This procedure is recommended only for an emergency.

WHISKING EGG WHITES

1. Egg whites whisked for soufflés or meringues in a copper bowl with a balloon whisk acquire a greater volume and denser texture than those beaten using any other equipment. Bowls of other metals and a balloon whisk or a heavy-duty electric beater, as opposed to a hand-held beater, are the next best choices.

2. Before using a copper bowl, always clean the inside by rubbing with one to two tablespoons salt and one to two tablespoons vinegar, or use salt rubbed on with a lemon half. Rinse and dry the bowl thoroughly. The copper should be bright and have a pinkish cast. The bowl can be cleaned one to two hours ahead but not more.

3. To whip properly, egg whites must be completely free of any trace of yolk, and the bowl and whisk must be equally free of grease.

4. To beat egg whites with a large balloon whisk: start slowly, working at first in the bottom of the bowl and then lifting the whisk high in a circle to beat in as much air as possible. As the whites break up and become frothy, increase the size of the circles until you are using the whole bowl area and whisking as fast as possible, still lifting the whisk high out of the bowl in a circle.

5. After the egg whites are quite stiff, whisk in large circles as fast as possible with the whisk kept down in the egg whites and in contact with the bowl. This stiffens and "tightens" the whites rather than beating air into them. For sweet soufflés, reserve a little of the sugar to add when tightening the whites.

6. Fully beaten egg whites are smooth and so stiff that they would not fall out if the bowl were turned upside down.

7. If beating egg whites in a machine, start beating slowly and only gradually increase the speed. Overbeaten egg whites, not generally a problem when beating by hand, will "grain" and become lumpy.

FOLDING EGG WHITES

1. Beaten egg whites blend more easily with a mixture of other ingredients if its consistency is similar to that of the whites.

2. The folding motion is as follows: With a spoon or rubber spatula, cut down into the center of the bowl, scoop under the contents, and turn them bottom to top in a rolling motion. Proceed in this fashion, working clockwise. While folding, turn the bowl in the opposite direction (counterclockwise) with the other hand.

3. Continue folding only until the whites and the other ingredients are blended; if the whites show signs of going liquid, stop at once. Better a few patches of egg white than a Soufflé Dishes heavy mixture.

 SOUFFLÉ DISHES

Originally, soufflés were cooked in pastry cases that had the same straight sides as today's standard dish; the pastry was not eaten. The classic soufflé dish is made of white ovenproof porcelain with straight sides ribbed on the outside. They come in several sizes; the small individual ones are called ramekins.

Soufflé dishes are available in many diameters, and it is the capacity or volume measure that is important. Standard soufflé dishes are available in 4-, 5-, and 6-cup (1, 1.25, and 1.5 L) sizes. For individual soufflés, ⅔-cup (160 ml) dishes are a useful size. Any of the recipes in this chapter can be made as individual soufflés. You can usually determine the size of the dish or the number of small dishes needed by figuring that a recipe will make the same number of cups of raw soufflé mixture as the number of egg whites it specifies. A four-egg-white mixture, then, will fill a 4-cup (1 L) soufflé dish or six ⅔-cup (160 ml) dishes. All sizes of soufflé dishes are useful for baking other mixtures such as crème caramel (p. 109) and for preparing frozen soufflés (p. 308).

If a soufflé dish is not available, a charlotte mold or any deep heatproof dish can be used instead. The handles on a charlotte mold make it easy to transport from oven to table, but because the mold is deeper than a soufflé dish, there is greater risk of collapse.

Eggplant Soufflé
(SOUFFLÉ AUX AUBERGINES)

Salt draws juices from the flesh of vegetables—a process called dégorger *in French. For eggplants this not only gets rid of extra moisture but bitterness as well.*

> 2 medium (¾ pound or 350 g) eggplants
> 2 tablespoons oil
> 3 tablespoons (45 g) butter
> béchamel sauce (p. 192) made with 1 cup (250 ml) milk,
>   salt and pepper, nutmeg, 2 tablespoons (30 g) butter,
>   and 2 tablespoons (15 g) flour
> 4 egg yolks
> 2 tablespoons dry bread crumbs

1 ounce or ¼ cup (30 g) grated Parmesan cheese
salt and pepper
6 egg whites

6-cup (1.5 L) soufflé dish

SERVES 4–6.

Trim the stems from the eggplants and cut each eggplant in half lengthwise. Run the point of a knife around the outside edge and then across the flesh of each cut surface. Sprinkle with salt and leave 30 minutes. Rinse the eggplants with cold water and dry on paper towels.

Set the oven at 375°F (190°C). Heat the oil in a frying pan, add 2 tablespoons (30 g) butter, and when it is hot, fry the eggplants, cut side down, until brown. Transfer them to the heated oven and bake until tender, 10–15 minutes. Let cool slightly, scoop out the flesh, and purée it in a food processor or mash it with a fork. Melt the remaining butter in a sauté pan and cook the eggplant purée over medium heat, stirring, to remove excess moisture.

Make the béchamel sauce and stir in the eggplant purée. Beat in the egg yolks, one by one, and cook the eggplant base over low heat, stirring, until the mixture thickens slightly. The soufflé base can be made ahead and kept, refrigerated, for up to a day.

Toast the bread crumbs in a 350°F (175°C) oven until browned, about 5 minutes, and let cool. Heat the oven to 425°F (220°C). Butter the soufflé dish generously and sprinkle it with the cooled bread crumbs.

To finish: Heat the eggplant base over low heat until hot to the touch. Take from the heat and stir in 3 tablespoons (20 g) of the cheese. Taste the mixture—it should be highly seasoned. Add more salt and pepper if needed. Beat the egg whites until stiff, preferably in a copper bowl. Stir a quarter of the egg whites into the eggplant base and then gently fold this mixture into the remaining egg whites. Pour the soufflé mixture into the prepared dish and smooth the surface. Bake in the heated oven until the soufflé is puffed and brown, 15–18 minutes. Serve at once.

Endive and Parmesan Soufflé
(SOUFFLÉ D'ENDIVES AU PARMESAN)

Endive is particularly tasty in this recipe, but many vegetables, for instance carrots or broccoli, could be substituted.

1 tablespoon (15 g) butter
½ pound (250 g) Belgian endive, sliced
salt and pepper
nutmeg
⅔ cup (160 ml) light cream
béchamel sauce (p. 192) made with ¾ cup (185 ml)
   milk, a slice of onion, a bay leaf, 6 peppercorns, 2
   tablespoons (30 g) butter, ¼ cup (30 g) flour
8 eggs
2 ounces or ½ cup (60 g) grated Parmesan cheese

1½-quart (1.5 L) soufflé dish

SERVES 4–6.

In a sauté pan melt the butter, add the sliced endive, salt and pepper, a grating of nutmeg, and cream. Cover and cook gently until the endive is tender, 10–15 minutes. Purée the vegetables in a blender or food processor or work them through a food mill. Return the purée to the pan and cook it gently, stirring constantly, until thick—the purée should fall lazily from the spoon.

Make the béchamel sauce and beat in the endive purée. Whisk in 2 whole eggs and 4 egg yolks and heat very gently, stirring, until the mixture thickens slightly. The endive base can be prepared ahead and kept, refrigerated, for up to a day.

Butter the soufflé dish generously and set the oven at 425°F (220°C).

To finish: Heat the endive base until hot to the touch. Take from the heat, stir in all but 2 tablespoons of the cheese, and taste for seasoning—it should be quite peppery. Beat the remaining 6 egg whites until stiff, preferably in a copper bowl. Stir a quarter of the egg whites into the endive base and then gently fold this mixture into the remaining whites. Pour the soufflé mixture into the prepared dish, smooth the top, and sprinkle with the remaining cheese. Bake in the heated oven until the soufflé is puffed and brown, 15–18 minutes. Serve at once.

Fish Soufflé with Curry Sauce
(SOUFFLÉ DE POISSON, SAUCE CURRY)

This soufflé is denser than most French soufflés and is cooked in a lower oven for a longer time so it is unusually firm in the center. Curry sauce provides a spicy contrast in flavor.

fish stock (p. 115) made with 1 tablespoon butter, 1
　　onion, 1½ pounds (750 g) bones, 1 quart (1 L) water,
　　10 peppercorns, a bouquet garni, and 1 cup (250 ml)
　　white wine
1½ pounds (750 g) white fish (cod or whiting)
velouté sauce (p. 193) made with 1 cup (250 ml) fish
　　stock, salt and pepper, nutmeg, 3 tablespoons (45 g)
　　butter, 2 shallots finely chopped, and 3 tablespoons
　　(25 g) flour
¼ cup (60 ml) heavy cream
pinch of dry mustard
salt and pepper
4 egg yolks
2 tablespoons bread crumbs
6 egg whites

For the curry sauce:
　　2 tablespoons (30 g) butter
　　2 shallots, finely chopped
　　1½ teaspoons curry powder
　　1½ tablespoons (18 g) flour
　　salt and pepper
　　nutmeg
　　1¼ cups (375 ml) cooking liquid from the fish
　　¼ cup (60 ml) heavy cream

6-cup (1.5 L) soufflé dish

SERVES 4–6.

Make the fish stock. Wash and clean the fish, scale it, and cut off the fins. Put the fish in a large pan, pour the stock over the fish; it should cover it, but if it doesn't, add more water. Cover the pan and bring the liquid just to a boil. Poach until the flesh can be pierced easily with a fork, 10–15 minutes. Leave to cool. Take the fish from the pan with a slotted spoon, remove the skin and bones, and flake the fish with a fork. Strain the cooking liquid and reduce by boiling to 2¼ cups (560 ml).

Make the velouté sauce, sautéing the shallots in the butter before adding the flour. Stir in the fish, cream, mustard, and salt and pepper and taste—the mixture should be highly seasoned. Add salt and pepper if needed. Beat the egg yolks into the hot mixture so it thickens. The soufflé can be prepared ahead to this point and kept, covered and refrigerated, for up to 6 hours.

For the curry sauce: In a heavy-bottomed saucepan melt the butter, add the shallots and curry powder, and cook gently until the shallots are soft but not brown, 3–4 minutes. Whisk in the flour, cook until foaming, and then add the remaining cooking liquid from the fish, salt and pepper, and a grating of nutmeg. Bring to a boil and then simmer, whisking constantly, for 2 minutes. Taste for seasoning and adjust if necessary. Rub the surface of the sauce with butter to prevent the formation of a skin. If you like, the sauce can be made to this point up to 4 days ahead and kept, covered and refrigerated.

Toast the bread crumbs in a 350°F (175°C) oven until browned, about 5 minutes, and let cool. Butter the soufflé dish generously and sprinkle it with the cooled crumbs.

To finish: Heat the oven to 375°F (190°C). Heat the fish mixture over low heat until hot to the touch. Beat the egg whites until stiff, preferably in a copper bowl. Stir a quarter of the egg whites into the fish base and then gently fold this mixture into the remaining egg whites. Pour the soufflé mixture into the prepared dish, smooth the top, and bake in the heated oven until the soufflé is puffed and brown, 20–25 minutes. Meanwhile, heat the curry sauce and stir in the cream. Taste for seasoning and adjust if necessary.

Serve the soufflé at once and pass the sauce separately.

Fresh Pear Soufflé
(SOUFFLÉ AUX POIRES FRAÎCHES)

This soufflé, made without flour, milk, or egg yolks, is exceptionally light.

> **3 medium pears (about 1 pound or 500 g)**
> **juice of ½ lemon**
> **2 tablespoons pear alcohol or kirsch**
> **½ cup (100 g) sugar**
> **5 egg whites**
>
> **5-cup (1.25 L) soufflé dish**

SERVES 4–6.

Peel and core the pears and purée them in a food mill or food processor with the lemon juice, alcohol, and half the sugar. Pour into a bowl and press a piece of plastic wrap over the top to prevent discoloration. The purée can be made ahead and kept, well covered and refrigerated, for 2 hours.

Butter the soufflé dish generously and heat the oven to 375°F (190°C).

To finish: Beat the egg whites until stiff, preferably in a copper bowl. Add the remaining sugar and beat until glossy, about 20 seconds. Stir a quarter of the egg whites into the pear purée and then gently fold this mixture into the remaining egg whites. Pour the mixture into the prepared dish and smooth the surface. Bake in the heated oven until the soufflé is puffed and brown, 12–15 minutes.

Cover the pear purée with plastic wrap if it is made ahead and refrigerated.

Grand Marnier Soufflé en Surprise
(SOUFFLÉ AU GRAND MARNIER EN SURPRISE)

You can use any favorite liqueur to flavor this soufflé and change the decorative topping and the name accordingly. In this case you might replace the orange zest with an appropriate flavoring or flavor the pastry cream with vanilla.

> **thick pastry cream (p. 229) made with 1 cup (250 ml)
> milk, a pinch of salt, 3 egg yolks, 2 tablespoons
> (25 g) sugar, and ¼ cup (30 g) flour
> grated zest of 2 oranges
> 6 tablespoons Grand Marnier
> 1 orange
> 4–6 ladyfingers—homemade (p. 279) or store-bought
> 5 egg whites
> 2 tablespoons (25 g) granulated sugar
> powdered sugar (for dusting)**
>
> ***5-cup (1.25 L) soufflé dish***

SERVES 4–6.

Make the pastry cream. Stir in grated orange zest and 4 tablespoons of the Grand Marnier. The soufflé base can be made ahead and kept, refrigerated, for up to a day.

Cut all the pith from the orange. Then cut the segments of flesh away from the membrane. Set the oven at 425°F (220° C). Butter the soufflé dish generously. Split the ladyfingers and moisten with the remaining Grand Marnier.

To finish: Heat the Grand Marnier base over low heat until hot to the touch. Beat the egg whites until stiff, preferably in a copper bowl. Add the 2 tablespoons sugar and beat until glossy, about 20 seconds. Stir a quarter of the egg whites into the base and then gently fold this mixture into the remaining egg whites. Pour half of the soufflé mixture into the prepared dish, set the soaked ladyfingers on top, add the remaining mixture, and smooth the surface. Bake in the heated oven until the soufflé is puffed and brown, 12–15 minutes.

Dust the soufflé with powdered sugar, arrange the orange segments on top, and serve at once.

Hot Lemon Soufflé
(SOUFFLÉ CHAUD AU CITRON)

The tangy lemon flavor really comes through in this flourless soufflé. Be sure to cook the lemon mixture until quite thick.

4 tablespoons (60 g) butter
6 tablespoons (95 ml) lemon juice
⅔ cup (135 g) sugar
4 egg yolks
grated zest of 2 lemons
5 egg whites
powdered sugar (for dusting)

4-cup (1 L) soufflé dish

SERVES 4.

In a heavy-bottomed pan heat the butter with the lemon juice and half the sugar until the butter and sugar are melted. Remove from the heat and beat in the egg yolks, one by one. Add the lemon zest. Heat very gently, whisking constantly, until the mixture thickens. (NOTE: Do not let it get too hot or it will curdle.) It can be made up to 3 hours before using and kept at room temperature.

Butter the soufflé dish generously and heat the oven to 425°F (220°C).

To finish: Gently heat the lemon base until hot to the touch. Beat the egg whites until stiff, preferably in a copper bowl. Add the remaining sugar and beat until glossy, about 20 seconds. Stir a quarter of the egg whites into the base and then gently fold this mixture into the remaining egg whites. Pour the mixture into the prepared dish and smooth the surface. Bake in the heated oven until the soufflé is puffed and brown, 10–12 minutes. Dust the soufflé with powdered sugar and serve at once.

Ginger Soufflé
(SOUFFLÉ AU GINGEMBRE)

I've found that people either hate or adore this unusual soufflé that is flavored with both candied and powdered ginger.

thick pastry cream (p. 229) made with 1 cup (250 ml)
milk, 3 egg yolks, ½ cup (100 g) sugar, and ¼ cup
(30 g) flour
½ teaspoon ground ginger
1 tablespoon chopped candied ginger
4 egg whites
2 tablespoons sugar

4-cup (1 L) soufflé dish

SERVES 4.

Make the pastry cream and stir in the ground and candied ginger. The soufflé base can be made ahead and kept, refrigerated, for up to a day.

Set the oven at 425°F (220°C). Butter the soufflé dish generously.

To finish: Heat the ginger base over low heat until hot to the touch. Beat the egg whites until stiff, preferably in a copper bowl. Add the 2 tablespoons sugar and beat until glossy, about 20 seconds. Stir a quarter of the egg whites into the base and then gently fold this mixture into the remaining egg whites. Pour the soufflé mixture into the prepared dish and smooth the surface. Bake in the heated oven until the soufflé is puffed and brown, 10–12 minutes, and serve at once.

Flour-based Sauces

"SAUCES ARE TO cookery what grammar is to language and melody is to music." Like so many catchy quotations, this lyrical outburst is attributed to at least three celebrities, in this case all of them chefs. It certainly sums up the Frenchman's almost reverential attitude toward a sauce. To a chef, sauces give structure—the grammar—to his repertoire, while defining the theme—the melody—of a particular dish. The analogy I would use is more mundane. I think of sauces as the mortar that holds a dish together, giving it coherence, so that cooks can build an almost infinite number of variations on a few basic ingredients.

God forbid, however, that a sauce should have the texture of cement! Even the trickiest of sauces, designed to give body to foods with a high water content like vegetables, should not have a glutinous quality. Sauces for coating should coat lightly, so that the shape and color of the food beneath are still discernible. And brown sauces to accompany roasts and grilled meats should be light, about the thickness of oil. Often they contain no thickener at all.

For centuries, the most common thickener has been a *roux*, a paste of melted butter and flour that is cooked until frothy (for white sauces) or until a rich brown (for brown sauces). But flour-based sauces are comparatively modern. In medieval times sauces were thickened with eggs, with bread crumbs, sometimes with vegetable purées, never with flour.

The first French cook who seems to have used flour for thickening a sauce was La Varenne in the mid-seventeenth century, and it was not until the following century that the familiar range of

SAUCE BÉCHAMEL
One of the most important and familiar of the "mother" sauces, it is made of seasoned milk and thickened with a white roux.

SAUCE ITALIENNE
This sauce consists of thickened brown veal stock flavored with wine, mushrooms, and ham.

SAUCE VELOUTÉ
One of the basic or "mother" sauces, made from chicken, veal, or fish stock and thickened with a light roux

white and brown sauces was developed. Some were named after contemporary personalities, such as the Marquis de Béchamel and Duc de Mornay. Brown sauce (flavored with ham) was called espagnole because the finest hams of the day came from Montanchez in the west of Spain. These basic sauces have continued up to the present, with more and more variations being added over the years.

All are based on flour mother (*mère*) sauces, two white and two brown: béchamel, made of milk thickened with a white roux; velouté, made of white stock; espagnole, made of brown stock with a brown roux; and *fond de veau lié*. This last one is a simple brown sauce, just veal stock thickened with arrowroot or potato starch, that has almost entirely replaced the long-cooked espagnole in everyday use.

On the foundation of these four sauces, innumerable others are constructed by adding such ingredients as wine, shallots, mushrooms, tomatoes, cheese, herbs, or garlic. Bordelaise sauce for serving with steak, for example, is a brown sauce with a little red wine, shallots, and marrow; bretonne, for roast lamb, is composed of brown sauce, white wine, onions, tomatoes, and garlic; the famous sauce suprême is a chicken velouté flavored with mushroom stems and enriched with cream.

A sauce does not exist in limbo—it is there to enhance other ingredients, to complement them without overwhelming. As with the selection of red or white wine, there is a recognized rule: the lighter the meat, the paler the sauce. Béchamel, as the lightest, is used for vegetables, eggs, fish, and sometimes chicken; velouté sauces, made from veal, chicken or fish stock, are ideal to serve with these meats; brown sauces are for dark meats, particularly beef and game. But jurisdictions overlap, and a rich red wine sauce may be just the thing with some fish, or a light cream sauce right with pheasant. The very origin of the word sauce, from the Latin *salsa* meaning salty, emphasizes its role in highlighting the flavor of a dish. This is why no sauce should taste right altogether on its own— its flavor should be too concentrated to be palatable in quantity.

The key to a good sauce is reduction: cooking down to concentrate the flavor and, at the same time, achieve just the right consistency. As a general rule, the longer a sauce is simmered, the more subtle and mellow it will be. The shortest cooking time is given to white sauces: five to ten minutes will suffice for béchamel, although there are chefs who like to give it half an hour to be absolutely sure any flavor of raw flour has disappeared. A velouté, particularly when made with veal or chicken stock, should simmer for at least fifteen minutes, preferably half an hour, while a good brown sauce needs an hour or more, three to four hours for espagnole. A good deal of the reduction process can take place before the sauce is thickened with any starch, thus decreasing the danger of scorching. This is one reason for the popularity of fond de veau lié, thickened at the end of cooking.

Although chefs who still make espagnole cook it in three or four hours, in its heyday preparation of the sauce took two days. First the roux was slowly browned, rather like roasting coffee beans, to develop the flavor. Then a rich brown stock—a day's work in itself—was added together with pieces of veal, ham, a stewing fowl, and sometimes game birds. The mixture was simmered with frequent stirrings, skimmings, and strainings to obtain a dark, rich, glossy sauce. Louis Diat, who was in charge of the kitchens of the old Ritz-Carlton Hotel in New York City from 1910 to 1951, describes his training in France: "The work with sauces was the most important part of a long and arduous apprenticeship. . . . I can see myself, a very young sous-chef, in front of a hot range pushing and turning a sturdy wooden spatula as the sauces reduced in the big copper pans, and standing with bated breath while the chef des cuisines went through his daily routine of tasting the sauces for the day. The practiced eye and sensitive tongue of this culinary expert could detect the slightest deviation from perfection, and his Gallic temper would soon let the kitchen know it. *Zut!* Down the drain would go what we had thought a perfectly good sauce, and to the tune of a torrent of French fury." No wonder young chefs, short of help, are adopting the traditional household solution of a fond de veau lié.

The eclipse of flour-based sauces is one of the major developments of nouvelle cuisine. More and more chefs are whipping up *petites sauces* at the last minute, using cooking juices, a dash of wine, and a ladle of the all-important well-reduced stock. Thickening, if it is added at all, is a teaspoon of arrowroot or a tablespoon of heavy cream. Sauces, even the traditionally thick white sauces, are getting thinner and thinner, relying on the gelatin in good stock to give body, with a generous swirl of butter added just before serving. One or two idealists have banned flour altogether from the cuisine section of the kitchen.

Flour-based sauces, however, are a long way from disappearing entirely. Too many favorite dishes, old and new, depend on full-bodied roux-thickened sauce for their excellence. French cuisine would be unimaginable without its browned gratins, based on creamy béchamel, or without its regional ragoûts with their rich brown sauces—the daubes of Provence and the wine-based stews of Burgundy. Flour-thickened sauces form the base of many fillings, and without them the fabled French soufflé could scarcely exist.

FOR SUCCESSFUL FLOUR-BASED SAUCES

1. Use a heavy-bottomed pan. Copper lined with tin or stainless steel is best. Sauce scorches easily in a thin pan.

2. The roux must be thoroughly cooked so that it does not impart an unpleasant taste of raw flour to the sauce. Even for béchamel, the roux should be cooked until frothing.

3. Stir a roux constantly to prevent scorching and uneven cooking.

4. For béchamel and velouté sauces, the roux must not brown, although it can be slightly darker for velouté than for béchamel.

5. The flavor of velouté and brown sauces depends very much on the quality of the stock. Reduce the stock well for full flavor.

6. Add hot liquid to shorten the time of whisking while the sauce comes to a boil, but first cool the roux slightly because if both elements are very hot lumps may form.

7. Add the liquid to the roux in a steady stream, whisking constantly.

8. To avoid lumps and give the sauce a gloss, whisk constantly as it comes to a boil. If lumps form, do not cook them. Take the sauce from the heat and whisk it well. If the lumps persist, strain the sauce.

9. If the sauce is to be reduced, season very lightly because the seasoning will become concentrated as the liquid reduces.

10. The right consistency for a sauce depends on its type and use. If it is too thin, simmer it to reduce until thick enough; if too thick, add liquid.

11. Brown sauces are strained in a chinois—a conical strainer. Press with a small ladle to extract all the juices from the vegetables. White sauces can also be strained to ensure smoothness and increase their gloss.

12. Always taste a sauce for seasoning before serving.

PREPARING AHEAD

1. If a flour-based sauce is not to be used immediately, rub the surface of the warm sauce with a small piece of butter or press a piece of waxed paper directly on the surface. This will prevent the formation of a skin.

2. Sauces based on béchamel or velouté can be stored, covered and refrigerated, for up to three days; brown sauces can be similarly kept for a week. Any butter, cream, or egg yolks used for enriching the basic sauce should be added when reheating.

3. Brown and velouté sauces freeze well, so it is worth making a large batch. White sauces containing egg yolks separate when defrosted, and all sauces containing cream tend to thin when thawed. If the consis-

tency of a defrosted sauce is not smooth, pass it through a fine strainer or work it in a blender or food processor.

LAST-MINUTE THICKENERS

ARROWROOT OR POTATO STARCH:

Arrowroot or potato starch is used in basic brown sauce and sauces made from cooking liquids. When short of time, a roux-based sauce that is too thin can also be thickened with arrowroot or potato starch. Arrowroot or potato starch is added at the end of the cooking time because both will thin if simmered for more than two or three minutes.

For every 2 cups (500 ml) liquid, mix two to three level teaspoons arrowroot or potato starch with two to three tablespoons cold water or cold liquid such as stock. Whisk enough of this liquid into the boiling sauce to thicken it slightly; it should be light and slightly syrupy.

CORNSTARCH:

Cornstarch is often used for thickening sweet sauces. It is used in the same proportion as arrowroot. The result is slightly more sticky, and the sauce can be cooked somewhat longer than one thickened with arrowroot or potato starch.

EGG YOLKS AND CREAM:

This liaison is used in velouté sauces and occasionally in béchamel. Egg yolks with cream should be added just before serving. A sauce with these additions may curdle if reheated or kept warm for too long.

Mix the yolks with about an equal volume of cream and then stir in some of the hot sauce to partially cook the mixture. Off the heat, whisk this mixture into the remaining sauce. Then cook, whisking constantly, until the sauce thickens slightly. If the sauce doesn't contain flour, do not boil or it will curdle. If it has a roux base, bring it just back to a boil after adding the egg yolks and cream.

BEURRE MANIÉ:

Beurre manié is rarely used nowadays, but it is a useful way of thickening both white and brown sauces. It is a roux of butter and flour added to a mixture at the end, rather than at the beginning, of cooking.

Cream the butter and work in an equal quantity of flour with a fork or whisk. Drop pieces of beurre manié into the boiling liquid, whisking hard. The butter will melt and distribute the flour evenly through the liquid. Keep adding pieces of beurre manié until the sauce is thick enough to coat a spoon and then simmer the sauce for at least five minutes to cook the flour.

Béchamel Sauce
(SAUCE BÉCHAMEL)

This multipurpose white sauce is made thin for preparing cream soups, medium for serving with eggs, vegetables, and pasta, and thick for binding soufflé mixtures.

1 cup (250 ml) milk
1 slice of onion
1 bay leaf
6 peppercorns
salt and white pepper
nutmeg

For the roux:

Thin:	**1 tablespoon (15 g) butter**
	1 tablespoon flour
Medium:	**1½ tablespoons (20 g) butter**
	1½ tablespoons flour
Thick:	**2 tablespoons (30 g) butter**
	2 tablespoons flour

MAKES 1 CUP (250 ml) SAUCE.

In a small saucepan bring the milk just to a boil. Add the onion, bay leaf, and peppercorns, cover, and leave to infuse 5–10 minutes. Meanwhile make the roux: In a heavy-bottomed saucepan melt the butter, whisk in the flour, and cook until the roux is foaming but not browned, 1–2 minutes. Let it cool a few moments and then strain in the hot milk, whisking. Bring the sauce to a boil, whisking constantly, and add salt, pepper, and nutmeg to taste. Reduce the heat and simmer for 5 minutes. If the sauce is not to be used immediately, rub the surface with butter to prevent the formation of a skin. Béchamel can be kept, covered and refrigerated, for 2–3 days.

A Béchamel Sauce Derivative

MORNAY SAUCE *(sauce mornay)*:

Mornay sauce is served with eggs, fish, white meats, and vegetables and is an important ingredient in most gratins. Well-aged Gruyère or Parmesan, or a mixture of both, are the best cheeses to use.

> **1 cup (250 ml) béchamel sauce (p. 192)**
> **1 egg yolk—optional**
> **1 teaspoon Dijon mustard—optional**
> **1 ounce or about ¼ cup (30 g) grated cheese**
> **1 tablespoon (15 g) butter**
> **salt and pepper**

MAKES ABOUT 1 CUP (250 ml) SAUCE.

Make the béchamel sauce. Off the heat, beat in the egg yolk, if using, stir in the mustard, the cheese, and finally the butter. Taste for seasoning and adjust if necessary.

Velouté Sauce
(SAUCE VELOUTÉ)

This basic sauce is usually enriched with egg yolks, cream, and/or butter just before serving. It can accompany eggs, fish, poultry, light meats, and vegetables.

> **1 cup (250 ml) fish (p. 115), chicken (p. 115), or white**
> **veal stock (p. 116)**
> **1½ tablespoons (20 g) butter**
> **1½ tablespoons flour**
> **salt and pepper**

MAKES 1 CUP (250 ml) SAUCE.

Bring the stock to a boil. In a heavy-bottomed saucepan melt the butter, whisk in the flour, and cook until the roux is foaming but not browned, 1–2 minutes. Let cool a few moments and then whisk in the hot stock. Bring the sauce to a boil, whisking constantly, and add just a little salt and pepper— the flavor of the sauce will be concentrated during cooking. Simmer, skimming occasionally, for 15–30 minutes. Taste for seasoning and adjust if necessary. If the sauce is not to be used immediately, rub the surface with butter to prevent the formation of a skin. Velouté can be kept, covered and refrigerated, for 2–3 days.

Velouté Sauce Derivatives

SAUCE SUPRÊME *(sauce suprême)*:

Sauce suprême is especially good with poultry.

> **1 cup (250 ml) velouté sauce (p. 193) made with
>   chicken stock**
> **¼ cup (2 ounces or 60 ml) chopped mushroom stems**
> **¼ cup (60 ml) heavy cream**
> **salt and pepper**
> **1 tablespoon (15 g) butter**

MAKES 1 CUP (250 ml) SAUCE.

Make the velouté sauce, adding the mushrooms before simmering. Strain the sauce, add the cream, and simmer another 2–3 minutes. Taste for seasoning and adjust if necessary. Remove from the heat and swirl in the butter.

ALLEMANDE SAUCE *(sauce allemande)*:

Much like sauce suprême but based on veal stock rather than chicken and enriched with an egg yolk rather than cream, this sauce is good with poultry, veal, and vegetables.

> **1 cup (250 ml) velouté sauce (p. 193) made with veal
>   stock**
> **¼ cup (2 ounces or 60 ml) chopped mushroom stems**
> **1 egg yolk**
> **few drops lemon juice**
> **salt and pepper**
> **nutmeg**
> **2 tablespoons (30 g) butter**

MAKES 1 CUP (250 ml) SAUCE.

Make the velouté sauce, adding the mushrooms before simmering. Strain the sauce, whisk part of the hot sauce into the egg yolk, and then whisk the yolk mixture into the sauce remaining in the pan. Bring the sauce just back to a boil and season to taste with lemon juice, salt and pepper, and nutmeg. Remove from the heat and add the butter.

Basic Brown Sauce I
(FOND DE VEAU LIÉ)

In French restaurants, basic brown sauce has largely replaced the classic espagnole sauce as the base for all brown sauces. This and the following Basic Brown Sauce II may be used interchangeably.

1 cup (250 ml) brown veal stock (p. 117)
2 teaspoons arrowroot or potato starch
1½ tablespoons Madeira or water
salt and pepper

MAKES 1 CUP (250 ml) SAUCE.

Bring the stock to a boil. Mix the arrowroot or potato starch to a paste with the Madeira or water. Whisk enough of the mixture into the stock to thicken the sauce to the desired consistency. Bring it back to a boil, taste for seasoning, and adjust if necessary. Strain and, if the sauce is not to be used immediately, rub the surface with butter to prevent the formation of a skin. The sauce can be kept, covered and refrigerated, for 3–4 days.

Basic Brown Sauce II

This richer version of the basic brown sauce resembles the traditional espagnole sauce.

1 tablespoon (15 g) butter
½ leek, chopped
½ carrot, chopped
½ onion, chopped
½ stalk celery, chopped
1 cup (250 ml) brown veal stock (p. 117)
1 tomato, chopped
1 bouquet garni (p. 118)
1 teaspoon tomato paste
2 teaspoons arrowroot or potato starch
1½ tablespoons Madeira or water
salt and pepper

MAKES 1 CUP (250 ml) SAUCE.

Heat the butter in a heavy-bottomed pan and brown the chopped leek, carrot, onion, and celery. Add the stock, tomato, and bouquet garni, bring to a boil, and then simmer until the vegetables are very tender, 30–45 minutes.

Add the tomato paste and return to a boil. Mix the arrowroot or potato starch to a paste with the Madeira or cold water. Whisk enough of the mixture into the stock to thicken it to the desired consistency. Bring it back to a boil, taste for seasoning, and adjust if necessary. Strain and, if the sauce is not to be used immediately, rub the surface with butter to prevent the formation of a skin. The sauce can be kept, covered and refrigerated, for 3–4 days.

Basic Brown Sauce Derivatives

SAUCE ITALIENNE *(sauce italienne)*:

Sauce italienne is a good complement for roast beef, steak, or veal.

> **2 teaspoons (10 g) butter**
> **¼ onion, finely chopped**
> **¼ cup (2 ounces or 60 g) finely chopped mushrooms**
> **½ cup (125 ml) white wine**
> **1 cup (250 ml) basic brown sauce (p. 195)**
> **1 ounce (30 g) slice cooked ham, cut in small dice**
> **salt and pepper**

MAKES ABOUT 1½ CUPS (375 ml) SAUCE.

    Melt the butter in a saucepan, add the onion, and cook slowly until soft but not brown, 7–10 minutes. Add the mushrooms and cook over high heat, stirring frequently, until soft, 4–5 minutes. Add the wine, bring to a boil, and boil until reduced to ¼ cup (60 ml). Stir in the basic brown sauce and bring to a boil. Add the ham, taste for seasoning, and adjust if necessary. The sauce can be kept, covered and refrigerated, for 3–4 days.

MADEIRA SAUCE *(sauce madère)*:

This sauce is a classic accompaniment to fillet of beef, veal, ham, and innards such as tongue and kidney.

> **1 cup (250 ml) basic brown sauce (p. 195)**
> **3 tablespoons Madeira**
> **salt and pepper**

MAKES ABOUT 1 CUP (250 ml) SAUCE.

    Heat the basic brown sauce in a saucepan, add 1½ tablespoons of the Madeira, and simmer for 10 minutes. Add the remaining Madeira and bring just to a boil. Taste for seasoning and adjust if necessary.

thoroughly cooked, and the wine or vinegar well reduced if the sauce is to avoid acidity; lemon juice must be added with a light hand. In consistency, butter sauces range from quite thick (béarnaise) to flowing (beurre blanc). Sometimes, as in eggs Benedict, the butter sauce is spooned over the food it accompanies, but more often it is served apart so that it doesn't separate on contact with very hot food.

Emulsified sauces are prone to separation if they are mixed too quickly, subjected to high temperatures, or allowed to stand for too long. When making egg yolk-based sauces, adding the butter to the base is easy enough: the critical element is the base itself. At La Varenne for egg yolk sauces we prefer the mousse method, in which the yolks are whisked with a tablespoon or two of liquid until they are light and then cooked slowly, whisking constantly, until they're thick enough to leave a ribbon trail. Then clarified butter is added, and not for French cooks the agonizing drop by drop suggested in some cookbooks. A half smile on his face, Chef Chambrette regularly draws gasps from his audience as he prepares hollandaise sauce: having briskly fluffed up his egg yolk mousse, he casually whisks in a panful of clarified butter in a steady stream. But there is method in this mad pouring and whisking, for he has saved himself time. And time is money for a professional cook.

Beurre blanc, however, is a different story because sauces based on reduced liquid separate even more easily than egg yolk-based sauces. They should be made at the last possible moment. This is not difficult since the reduction of the wine and vinegar to a syrupy glaze is simplicity itself and can be done ahead. The sauce is finished in a few moments by "mounting" it with butter—that is, whisking chunks of butter into the base over very low heat or off the heat altogether. The butter should not melt, but soften to form a creamy sauce. (The same method is often used to enrich brown and velouté sauces just before serving with a little, and often more than a little, butter.) Once "mounted," the sauce cannot be reheated successfully.

A sweet emulsified sauce also exists—*sauce sabayon,* which is the French version of Italian zabaglione. It is made rather like hollandaise by whisking egg yolks with liquid (usually white wine) and sugar to a light fluffy mousse that is still thin enough to pour. Sauce sabayon is often served with poached fruit or with cake. It, too, separates easily.

If emulsified sauces are so tricky, why are they so popular? They complement a wide variety of dishes from vegetables to eggs to fish, steak, lamb, and kidneys. Perhaps even more important is that they are so quick to make: they require no advance preparations such as the long simmering of stock, little equipment, and a minimum of ingredients.

FOR SUCCESSFUL HOT EMULSIFIED SAUCES

1. A good heavy pan, preferably tin-lined, makes preparing hot emulsified sauces much easier.

2. For richer hollandaise or béarnaise sauce, increase the butter up to about 6 tablespoons (about 3 ounces or 95 g) per egg yolk. Do not use less than 4 tablespoons (2 ounces or 60 g), or the taste of egg will be too strong.

3. Clarify butter and then cool it slightly before adding to egg yolks. Hot butter will curdle yolks.

4. Thoroughly cook the egg yolk mousse that forms the base of hollandaise and béarnaise. Use low heat and whisk for several minutes so the mousse thickens evenly and becomes fluffy. Sudden heat will make the eggs granular.

5. Remove egg yolk mousse from the heat as soon as it is thick enough; overcooking will scramble it.

6. Reduce wine and vinegar thoroughly or the sauce will be too acid.

7. Add butter to yolks in a slow but steady stream and to reduced liquid in small pieces so it thickens the sauce without separating from it.

8. Never stop whisking while cooking yolks or when adding butter to either a yolk or a reduced liquid base.

9. In making a liquid-based butter sauce, work over very low heat and, if necessary, move the pan off the heat occasionally to lower the temperature of the sauce. The butter must soften enough to form a sauce but must not melt.

10. If a hollandaise or béarnaise sauce is too thick, add a tablespoon of tepid water. If the sauce is too thin, but not separated, continue cooking over low heat, whisking constantly, until it thickens.

11. Add lemon juice to sauce just before serving. If it is added too soon to a sauce that is kept warm for some time, it may cause fermentation.

PREPARING AHEAD

1. It is best to make emulsified sauces just before serving. However, egg-yolk based sauces can be made up to thirty minutes ahead and kept in a warm, not boiling, water bath. Whisk the sauce often, checking to be sure it has not curdled. If the sauce was made in a tin-lined copper pan, remove it to another pan to keep warm. Never leave a warm sauce in a copper pan.

2. The liquid base for a butter sauce can be reduced well ahead of time.

However, once finished, a liquid-based sauce can be kept warm for only a short time.

3. Leftover hollandaise and béarnaise can be kept, covered and refrigerated, for up to two days. They can be reheated gently, by whisking them constantly in a warm water bath, but the risk of separation is high.

TO RESCUE SEPARATED EMULSIFIED SAUCES

1. Emulsified sauce almost always separates because it has been overheated. If an egg yolk-based sauce separates:

   a. Remove the sauce at once from the heat and whisk in an ice cube.

   b. If this doesn't work, in a clean pan gradually whisk the separated mixture into one tablespoon of cold water.

   c. If still unsuccessful, start the sauce again: whisk one egg yolk and one tablespoon water over low heat to a mousse consistency and then gradually whisk in the separated mixture, drop by drop.

   d. If the sauce is so curdled that the egg yolks have cooked into granules, the sauce is irretrievable.

2. A yolk-based sauce can separate because it is too cool and has not been sufficiently cooked. Try bringing a tablespoon of water to a boil and then whisking in the turned sauce drop by drop over low heat.

3. Sauces based on reduced liquid rather than egg yolks cannot be rescued once separated.

Hollandaise Sauce
(SAUCE HOLLANDAISE)

The mysteriously named hollandaise is an entirely French invention. Serve it with poached fish, with luxurious vegetables such as asparagus and artichokes, and with eggs.

    6 ounces (180 g) butter
    3 tablespoons water
    3 egg yolks
    salt and white pepper
    juice of ½ lemon, or to taste

MAKES ABOUT 1 CUP (250 ml) SAUCE.

Melt the butter, skim the froth from the surface, and let it cool to tepid. In a small heavy-bottomed saucepan whisk the water and egg yolks with a little salt and pepper until light, about 30 seconds. Set the pan over very low heat and whisk constantly until the mixture is creamy and thick enough to form a ribbon trail.

Take from the heat and whisk in the tepid butter a few drops at a time. When the sauce has started to thicken, the butter can be added a little faster. Do not add the milky sediment at the bottom of the butter. When all the butter is added, stir in the lemon juice and add salt and pepper and lemon juice to taste. Hollandaise is served warm, not hot. It can be kept in a warm water bath for up to half an hour.

Skimming foam from the melted butter

Heat and whisk the egg-yolk base until thick.

Add the clarified butter a little at a time, and when the sauce thickens add the remaining butter in a steady stream. Stir in seasonings and lemon juice at the end.

Hollandaise Sauce Derivatives

CHANTILLY SAUCE *(sauce Chantilly)*:

Sauce Chantilly, also called sauce mousseline or sauce vierge, is served with fish, chicken, sweetbreads, and broccoli.

1 recipe hollandaise sauce (p. 201)
¼ cup (60 ml) heavy cream, stiffly whipped
salt and white pepper

MAKES ABOUT 1¼ CUPS (310 ml) SAUCE.

Make the hollandaise and fold the whipped cream into it. Taste for seasoning, adjust if necessary, and serve immediately.

NOISETTE SAUCE *(sauce noisette)*:

Serve noisette sauce with eggs, fish, and vegetables.

1 recipe hollandaise sauce (p. 201) made as below
MAKES ABOUT 1 CUP (250 ml) SAUCE.

Clarify the butter for the hollandaise sauce by melting, skimming off the froth, and carefully pouring it into a heavy-bottomed pan, leaving the milky sediment behind. Cook the clarified butter over medium heat until fragrant and nut brown. Let cool to tepid and proceed as for regular hollandaise.

MALTESE SAUCE *(sauce maltaise)*:

Maltese sauce is most often served with asparagus.

½ orange
1 recipe hollandaise sauce (p. 201)

MAKES ABOUT 1¼ CUPS (310 ml) SAUCE.

Pare the zest from the orange being careful to cut off only the orange layer and none of the bitter white skin beneath. Cut the zest into needle-like shreds, blanch them in boiling water for 1–2 minutes, and drain. Squeeze the juice from the orange. Make the hollandaise sauce and add the zest and juice. Taste for seasoning and adjust if necessary. The sauce can be kept in a warm water bath for up to half an hour.

MUSTARD SAUCE *(sauce moutarde):*

Sauce moutarde is particularly good with eggs, fish, and kidneys.

> **1 recipe hollandaise sauce (p. 201)**
> **1–2 teaspoons Dijon mustard**

MAKES ABOUT 1 CUP (250 ml) SAUCE.

Make the hollandaise sauce and whisk in the mustard to taste. The sauce can be kept in a warm water bath for up to half an hour.

Béarnaise Sauce
(SAUCE BÉARNAISE)

Some writers argue that sauce béarnaise was originally made in Béarn, in southwestern France. Others think the name honors Béarn-born King Henri IV, "Le Grand Béarnais," who loved spicy food. But most agree that the sauce became famous at a restaurant that was named after the king—the Pavillon Henri IV in Saint-Germain-en-Laye. It is served with steaks, lamb, kidneys, and rich fish such as salmon.

> **6 ounces (180 g) butter**
> **3 tablespoons vinegar**
> **3 tablespoons white wine**
> **10 peppercorns, crushed**
> **2 shallots, chopped**
> **1 tablespoon chopped fresh tarragon stems or**
>   **tarragon preserved in vinegar**
> **3 egg yolks**
> **salt and white or cayenne pepper**
> **1 tablespoon chopped chervil or parsley**
> **1–2 tablespoons finely chopped fresh tarragon leaves**
>   **or tarragon preserved in vinegar**

MAKES ABOUT 1 CUP (250 ml) SAUCE.

Melt the butter, skim the froth from the surface, and let cool to tepid. In a heavy-bottomed pan boil the vinegar and wine with the peppercorns, chopped shallots, and the 1 tablespoon tarragon until reduced to 2 tablespoons. Let cool. Add the egg yolks and a little salt and pepper and whisk until light, about 30 seconds. Set the pan over very low heat and whisk constantly until the mixture is creamy and quite thick. Take from the heat and whisk in the tepid butter, a few drops at a time. When the sauce has thickened, the butter can be added more quickly. Do not add the milky sediment at the bottom of the pan.

When all the butter has been added, strain the sauce. Add the chervil or parsley and the tarragon leaves, taste for seasoning, and adjust if necessary—béarnaise should be quite piquant with pepper. It is served warm, not hot, and can be kept in a warm water bath for up to half an hour.

Béarnaise Sauce Derivatives

CHORON SAUCE *(sauce Choron)*:

This tomato-flavored béarnaise is good with eggs, fish, steak, and lamb.

> **1 recipe béarnaise sauce (p. 204)**
> **1½ tablespoons tomato paste**
> **salt and white or cayenne pepper**

MAKES ABOUT 1 CUP (250 ml) SAUCE.

Make the béarnaise sauce and stir the tomato paste into it. Taste for seasoning and adjust if necessary. The sauce can be kept in a warm water bath for up to half an hour.

FOYOT SAUCE *(sauce Foyot)*:

Sauce Foyot is particularly good for steak.

> **1 recipe béarnaise sauce (p. 204)**
> **1 teaspoon meat glaze (p. 118)**

MAKES ABOUT 1 CUP (250 ml) SAUCE.

Make the béarnaise sauce and stir the meat glaze into it. The sauce should be the color of café au lait. It can be kept in a warm water bath for up to half an hour.

White Butter Sauce
(SAUCE BEURRE BLANC)

White butter sauce comes from the Loire valley and traditionally is served with pike from the river, but it is delicious with any poached or steamed fish, with vegetables, and the nouvelle cuisine chefs serve it with almost anything, even pasta.

3 tablespoons white wine vinegar
3 tablespoons dry white wine
2 shallots, finely chopped
½ pound (250 g) butter
salt and white pepper

White butter sauce at the right consistency; the butter is creamy rather than melted.

MAKES 1 CUP (250 ml) SAUCE.

In a heavy-bottomed saucepan boil the vinegar, wine, and shallots until reduced to 1 tablespoon. Set the pan over very low heat and gradually whisk in the butter in small pieces to make a smooth creamy sauce. Move the pan off the heat, if necessary, so the butter doesn't melt completely but softens to form a smooth sauce. Season to taste and serve as soon as possible. If it must be held for a few minutes, keep it in a barely warm water bath.

RED BUTTER SAUCE *(sauce beurre rouge)*:

This very pretty sauce is an interesting variation on sauce beurre blanc.

Make exactly as white butter sauce except in place of the 3 tablespoons vinegar and 3 tablespoons white wine use ⅓ cup (80 ml) red wine.

White Wine Sauce
(SAUCE VIN BLANC)

White wine sauce can be made in various ways but always includes fish stock, usually in a reduced form. It is always served with fish.

2 shallots, finely chopped
½ pound (250 g) butter
⅓ cup (80 ml) white wine
1 tablespoon heavy cream
juice of ¼ lemon
½ teaspoon fish glaze (p. 118)
salt and pepper

MAKES 1 CUP (250 ml) SAUCE.

In a heavy-bottomed saucepan cook the shallots slowly in 1 tablespoon (15 g) of the butter until soft but not brown. Add the wine and boil until reduced to 1–2 tablespoons. Add the cream and reduce again to 1–2 tablespoons. Set the pan over low heat and gradually whisk in the rest of the butter in small pieces to make a smooth creamy sauce. Move the pan off the heat, if necessary, so the butter doesn't melt completely but softens to form a smooth sauce. Whisk in the lemon juice and fish glaze and season to taste with salt and pepper. The sauce can be kept warm for a few minutes in a barely warm water bath.

Sabayon Sauce
(SAUCE SABAYON)

Sabayon sauce can be served warm or cold over fresh or poached fruit, plain sponge cake, or ice cream.

4 egg yolks
½ cup (100 g) sugar
⅔ cup (160 ml) white wine
grated zest of 1 orange or 1 lemon

MAKES ABOUT 1 CUP (250 ml) SAUCE.

Put the yolks, sugar, and wine in a bowl, preferably copper, and set it over a pan of hot but not boiling water. Whisk until the sauce is frothy and almost thick enough to leave a ribbon trail, 15–20 minutes. Fold in the grated zest, and if serving warm, do so as soon as possible. If serving the sauce cold, whisk it until cool and then set the bowl in a pan or bowl of ice water and continue whisking until the sauce is cold. It will hold up without separating for about an hour.

Sauce sabayon at just the right thickness

Sabayon Sauce with Madeira
(SAUCE SABAYON AU MADÈRE)

Madeira is a favorite variation on basic wine-flavored sabayon. Actually, almost any wine or fortified wine can be used.

4 egg yolks
⅓ cup (65 g) sugar
¼ cup (60 ml) Madeira

MAKES ABOUT 1 CUP (250 ml) SAUCE.

Put the yolks, sugar, and Madeira in a bowl, preferably copper, and set it over a pan of hot but not boiling water. Whisk until the sauce is frothy and almost thick enough to leave a ribbon trail, 15–20 minutes. If serving warm, do so as soon as possible. If serving the sauce cold, whisk it until cool and then set the bowl in a pan or bowl of ice water and continue whisking until the sauce is cold. It will hold up without separating for about an hour.

CRÊPES SOUFFLÉES AU CITRON
The filling is a lemon soufflé mixture, which puffs up in the oven; the sauce is a raspberry purée flavored with kirsch.

Crêpes

THERE SEEMS TO BE something provocative about a crêpe that tempts the most phlegmatic of adults to indulge in childish games. If you toss a crêpe on New Year's Day, a French saying goes, a coin in your hand will multiply each day of the year. At Candlemas, count the stars in the sky as you toss your crêpes, and you'll find the same number of eggs in the hen house next morning. And it's a dull chef indeed who does not occasionally forget his training and toss a crêpe blithely in the air instead of turning it prudently with a metal spatula.

But crêpes offer far more than fun and games to a cook. They can be made at a moment's notice from three basic ingredients— eggs, flour, and milk. They can equally well be prepared ahead against the arrival of an unexpected guest. They adapt to sweet or savory fillings; they can be dressed up by flaming or dressed down with just a dusting of sugar or a spoonful of jam.

Eggs are the most important ingredient in crêpes. Flour provides the base and milk the liquid, but it is the eggs that give richness and flavor and bind the crêpes together in the pan. Usually white flour is used, but in Brittany crêpes are often made with buckwheat flour and then are called *galettes;* the buckwheat flour has a low gluten content, so these crêpes are very light. Cooks in Alsace sometimes replace the milk with beer, which also has a lightening effect. Salt is an indispensable seasoning in crêpe batter, and sugar can be added for sweetness.

The vanilla, rum, or liqueur called for in some recipes is gilding the lily, I think, since their flavor is inevitably lost during cooking. Much more important is the final ingredient, melted butter—almost the more the better. The more melted butter in the batter, the less often the pan needs to be greased, and the easier the frying.

Before you start frying, it is best to be organized. Assemble a bowl of melted butter or oil, a plate, and a metal spatula. Put a small ladle in the batter—it should scoop just enough batter to cover the bottom of the crêpe pan. Heat the pan, coat it with melted butter or oil, and pour the excess back into the bowl. Heat the pan again and test with a few drops of batter—if they splutter, the pan is ready. Add a ladle of batter, turning the pan with a sweep of the wrist and shaking at the same time so the bottom is coated. This movement is the key to thin even crêpes, and it takes a bit of practice.

Put the pan back on the heat, brown one side of the crêpe, turn it over, brown the other side, and then turn the crêpe onto the plate. A good crêpe is easy to recognize: it is flexible and paper-thin with a pretty marbled surface where it has browned in the pan. (The second side of a crêpe is never as handsome as the first and is turned to the inside.) If the crêpe is heavy, the batter was too thick. If the crêpe split when it was turned, the batter was too thin.

Continue frying, piling the crêpes one on top of another to keep them warm and moist. Add more butter to the pan only when the crêpes start to stick; you should be able to fry at least six crêpes and probably more without adding more butter. With a bit of experience, you will soon get into a rhythm and will be able to keep two pans going at once; I can manage three, and the chefs juggle with four, though the pace gets a little hectic and I've learned a colorful oath or two as a result.

With crêpes in hand, the sky is the limit. As versatile a wrapping as pastry, crêpes lend themselves to any filling from the simplest grated cheese and scrambled egg to the luxury of lobster or sweetbreads moistened with a sauce. Dessert ideas range from a sprinkling of sugar and liqueur to fruit mixtures or pastry cream or, grandest of all, a soufflé mixture that puffs within the crêpes.

Crêpes, either as haute cuisine or fast-food, are very popular in France, and the infinite variety of possible fillings for them has inspired chefs from Escoffier downward. Crêpes are as likely to appear flamed at tableside in a three-star restaurant as wrapped in paper at a street stand. Crêpe makers can be seen expertly tossing crêpes the size of small pizzas on city street corners, where pedestrians will stop at all times of the day and in any weather to buy a simple snack of a crêpe with sugar, jam, or chocolate. In between the posh restaurant and the simple stand is the *crêperie*—a small restaurant that serves only crêpes. And, of course, every region has its own special version of crêpes. There are seafood crêpes from Brittany, crêpes normande stuffed with caramelized apples and cream and flamed in Calvados, and crêpes belle Angevine filled with pears from the Loire valley and flamed with Curaçao.

A few extra crêpes pose no problem: they can be eaten cold

with jam for breakfast; they can be shredded and scrambled with eggs or added to soup as a garnish. Judging by the trainees and students at La Varenne, extra crêpes are best eaten on the spot spread with butter and sprinkled with sugar. And the last misshapen crêpe of a batch, called a *galichon*, is given to the dog.

FOR SUCCESSFUL CRÊPES

1. The basic batter—flour, milk, and egg—must be smooth. To avoid lumps, add only *part* of the milk to the flour at the beginning of mixing and then gradually stir in the rest. If the batter is lumpy, strain it.

2. Let batter stand at room temperature for at least half an hour and preferably longer to allow the grains of starch in the flour to swell. It will thicken on standing.

3. If the batter is too thick, add more liquid. However, do this with care because batter that is too thin is hard to rectify.

4. Use medium heat for cooking. Crêpes should be cooked briskly, but a very high heat sets the batter too fast so the crêpe will be thick. Also the crêpe may scorch.

5. Before making each crêpe, stir the batter a little with the ladle to be sure the mixture has not separated.

6. Grease the pan as little as possible: crêpes fried in too much butter are heavy and greasy. You can give an extra light coating of butter to the pan with a pastry brush.

PREPARING AHEAD

1. Crêpe batter can be made up to a day ahead and kept, covered, in the refrigerator. Melted butter should be added just before cooking or it will solidify into granules.

2. Unfilled crêpes can be made up to three days ahead, layered in waxed paper, and stored in a plastic bag in the refrigerator. They can also be wrapped and frozen, but they tend to become brittle if kept for more than a month.

3. Filled crêpes, especially when coated with sauce, can be kept in the refrigerator or can be frozen for two to three months.

CRÊPE PANS

1. Crêpe pans once had handles as much as 1½ yards (about 1.5 meters) long for use over an open fire, but now the handles have shrunk to a standard 7–8 inches (18–20 cm). The pans themselves are made of cast iron with shallow sides to make turning easier, and most are 9 inches (23 cm) across the rim. Larger sizes are available, but big crêpes need an expert touch.

2. A regular frying pan can be used for crêpes. It must be heavy enough to distribute the heat evenly, yet light enough to handle easily.

3. Like omelet pans, crêpe pans should never be washed. They should be thoroughly seasoned when new, and again each time they stick or have to be washed. After each use and while still hot, wipe them thoroughly with a cloth or paper towel.

FLAMING FOOD

Foods are flamed for two reasons: one is to add flavor, and sometimes color; the other, frowned on by chefs but applauded by head waiters in slightly flashy restaurants, is that flaming makes a good show.

To flame food successfully, a spirit or wine with a high alcohol content is needed. This is found in brandy or rum, in fortified wines like sherry and Madeira, and in liqueurs like Cointreau and Grand Marnier. Plain wine will not do. The alcohol must be hot before it will light, and so must the food to be flamed—don't forget to use a flameproof dish. When all the alcohol has burned off, the flame dies away naturally, leaving only the essence.

One method is to warm the alcohol slightly at first, pour it over the food, and then heat both together on top of the stove or a table burner. The alcohol is then lit either with a match or by tipping the dish over a gas flame until the fumes ignite. However, this method occasionally fails if the alcohol has been absorbed by the food before it can be lit. More reliable, I think, is another method. Heat the alcohol separately in a small pan, flame it, and then pour it—flaming—over the hot food. This way the flames are easier to control. Baste the food with the flaming juices until the flames die; then serve at once.

VITAL PRECAUTIONS:

1. Stand back when flaming.

2. Never pour alcohol straight from the bottle onto very hot food because the alcohol in the bottle can catch fire.

Crêpes
(CRÊPES)

This neutral batter can be used for savory or sweet crêpes.

> **1 cup (130 g) flour**
> **½ teaspoon salt**
> **1 cup (250 ml) milk**
> **3 eggs**
> **2 tablespoons (30 g) melted butter or oil**
> **5 tablespoons (80 g) clarified butter or oil (for frying)**

MAKES 12–15 CRÊPES.

Sift the flour into a bowl, make a well in the center, and add the salt and half the milk. Gradually whisk in the flour to make a smooth batter. Whisk in the eggs. (NOTE: Do not beat the batter too much, or it will become elastic and the finished crêpes will be tough.) Stir in the melted butter or oil with half the remaining milk, cover, and let the batter stand 1–2 hours. The batter can be kept, refrigerated, for up to a day.

Just before using, stir in enough of the remaining milk to make a batter the consistency of heavy cream. Brush or rub the crêpe pan with butter or oil and heat until very hot (a drop of batter will sizzle at once). Add 2–3 tablespoons of the batter to the hot pan, turning it quickly so the bottom is evenly coated. Cook over moderately high heat until browned and then turn the crêpe over. Cook for about 10 seconds to brown the other side and turn out onto a warm plate. Continue cooking the remaining batter in the same way, greasing the pan only when the crêpes start to stick.

As the crêpes are cooked, pile them one on top of the other to keep the first crêpes moist and warm. Crêpes can be made ahead, layered with waxed paper, and stored in a plastic bag. They can be kept in the refrigerator for up to 3 days, or they can be frozen.

Seafood Crêpes
(CRÊPES AUX FRUITS DE MER)

Any combination of fish and shellfish can be used in these crêpes, which are typical of Brittany, a region famous for its excellent seafood.

8 crêpes (p. 213)

fish stock (p. 115) made with 1 tablespoon (15 g) butter,
1 onion, 1½ pounds (750 g) fish bones, 1 quart (1 L)
water, 10 peppercorns, 1 bouquet garni (p. 118), 1
cup (250 ml) white wine

½ pound (250 g) sole fillets, cut in strips

¼ pound (125 g) scallops

salt and pepper

¼ pound (125 g) mushrooms, quartered

juice of ½ lemon

velouté sauce (p. 193) made with 2 cups (500 ml) of the
cooking liquid from the fish and mushrooms, 3
tablespoons (45 g) butter, 3 tablespoons (25 g) flour,
and salt and pepper

¼ pound (125 g) cooked lobster or crab meat

¼ pound (125 g) cooked peeled shrimps, halved
lengthwise

½ cup (125 ml) heavy cream

2 egg yolks

SERVES 4.

Make the crêpes.

Bring the fish stock to a boil, add the sole strips, the scallops, and salt and pepper, lower the heat, and poach for just 2 minutes. Drain and reserve the cooking liquid. Put the mushrooms in a saucepan with the lemon juice, salt and pepper, add ½ inch (1.25 cm) of water. Cover and cook over high heat until the liquid boils to the top of the pan and the mushrooms are tender, 2–3 minutes. Drain and add the cooking liquid to the reserved fish stock.

Make the velouté sauce and mix half the sauce with the sole, scallops, lobster or crab meat, shrimps, and mushrooms. Beat together the cream and the egg yolks, add a little of the velouté sauce, and stir this mixture back into the remaining sauce. Heat gently, stirring, until the sauce thickens slightly. Taste for seasoning and adjust if necessary.

Set the oven at 375°F (190°C) and butter a heatproof platter. Fill the crêpes, allowing 2 per person, roll them like cigars, and arrange them diagonally on the prepared platter. Spoon the sauce over the crêpes and bake in the heated oven until hot, 10–15 minutes.

Ham and Cheese Soufflé Crêpes
(CRÊPES SOUFFLÉES AU JAMBON
ET AU FROMAGE)

These crêpes are typical of the French crêperie, which serves crêpes for first course, main course, and dessert.

8 crêpes (p. 213)

For the soufflé mixture:
béchamel sauce (p. 192) made with ⅔ cup (160 ml) milk, salt and pepper, nutmeg, 2 tablespoons (30 g) butter, and 2 tablespoons (15 g) flour
1 teaspoon Dijon mustard
3 egg yolks
1½ ounces or about ½ cup (45 g) grated Gruyère cheese
3 ounces (90 g) ham, finely diced
salt and pepper
4 egg whites

SERVES 4.

Make the crêpes.

For the soufflé mixture: Make the béchamel sauce and beat in the mustard and egg yolks over low heat until the mixture thickens, about 1 minute. The mixture can be prepared ahead up to this point and kept, covered and refrigerated, for up to a day.

Set the oven at 425°F (220°C) and butter a heatproof platter. Heat the soufflé base over low heat until hot to the touch. Take from the heat and stir in the grated cheese and ham. Taste for seasoning and adjust if necessary—it should be highly seasoned. Beat the egg whites until stiff. Stir a quarter of the egg whites into the soufflé base and then gently fold this mixture into the remaining egg whites.

Fill the crêpes with the soufflé mixture, allowing 2 per person, fold in half loosely, and arrange in one layer on the platter. Bake in the heated oven until the crêpes are puffed, 5–6 minutes, and serve immediately.

Chocolate Crêpes
(CRÊPES AU CHOCOLAT)

These simple crêpes are very popular at the crêpe stands dotted all over Paris.

12 crêpes (p. 213)

For the chocolate sauce:
3 ounces (90 g) semisweet chocolate
⅓ cup (80 ml) water

SERVES 4.

Make the crêpes.

For the chocolate sauce: Melt the chocolate in the water over very low heat, stirring occasionally. Do not allow to boil. The sauce can be made well ahead and kept in the refrigerator.

Set the oven at 375°F (190°C) and butter a heatproof platter. Spread the crêpes with the chocolate sauce, allowing 3 per person, fold in quarters, and arrange in one layer on the prepared platter. Bake in the oven until hot, 10–15 minutes, and serve.

Nectarine Crêpes
(CRÊPES AUX NECTARINES)

Use this basic recipe for other fruits in season and vary the liqueur as well, if you like. Substitute peaches, apples, or pears for the nectarines or combine such fruits as peaches and bananas.

12 crêpes (p. 213)
¼ cup (60 ml) Cointreau

For the nectarine filling:
6 tablespoons (95 g) butter
2 pounds (1 kg) nectarines, peeled and sliced
½ cup (100 g) sugar
¼ cup (60 ml) Cointreau

SERVES 4.

Make the crêpes.

For the nectarine filling: Melt the butter in a shallow pan, add the sliced nectarines, and cook over low heat, stirring often, until very soft and thick, about 20 minutes. Add the sugar and continue to cook gently, stirring constantly, until the mixture begins to stick to the pan, about 5 minutes. Remove from the heat and stir in the Cointreau. The filling can be kept, covered and refrigerated, for several days.

Set the oven at 375°F (190°C) and butter a heatproof platter. Spoon a strip of filling on each crêpe, allowing 3 per person, roll them like cigars, and arrange in one layer on the prepared platter. Bake until hot, 10–15 minutes.

To flame the crêpes, heat the Cointreau in a small pan. Light the Cointreau, pour it flaming over the crêpes, and serve at once.

Crêpes rolled like cigars, as in Nectarine Crêpes and Praline-filled Crêpes

Praline-filled Crêpes
(CRÊPES FOURRÉES À LA PRALINE)

Each element of this recipe—crêpes, praline, and pastry cream—can be made ahead. The crêpes could even be filled a day before serving and simply heated and flamed at the last moment.

12 crêpes (p. 213)
¼ cup (60 ml) rum

For the filling:
praline (p. 425) made with ⅔ cup (100 g) almonds and ½ cup (100 g) sugar
pastry cream (p. 229) made with 2 cups (500 ml) milk, a pinch of salt, a vanilla bean OR 1 teaspoon vanilla extract, 6 egg yolks, ½ cup (100 g) sugar, and ¼ cup (30 g) flour
1 tablespoon rum

SERVES 4.

Make the crêpes.

For the filling: Make the praline and pastry cream and, while the cream is still hot, beat in the praline and rum.

Set the oven at 375°F (190°C) and butter a heatproof platter. Spoon a strip of filling on each crêpe, allowing 3 per person, roll them like cigars, and arrange in one layer on the prepared platter. Bake in the oven until hot, 10–15 minutes.

To flame the crêpes, heat the rum in a small pan. Light the rum, pour it flaming over the crêpes, and serve at once.

Lemon Soufflé Crêpes
(CRÊPES SOUFFLÉES AU CITRON)

The crêpes are gently folded over the soufflé mixture and need to be baked only briefly until the filling puffs.

8 crêpes (p. 213)

For the raspberry purée:
1 pint (250 g) fresh raspberries or 8 ounces (250 g) frozen raspberries, thawed
1 tablespoon kirsch
powdered sugar to taste

For the soufflé filling:
juice and finely chopped zest of 4 lemons
¾ cup (150 g) sugar
pastry cream (p. 229) made with 1 cup (250 ml) milk, a pinch of salt, a vanilla bean OR ½ teaspoon vanilla extract, 3 egg yolks, ¼ cup (50 g) sugar, and ¼ cup (30 g) flour
4 egg whites

SERVES 4.

Make the crêpes.

For the raspberry purée: Work the raspberries through a sieve or purée them in a food processor and then strain. Stir in the kirsch and the powdered sugar to taste, and chill. The purée can be kept, covered and refrigerated, for up to a week, or it can be frozen.

For the soufflé filling: Heat the lemon juice and zest and the sugar over low heat until the sugar dissolves. Continue cooking, stirring, until the mixture thickens but still falls easily from the spoon, 20–25 minutes. (NOTE: The mixture will become light brown, but do not let it turn dark brown or it will be bitter.) Make the pastry cream and beat in the lemon mixture.

Set the oven at 375°F (190°C) and butter a heatproof platter. Heat the lemon pastry cream over low heat until hot to the touch. Beat the egg whites until stiff. Stir a quarter of the egg whites into the pastry cream and then gently fold this mixture into the remaining egg whites.

Fill the crêpes with the soufflé mixture, allowing 2 per person, fold them in half loosely and arrange in one layer on the prepared platter. Bake in the oven until the crêpes are puffed, 10–15 minutes. Spoon some of the cold raspberry purée around the crêpes and serve immediately. Pass the remaining sauce separately.

PROFITEROLES AU CHOCOLAT
Choux puffs filled with a mixture of crème pâtissière and crème Chantilly and finished with chocolate sauce

GÂTEAU PARIS-BREST
The ring of choux pastry is filled with a praline-flavored mixture of crème pâtissière and butter cream.

Choux Pastry

To me choux pastry always smacks of a conjuring trick. I can't get over my mistrust of the power of plain eggs to transform gluey butter, flour, and water paste into crisp balloons of pastry with hollow centers so neatly designed to hold rich fillings. I find a certain challenge in baking choux and suffer a sneaking fear that, despite my best efforts, the dough may not rise. In fact, this feeling is quite unfounded, for choux is perhaps the easiest of all doughs to make.

Choux pastry is unlike any other, for it is cooked twice—its original name was *pâte à chaud*, or "heated pastry." In the first cooking, butter is melted in water and brought to a boil; then flour is beaten in off the heat. The heat of the butter and water mixture cooks the flour to a solid dough, which is usually dried slightly over the heat for half a minute. Next eggs are beaten, one by one, into the dough, which should be warm enough to cook them slightly.

Adding the eggs is the only tricky part in making choux pastry. The beating is quite hard work, and each egg must be thoroughly incorporated before the next is added. At first the dough thickens, and then it starts to thin and look glossy. At this point, the last egg is lightly beaten with a fork and added—little by little—until the dough just falls easily from the spoon.

Eggs make the pastry light, so it's desirable to use as many as possible, but the dough mustn't be so soft that it won't hold its shape. For this reason, no recipe states exactly how many eggs to use when making choux. Quantities can vary depending on the size of the eggs, the dryness of the flour, the amount of water that evaporated as it was brought to a boil, and how much the dough was dried. I had a nasty moment giving a demonstration in Seattle when my four-to-five-egg quantity of choux dough absorbed seven eggs. The flour of the Northwest is notoriously dry, but nonetheless, I was relieved when the pastry rose in the oven on schedule.

The choux dough puffs both from the action of the eggs and from that of the steam created within the dough by the oven heat because the dough has such a high water content. The choux must dry as well as puff while cooking, and in an electric oven, which has no ventilation, the door should be propped open with a wooden spoon halfway through the baking time to allow steam to escape.

Do not, by the way, despise the spoon as an oven control. A generous chink in the door is much the quickest way to cool an overheated oven, though the drafts when it is fully open will endanger cakes and soufflés. When I was training in Paris, we had ovens that heated red-hot top and bottom, all or nothing, and the only way to control them was by adjusting the gap in the door.

Baked choux pastry quickly loses its crispness, so it should be stored in an airtight container and filled not more than an hour or two before serving. It is edible, of course, for much longer. Frankly, a truly fresh crisp choux pastry with a melting filling is rare outside a home kitchen. That may explain the most expensive snack I ever had. It was at a grand hotel in Paris—tea for two with a couple of choux pastries, admittedly spanking fresh, for $20 without the tip.

Like all pastry, baked choux is used primarily as a container for other ingredients. For choux gâteaux, the most common fillings are pastry cream and whipped cream, with pastry cream in the lead, partly because it keeps better than whipped cream, partly because it has less tendency to soak into the pastry. French flavors lean heavily toward the traditional vanilla, chocolate, and coffee. The ring-shaped cake called gâteau Paris-Brest (p. 230) is filled with praline-flavored pastry cream. One excellent variation on the standard flavors, choux normande, calls for pastry cream mixed with a third its weight in Calvados-spiked apple purée, while in choux Montmorency the cream is flavored with chopped cherries and cherry brandy.

But choux pastry is much more than just the basis of rich gâteaux. Savory choux puffs can be made with a hot filling such as cubes of ham in mornay sauce. Cold puffs are often stuffed with mayonnaise-bound meat mixtures. Baby choux puffs, plain or cheese flavored, are a good accompaniment to soup, and leftover dough mixed with double the quantity of mashed potato then deep fried makes one of my favorites—pommes dauphine (p. 71). The dough can also be deep fried on its own, flavored with mushrooms or cheese for savory fritters or with sugar for sweet ones.

The most famous of all choux creations is the croquembouche—the standard *pièce montée* used as the table centerpiece at

French weddings and anniversaries. To make it, small choux puffs are glued together with light caramel to form a towering cone as much as a yard (1 meter) high, which is then embellished with nougatine shapes, sugared almonds, and so forth. Most pastry chefs develop their own variant of croquembouche, and Chef Jorant of La Varenne recalls that, whenever he was commissioned to make one at his pastry shop, he would make it an hour or two ahead so he could display it for a while in the shop window—the best possible advertisement of his skill.

Add as much of the last egg as is needed to make the choux dough shiny and fall easily from the spoon.

FOR SUCCESSFUL CHOUX PASTRY

1. Use a heavy-bottomed pan so the dough does not scorch.

2. When heating the butter and water, cut the butter in pieces so it will melt quickly. Take from the heat as soon as the water comes to a boil so dough proportions are not altered by water evaporation.

3. Add flour to the butter/water mixture all at once and beat vigorously. Flour added little by little will cook into lumps.

4. Do not dry the dough over heat for more than one-half to one minute or water may evaporate and the butter may separate from the dough.

5. If the flour, water, and butter mixture looks grainy, too much water has evaporated. Try beating in a little water to make it smooth. If it is still grainy, make another mixture rather than proceeding to the next step—there's no point in wasting eggs.

6. Baking sheets for choux dough should be very lightly buttered: if they are too dry, the dough will stick; if too greasy, the choux puffs will slide and become misshapen.

7. Brush shaped choux carefully with beaten egg. If it drips onto the baking sheet, it will glue the pastry to the sheet and hinder rising.

8. Score the egg-glazed dough with the tines of a fork so it will rise evenly. Choux pastry cracks as it puffs and will rise best if it cracks in a regular pattern.

9. An ideal heat for baking choux pastry is 400★°F (200°C). If the oven is not hot enough, choux will not puff well but will dry out and become brittle. If the oven is too hot, the dough will rise quickly but often flattens again during baking.

After brushing small choux puffs with egg, score the tops lightly with a fork.

PREPARING AHEAD

1. Choux dough can be made up to eight hours before being baked, but it will not puff quite so well as when used fresh. The surface of the dough should be rubbed with butter while still warm to prevent the formation of a crust. When the dough is cool, cover it and keep refrigerated.

2. Baked choux pastry is best eaten the day it is made, but it can be stored in an airtight container for a day.

3. Filled choux can be kept for only a couple of hours before becoming soggy.

Choux Pastry
(PÂTE À CHOUX)

For a larger quantity of pastry, you can multiply the amounts of ingredients, but this is the smallest size batch of choux that can be made easily.

½ cup (65 g) flour
½ cup (125 ml) water
¼ teaspoon salt
4 tablespoons (60 g) unsalted butter
2–3 eggs

MAKES TWELVE 3-INCH (7.5 cm) BAKED PUFFS.

Sift the flour onto a piece of waxed paper. In a saucepan heat the water, salt, and butter until the butter is melted, then bring to a boil, and take from the heat. (NOTE: Prolonged boiling evaporates the water and changes the proportions of the dough.) As soon as the pan is taken from the heat, add all the flour and beat vigorously with a wooden spoon for a few seconds until the mixture is smooth and pulls away from the sides of the pan to form a ball. Beat over low heat for about 30 seconds to dry the mixture.

Beat 1 egg in a bowl until mixed and set aside. With a wooden spoon, beat the remaining eggs into the dough, one by one, beating thoroughly after each addition. Now beat enough of the reserved egg into the dough to make a mixture that is very shiny and just falls from the spoon.

Though the dough puffs better if it is used immediately, choux pastry can be stored up to 8 hours. To prevent the formation of a skin, rub the surface with butter while the dough is still warm. When cool cover tightly and refrigerate.

Filled Cocktail Choux Puffs
(PETITS CHOUX FARCIS POUR COCKTAIL)

The filling for these little mouthfuls can be determined by whatever you have on hand. The two suggestions here are quick and very good.

1 recipe choux pastry (above)
1 egg, beaten to mix with salt
chosen filling (see below)

pastry bag with ⅜-inch (1 cm) plain tip—optional

MAKES ABOUT 2 DOZEN PUFFS.

Butter 2 baking sheets very lightly and heat the oven to 400°F (200°C). Make the choux pastry, put it into the pastry bag, and pipe ¾-inch (2 cm) mounds well apart on the prepared baking sheets or, alternatively, shape the choux with 2 spoons. Brush the tops of the mounds with the beaten egg and score lightly with the tines of a fork. Bake in the heated oven until the puffs are firm and brown, 20–25 minutes. Transfer to a rack and split each one to release steam.

Not more than 2 hours before serving, spoon the filling into the puffs and arrange them on a platter.

Fillings

CHEESE WITH BUTTER *(fromage au beurre):*

> béchamel sauce (p. 192) made with ½ cup (125 ml)
>   milk, a slice of onion, 1 bay leaf, 3 peppercorns, salt
>   and pepper, nutmeg, 1 tablespoon (15 g) butter, and
>   1 tablespoon flour
> 2 ounces or ½ cup (60 g) grated Parmesan cheese
> 1 ounce or about ¼ cup (30 g) grated Gruyère cheese
> ½ teaspoon Dijon mustard
> salt and pepper
> nutmeg
> ¼ pound (125 g) butter, softened

Make the béchamel sauce and let cool slightly. Beat in the Parmesan and Gruyère cheese, mustard, salt and pepper, and a grating of nutmeg. Let the mixture cool completely and then beat in the butter. Taste for seasoning and adjust if necessary.

CHICKEN AND PISTACHIO *(sultane):*

> ¼ cup (40 g) pistachios
> mayonnaise (p. 351) made with 1 egg yolk, salt and
>   pepper, 1 tablespoon lemon juice, ¼ teaspoon Dijon
>   mustard, and ½ cup (125 ml) oil
> ¾ cup (about ¼ pound or 125 g) chopped cooked
>   chicken breast
> salt and pepper

Blanch the pistachios in boiling water for 1 minute, drain, peel, and split them in half. Make the mayonnaise. Combine mayonnaise, chicken, and pistachios, taste for seasoning, and adjust if necessary.

Choux Puffs with Poached Eggs and Green Bean Purée
(PROFITEROLES D'OEUFS À LA PURÉE DE HARICOTS VERTS)

A light yet satisfying first course from nouvelle cuisine.

1 recipe choux pastry (p. 225)
1 egg, beaten to mix with salt
½ pound (250 g) green beans
8 eggs
1 tablespoon (15 g) butter
salt and pepper

For the tomato sauce:
6 tomatoes, peeled, seeded, and chopped
salt and pepper
sprig of thyme
1 tablespoon (15 g) butter

pastry bag with ⅜-inch (1 cm) plain tip—optional

SERVES 8.

Butter a baking sheet very lightly and heat the oven to 400°F (200°C). Make the choux pastry, put it into the pastry bag, and pipe eight 2-inch (5 cm) mounds well apart on the prepared baking sheet or, alternatively, shape the choux with 2 spoons. Brush the tops of the mounds with the beaten egg and score lightly with the tines of a fork. Bake in the heated oven until the puffs are firm and brown, 25–30 minutes. Transfer to a rack and cut the top third from each puff to release steam.

For the tomato sauce: Put the tomatoes, salt and pepper, and thyme in a saucepan and simmer until the excess moisture has evaporated, about 20 minutes. Purée the tomatoes in a food processor and return to the pan. The sauce can be made to this point up to 3 days ahead. Keep covered and refrigerated.

Cook the green beans in a large pan of boiling salted water until just tender, 7–10 minutes. Drain them, purée in a food processor or work them through a food mill, and strain to remove any strings. The purée can be made to this point up to 3 days ahead and kept, covered and refrigerated. Poach the eggs in simmering water (see p. 368) for about 3 minutes and transfer to a bowl of cold water. The eggs can be cooked up to 2 days ahead and kept, refrigerated, in water.

To finish: Reheat the choux puffs in a 350°F (175°C) oven. Transfer the eggs to a bowl of warm water to heat them. Cook 1 tablespoon (15 g) butter in a saucepan until nut brown, add the green bean purée, salt and pepper, and cook, stirring, until nearly all the moisture has evaporated, 3–5 minutes. Taste for seasoning and add more salt and pepper if needed. Reheat the tomato sauce, remove it from the heat, and whisk in the 1 tablespoon (15 g) butter. Taste for seasoning and adjust if necessary.

To serve, drain the eggs. Spoon some green bean purée into the bottom of each choux puff, top with a poached egg, spoon a little of the tomato sauce over the egg, and set the choux puff top over all. Serve immediately and pass the remaining sauce separately.

Coffee Cream Puffs
(CHOUX AU CAFÉ)

These are best assembled at the last minute to ensure a pleasant contrast between the crisp pastry and the creamy filling.

> **1 recipe choux pastry (p. 225)**
> **1 egg, beaten to mix with salt**
> **coffee fondant (p. 324) made with 1 cup (200 g) sugar,**
> **½ cup (125 ml) water, 1 tablespoon corn syrup, and**
> **½ teaspoon instant coffee dissolved in 2 teaspoons**
> **warm water**

For the filling:
> **1 recipe pastry cream (p. 229)**
> **1 tablespoon instant coffee**

> ***pastry bag and ⅜-inch (1 cm) plain tip***

MAKES 12 PUFFS.

Butter a baking sheet very lightly and heat the oven to 400°F (200°C). Make the choux pastry, put it into the pastry bag, and pipe 1½-inch (4 cm) mounds well apart on the prepared baking sheet or, alternatively, shape the choux with 2 spoons. Brush the tops of the mounds with the beaten egg and score lightly with the tines of a fork. Bake in the heated oven until the puffs are firm and brown, 20–25 minutes. Transfer to a rack and make a hole with the pastry tip in each one to release steam.

For the filling: Make the pastry cream, dissolving the coffee in the hot milk.

Make the fondant, heat, and flavor with the coffee. Keep the fondant warm in a water bath. Dip the top of each choux puff into the fondant to coat and then leave to set.

Not more than 2 hours before serving, put the pastry cream into the pastry bag and pipe the cream into the puffs through the hole made earlier.

Pastry Cream
(CRÈME PÂTISSIÈRE)

Besides being a standard filling for choux puffs, pastry cream is commonly spread on the bottom of fruit tarts and between layers of cake, and an especially thick version of pastry cream is the base for most sweet soufflés.

2 cups (500 ml) milk
pinch of salt
1 vanilla bean OR 1 teaspoon vanilla extract—optional
6 egg yolks
½ cup (100 g) sugar
¼ cup (30 g) flour

MAKES ABOUT 2½ CUPS (625 ml) PASTRY CREAM.

In a saucepan bring the milk just to a boil. Add the salt and vanilla bean, if using, cover, and leave to infuse, 10–15 minutes. Remove the bean and wash it to use again. Reheat the milk to boiling.

Beat the egg yolks with the sugar until thick and light, add the flour, and whisk in a little of the boiling milk. Add this mixture to the pan of milk and whisk over gentle heat until boiling. (NOTE: Be sure the pastry cream is smooth before letting it boil.) If lumps form as the mixture thickens, take the pan from the heat and beat until smooth.

Cook the cream gently, whisking constantly, for 2 minutes or until it thins slightly showing that the flour is completely cooked. If using vanilla extract, add it now. Take the cream from the heat, transfer it to a bowl, and rub a piece of butter over the surface or sprinkle with powdered sugar to prevent the formation of a skin. Cover only after it has cooled. Pastry cream can be stored, tightly covered and refrigerated, for up to a day.

Chocolate Profiteroles
(PROFITEROLES AU CHOCOLAT)

The combination of Chantilly cream and pastry cream in the filling for these profiteroles is especially good, but either cream could be used alone. The puffs could also be filled with vanilla ice cream.

1 recipe choux pastry (p. 225)
1 egg, beaten to mix with salt

For the filling:

½ recipe pastry cream (p. 229)
Chantilly cream (p. 285) made with ½ cup (125 ml)
cream, 1 tablespoon sugar, and ¼ teaspoon vanilla
extract

For the chocolate sauce:

3 ounces (90 g) semisweet chocolate
2 tablespoons (30 g) butter
5 tablespoons water
1 tablespoon cognac

pastry bag with ⅜-inch (1 cm) plain tip—optional

SERVES 4.

Butter a baking sheet very lightly and heat the oven to 400°F (200°C). Make the choux pastry, put it into the pastry bag, and pipe 1-inch (2.5 cm) mounds well apart on the prepared baking sheet or, alternatively, shape the choux with 2 spoons. Brush the tops of the mounds with the beaten egg and score lightly with the tines of a fork. Bake in the heated oven until the puffs are firm and brown, 20–25 minutes. Transfer to a rack and split each one to release steam.

For the filling: Make the pastry cream and let cool. Make the Chantilly cream and fold into the cooled pastry cream. The filling can be made up to 4 hours ahead and kept in the refrigerator.

For the chocolate sauce: Melt the chocolate and the butter in the water over very low heat, stirring occasionally. Do not allow to boil. Stir in the cognac. The sauce can be made up to a week ahead and kept in the refrigerator. Bring to room temperature before using.

Not more than 2 hours before serving, spoon the filling into the puffs. Just before serving, arrange the puffs in dessert bowls and top with the chocolate sauce.

Gâteau Paris-Brest
(GÂTEAU PARIS-BREST)

Gâteau Paris-Brest can be made with several different fillings—just so the flavoring is praline. Praline butter cream is the classic filling. However, by today's standards the quantity of rich butter cream is almost too much of a good thing. Simply praline-flavored Chantilly cream could be used, but La Varenne's pastry chef, Chef Jorant, says the ideal filling is a mixture of butter cream and pastry cream.

1 recipe choux pastry (p. 225)
1 egg, beaten to mix with salt
2 tablespoons sliced almonds
powdered sugar (for dusting)

For the filling:
> **praline (p. 425) made with ⅓ cup (50 g) almonds and ¼
>   cup (50 g) sugar**
> **½ recipe pastry cream (p. 229)**
> **butter cream (p. 282) made with 3 egg yolks, ½ cup
>   (100 g) sugar, ¼ cup (60 ml) water, and 6 ounces (180
>   g) butter**

pastry bag with ¾-inch (2 cm) plain and large star tip

SERVES 6.

Heat the oven to 400°F (200°C) and butter a baking sheet very lightly. Make the choux pastry. Put the dough into the pastry bag fitted with the plain tip and pipe an 8-inch (20 cm) ring on the prepared baking sheet. Pipe a second ring of dough just inside the first. Pipe another ring of dough on top, on the crack between the first 2 rings. Brush it with the beaten egg, score with the tines of a fork, and sprinkle with the sliced almonds. Bake in the oven until the cake is firm and brown, 30–35 minutes. Transfer to a rack and split the cake in half horizontally to allow steam to escape.

For the filling: Make the praline, pastry cream, and butter cream and, when all are cool, mix them together. The filling can be made ahead and kept, covered and refrigerated, for up to a day.

To finish: Not more than 2 hours before serving, put the filling into the pastry bag fitted with the star tip and pipe onto the lower half of the ring. Cover with the top half—the cream should show around the sides. Dust with powdered sugar before serving. The gâteau may also be decorated with rosettes of the filling and candied violets.

**Piping the third ring of
choux dough for Gâteau
Paris-Brest**

Puff Pastry

To the aspiring cook, puff pastry, or *pâte feuilletée*, is the ultimate challenge. The word *feuilleté* means multileaved—as good puff pastry should be, with its feather-light flaky layers that seem to defy the weight of the butter that flavors them. Apprentices are trained for months before their puff pastry technique is acceptable, and some full-fledged chefs never achieve quite the right touch. For in making puff pastry, it is the *tour de main* that counts, the feeling in the hands that tells you if the dough is too sticky or too dry, too hot or too cold. Recipes—and there are several variants—are secondary.

Puff pastry is raised by literally hundreds of layers of butter (729 to be precise) that are interspersed with flour-and-water dough. In the oven, the butter melts, detaching the dough layers, while the water in the dough and in the butter turns to steam, raising the pastry three to four times its original thickness. It is hard to believe that puff pastry is made with exactly the same basic ingredients as pie pastry, though admittedly the butter content is much higher, often equalling the weight of the flour. Exact quantities are difficult to fix because the amount of water absorbed by the flour can depend on its type, dryness, and even the humidity of the day. Some chefs prefer to weigh the dough after mixing and then add half its weight in butter.

To make the flour-and-water dough—graphically called the *détrempe*, or soaking—the flour is sifted onto a marble slab, and the

FEUILLETÉS DE FRUITS DE MER AUX ÉPINARDS
In the nouvelle cuisine style, diamonds of puff pastry are filled with mussels, sole, scallops, shrimp, and spinach—all in a white wine and butter sauce.

GÂTEAU PITHIVIERS
Two rounds of puff pastry are filled with a rich almond mixture, sealed together, glazed, and scored in the traditional pattern before baking.

water, salt, and a little butter are added. (Puff pastry is disappointingly bland without a good dose of salt.) Some chefs like to add a spoonful of lemon juice to the détrempe to discourage the development of gluten. Gluten gives elasticity, a quality vital to good bread, but a problem in puff pastry in which it makes dough "fight back" so it is hard to roll and toughens the finished pastry.

Once the dough has been mixed as gently as possible to a soft, slightly sticky mass, the butter is incorporated. A block of cold butter is pounded with a rolling pin until it is as pliable as putty and then shaped into a large square. The détrempe is rolled to a rough circle, just large enough to enclose the butter, and the butter is wrapped in the dough ready for the real rolling.

It is this phase that gives puff pastry its many layers. Practice and a heavy rolling pin are required to roll the stolid square of dough to a rectangle almost three times as long as it is wide. The width and length of the rectangle vary depending on the quantity of dough. Half a pound (250 g) of flour is a minimum, and I've seen our chefs, who are accustomed to heavy work in the kitchen, rolling 4 pound (2 kg) quantities, though this works even their biceps to the limit. Pastry shops dealing in bulk have mechanical rollers.

Then the rectangle of dough is folded in three to form a square again and turned ninety degrees so that three layers rather than a folded edge face the person rolling. This is called a "turn" and ensures that the dough is rolled first in one direction and then in the other. The dough is rolled and folded again, and already it has nine layers. Each subsequent rolling multiplies them three times. After the first two turns, a rest in the refrigerator is mandatory before the dough receives a further two turns, bringing the total to four. Finally, it must be given two last turns just before it is used.

Throughout this process, low temperature is crucial. A marble slab is ideal for making puff pastry, though in cool weather a smooth Formica or stainless steel surface can be used. In well-equipped pastry shops, the marble is refrigerated, and in summer in Paris we improvise by cooling the marble beforehand with a pan of ice, and by chilling the flour and the rolling pin. In a restaurant, puff pastry is always made first, before the kitchen heats up, and in the hotel in Venice where I taught for one season, the pastry chef rose (he said) at five A.M. to make puff pastry in the cool early morning.

To this point, every step in making puff pastry is geared to producing a dough that is stacked in even layers. Once in the oven, the layers must detach from each other so they rise and cook. A quick boost of heat is the ideal way to begin, so as to melt the butter layers and at the same time convert the water to steam, raising the dough. Then, once the dough has risen, the heat can be lowered to

cook it thoroughly inside. If the oven is too low, or the dough is not chilled before baking, the butter tends to melt and run from the pastry, which then cooks into a solid gummy mass without rising.

Once cooked, puff pastry makes the perfect airy container for shellfish, the traditional creamed chicken, or ham and mushrooms. It makes special turnovers or a luxurious wrapping for whole baked fish or classic boeuf en croûte. Puff pastry is equally at home in nouvelle cuisine where it forms the foundation of little feuilletés of crayfish and spinach in a butter sauce, asparagus with chervil butter, or green beans with hot foie gras. The only concession to the new spirit of lightness is in the shaping of the dough, which is baked in thin diamonds, rather than being cut in traditional round bouchées and topped with an extra ring of dough to form their sides. The young chefs claim that their feuilletés use less dough, without so much as a mention of the other advantage of the new shape: it is much quicker to make.

Sweet puff pastries are numerous—gâteau Pithiviers with its almond filling and distinctive circular shape; *jalousie* filled with jam and slashed on top so it looks like the shutters of a window; *dartois*— a jalousie without the slashes; and of course *millefeuilles*, or Napoleons.

Almost as important, as the original pastry are the trimmings, which can amount to half the original dough. Leftovers should be piled side by side or one on another so the layers are maintained, never crushed in a ball. All sorts of ways to use them have been devised, both savory cocktail tidbits and sweet petits fours.

Puff pastry is one of the few preparations tackled by both pastry and cuisine chefs. At La Varenne it is always a special moment when Chef Jorant (in the pastry corner) and Chef Chambrette (in the cuisine corner) can be persuaded to fight it out in the ring. Like a true pastry chef, Jorant weighs each pat of butter and gram of salt; he rolls his corners with geometric precision and calculates his timing with the clock. Chef Chambrette relies on instinct for measurements and makes a dreadful mess when rolling out. He slashes his dough in a fury and bangs his baking sheet into the oven. Yet the result of the contest is always a draw—a victory for the diversity of approach in French cooking that enriches every meal in France.

FOR SUCCESSFUL PUFF PASTRY

1. Ideally, the butter and the détrempe should be of the same consistency. This will make rolling them together easier.

2. Before rolling and folding the dough, be sure that the work surface is cleaned of any leftover flour or scraps of dough.

3. When rolling the dough out, move it often, lifting it and flouring the work surface. However, do not add more flour than is needed to prevent sticking, because this would change the proportions of the dough.

4. When rolling the dough into a rectangle, keep the sides straight and corners square so that the layers can be aligned when it is folded.

5. It is often easier to roll the folded dough to an even rectangle if the seam side of the dough faces downward.

6. Always roll dough to an even thickness, both for folding and before shaping.

7. When rolling out the folded dough, roll only away from, or toward you, not sideways. However, when dough is rolled for the last time before shaping, it can be rolled in any direction.

8. Puff pastry should be rolled to quite a thin sheet, no more than ¼ inch (6 mm) thick. If it is too thick, the dough weighs itself down and does not rise well.

9. Use a sharp knife or cutter to cut the dough so the layers are not torn or pulled.

10. When cutting shapes from dough, brush each piece separately with beaten egg, rather than glazing the whole surface of dough. Glaze on leftover pastry trimmings prevents them from rising.

11. Sprinkle the baking sheet with water. It holds the dough in place, helping to reduce shrinkage.

12. Use heavy baking sheets so that the pastry does not burn on the bottom. If the bottom does brown too much, put another cold baking sheet directly underneath the first one for protection. If the top of the pastry browns too much, cover it with foil.

PREPARING AHEAD

1. The flour-and-water dough can be made ahead and kept overnight, tightly wrapped, in the refrigerator.

2. After the puff-pastry dough is rolled and folded four times, it can be kept, tightly wrapped and refrigerated, for four to five days, or it can be

frozen for up to three months. It can also be kept after six turns, but will not rise quite so well. Be sure to wrap the dough tightly; if the surface dries, the dough will crack when rolled out.

3. If chilled for a long time, let the dough come to room temperature before rolling, otherwise it will tear. Defrost frozen pastry thoroughly before use.

4. Puff pastry can be shaped a day ahead and kept, refrigerated; it can also be shaped and then frozen. Small shapes can be baked from the frozen state, though large ones should be defrosted first.

5. Because puff-pastry dough freezes so well, it is useful to make a double quantity and freeze what dough you do not need for immediate use.

6. Puff pastry is best eaten the day it is baked. However, it can be stored in an airtight container or frozen. Do not attempt to refrigerate baked puff pastry or it will turn soggy.

7. Baked puff pastry reheats well in a low oven. However, any creamy filling should be added at the last minute so that the pastry stays crisp.

Puff Pastry
(PÂTE FEUILLETÉE)

This is the smallest amount of puff pastry that can be handled easily. If you need less, simply cut off what is required before the final rolling and shaping, and store the rest. Choose a cool day to make puff pastry for the first time, and if the dough is hard to handle because of elasticity, try chilling it for a longer time between rollings. If only salted butter is available, reduce the quantity of salt in the recipe.

     ½ **pound (250 g) unsalted butter**
     1⅓ **cups (175 g) all-purpose flour**
     ⅔ **cup (80 g) cake flour**
     1 **teaspoon salt**
     1 **teaspoon lemon juice**
     ½–¾ **cup (125–185 ml) cold water**

MAKES 1 POUND (500 g) PASTRY.

     Melt or soften 1½ tablespoons (20 g) of the butter but keep the rest cold. Sift the flour onto a cool surface, make a well in the center, and add the salt, lemon juice, ½ cup (125 ml) of the water, and the melted or softened

butter. Work together with the fingertips until well mixed. Gradually work in the flour, pulling the dough into large crumbs with the fingertips. If the crumbs are dry, add more water. Cut the dough several times with a dough scraper to ensure that the ingredients are evenly blended, but do not knead it. Press the dough to form a ball. It should be quite soft. Wrap and chill for at least 15 minutes.

Lightly flour the cold butter, flatten it with a rolling pin, and fold it in half. Continue pounding and folding until it is pliable but not sticky—the butter should be the same consistency as the dough. Shape the butter into a 6-inch (15 cm) square. Roll out the dough on a floured surface to a 12-inch (30 cm) circle that is thicker in the center than at the edges. Set the square of butter in the middle. Fold the dough over the butter like an envelope, stretching the dough slightly so it meets in the center of the butter. Pound the seams lightly with the rolling pin to seal them.

Put the dough-wrapped butter, seams down, on a floured surface and tap the dough 3–4 times with the rolling pin to flatten it slightly. Roll it out to a rectangle about 6 inches (15 cm) by 18 inches (45 cm). Fold the rectangle in 3 as if folding a business letter, aligning the layers as accurately as possible. Seal the edges with taps of the rolling pin and turn the dough a quarter turn (90°) to bring the fold to your left so the dough could be opened like a book. Roll out again and fold in 3. Mark the dough with 2 fingerprints to show that it has been rolled twice. Wrap the dough and chill at least 30 minutes.

Roll out and fold in three 2 more times. Mark the dough with 4 fingerprints and chill at least 30 minutes.

At this point, the dough can be kept, tightly wrapped, in the refrigerator for up to a week, or for up to 3 months in the freezer. Roll and fold the dough 2 more times just before rolling out and shaping according to the recipe for which it is being used.

Wrapping the détrempe around the square of butter

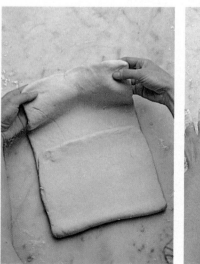

Folding the dough in three like a letter after rolling it out

Give the "letter" the first quarter turn, bringing the folded side to the left . . .

. . . and roll it out again.

Fold the dough again and mark it with two fingerprints to show it has been rolled twice.

Cocktail Puff Pastries
(FEUILLETÉS DE COCKTAIL)

Make these small pastries as uniform as possible. The fillings can be varied. For example, you can make cheese fingers by topping the dough with grated Parmesan, or adapt the ham crescents by substituting chopped cooked chicken or fish for the ham and binding with béchamel sauce (p. 192) or cream.

**1 pound (500 g) puff pastry (p. 237) or the equivalent
    amount in puff-pastry trimmings
filling (see below)
1 egg, beaten to mix with salt**

Make the puff pastry. Sprinkle 2 baking sheets with water. Roll the pastry on a floured surface to a rectangle about 12 inches (30 cm) wide and as long as necessary to achieve a thickness of ³⁄₁₆ inch (4.5 mm). Trim the edges, and cut the rectangle in half lengthwise to make two 6-inch (15 cm) strips. Fill, shape, and glaze according to the individual recipe. Set the pastries on the prepared baking sheet and chill for at least 15 minutes.

Heat the oven to 425°F (220°C). Bake the pastries in the heated oven until puffed and brown, 8–12 minutes, and transfer them to a rack to cool.

Anchovy Fingers
(FEUILLETÉS AUX ANCHOIS)

24 anchovy fillets

MAKES ABOUT 2 DOZEN FINGERS.

Cut each 6-inch (15 cm) strip in half lengthwise so there are four 3-inch (7.5 cm) strips. Brush 2 of the strips with the beaten egg and lay an anchovy fillet crosswise on the dough ¾ inch (2 cm) from one end of each strip and the rest of the fillets along the strips at 1½-inch (4 cm) intervals. Top with the unglazed strips and press gently to outline the anchovies. Brush with beaten egg and cut between each fillet to make 1½-inch (4 cm) fingers. Score each finger in a lattice pattern with the back of a knife.

Chicken Liver Fingers
(FEUILLETÉS AUX FOIES DE VOLAILLE)

**2 tablespoons (30 g) butter
1 onion, chopped
½ pound (250 g) chicken livers
2 tablespoons brandy
pinch of cayenne pepper
salt and pepper**

MAKES ABOUT 3 DOZEN FINGERS.

Melt the butter in a frying pan and cook the onion until soft but not brown, 7–10 minutes. Add the chicken livers and sauté over medium heat for just a few minutes until brown on all sides but still pink in the center—the exact time will depend on the size of the livers. Add the brandy, cayenne pepper, and salt and pepper and cook for 1 minute. Leave to cool and then chop. Spread the chicken liver mixture lengthwise on half of each 6-inch (15 cm) strip, leaving a border of pastry around the edge. Brush the edges with beaten egg, fold the strip lengthwise covering the filling, and press the edges to seal. Brush the top with beaten egg and cut into 1-inch (2.5 cm) fingers.

Ham Crescents
(FEUILLETÉS AU JAMBON)

**1 cup (6 ounces or 180 g) finely chopped cooked ham
1 tablespoon Dijon mustard**

MAKES ABOUT 40 CRESCENTS.

Mix together the ham and mustard. Cut each 6-inch (15 cm) strip in half lengthwise so there are four 3-inch (7.5 cm) strips. Cut the strips into triangles and put a teaspoon of filling on each one. Roll up each triangle starting with a side rather than a point, roll on the work surface with the hand to seal and elongate it slightly, and shape it into a crescent. Brush with the beaten egg.

Mushroom Turnovers
(CHAUSSONS AUX CHAMPIGNONS)

Be sure to press the edges of these pastries together firmly so the filling won't leak out during baking.

1 pound (500 g) puff pastry (p. 237)
1 egg, beaten to mix with salt

For the filling:
2 tablespoons oil
2 tablespoons (30 g) butter
1 pound (500 g) mushrooms, chopped
1½ cups (375 ml) heavy cream
3 shallots, finely chopped
2 cloves garlic, finely chopped
salt and pepper
2 egg yolks

2½–3-inch (6–7.5 cm) fluted pastry cutter

MAKES ABOUT 2 DOZEN TURNOVERS.

Make the puff pastry.

For the filling: Heat the oil in a frying pan and add the butter. Put in the mushrooms and sauté them over high heat, tossing often, for about 5 minutes. Bring the cream to a boil in a heavy-bottomed pan. Stir in the mushrooms, shallots, and garlic and boil until the mushrooms have absorbed all the cream. Season to taste with salt and pepper and let cool slightly. Beat in the egg yolks and leave to cool.

Sprinkle a baking sheet with water. Roll out the puff pastry on a floured surface to a sheet ¼ inch (6 mm) thick and stamp out rounds with the pastry cutter. Put a spoonful of the cold filling in the center of each round, brush the border with the beaten egg, and fold the dough over to make a semicircular turnover. Press the edges to seal them and put the pastries on the prepared sheet. Chill at least 15 minutes more. The chaussons can be made to this point up to a day ahead and kept, refrigerated, or they can be frozen.

Heat the oven to 425°F (220°C). Brush the top of each turnover with beaten egg and cut 3 slits in the top with the point of a knife. Bake the turnovers 8 minutes. Lower the heat to 375°F (190°C) and bake until puffed and brown, 12–15 minutes more. Serve hot, warm, or at room temperature.

Seafood Feuilletés with Spinach
(FEUILLETÉS DE FRUITS DE MER AUX ÉPINARDS)

These nouvelle cuisine feuilletés are normally served as a first course in France, although they'd make a lovely luncheon dish. If serving them as a main course, make one and a half to two times the quantity specified.

> 1 pound (500 g) puff pastry (p. 237)
> 1 egg, beaten to mix with salt
> 1½ pounds (750 g) spinach
> 1½ pints (750 ml) mussels
> 1 shallot, chopped
> 3 tablespoons white wine
> ¾ pound (250 g) sole fillets, cut in ¾-inch (2 cm)
>   diagonal strips
> 6 ounces (180 g) scallops
> 2 ounces (60 g) shelled shrimps
> 1 tablespoon (15 g) butter
> salt and pepper
> nutmeg
> white wine sauce (p. 206) made with 2 shallots, ½
>   pound (250 g) butter, ⅓ cup (80 ml) white wine, the
>   cooking liquid from the mussels, 1 tablespoon
>   cream, the juice of ¼ lemon, and salt and pepper

⅜-inch (1 cm) plain pastry tip—optional

SERVES 6.

Make the puff pastry. Sprinkle a baking sheet with water. Roll the dough on a floured surface to as thin a sheet as possible and cut 6 diamonds that measure 4 inches (10 cm) on each side. Set them on the prepared baking sheet and brush with the beaten egg. With a sharp knife trace a line around the perimeter of each diamond about ½ inch (1.25 cm) from the edge, cutting halfway through the dough. In the same way, but not quite so deeply, mark a design on each pastry—a fish would be appropriate; scales can be made quickly with the pastry tip. Chill for at least 15 minutes. Heat the oven to 425°F (220°C) and bake the feuilletés for 8 minutes. Lower the heat to 375°F (190°C) and continue baking until puffed and brown, 12–15 minutes. Transfer to a rack, cut through the line traced earlier and lift out the diamond of pastry, thus forming a shell with a decorated lid.

Remove the stems from the spinach and wash the leaves in several changes of water. Cook in a large pan of boiling salted water until just tender, 2–3 minutes, and drain well.

Scrub the mussels, discarding any that are open and do not close when handled. Put the chopped shallot and wine in a saucepan and bring to a boil. Add the mussels, cover, and cook over high heat, stirring once, until the shells

Pâte Brisée and Pâte Sucrée

To think of French cooking without pastry is like imagining a house without beams—half the structure would fall apart. Where would be the mouth-watering open-faced fruit tarts that form the centerpiece of every pâtisserie window? Where would be the sweet custard flans and the quiches crammed with onions, bacon, cheese, mushrooms, or shellfish? What about the innumerable kinds of meat and poultry pâtés? (Technically speaking, a pâté should be wrapped in pâte, that is, pastry.) The foundation of all these creations, cornerstone of home and professional kitchen alike, is pâte brisée.

Pâte brisée means "broken dough," so called because the ingredients are worked and "broken" until they are as pliable as putty. And here lies the main difference between pâte brisée and American piecrust: the French regard their pâte brisée as a container. They want it to be thin yet sturdy, with none of the flaky texture that is the rightful pride of American cooks. For these qualities, French cooks turn to puff pastry. The similarity between piecrust and pâte brisée is, in fact, deceptive, since the flavor differs—the French use only butter rather than lard or shortening—as well as the consistency. They always finish the preparation of the dough by kneading it with the heel of the hand in a movement called *fraiser*, which thoroughly incorporates the butter and gives the dough its characteristic firm texture.

Basic pâte brisée consists of four or five ingredients: flour, butter, salt, water, and often, but not necessarily, egg yolks. The butter can be salted or unsalted, and the amount of water needed will vary with such factors as the age and brand of the flour, the quality of the butter, and even the humidity of the kitchen. Egg yolks give richness to the dough and make patching easy. For sweet tarts, a touch of sugar is sometimes added.

The preparation of pâte brisée is a good example of French economy in ingredients and utensils. No bowl, no pastry cutter; all that is needed is a metal or plastic scraper, a cup of cold water, and for the fainthearted, a spoon for measuring. Flour is sifted in a heap on the table and swept into a ring with a quick movement of the hand. Into this "well" are put the remaining ingredients: butter, egg yolk, salt, and, for sweetened pâte brisée or for pâte sucrée, some sugar. These ingredients are worked with the fingertips, and then the flour is incorporated. More water is added if the dough is dry. Just before pressing it into a ball, the hands are dipped in the flour box and rubbed together to loosen every errant morsel of dough—no waste is countenanced. Then it is time to *fraiser* before putting the dough in the refrigerator to chill.

Making pâte brisée is a quick process. From start to finish, Chef Jorant, our pastry chef at La Varenne, takes about two minutes. My personal record is three minutes, and even a novice takes no more than ten minutes.

The quicker the better, not only to save time but because the longer the dough is worked, the more elastic it becomes as the gluten in the flour is developed. Elastic dough is difficult to roll, it shrinks during cooking, and the texture is tough. To a certain extent, elasticity is lost when the dough is left to "relax" in the refrigerator, but once really overworked, dough will never have precisely the right texture.

Pâte brisée is often used for tarts or for making tartlets or *barquettes* (little boats). It can also be used to wrap a pâté. Here the ingredients of the dough may be changed, transforming it into a pâte à pâté (see p. 153) by substituting lard for butter and using whole eggs so the pastry sets firmly in the oven. *Pâte à foncer* (lining pastry), a plain version of pâte brisée, has a lower proportion of butter and no egg yolks and is used for lining molds as well as tart pans.

By far the most popular—and delectable—variation of pâte brisée is pâte sucrée, sometimes called pâte sablée, or "sandy" pastry. For this, so much sugar is added that it totally changes the character of the dough, making it crumbly and as crisp as a cookie. Its sweetness makes it a favorite for fruit tarts, particularly for little tartlets filled with berries.

TARTELETTES AUX FRUITS
Small pâte sucrée shells are simply filled with fresh fruit and glazed with red
currant or apricot glaze.

TARTE DE POMMES À LA NORMANDE
A pâte brisée shell is spread with frangipane (almond cream) and topped with
halved, thinly sliced apples arranged like the petals of a large flower. During
baking, the frangipane rises to fill the spaces.

In Normandy the excellent butter has made pâte sucrée cookies (called *sablés*) a local specialty, and the little pastry shop near our house on the coast always displays a pile of them topped by the reassuring sign *guaranti pur beurre*.

These variations of basic pâte brisée date back to the Renaissance. In early days, pastry was literally a paste, a flour and water dough used to enclose and protect food while it was baking. Recipes for baking birds in a pastry made of flour and oil were recorded by Apicius, who lived in ancient Rome. Even as late as the nineteenth century, the straight-sided dishes called timbales were normally made of pastry, instead of the biscuit-colored pottery that is often used today. And now, despite the current preoccupation with calories, quiche is invariably a popular item on any menu, and an open tart, filled with the fruits of the season, is the undisputed queen of the dessert trolley. Pastry will never lose its appeal—or its convenience.

 FOR SUCCESSFUL PÂTE BRISÉE AND PÂTE SUCRÉE

1. Keep the dough cool. Butter should be cold, though soft enough to knead. Use cold water, in summer ice-cold water. Work the dough as rapidly as possible, using a pastry scraper to minimize contact with the hands.

2. Salt and sugar should be sprinkled over the water in the "well" so they dissolve completely.

3. To avoid developing elasticity in the dough, work it as lightly as possible, using the fingertips rather than the whole hand until the *fraiser* stage. All dough is somewhat elastic and should be left to "relax" in the refrigerator for at least 15 minutes before rolling. To test for elasticity, press with a fingertip—the dough should not spring back.

4. Use a heavy rolling pin—chefs favor the long, straight, cylindrical kind without handles. Start with the dough in the shape you want in the end; for a circle, start with a ball, and for a square or rectangle, start with a square.

5. Roll out only as much dough as you need to avoid excess trimmings. Dough toughens on repeated rollings.

6. Pâte sucrée is more difficult to handle than pâte brisée and cannot be rolled to as thin a sheet.

7. Chill the dough thoroughly in the refrigerator or freezer after rolling and shaping; it should be firm, showing that the butter has set. Chilling helps the dough to hold its shape during baking and reduces shrinkage.

8. Baking is usually begun at a fairly high heat to set the dough so it does not melt out of shape.

9. Watch pâte sucrée carefully after it begins to brown. Because of the high sugar content, it scorches easily.

10. To avoid a soggy crust, moist fillings are best put into a shell that is already at least partly baked. Do not fill pastry with a hot mixture, and once filled bake immediately.

PREPARING AHEAD

1. Pâte brisée and pâte sucrée can be made ahead and stored, wrapped and refrigerated, for up to three days. They can also be frozen for about a month if tightly sealed. If frozen too long, they tend to dry out. Thaw them thoroughly before rolling.

2. Shaped unbaked tart and tartlet shells can also be kept refrigerated or frozen.

3. Pastry shells are best eaten the day they are baked, but they can be kept in an airtight container for up to two days, or they can be frozen. Reheat to crisp them before using.

TO LINE TART AND TARTLET PANS

1. To line a tart pan, roll the sheet of dough loosely onto the rolling pin and then unroll it over the pan. A sheet of dough can be unrolled over tartlet pans in the same way—group them close together. Or you can stamp out rounds slightly larger than the tartlet pans with a pastry cutter and fit these into the pans.

2. With a small ball of dough dipped in flour, gently press the dough into the pan or pans.

3. For a tart pan or for tartlets lined with a single sheet of dough, roll the rolling pin across the pan or pans to cut off the dough.

4. With finger and thumb, press up the edge of the dough all around each pan so it extends slightly above the rim. Pastry shells generally shrink somewhat, and this will counteract the effect.

Pie Pastry
(PÂTE BRISÉE)

This is the basic pastry of French cooking, found in the simplest as well as the most elegant kitchens and used with sweet or savory fillings, to wrap pâtés, as a shell for quiches, as a base for some gâteaux and small pastries, and of course, for a multitude of sizes and shapes of tarts and tartlets.

> **1½ cups (195 g) flour**
> **6 tablespoons (95 g) butter**
> **1 egg yolk**
> **½ teaspoon salt**
> **4–5 tablespoons cold water**

MAKES UP TO A 10-INCH (25 cm) TART SHELL OR SIX 3½-INCH (9 cm) TARTLET SHELLS.

Sift the flour onto a work surface and make a large well in the center. Put the butter, egg yolk, salt, and 4 tablespoons of water in the well and work together with the fingertips until partly mixed. Gradually draw in the flour, working the dough lightly between the fingers so it forms large crumbs. If some dry crumbs remain that don't stick together to form large ones, sprinkle up to a tablespoon additional water over them. Press the dough together into a ball. It should be soft but not sticky. Now, on a floured surface, push a portion of the dough away from you with the heel of the hand in a long sliding motion. Work all of the pastry in this way and then gather it together again with a dough scraper. Repeat this process, if necessary, continuing until the dough is completely mixed, smooth, and pliable. Press the dough into a ball, wrap, and chill for at least 15 minutes. It can be stored, wrapped and refrigerated, for up to 3 days, or it can be frozen.

In the flour well, work together the butter, egg yolk, salt, and water.

Gradually draw in the flour . . .

. . . working the dough lightly between the fingers so it forms large crumbs.

Sweet Pie Pastry
(PÂTE SUCRÉE)

Use leftover dough to make cookies—just cut the rolled dough into rounds, brush them with beaten egg, and bake.

1 cup (130 g) flour
¼ teaspoon salt
⅓ cup (65 g) sugar
3 egg yolks
¾ teaspoon vanilla extract
5 tablespoons (80 g) butter

MAKES UP TO A 10-INCH (25 cm) TART SHELL OR SIX 3½-INCH (9 cm) TARTLET SHELLS.

Sift the flour onto a work surface and make a large well in the center. Put the salt, sugar, egg yolks, and vanilla extract in the well and stir them with the fingertips until the sugar dissolves. Add the butter to the well and work it with the other ingredients until partly incorporated. Gradually draw in the flour, working the dough lightly between the fingers until it begins to hold together. Form it into a ball. Now, on a floured surface, push a portion of the dough away from you with the heel of the hand in a long sliding motion. Work all of the pastry in this way and then gather it together again with a dough scraper. Repeat this process, if necessary, continuing until the dough is completely mixed, smooth, and pliable. Press the dough into a ball, wrap, and chill for at least 15 minutes. It can be stored, wrapped and refrigerated, for up to 3 days, or it can be frozen.

Shrimp Boats Mornay
(BARQUETTES AUX CREVETTES, SAUCE MORNAY)

These are perhaps best served as a sit-down first course, but they might be adapted for use as hors d'oeuvres by making them as very tiny tartlets rather than as barquettes.

1 recipe pie pastry (p. 254)
mornay sauce (p. 193) made with 1 cup (250 ml)
béchamel sauce, 1 egg yolk, 1 teaspoon mustard, 1
ounce or about ¼ cup (30 g) grated Gruyère cheese,
1 tablespoon (15 g) butter, and salt and pepper
½ pound (250 g) cooked shrimps, peeled and coarsely
chopped
salt and pepper
1 ounce or about ¼ cup (30 g) grated Gruyère cheese
2 tablespoons (30 g) butter, melted

twelve 3-inch (7.5 cm) boat molds

MAKES ABOUT 1 DOZEN BARQUETTES.

Make the pie pastry. Butter the boat molds. Roll the pastry on a floured surface to a sheet ³⁄₁₆ inch (4.5 mm) thick, line the molds with the dough, and set them on a baking sheet. Chill until firm, at least 15 minutes. The barquettes can be shaped up to 3 days ahead.

Heat the oven to 400°F (200°C). Prick the dough with a fork, line the shells with aluminum foil, and fill with dried beans or rice. Bake in the heated oven until the pastry is set and beginning to brown, 8–10 minutes. Remove the foil and beans or rice, return the boat molds to the oven, and continue baking until crisp and brown, 5–7 minutes. Let cool slightly and then remove the shells from the molds and set them on a rack.

Make the mornay sauce. Add the chopped shrimps, taste for seasoning, and adjust if necessary. This filling can be made up to a day ahead and kept, covered and refrigerated.

To finish: Heat the oven to 425°F (220°C). Set the pastry boats back on the baking sheet and spoon the shrimp filling into them. Sprinkle with the grated cheese, drizzle the melted butter over the cheese, and bake until bubbling and brown, about 10 minutes. Serve hot.

Roquefort and Onion Quiche
(QUICHE AU ROQUEFORT ET AUX OIGNONS)

Quiche is one of the most popular snacks in France, along with croque-monsieur and "le hotdog." It is also served at fine restaurants as a first course.

1 recipe pie pastry (p. 254)
2 tablespoons (30 g) butter
3 large onions, thinly sliced
salt and pepper
pinch of thyme
7 ounces (200 g) Roquefort, crumbled

For the custard filling:
1 egg
2 egg yolks
¼ cup (60 ml) milk
¾ cup (185 ml) heavy cream
salt and pepper
nutmeg

9-inch (23 cm) tart pan

SERVES 6.

Make the pie pastry. Butter the tart pan. Roll the pastry on a floured surface to a sheet ³⁄₁₆ inch (4.5 mm) thick, line the pan with the dough, and chill until firm, at least 15 minutes. The tart shell can be shaped up to 3 days ahead.

Heat the oven to 400°F (200°C). Prick the base of the shell with a fork, line the dough with aluminum foil, and fill with dried beans or rice. Bake in the heated oven until the pastry is set and beginning to brown, 12–15 minutes. Remove the foil and beans or rice, return the tart to the oven, and continue baking until crisp and brown, 5–7 minutes.

Melt the butter in a heavy-bottomed pan, add the onions, salt and pepper, and thyme. Press a piece of buttered aluminum foil over the onions and cover with the lid. Cook very gently, stirring occasionally, until the onions are soft but not brown, 7–10 minutes. Add the Roquefort and stir with a wooden spoon over low heat until melted and smooth. Spread the onion and cheese mixture in the bottom of the tart shell. Heat the oven to 375°F (190°C).

For the custard filling: Beat the egg and egg yolks with the milk and cream. Season to taste with salt and pepper and grated nutmeg.

Pour the custard filling into the shell and bake in the heated oven until the custard is set and the top puffed and brown, 40–45 minutes. Serve hot, warm, or at room temperature.

Fruit Tartlets
(TARTELETTES AUX FRUITS)

Any soft fruit that doesn't brown quickly after cutting can be used to fill tartlet shells. Red and purple fruits should be coated with red currant jelly glaze, and green, yellow, and orange fruits with apricot jam glaze.

1 recipe sweet pie pastry (p. 255)
½–¾ pound (250–350 g) fresh fruit (berries, grapes,
   cherries, apricots, peaches, and so on)
¾ cup (185 ml) apricot or red currant glaze (p. 259)

six 3½-inch (9 cm) tartlet pans

4-inch (10 cm) fluted pastry cutter—optional

MAKES 6 TARTLETS.

Make the sweet pie pastry. Butter the tartlet pans. Roll the dough on a floured surface to a sheet ¼ inch (6 mm) thick and line the tartlet pans. Chill until firm, at least 15 minutes. The tartlets can be shaped up to 3 days ahead.

Heat the oven to 400°F (200°C). Prick the dough with a fork, line the shells with aluminum foil, and fill with dried beans or rice. Bake in the heated oven until the pastry is set and beginning to brown, 8–10 minutes. Remove the foil and beans or rice, return the tartlet pans to the oven, and continue baking until crisp and brown, 5–7 minutes. Let cool slightly, and then remove the shells from the pans and set them on a rack.

For the filling: Clean the fruit and remove any pits or seeds. Halve strawberries if they are large and slice apricots and peaches.

Not more than 4 hours before serving, melt the glaze in a small pan over low heat and brush the inside of each tartlet shell with it. Arrange the fruit in the tartlet shells. It is possible to combine fruits in a single shell, but because they are so small, one-fruit tartlets are considered more attractive. However, several kinds of tartlets are often mixed on a tray. Coat the fruits thoroughly with glaze.

Apricot Glaze
(NAPPAGE À L'ABRICOT)

Use glaze to give pastry shells a protective coating against the moisture of the filling and to give the filling a bright shine. It can be kept almost indefinitely.

1 cup (300 g) apricot preserves
2 tablespoons water

MAKES 1 CUP (250 ml) GLAZE.

In a small heavy-bottomed pan heat the apricot preserves with the water. Work the hot preserves through a strainer. The glaze can be kept, covered and refrigerated, for several months. Reheat to melt before using.

Red Currant Glaze
(GELÉE DE GROSEILLE)

Though simplicity itself to make, glaze adds a professional touch to desserts.

1 cup (300 g) red currant jelly
1 tablespoon water

MAKES 1 CUP (250 ml) GLAZE.

In a small heavy-bottomed pan heat the red currant jelly with the water, stirring gently, until the jelly melts. The glaze can be kept, covered and refrigerated, for several months. Reheat to melt before using.

Normandy Apple Tart
(TARTE DE POMMES À LA NORMANDE)

In Normandy, where apples abound, the variations of apple pie are as numerous as the cooks who make them.

> **1 recipe pie pastry (p. 254)**
> **3–4 Golden Delicious apples**
> **sugar (for sprinkling)**
> **½ cup (125 ml) apricot glaze (p. 259)**

> *For the frangipane:*
> **6 tablespoons (95 g) butter**
> **½ cup (100 g) sugar**
> **1 egg**
> **1 egg yolk**
> **1 tablespoon Calvados or applejack**
> **⅔ cup (100 g) blanched whole almonds, ground**
> **2 tablespoons flour**
>
> **10-inch (25 cm) tart pan**

SERVES 8.

Make the pie pastry. Butter the tart pan. Roll the dough on a floured surface to a sheet ³⁄₁₆ inch (4.5 mm) thick and line the tart pan with the dough. Chill until firm, at least 15 minutes. The tart shell can be shaped up to 3 days ahead.

For the frangipane: Cream the butter, gradually beat in the sugar, and continue beating until the mixture is light and soft. Beat in the egg and then the yolk. Add the Calvados or applejack and then stir in the ground almonds and the flour. The frangipane can be made up to 4 hours ahead and kept, covered, in the refrigerator.

Heat the oven to 400°F (200°C). Spread the frangipane in the bottom of the chilled pastry shell. Peel the apples, halve them, and scoop out the cores. Cut each half crosswise into very thin slices and arrange the slices of each half apple, spread out and flattened slightly but kept together, on the frangipane like the spokes of a wheel. Press them down gently until they touch the base of the tart.

Bake the tart in the bottom third of the hot oven until the pastry begins to brown, 10–15 minutes. Lower the oven heat to 350°F (175°C) and cook until the apples are tender and the frangipane is set, 15–20 minutes.

Ten minutes before the end of cooking, sprinkle the tart with sugar and continue cooking until the sugar melts and caramelizes slightly. Transfer to a rack. When the tart is cool, melt the apricot glaze and brush the top of the tart with it. Serve at room temperature.

Yeast Doughs

No food has so captured our imagination as bread. The staff of life, the symbolic link between God and man—the imagery surrounding the humble household loaf is unending. Perhaps this fascination reflects our dependence on bread as a staple, or perhaps it arises from the seeming magic of yeast, which transforms an apparently inert lump of dough into a puffy aromatic loaf.

The French tend to be conservative about their bread. With the exception of a few country breads made with whole-wheat or rye flour, they stick to their famous *baguettes*, *flutes*, and *ficelles* plus the plumper family loaves, all made from a basic dough of water and white flour, raised with yeast, and baked to a crisp brown. Each is made (as are the butter-layered *croissants*) to a standard recipe and depends for its quality on the *tour de main*—the technique—of its maker. These are baker's breads: no restaurant chef or household cook would dream of competing with the *boulanger*, who has been at his trade from the age of fourteen.

It is the luxury breads that are made at home, such as brioche, golden with butter, and syrup-soaked savarin. Brioche is the most versatile of the made-at-home yeast doughs. It can be used to wrap sausages, foie gras, or fillet of beef; made into sweet breads; and of course, it can become the characteristic round loaf, baked in a fluted mold and crowned with a ball of dough.

Some bakers, pushing luxuriance to the limit and ignoring the usual rule of a half kilo of butter per kilo of flour, match every kilo of flour in their brioche with a kilo of butter. No wonder the Abbé Perrin, director of the first Paris opera in the 1600's, imposed on delinquent musicians fines that were used each month to finance a giant brioche for the whole orchestra. The culprits had to sew brioche-shaped emblems on their coats, and soon *brioche* entered the language as slang for mistake.

Breadmaking can never be an exact science, because it depends so much on the idiosyncracies of yeast, its vital ingredient. Yeast is a living plant that can produce tiny bubbles of carbon dioxide and thus expand the volume of a flour and water dough. Like any plant, yeast is particular about its environment. It thrives at about 85°F (27°C); at lower temperatures it works more slowly or simply goes to sleep, and at 130°F (54°C), it expires.

The salt used in breadmaking is another essential, but it must be mixed with the flour and never added directly to the yeast because salt kills yeast. Salt not only gives flavor to bread, but also slows the rising, giving the dough a more even texture and a mellower flavor. The usual proportion of salt to flour is 20–25 grams per kilo (about 2 teaspoons per pound). Saltless bread is a disaster.

Sugar, on the other hand, activates yeast. It, too, is usually added to the flour along with the salt, since sugar tends to overstimulate the yeast if mixed directly into it. Eggs and butter (for richness) are common in many French yeast doughs, but milk is rarely used.

These ingredients are combined and mixed, according to the recipe instruction, to doughs of varying consistencies: soft but not sticky (for pissaladière and sweet breads), very soft (for brioche), and almost pourable (for savarins). Next comes kneading, the all-important exercise that develops the gluten in the flour and distributes the yeast throughout the dough so that the bread rises with a close even texture. Ideally, kneading is done by hand, but if you are making large quantities of dough, an electric mixer with a dough hook will ease the task.

For firm doughs, kneading is done on a floured board, pushing the dough away with one hand, folding it, turning, and pushing again—this procedure is often called the American or English method. The French lift brioche in the air and throw it down on the board, and savarin dough is kneaded in a bowl, using the hand cupped like a spoon to pick up the dough and then slap it back into the bowl. Whatever the method, kneading should last several minutes, and the finished dough should look smooth and slightly shiny and have a characteristically elastic texture.

Most recipes say that the dough should double in bulk during the first rising. Actually it may rise less than that—La Varenne's pâtissier Chef Jorant says one and a half times the original bulk is ideal. Again, experience will tell you when dough has risen to the

PISSALADIÈRE (top)
The famous Provençal specialty, a yeast dough shell topped with tomatoes, onions, anchovies, and olives

SAUCISSON EN BRIOCHE (right)
French garlic sausage baked in a savory brioche dough

SAVARIN (bottom)
A traditional classic. The baked ring of sweet yeast dough is soaked with lemon- or liqueur-flavored syrup.

proper height. A savarin should look bubbly, and the test of a firmer dough is that it does not spring back when pressed with a fingertip.

Left to its own devices, dough will go on rising and rising, as I discovered one morning when I found an amorphous sprawling mass had taken charge of the kitchen table—the bread dough I had started the night before. When sufficiently risen, the dough is punched down, shaped or poured into a mold, left to rise again, and then baked.

Mixing, kneading, shaping, baking. The effort yields the common yet magical breads and yeast cakes that have become part of traditional ceremonies. It was usual for an Alsatian bride, as part of her trousseau, to bring a mold for baking raisin-studded yeast bread, and in Lorraine a braided brioche is still served as part of a baptismal celebration. Such customs testify to our fascination with this staff of life made from flour, water, the simplest of flavorings— and yeast.

 FOR SUCCESSFUL YEAST DOUGHS

1. Have all the ingredients at room temperature or, in winter, slightly warm. Take eggs from the refrigerator well ahead of time.

2. To hurry rising, or on cold days, add a little more yeast.

3. Yeast is relatively more active in a large quantity of dough, so when doubling a recipe, use a little less than double the yeast.

4. If dough rises too fast, the texture of the finished bread will be uneven and the flavor poor.

5. Chill brioche thoroughly between rising and shaping and keep it cool while working with it. If your hands are particularly warm, try lowering their temperature by holding them under cold water.

6. So steam can escape, transfer bread to a rack immediately after baking.

 PREPARING AHEAD

1. If you wish to mix the dough well ahead of time, slow its rising by refrigerating.

2. After rising once, yeast doughs can be punched down, refrigerated, and then shaped the next day. On warm days, let the yeast dough rise not more than one and one-half times its volume before punching down

and refrigerating. The dough will continue to rise very slowly in the refrigerator.

3. Dough can be shaped and then kept overnight in the refrigerator. Let the dough finish rising just before baking.

4. If you want to keep the dough for more than a day, wrap it tightly after the first rising and freeze it for up to a week. Defrost slowly in the refrigerator.

5. Unbaked yeast dough that has been shaped can be kept a day in the refrigerator. It will continue to rise very slowly.

6. Unbaked dough that has been shaped and has risen for the last time can be frozen for one to two weeks. Let the dough thaw slowly in the refrigerator and then bake it as soon as it shows signs of rising. Do not bake the dough while it is still frozen or the middle will not cook properly.

7. Baked yeast breads and cakes freeze well. To thaw, let them come to room temperature, or defrost them more quickly by warming in a low oven. Savarin keeps especially well, because it can be reheated and moistened with syrup just before being served.

Brioche
(BRIOCHE)

More than any other bread, brioche puts butter in the limelight. Make it with the best quality available.

> **2 cups (260 g) flour**
> **1¼ teaspoons salt**
> **1 tablespoon (15 g) sugar**
> **½ package (⅛ ounce or 3.5 g) dry OR ½ cake (about ⅓**
>   **ounce or 10 g) compressed yeast, crumbled**
> **1 tablespoon lukewarm water**
> **3–4 eggs**
> **¼ pound (125 g) unsalted butter, cold**
> **1 egg, beaten to mix with salt (for glaze)**
>
> ***6-inch (15 cm) brioche mold OR 6 small brioche molds***

MAKES 1 LARGE BRIOCHE OR 6 SMALL BRIOCHES.

Sift the flour onto a work surface and make a large well in the center. Place the salt and sugar in little piles on one side of the well and the yeast

The French method for kneading brioche dough: scoop the dough up with both hands . . .

opposite them, as far from the salt and sugar as possible. Pour the water over the yeast and, using your fingertips, combine the yeast and the water. Draw about ⅛ of the flour into the yeast, keeping the mixture on one side of the flour well. Leave to rise 5–10 minutes.

Break 2 of the eggs into the well. With your fingertips, mix together the eggs, salt, sugar, and the yeast mixture. Draw in the rest of the flour with both hands and work the mixture lightly with your fingers until it forms large crumbs. Beat the third egg to mix and add it. If the dough is dry, beat the fourth egg and add as much of it as is necessary to make a softy sticky dough.

Knead the dough by scooping it up from underneath with the fingers of both hands and then slinging it forcefully back down onto the work surface, pulling the fingers sideways out of the dough at the same time. Repeat this motion until the dough is elastic and very smooth, about 10 minutes.

Flatten the cold butter with a rolling pin, fold it in half, and continue pounding and folding until it is soft and pliable—it should still be cool. Put the softened butter on the dough and mix it in by pinching off a small portion from the far end of the dough and of the butter and sticking them onto the end closest to you. Do this repeatedly until the butter is fairly well mixed into the dough. Finish the mixing by slapping the dough down onto the work surface as before, but this time as lightly as possible.

Dust the dough very lightly with flour, shape into a smooth ball, put it in a buttered bowl, and turn the dough over to coat all sides. Cover the bowl with a damp cloth and leave to rise at room temperature until nearly doubled in bulk, about 2 hours.

Put the dough on a floured surface and fold in three, patting it to knock out the air. Return to the bowl, cover with a damp cloth, and leave to rise again, either at room temperature or overnight in the refrigerator, until doubled in bulk. Brioche dough is much easier to handle if thoroughly chilled.

. . . and throw it back down, pulling the fingers sideways out of the dough.

To make the dough into a large brioche or several small ones: Butter the brioche mold or molds. Knead the dough lightly to knock out the air and, if making individual brioches, divide it into 6 pieces. Pinch off ⅓ of each piece of dough and roll both large and small pieces into balls. Put each large ball in a mold, cut a deep cross in the top, and nestle the small ball into it. Let the shaped brioche rise until the mold or molds are almost full; allow 15 minutes for the small ones and 20–25 minutes for a large loaf.

Heat the oven to 425°F (220°C). Brush the brioche with beaten egg and bake in the heated oven until well browned, 15–20 minutes. The small brioches should be done. For a large brioche, lower the heat to 375°F (190°C) and continue baking until it shrinks from the sides of the mold and emits a hollow sound when tapped on the bottom, 30–40 minutes. Remove to a rack to cool.

Sausage in Brioche
(SAUCISSON EN BRIOCHE)

This is usually served as a first course in France and also makes excellent picnic fare.

1 recipe brioche dough (p. 265)
**1½ pound (750 g) French garlic sausage or Polish
   kielbasa**
1 egg, beaten to mix with salt

9 × 5 ×4 inch- (23 × 13 × 10 cm) loaf pan

SERVES 6.

Make the brioche dough, letting it rise according to instructions, and chill so it will be easier to roll out. Put the sausage in a saucepan with enough water to cover, bring to a boil, and then simmer for 20 minutes. Drain, remove the skin, and cool completely. Butter the loaf pan. Roll the dough on a lightly floured work surface to a 12 × 6 inch- (30 × 15 cm) rectangle and brush it with beaten egg. Brush the sausage with the beaten egg and roll it lightly in flour. Set the sausage lengthwise in the center of the dough and roll the dough around it. Pinch the edges to seal well, turn it over so that the seam is underneath, and put the loaf in the prepared pan. Let the brioche rise until the pan is almost full, 25–30 minutes.

Set the oven at 400°F (200°C). Brush the dough with beaten egg and make 3 holes in the top to let the steam escape. Decorate the top with dough trimmings, if you like. Bake in the heated oven until the brioche is well browned and starts to pull away from the sides of the pan, 30–35 minutes. Turn out onto a rack. Serve warm or at room temperature.

Pissaladière
(PISSALADIÈRE)

This tart, a specialty of Provence, profits from many of the regional products.

4 tablespoons olive oil
4 large onions
2 teaspoons mixed herbs (basil, thyme, rosemary)
salt and pepper
**1 small can anchovy fillets, soaked in a little milk for
   20–30 minutes and then drained**
4 tomatoes, peeled, seeded, and sliced
15–20 black olives, pitted

For the yeast dough:
> ½ **package (⅛ ounce or 3.5 g) dry OR ½ cake (⅓ ounce**
> **or 10 g) compressed yeast**
> ⅓ **cup (80 ml) lukewarm water**
> 1½ **cups (200 g) flour**
> 1 **egg, beaten to mix**
> ¾ **teaspoon salt**

> **11–12-inch (28–30 cm) tart pan**

SERVES 6–8.

For the yeast dough: Sprinkle or crumble the yeast over the lukewarm water and leave until dissolved, about 5 minutes. Sift the flour into a bowl and make a well in the center. Put the dissolved yeast, egg, and salt in the well, mix them together with the fingertips, and then draw in the flour. Work the mixture lightly with the fingers until it forms large crumbs. The dough should be soft but not sticky. Add more flour if needed. Turn it out on a floured work surface and knead until elastic and very smooth, about 5 minutes. Transfer the dough to a buttered bowl, cover with a damp cloth, and leave to rise in a warm place until doubled in bulk, about 45 minutes.

Heat the oil in a saucepan, add the onions, herbs, and salt and pepper, and press a piece of foil on top. Cover the pan with the lid and cook, stirring occasionally, over low heat until the onions are very soft but not brown, 7–10 minutes.

When the dough has risen, knead it lightly to knock out the air. Butter the tart pan and pat the dough out in the pan, pushing it up the sides. Spread the onion mixture over the bottom of the dough shell, spread the tomatoes on top, and sprinkle with pepper. Arrange the anchovy fillets over all and complete the pissaladière with the olives. Leave to rise in a warm place for about 15 minutes.

Set the oven at 375°F (190°C). Bake the tart in the heated oven until browned, 40–50 minutes. Serve hot, warm, or at room temperature.

Raisin Sweet Rolls
(PETITS PAINS AUX RAISINS)

Pains aux raisins are a popular snack all over France.

> 1 **recipe brioche dough (p. 265)**
> **pastry cream (p. 229) made with 1 cup (250 ml) milk, a**
> **pinch of salt, 1 vanilla bean OR ½ teaspoon vanilla**
> **extract, 3 egg yolks, 4 tablespoons (50 g) sugar, 2**
> **tablespoons (15 g) flour**

1¼ cups (175 g) raisins
1 egg, beaten to mix with salt
¼ cup (60 ml) apricot glaze (p. 259)

MAKES ABOUT 20 PETITS PAINS.

Make the brioche dough, letting it rise according to instructions, and chill so it will be easier to roll out. Make the pastry cream and chill it also. Roll the dough to a rectangle of about 10 × 15 inches (25 × 38 cm). Spread the dough with the pastry cream, leaving a 1-inch (2.5 cm) border on one long side, and sprinkle with the raisins. Brush the border with beaten egg, roll the dough up from the opposite side, and press along the glazed border to seal. Cut the roll of dough into ¾-inch (2 cm) slices and lay the slices on a baking sheet. Let the petits pains rise until doubled in bulk, about 2 hours.

Set the oven at 400°F (200°C). Brush each roll with beaten egg and bake in the heated oven until golden brown, 25–30 minutes. Transfer to a rack to cool. When the rolls are cool, brush them with melted apricot glaze.

Galette Vieux Pérouges
(GALETTE VIEUX PÉROUGES)

This broad flat cake is cut like a pie. It is a simple homey dessert, and there never seems to be enough of it.

1 package (¼ ounce or 7 g) dry OR 1 cake (⅝ ounce or
  18 g) compressed yeast
¾ cup (185 ml) lukewarm water
3–3½ cups (400–450 g) flour
1½ teaspoons salt
1 tablespoon (15 g) sugar
1 egg
1 egg yolk
5 tablespoons (80 g) butter, softened

For the topping:
  5 tablespoons (80 g) butter, softened
  ⅔ cup (135 g) sugar
  grated zest of 1 lemon

SERVES 10–12.

Sprinkle or crumble the yeast over the lukewarm water and let stand until dissolved, about 5 minutes. Sift the flour with the salt and sugar into a bowl and make a well in the center. Break the egg into the well and add the egg yolk and the dissolved yeast. Mix the eggs and dissolved yeast together with the fingertips and then draw in the flour and work the mixture lightly with the fingers until it forms large crumbs. If the dough is too moist, add more flour to make a dough that is soft but not sticky. Turn the dough onto a floured surface and knead until it is elastic and very smooth, about 10 minutes. Mix the softened butter into the dough.

Dust the dough with flour, shape into a smooth ball, and put it in a buttered bowl. Cover the bowl with a damp cloth and leave to rise at room temperature until doubled in bulk, about 45 minutes.

Dust a large baking sheet or pizza pan with flour. Knead the dough lightly to knock out the air and then roll it to a ¼-inch (6 mm) thick round 20 inches (50 cm) in diameter.

For the topping, spread the dough with the softened butter and sprinkle with sugar and grated lemon zest. Let the galette rise in a warm place for 10–15 minutes.

Heat the oven to 450°F (230°C). Bake the galette in the heated oven until the dough is browned and the sugar has melted, 7–10 minutes. Serve warm.

Savarin
(SAVARIN)

Savarin holds many possibilities: The syrup can be flavored, perhaps with kirsch or orange zest. The center of the cake might be filled with fresh fruit, Chantilly cream, or both.

> 1 package (¼ ounce or 7 g) dry OR 1 cake (⅝ ounce or
>   18 g) compressed yeast
> 4 tablespoons lukewarm water
> 2⅓ cups (300 g) flour
> 4 eggs
> 1 teaspoon salt
> 2 tablespoons (25 g) sugar
> 5 ounces (150 g) butter, softened
> 3 tablespoons kirsch

For the syrup:
> 1¼ cups (250 g) sugar
> 2 cups (500 ml) water
> zest and juice of ½ lemon

For the garnish—optional:
½ cup red currant glaze (p. 259)
2 candied cherries
1 piece angelica

1¼-quart (1.25 L) ring mold

SERVES 8–10.

Sprinkle or crumble the yeast over the lukewarm water and let stand until dissolved, about 5 minutes. Sift the flour into a bowl and make a well in the center. Pour in the dissolved yeast and add the eggs, salt, and sugar. Mix them together with the fingertips and then draw in the flour and work the mixture lightly with the fingers until it forms large crumbs. The dough should be soft but not sticky. Knead with a cupped hand, lifting the dough and throwing it back into the bowl so it hits with a slap, until it is elastic and very smooth, about 5 minutes. Cover the bowl and leave in a warm place until the dough has doubled in bulk, about 45 minutes.

Butter the ring mold generously. Mix the softened butter into the dough. Spoon the dough into the prepared mold, cover with a towel, and leave in a warm place to rise until the dough fills the mold, 30–35 minutes.

Heat the oven to 400°F (200°C). Bake in the heated oven until the savarin is brown and shrinks from the sides of the pan, 20–25 minutes. The savarin can be baked ahead and stored, in a airtight container, for up to 3 days, or it can be frozen. Heat it gently in the oven before soaking with syrup.

Kneading savarin dough: lift the dough out of the bowl . . .

. . . and throw it back so it hits with a slap.

The risen savarin dough is slightly bubbly.

Spooning hot syrup over the baked savarin: the syrup will make it swell.

For the syrup: In a large sauté pan dissolve the sugar in the water over low heat, bring to a boil, add the lemon zest, and simmer for 5 minutes. Take from the heat, add the lemon juice, and, if possible, put the savarin into the hot syrup in the sauté pan. Spoon the syrup over the savarin until it is saturated. If the savarin cannot be placed directly into the hot syrup, put it on a rack over a tray and spoon hot syrup over it, reheating any that falls into the tray, until all the syrup is absorbed. The savarin will swell and become shiny.

Sprinkle the kirsch over the savarin. Melt the red currant glaze and brush the savarin with it. Slice the cherries in half and cut diamond shapes from the angelica. Arrange the 4 cherry halves on top of the savarin and flank each with angelica.

Génoise and Biscuit

GÉNOISE BEARS the same relation to pastry as brown sauce to savory dishes—it is the cornerstone of innumerable classic recipes. Hundreds of gâteaux are built up from a foundation of génoise (or its cousin, *biscuit*, pronounced bee-skwi) elaborated with butter cream, pastry cream, whipped cream, fondant, Italian meringue, and various flavorings. Happily no one, not even a master pâtissier, is expected to have every possible gâteau at his fingertips, and most chefs keep to a dozen or so popular favorites.

There is little to choose between génoise and biscuit. Both are made with the same ingredients of eggs, sugar, flour, and butter and in the same proportions. The only difference is in the method of mixing: génoise uses whole eggs, whereas for biscuit, the eggs are separated. When baked, biscuit is slightly drier and lighter because of the beaten egg whites. Perhaps the most common form of biscuit is ladyfingers whose main role is to line the mold and provide a plain background for creamy charlotte fillings.

Once mixed, génoise and biscuit will not wait, so advance preparation is at least as important as the mixing itself. The oven must be preheated. The shelf should be set two-thirds down in the oven, and a cake pan of the right size prepared. Equipment must be assembled: strainer to sift the flour, bowl and whisk for the eggs, wooden spatula or metal spoon for folding, and rubber spatula for scraping the bowl. After the ingredients are measured, the butter is melted slightly to make it easier to mix. Some chefs like it to be pourable but still creamy, others melt it completely, and still others flavor it by cooking it to a nut brown. Whatever the stage of cooking, the butter must be left to cool before adding it to the mixture.

At last comes the action, designed to give the maximum of air to the cake. Two points are crucial: whisking the eggs and sugar to the right consistency and folding in the flour and butter as lightly as possible. The egg and sugar mixture for génoise is ready, say the chefs at La Varenne, when you can write your name with the ribbon trail from the whisk, but I think they exaggerate, particularly when the mixture has been whisked over heat and will thicken as it cools. I whisk only until the trail shows for a few seconds then disappears.

As for folding, génoise and biscuit rival a soufflé for capriciousness: the classic cutting and scooping motion that turns over the ingredients with the minimum of disturbance works well when adding the flour, but the whisked mixture visibly loses volume when the butter is added. One way to mix it quickly is to add a couple of spoonsful of whisked mixture to the melted butter, fold both together, and then fold this mixture into the rest.

Baking time depends on the size of the cake: when it starts to shrink from the sides of the pan, it is nearly ready, and when the center springs back after being pressed with a fingertip, the cake is done. Tip the cake upside down on a rack covered with paper so the cake cannot stick. If a cake sticks to the pan, ease it away from the sides being careful not to damage the crust. A pan that habitually sticks is a nuisance, and La Varenne's pâtissier, Chef Jorant, jokes that he used to sell cakes still attached to such bugbears.

The filling and decoration are where the fun begins. To keep cake moist, pastry chefs often brush the layers with liqueur-flavored syrup; for simplicity and more alcoholic kick, I often just sprinkle the cake with liqueur. For filling and coating there are many possibilities. Butter cream is the clear favorite because its richness complements the plainness of the cake and it lends itself to almost any flavor. Pastry cream is lighter, especially when mixed with whipped cream, but it does not keep well. Plain whipped cream separates within a few hours, but it's also quick and easy. Recently, young chefs have been filling cakes with mousse mixtures. The most popular of these new cakes is sandwiched and coated with chocolate mousse and decorated with chocolate curls—hardly bearing out nouvelle cuisine's reputation for lightness.

Decorations for génoise and biscuit could fill a whole book, and the more obvious include piped rosettes of butter cream and the mundane candied cherry. The chefs whip up little paper piping cones and trace delicate patterns with melted chocolate. Less artistically gifted, I'm a great devotee of wafer-thin rounds or ovals of chocolate

GÂTEAU À LA MOUSSE AU CHOCOLAT
A chocolate génoise filled and frosted with chocolate mousse and decorated with shaved chocolate, whipped cream, and chocolate ovals

SUISSES (back)
Small rounds of génoise topped with a mound of butter cream and a candied cherry, covered with fondant icing

PRINTANIERS (center)
Thin layers of génoise sandwiched with vanilla butter cream and decorated with stripes of pistachio-, vanilla-, and chocolate-flavored butter cream

NOISETTES (front)
Small squares of génoise filled with coffee butter cream, coated with coffee-flavored fondant icing, and topped with a whole hazelnut

(see the recipe for chocolate mousse cake, p. 284), and other ready-made little nothings like candied violets that cost a small fortune but go a long way.

Possible variations for génoise and biscuit even within the classic repertoire seem almost endless—and indeed they are. I once demonstrated a different French gâteau every afternoon for three months, and I still had scarcely scratched the surface. The best pictorial record I know of these cakes is in *Recettes d'un Compagnon du Tour de France* by Yves Thuries. (M. Thuries is referring to the gastronomic society, not the bicycle race.) The great strength of génoise cakes is that they include something for everyone, from the challenges of tiny petits fours to a simple cake with fresh berries and whipped cream.

FOR SUCCESSFUL GÉNOISE AND BISCUIT

The first step of a génoise: eggs and sugar beaten to the ribbon stage

1. It is better to slightly overbeat the eggs and sugar for génoise than to underbeat them. When they reach the ribbon stage, they will be completely smooth; if they still have bubbles, they have not been beaten enough.

2. For points on folding beaten egg whites, see page 177.

3. After pouring the batter into the pan, hollow the center slightly because it tends to rise more than the edges. The pan should be about two-thirds full.

4. Before baking, bang the pan briskly once on the table to knock out any large air bubbles.

5. If the top browns too quickly, cover the cake loosely with foil and, if the cake is firm enough to be moved, lower the oven shelf.

6. If the génoise or biscuit does not come out of the pan easily, turn it upside down and leave for a minute to allow its own steam to loosen it. You can also run a knife between the cake and the sides of the pan, but be careful not to cut into the crust.

7. Let a cake cool thoroughly before cutting it into layers. It will tend to fall apart if cut while still warm.

8. To split a cake easily, set it flat on a table, steady it with one hand on top, and cut horizontally with a long serrated knife.

wary when cooked meringue is mentioned and tend to reserve it for boisterous students who regard cooking as an active sport.

Once prepared, any meringue is invaluable (and remarkably inexpensive). With no addition save a few drops of vanilla for flavor, Swiss meringue can be baked and sandwiched with cream to make meringues Chantilly, piped into individual baskets to fill with fruit, or spread on a tart as a topping. Swiss meringue makes delicious cakes when mixed with ground almonds or hazelnuts and filled with various flavors of butter cream. Classics include *japonais* (made with ground almonds and filled with kirsch-flavored butter cream) and *succès* (made with ground almonds and filled with praline butter cream).

Italian meringue, too, is versatile. It can be substituted for Swiss meringue in any recipe, though the texture is somewhat finer and softer. Italian meringue is the basis for a multitude of petits fours such as *noix au café*—hemispheres of coffee-flavored meringue sandwiched with the same meringue, uncooked. Equal parts of Italian meringue, whipped cream, and fruit purée make the perfect iced soufflé, and pâtissiers keep a jar of Italian meringue on hand to sweeten pastry cream and whipped cream (the results are lighter and smoother than when sugar is used).

Above all, Italian meringue is the mortar for a *vacherin*—that dazzling operetta castle turreted with whipped cream and emblazoned with fresh fruit. The bricks of these castles are normally made of Swiss meringue, with a solid round of meringue as base. When baked, the "bricks" are mounted on the base and mortared with Italian meringue; the shell is recooked until crisp and finally filled with a cream.

Such fanciful confections hark back to another age. Marie Antoinette whipped up meringues for her friends when at the Trianon, and it was the greatest pâtissier of all time, Carême, chef to Tsar Nicholas I, to the Prince Regent, and to Talleyrand, who remarked, "Of the five fine arts, the fifth is architecture, whose main branch is confectionery." Today's trend toward simplicity in cooking belies his words, but the vacherin has survived triumphantly to attest to his claim.

FOR SUCCESSFUL MERINGUES

1. For points on beating egg whites, see p. 177.

2. When making Swiss meringue, do not fold in the sugar too vigorously or for too long. When the egg whites are stiff enough to hold peaks, add a couple of tablespoons of sugar and beat vigorously for a few seconds to "cook" the whites, giving them body and gloss. Carefully fold the remaining sugar into the mixture. The meringue should still be stiff enough to retain peaks so it can be piped.

3. To prevent meringues from sticking during cooking, butter baking sheets, chill to set the butter, and then sprinkle evenly with flour. Do not add flour while the butter is still soft.

4. A perfect meringue is thoroughly dried but is not at all browned. Reduce the oven heat if meringues begin to color during cooking.

Swiss meringue stiff enough to retain peaks, ready to be put in a pastry bag for piping

PREPARING AHEAD

1. Although Swiss meringue must be baked as soon as it is made, Italian meringue can be kept for up to a week in a covered container in the refrigerator.

2. All baked meringues keep well for up to one week in an airtight container.

3. If for some reason a meringue loses its crispness (this can happen in damp weather), reheat in a 225°F (105°C) oven for 25–30 minutes to dry it.

Swiss Meringue
(MERINGUE SUISSE)

This much-used French meringue is the most common type in America. It bakes to a light, crisp shell or layer—it should never be hard.

> **4 egg whites**
> **1¼ cups (250 g) sugar**
> **1 teaspoon vanilla extract**

MAKES ABOUT 2½ CUPS (625 ml) MERINGUE.

Beat the egg whites until stiff, preferably in a copper bowl. Add 2 tablespoons (25 g) of the sugar and continue beating until the egg whites are glossy, about 20 seconds. Fold in the remaining sugar a few tablespoons at a time. Fold in the vanilla with the last spoonful of sugar. (NOTE: Do not mix too much or the meringue will become liquid as the sugar dissolves.)

Almond Swiss Meringue
(MERINGUE SUISSE AUX AMANDES)

This variation on Swiss meringue makes delicious layers for gâteaux. It can also be made with hazelnuts.

1¼ cups (185 g) blanched whole almonds
2 tablespoons potato starch or cornstarch
1 cup (200 g) sugar
6 egg whites

MAKES 4–5 CUPS (1–1.25 L) MERINGUE.

In a rotary cheese grater or food processor grind the almonds to a powder a few at a time. Mix together the almonds, potato starch or cornstarch, and all but 2 tablespoons of the sugar. Beat the egg whites until stiff, preferably in a large copper bowl. Add the remaining 2 tablespoons (25 g) of the sugar and beat until the egg whites are glossy, about 20 seconds. Gradually fold in the almond mixture as quickly and lightly as possible.

Italian Meringue
(MERINGUE ITALIENNE)

Italian meringue is most often used to make petits fours, as an ingredient in other desserts, or by itself as a frosting.

1 cup (200 g) sugar
½ cup (125 ml) water
4 egg whites
1 teaspoon vanilla extract

MAKES ABOUT 2½ CUPS (625 ml) MERINGUE.

Heat the sugar with the water over low heat until dissolved. Bring to a boil and boil without stirring until the syrup reaches the hard-ball stage (248°F or 120°C). If crystals form on the sides of the pan during boiling, wash them down with a brush dipped in water. Meanwhile, beat the egg whites, preferably in a copper bowl, until stiff. Gradually pour in the hot syrup, whisking constantly, and continue whisking until the meringue is completely cool. Beat in the vanilla. Alternately, the meringue can be beaten in an electric mixer. It will keep, covered and refrigerated, for up to 1 week.

To test for the hard-ball stage by hand, lift a bit of syrup from the pan with a spoon and plunge it into cold water. If it can be rolled into a firm ball, it is sufficiently cooked.

Petits Turquois
(PETITS TURQUOIS)

The chocolate mousse filling will firm in the refrigerator and the meringue will soften, making the turquois easy to cut into neatly.

1 recipe almond Swiss meringue (p. 293)
½ cup (100 g) chocolate sprinkles
2 ounces (60 g) semisweet chocolate
powdered sugar (for dusting)

For the chocolate mousse:
½ pound (250 g) semisweet chocolate, chopped
4 eggs, separated
6 tablespoons (95 g) butter, softened
1 tablespoon Grand Marnier
2 tablespoons (25 g) sugar

2½-inch (6 cm) plain pastry cutter

pastry bag with ⅜-inch (1 cm) tip

MAKES ABOUT 1 DOZEN TURQUOIS.

Butter and flour 2 baking sheets and mark at least 24 circles on the floured sheets with the pastry cutter, spacing them slightly apart. Set the oven at 250°F (120°C).

Make the almond meringue, scoop it into the pastry bag, and pipe 2½-inch (6 cm) rounds on the prepared baking sheets. Bake in the heated oven until the meringue is crisp and dry, 30–40 minutes. While they are still warm, trim with the pastry cutter to perfect rounds. Transfer to a rack to cool. The meringue rounds can be made ahead and kept in an airtight container for up to 1 week.

For the chocolate mousse: Melt the chocolate in a water bath. Remove from the heat and beat in the egg yolks one by one. Beat in the butter and the Grand Marnier. Allow to cool slightly. Beat the egg whites until stiff. Add the 2 tablespoons (25 g) sugar and beat until glossy, about 20 seconds. Fold the egg whites into the warm chocolate mixture as lightly as possible. Leave to cool to room temperature.

Sandwich pairs of the rounds with a thick layer of chocolate mousse. Spread the tops and sides with mousse. Press the chocolate sprinkles around the edges. With a vegetable peeler or small knife scrape curls from the chocolate directly onto the top of each turquois, and then dust with powdered sugar. Chill thoroughly before serving. They keep well for up to 3 days.

Cherry Dacquoise
(DACQUOISE AUX CERISES)

Everyone loves the contrasting flavors and textures of a dacquoise: the nutty crisp almond meringue, the mellow fluffy cream, and the sweet firm fruit.

> **almond Swiss meringue (p. 293) made with ¾ cup (110
>   g) almonds, 1½ tablespoons (15 g) cornstarch, ⅔ cup
>   (135 g) sugar, and 4 egg whites**
> **½ pound (250 g) black cherries**
> **Chantilly cream (p. 285) made with 1 cup (250 ml)
>   heavy cream, 1 tablespoon sugar, and ½ teaspoon
>   vanilla extract**
> **powdered sugar (for dusting)**
>
> ***pastry bag with ⅝-inch (1.5 cm) plain and medium star
>   tips***

SERVES 6.

Butter and flour a baking sheet and mark two 8-inch (20 cm) circles on the sheet using a pan lid or cake pan as a guide. Set the oven at 250°F (120°C).

Make the almond meringue, scoop it into the pastry bag fitted with the plain tip, and pipe in 2 rounds on the prepared baking sheet. Bake in the heated oven until crisp and dry, 40–50 minutes. While the meringue is still warm trim the rounds neatly with a sharp knife. Transfer to a rack to cool. The meringue layers can be made ahead and kept in an airtight container for up to 1 week.

Halve and pit the cherries and make the Chantilly cream. When the meringue layers are cool, spread ¾ of the Chantilly cream on 1 meringue layer and arrange the fruit on top, reserving 6 cherry halves. Cover with the other meringue round, press lightly, and dust the top with powdered sugar. Refrigerate the cake for 3–4 hours before serving so that it softens and can be cut into neat slices.

Shortly before serving, put the remaining Chantilly cream into the pastry bag fitted with the star tip and pipe 6 rosettes on the top of the cake. Top the rosettes with the reserved cherries.

Gâteau Succès
(GÂTEAU SUCCÈS)

The separate elements of this cake can be made well ahead of time, and the finished cake tastes even better if it is assembled a day before serving.

1 recipe almond Swiss meringue (p. 293)
butter cream (p. 282) made with 4 egg yolks, ⅔ cup
    (135 g) sugar, ⅓ cup (80 ml) water, and ½ pound
    (250 g) butter
praline (p. 425) made with ⅔ cup (100 g) almonds and
    ½ cup (100 g) sugar
powdered sugar (for dusting)
1 cup (135 g) chopped almonds, toasted

pastry bag with ⅝-inch (1.5 cm) plain tip

SERVES 8.

Butter and flour 2 baking sheets and mark three 8-inch (20 cm) circles on the sheets using a pan lid or cake pan as a guide. Set the oven at 250°F (120°C).

Make the almond meringue, scoop it into the pastry bag, and pipe 3 rounds on the prepared baking sheets. Bake in the heated oven until crisp and dry, 40–50 minutes. While the meringue is still warm, trim the rounds neatly with a sharp knife. Transfer to a rack to cool. The meringue layers can be made ahead and kept in an airtight container for up to 1 week.

Make the butter cream and the praline and combine them. This can be made ahead and kept, covered and refrigerated, for up to 1 week.

To assemble the gâteau: Spread about ¼ of the praline butter cream on a meringue layer. Add the second layer, spread with another ¼ of the butter cream, and top with the third meringue layer. Spread the remaining butter cream over the top and sides. The cake can be kept, refrigerated, for up to 1 week depending on the freshness of the butter cream. Shortly before serving, dust the top with powdered sugar and press the toasted almonds around the sides.

Petits Monts Blancs
(PETITS MONTS BLANCS)

This dessert is a white mountain of cream fenced in by chestnut purée, all on a meringue base. Rather than making the chestnut purée yourself, you can substitute canned sweetened purée.

1 recipe Swiss meringue (p. 292)
½ ounce (15 g) semisweet chocolate, grated

For the chestnut purée:
2 pounds (1 kg) fresh chestnuts OR 1½ pounds (750 g)
  unsweetened canned chestnuts
1 vanilla bean OR 1 teaspoon vanilla extract
⅔ cup (135 g) sugar

For the cream:
Chantilly cream (p. 285) made with 1 cup (250 ml)
  cream, 1 tablespoon sugar, and ½ teaspoon vanilla
  extract
1 egg white
1 tablespoon sugar

3½-inch (9 cm) pastry cutter

pastry bag with ⅜-inch (1 cm) and ⅛-inch (3 mm) plain
  tips

MAKES 6 MONTS BLANCS.

Butter and flour a baking sheet and mark six 3½-inch (9 cm) circles on the sheet with the pastry cutter, spacing them slightly apart. Set the oven at 250°F (120°C).

Make the meringue, scoop it into the pastry bag fitted with the ⅜-inch (1 cm) tip, and pipe 3½-inch (9 cm) rounds on the prepared baking sheet. Bake in the heated oven until the meringue is crisp and dry, 30–40 minutes. While still warm, trim with the pastry cutter to perfect rounds. Transfer to a rack to cool. The meringue rounds can be made ahead and kept in an airtight container for up to 1 week.

For the chestnut purée: Prick the shell of each nut with a knife. Put the nuts in a pan of cold water, bring to a boil, and then take from the heat and peel while still hot. Remove both outer and inner skin. Put the peeled nuts in a saucepan with the vanilla bean, if using, and water to cover and bring to a boil. Cover and simmer until the nuts are tender, 25–30 minutes. Canned nuts needn't be cooked. Lift the nuts out of the liquid and work in a food processor or through a food mill to purée them. Reduce the cooking liquid to 1 cup (250 ml). If using canned nuts, use 1 cup (250 ml) plain water. Add the sugar, bring to a boil, and let cool. If using the vanilla extract, add it to the syrup. Beat enough of the syrup into the purée to make it thin enough to pipe but still thick enough to hold its shape. The purée can be made ahead and kept, covered and refrigerated, for up to 5 days.

For the cream: Make the Chantilly cream. Beat the egg white until stiff, add the sugar, and beat until glossy, about 20 seconds. Fold into the cream.

To assemble: Using the pastry bag fitted with the ⅛-inch (3 mm) tip, pipe chestnut purée in the shape of a nest around the edge of each meringue round. Pile the cream in the center and sprinkle the top with the grated chocolate. Refrigerate until serving. The Monts Blancs can be kept for up to 3 hours.

Vacherin
(VACHERIN)

A vacherin is a fairytale concoction of Swiss meringue, held together and decorated with Italian meringue. This one is filled with Chantilly cream and topped with strawberries.

**Swiss meringue (p. 292) made with 5 egg whites, 1½
    cups (300 g) sugar, and ½ teaspoon vanilla extract
1 recipe Italian meringue (p. 293)
Chantilly cream (p. 285) made with 2 cups (500 ml)
    heavy cream, 2 tablespoons sugar, and 1 teaspoon
    vanilla extract
½ pint (100 g) strawberries, hulled**

***pastry bag with ⅝-inch (1.5 cm) plain and medium star
    tips***

With a pastry scraper, scoop the Italian meringue into a pastry bag. It is used to "mortar" together and decorate the Swiss meringue shell.

SERVES 8.

Butter and flour 2 baking sheets and on 1 of the sheets mark an 8-inch (20 cm) circle, using a pan lid or cake pan as a guide. Set the oven at 250°F (120°C).

Make the Swiss meringue. Put it into the pastry bag fitted with the plain tip and pipe an 8-inch (20 cm) round and 16–20 fingers 4 inches (10 cm) long. Bake in the heated oven until crisp and dry, 40–50 minutes. While the meringue is still warm, trim the round neatly with a sharp knife. Transfer the round and the fingers to a rack to cool.

Make the Italian meringue. Cut a small piece from 1 end of each meringue finger to make the end square. Put the meringue round, flat side down, on a work surface. Scoop the Italian meringue into the pastry bag fitted with the star tip. Pipe a line of meringue around the edge of the round. Press meringue fingers side by side into the Italian meringue, square ends down and rounded sides outward; do this two or more fingers at a time. Pipe 2 lines of Italian meringue between all the fingers, one outside and one inside to hold them in place. Continue all the way around to complete the vacherin case.

Decorate the top and sides of the vacherin with rosettes and swags of the remaining Italian meringue. Bake the vacherin case in the heated oven until dry, about an hour. Leave it to cool on a rack. The case for the vacherin can be baked up to 1 week ahead and kept in an airtight container.

To finish: Make the Chantilly cream. Not more than 3 hours before serving, fill the vacherin case with the cream and arrange the strawberries on top.

Starting the Swiss meringue base

Meringue fingers are set upright in the Italian meringue that has been piped around the base.

Coffee Nuts
(NOIX AU CAFÉ)

For these petits fours the same mixture is used cooked for the meringues and raw for the filling.

> **1 recipe Italian meringue (p. 293)**
> **2 teaspoons instant coffee, dissolved in 1 tablespoon warm water**
>
> **pastry bag with ⅜-inch (1 cm) plain tip**

MAKES ABOUT 1 DOZEN COFFEE NUTS.

Butter and flour a baking sheet. Set the oven at 250°F (120°C).

Make the Italian meringue and beat in the dissolved coffee. Reserve about a quarter of the mixture for filling and scoop the rest into the pastry bag. Pipe walnut-sized mounds on the prepared baking sheet. Bake in the heated oven until crisp and dry, 40–50 minutes. Transfer the meringues to a rack to cool. They can be made ahead and kept in an airtight container for up to 1 week.

When the puffs are completely cool, spread the flat side of half of them with the remaining coffee meringue and stick each of these together with an uncoated meringue puff. The coffee nuts will stay crisp for 3–4 hours.

**Piping out Italian meringue
puffs for Coffee Nuts**

Frozen Desserts

THE FIRST FROZEN DESSERT I ever ate was a dingy pink block of rock-hard ice in which there were imprisoned a few parched strawberries, thirsting for release. It was a children's party in the early 1940's for which a kind great-aunt had done her best to re-create a peacetime treat during an ice-cream-less war. I'm afraid the effect was the opposite from what she had intended: we dispiritedly spooned the puddles of melting ice onto our plates. My aunt had, unwittingly, picked one of the most difficult of all frozen desserts—a fruit-based sorbet.

Sorbets were the original frozen desserts—the name comes from the Turkish word for a refreshing wine or fruit drink, no doubt originally chilled with snow. The Turks were by no means the first to appreciate the pleasure of chilled treats—Xenophon remarked on the Greek soldiers' taste for cold desserts made of honey and fruit juice, and Nero apparently regaled himself with rose water, honey, and raisins. But it was not until the Renaissance that ice creams really came into their own, when Italian cooks discovered how to deal with the great enemy—water. During freezing, the water in an ice-cream mixture forms crystals or, in extreme cases like that of my great-aunt, a solid block of ice. To break up crystals and give a smooth texture, the mixture must be frozen as quickly as possible and stirred constantly while it is freezing. In the sixteenth century, a Sicilian found he could chill a mixture more quickly by adding saltpeter to ice, thus lowering its melting point, an effect modern cooks accomplish by adding salt. The idea was slow to spread north, but by 1782 the Café Procope in Paris was serving eighty different

301

flavors, including the classics such as vanilla, chocolate, and coffee as well as the more unusual rose and chestnut. (The Café Procope still exists, but its menu is now regrettably pedestrian.)

The invention of the churn freezer further simplified the making of frozen desserts. The principle is simple: a cylindrical receptacle, equipped with a paddle, is surrounded by ice and salt packed into a bucket. A crank handle turns the paddle so that the mixture in the container is churned constantly while being cooled by the salted ice. Making ice cream this way can be tedious, messy work—a good outdoor occupation for children on a hot day, but there are now several versions of electrically driven freezers.

Given constant churning at a low temperature, it is possible to freeze a wide range of mixtures. They fall into two main categories: sorbets made of fruit juice or purée, wine or liqueur, plus sugar and various flavorings, and richer mixtures based on eggs, milk, and/or cream. Of the latter, by far the most common are custard-based ice creams made of milk thickened with eggs.

Even richer than ice cream are the iced desserts that reached their zenith in the nineteenth century. There are the bombes and the parfaits, made with up to thirty-two egg yolks and a quart of whipped cream, and those can still be frozen in a regular freezer. During the Belle Époque, a chef was scarcely worthy of the name if he did not invent a new *coupe* of ice cream or sorbet with some combination of fruit, sweet sauce, nuts, Chantilly cream, or candied fruits—creations such as Escoffier's famous *poires belle Hélène* and *pêches Melba*.

The relative popularities of the various frozen desserts are as changeable as is fashion. Now we are back at the beginning with sorbets: fruit sorbets, spiced sorbets, wine sorbets, or even vegetable sorbets are a mandatory part of an up-to-date French menu. One reason is that they epitomize the current vogue for lightness, color, and clarity of flavor, and the recent development of small commercial ice-cream machines certainly has helped.

Sorbets offer a good deal of scope for experiment, but finding just the right balance of flavor and sweetness is not easy. Professional *glaciers* measure the density of sorbet mixtures (which varies according to the proportion of sugar) with a hydrometer and debate the relative merits of stirring sugar directly into a mixture as compared with using a sugar syrup. All agree that, in practice, there is no substitute for tasting and then adjusting ingredients until the combination is just right.

As with all cooking, good frozen desserts require the finest ingredients. Cheating is easy, and the manufacturing of commercial ice cream in France is surrounded by regulations about the use of animal fat instead of cream, of additives such as cornstarch, gelatin, and gums. Also, the bulk of an ice cream can be increased enormously by whipping in air—compare the weight of a pint of homemade ice cream with that of a commercial ice cream and you will see. In France, commercially prepared fruit sorbets can contain as little as fifteen percent fruit (ten percent for acid fruits like red currants or lemon). Since the rest is mainly sugar and water, no wonder they don't taste the same as homemade!

Given a good mixture and an ice-cream churn, whether electric or hand-operated, making ice cream or sorbet is simple. Fill the container not more than two-thirds full (all mixtures expand when frozen), pack with ice, add salt, and churn until the mixture is set. This can take anywhere from ten minutes to half an hour depending on the amount and type of the mixture.

Whipped cream is often added to ice cream halfway through. And a very little egg white or meringue can be added to a sorbet to lighten the mixture and make it smoother. Egg white can give a slightly pasty texture, though, and detract from the flavor. At La Varenne we find that we're using it less and less.

In the old days, ice creams were often molded and turned out onto a white napkin (to absorb the drips); sorbets were invariably served in stemmed glasses. But now the only limit on possible serving containers is your imagination. One of the prettiest nouvelle cuisine presentations I have seen was an arrangement of five tiny scoops of different-colored sorbets, five fruits to match, and a vine leaf—a far cry from my first rock-hard strawberry ice.

FOR SUCCESSFUL FROZEN DESSERTS

1. When making the custard base for ice cream, never leave the yolks in contact with the sugar without mixing, or the sugar will break down the yolks—the French call the reaction "burning."

2. Make a richer ice cream by adding more egg yolks to the custard base. The usual proportions are from 5–12 yolks per quart (1 L) of ice cream. Mixtures should be highly flavored as freezing diminishes the taste.

3. Sugar and alcohol lower the freezing point of a mixture; if too much of either is added, it may not freeze at all. On the other hand, a sorbet with too little sugar will be hard and tasteless when frozen.

4. The mixture for fruit sorbets should be slightly sweeter than for one flavored with wine or eau-de-vie. Lemon juice is added to most fruit sorbets to bring out their flavor.

5. To add flavor to citrus sorbets, rub a cube of sugar on the rind of the fruit to extract the oils from the zest and then use the sugar to sweeten the juice.

6. Prepare the ice-cream freezer with salt and ice ten to fifteen minutes before using so the mixture is chilled as soon as it is put in. Proportions of ice to salt should be about three to one. If too much salt is used, the mixture will freeze too quickly and will not be smooth. Take great care not to drop any salt into the container. If a mixture takes more than thirty minutes to freeze, add more salt.

7. Mixtures that have just been frozen thaw very quickly (sorbet melts even more quickly than ice cream), so handle as speedily as possible and always chill any spoon or other equipment used.

8. When filling fruit shells such as tangerines with ice cream or sorbet, freeze the shells before filling.

 PREPARING AHEAD

1. Fruit jucies and fruit purée can be prepared and frozen for later use in making sorbet.

2. A freezer should not be set at its lowest temperature for storing ice cream or sorbet; the lower the temperature, the quicker they crystallize.

3. Rich ice creams can be stored well, but mixtures such as sorbet that contain a high proportion of water tend to crystallize on standing and should be used as soon as possible. If a sorbet does crystallize, churn it again for fifteen minutes.

4. Ice cream or sorbet that has been in the freezer for more than twelve hours should be left in the refrigerator for an hour to soften before serving.

Tea and Lime Sorbet
(SORBET DE THÉ AU CITRON VERT)

Nouvelle cuisine has launched the two-flavored sorbet, an oddity in France, and what's more, proposes unusual flavors such as tea.

> 3–4 limes
> 1 cup (250 ml) water
> 10 high-quality tea bags

For the syrup:
> **1 quart (1 L) water**
> **1¼ cups (250 g) sugar**

ice-cream freezer

MAKES ABOUT 1 QUART (1 L) SORBET.

For the syrup: In a heavy-bottomed pan dissolve the sugar in the water over low heat. Bring to a boil and boil steadily until the syrup is clear, 2–3 minutes.

Pare the zest from the limes and chop into the smallest possible pieces. Blanch by putting them into cold water and bringing to a boil. Refresh under cold running water and drain thoroughly. Simmer the blanched zest in ½ cup (125 ml) of the syrup, stirring frequently, until tender, about 15 minutes.

Bring the 1 cup (250 ml) of water to a boil, add the tea bags, take from the heat, and leave to infuse for 5 minutes. Remove the tea bags.

Squeeze and strain the juice from 3 of the limes. Mix together the syrup, infused tea, cooked zest with any remaining syrup, and the lime juice. Taste the mixture and add sugar or lime juice to taste. Pour into a freezer and churn until firm.

Sorbet-filled Tangerines
(MANDARINES GIVRÉES)

Besides tangerines, hollowed-out oranges, lemons, grapefruit, or melon halves also make attractive givrées.

> **20 tangerines**
> **juice of ½–1 lemon**
> **⅓ cup (80 ml) water**
> **powdered sugar to taste—optional**

For the syrup:
> **¾ cup (150 g) granulated sugar**
> **½ cup (125 ml) water**
> **juice of ¼ lemon**

ice-cream freezer

MAKES ABOUT 1 QUART (1 L) SORBET, WHICH FILLS 8 TANGERINES.

For the syrup: In a heavy-bottomed saucepan gently heat the sugar in the water and juice of ¼ lemon until the sugar dissolves. Bring to a boil and boil steadily until the syrup is clear, 2–3 minutes. Leave to cool.

Grate the zest of 12 tangerines, squeeze them, and strain the juice. Cut the remaining tangerines so as to form a bottom section that is ⅔ of the tangerine and a small "lid." Squeeze and strain the juice from these tangerines, being careful not to damage the skins. You will need 3 cups (750 ml) juice. Add the grated zest, juice, juice from ½ lemon, and the ⅓ cup (80 ml) water to the cooled syrup. Taste and add powdered sugar or lemon juice if needed. Pour into the freezer and churn until firm.

Meanwhile, scoop out the remaining membrane and flesh from the tangerine shells and chill the shells in the freezer. Mound the sorbet in the bases and cover with the lids.

Pistachio Ice Cream
(GLACE AUX PISTACHES)

This ice cream is delicious on its own, or it can be used as the outside layer of bombe Véronique (p. 309).

> **1 cup (150 g) shelled pistachios**
> **custard sauce (below) made with 2 cups (500 ml) milk,**
> **   6 egg yolks, and ⅔ cup (135 g) sugar**
> **1 cup (250 ml) heavy cream, lightly beaten**
>
> **ice-cream freezer**

MAKES ABOUT 1 QUART (1 L).

Blanch the pistachios in boiling water for 1 minute, drain, and peel. Grind them in a food processor or pound to a powder in a mortar with a pestle.

Make the custard sauce, infusing the milk with the finely ground pistachios. Strain, cool, and pour into the freezer. Churn until the ice cream begins to set, add the lightly beaten cream, and continue churning until set.

Custard Sauce
(CRÈME ANGLAISE)

This basic sauce is served as a dessert topping and is used as the base for ice cream and for Bavarian cream. The milk is most frequently infused with a vanilla bean, but other flavorings can be used instead. When the sauce is used as a base for ice cream, the proportion of sugar is increased because unsweetened cream is added before freezing.

2 cups (500 ml) milk
1 vanilla bean OR 1½ teaspoons vanilla extract OR
   other flavoring according to individual recipes
6 egg yolks
4 tablespoons (50 g) sugar

MAKES ABOUT 2 CUPS (500 ml) CUSTARD SAUCE.

Bring the milk with the vanilla bean, if using, to a boil and leave in a warm place to infuse 10–15 minutes. Remove the bean and wash it to use again. Beat the egg yolks with the sugar until thick and light. Reheat the milk to boiling. Whisk half the hot milk into the yolks and whisk this mixture back into the remaining milk. Heat gently, stirring constantly with a wooden spoon, until the custard thickens slightly; if you draw a finger across the back of the spoon, it should leave a clear trail. (NOTE: Do not overcook, or the sauce will curdle.)

Take the sauce from the heat as soon as it thickens and strain. If using vanilla extract, add it now. Stir often as the hot sauce cools. If serving cold, let cool completely, cover tightly, and chill. The sauce can be kept up to 2 days in the refrigerator.

**The test for the correct
thickness
of custard sauce**

Ginger Ice Cream
(GLACE AU GINGEMBRE)

The strong flavor of ginger mellowed by the rich ice cream is delicious, and the candied ginger adds textural interest.

   custard sauce (p. 306) made with 2 cups (500 ml) milk,
      6 egg yolks, and ⅔ cup (135 g) sugar
   1½ teaspoons ground ginger
   2 tablespoons chopped candied ginger
   1 cup (250 ml) heavy cream, lightly beaten

ice-cream freezer

MAKES ABOUT 1 QUART (1 L) ICE CREAM.

Make the custard sauce, remove from the heat, stir in the ground ginger, and strain the custard. Stir in the chopped ginger, leave the mixture to cool, and then pour into the freezer. Churn until the ice cream begins to set, add the lightly beaten cream, and continue churning until set.

Frozen Strawberry Soufflé
(SOUFFLÉ GLACÉ AUX FRAISES)

This classic frozen soufflé, a combination of meringue, fruit purée, and whipped cream, does not need to be churned during freezing. Frozen in individual soufflé dishes heightened by paper collars, the dessert stands high above the rims when the collars are removed and look like soufflés that have puffed in the oven.

Italian meringue (p. 293) made with ½ cup (100 g)
**   sugar, ¼ cup (60 ml) water, and 2 egg whites**
1 pint (200 g) strawberries, hulled
1 tablespoon kirsch or lemon juice
1 cup (250 ml) heavy cream, lightly beaten

four ½-cup (125 ml) ramekins

MAKES 4 INDIVIDUAL SOUFFLÉS.

Wrap a strip of waxed paper around each ramekin so that it extends 2 inches (5 cm) above the rim of the dish and tie with a string.

Make the Italian meringue. Purée the strawberries in a food processor or push them through a sieve. Gently fold the strawberry purée and the beaten cream into the meringue, pour the mixture into the prepared ramekins, and smooth the tops. Freeze, until firm, at least 2 hours.

**Removing
the paper collar
of a frozen soufflé**

Bombe Véronique
(BOMBE VÉRONIQUE)

Bombes were named for their shape. They were traditionally made in rounded molds with flat bottoms, which made it easy to bury them in snow, flat side up. Now, however, bombes are usually put in a freezer, and a mold of any shape can be used—a charlotte mold, a stainless steel bowl, or even a cake pan.

3 cups (750 ml) pistachio ice cream (p. 306)
2 tablespoons brandy
1½ ounces (45 g) candied orange peel, chopped
3 ounces (90 g) semisweet chocolate, chopped
⅓ cup (65 g) sugar
6 tablespoons (95 ml) water
3 egg yolks
1 cup (250 ml) heavy cream, lightly beaten

1½-quart (1.5 L) mold

SERVES 8–12.

Using a metal spatula, line the mold with the ice cream and put in the freezer to set firmly. Pour the brandy over the candied orange peel and leave to macerate. Melt the chocolate in a water bath and let cool.

In a heavy-bottomed pan gently dissolve the sugar in the water. Bring to a boil and boil steadily until the syrup forms a thread when tested between forefinger and thumb (232°F or 111°C). Pour the hot syrup over the egg yolks, beating constantly, and continue beating until the mixture is cool and thick. Set the bowl of sweetened yolks in a pan or bowl of ice water and beat until chilled. Stir in the macerated orange peel, brandy, and chocolate and then fold in the beaten cream. Spoon the mixture into the lined mold, cover with the lid or with aluminum foil, and freeze until firm, at least 3 hours.

To serve, dip the mold into a bowl of cold water for 5 seconds. Uncover the bombe and set a serving dish on top. Turn the mold upside down and give a sharp shake so the bombe slips out onto the plate.

Lining a square ice-cream mold with pistachio ice cream for Bombe Véronique

Petits Fours Secs

PETITS FOURS ARE named, so goes the story, after the little ovens (*fours*) invented in the seventeenth century for baking them. It is a beguiling name for what I have to confess are one of my greatest weaknesses. I can resist the allure of an overladen dessert trolley with hardly a pang, but set a plate of fresh, innocent petits fours in front of me and I am overcome. Should I choose one of the curved *tuiles*, or a crisp *cigarette russe*, or a miniature fruit tartlet, or a tiny génoise cake, or one of those fruits dipped in sugar that seem to explode in your mouth? On reflection, what better way to accompany a second cup of coffee than with one of each?

Tempting they certainly are, innocent they may look, but do not be deceived. Petits fours have been the undoing of many an ambitious chef. When properly made, each type should conform to exact standards: they should all be of the same size, baked to the same color, shaped to the same characteristic form, and decorated in precisely the same way. And they must be absolutely fresh.

There are literally hundreds of different petits fours, since most large pastries and cakes can be made in a small size, as well as the cookies, glazed fruits (see p. 322), and other "bonnes bouchées" that are specifically petits fours. Pâtissiers divide them into two categories: fresh and dry. Fresh petits fours cannot be kept for more than twenty-four hours; they may contain fruit, butter cream or pastry cream, or involve some kind of sugar coating that softens in humid air. Often they are based on génoise (see p. 281 for example). Dry petits fours can include little meringues (see p. 299), miniature puff pastries (see p. 247), and the cigarettes, tuiles (tiles), and other

310

PETITS FOURS SECS
From top left: Palets de Dames, thin round cookies topped with currants; Tuiles aux Amandes, curved in the shape of traditional roof tiles; Cigarettes Russes, very thin rolled cookies; and Petits Fours aux Amandes, made of an egg white and ground almond mixture piped into classic shapes

piped and shaped cookies that are the subject of this chapter. Unfortunately, even dry petits fours cannot be kept for more than a week; most are best eaten within a day or two.

Cigarette russes and *palets de dames* are made of essentially the same rich mixture of flour, butter, egg whites, and sugar that is piped onto a baking sheet. Possible flavorings include vanilla, lemon or orange rind, chocolate, finely chopped candied fruit, and finely slivered or ground almonds. For tuiles the mixture is dropped, rather than piped, on the baking sheet and then spread to wafer thinness with a fork.

When baked, palets de dames remain small round cookies, but cigarette russes and tuiles spread, so while they are still hot they can be curled to the shapes their names suggest. The mixture for cigarettes, which is slightly thicker than the other mixtures, is particularly versatile; it can be twisted into a cone or pressed over a glass or into a brioche mold to make *tulipes*, edible containers for serving ice cream or sorbet. Chef Jorant, La Varenne's pâtissier, even makes a confection called *Paris paquet,* for which génoise is soaked in liqueur, filled with pastry cream, and then wrapped in a warm sheet made of cigarette russe batter, a tour de force that requires—as do all these rolled cookies—a mixture of just the right consistency that has been baked to just the right stage.

Because the consistency can vary with the dryness of the flour or the size of the egg whites used, it is best to bake a trial cigarette russe or tuile to test the mixture. If it barely spreads and does not cook in the middle, it is too thick and a little more egg white should be added. If, on the other hand, the batter is too thin and spreads all over the baking sheet or if it is too brittle, stir in a little

Rolling Cigarettes around the handle of a wooden spoon and (right) Tuiles shaped over a rolling pin

more flour. If it is not crisp, add a spoonful of melted butter. Bake only one sheet of petits fours secs at a time because they must be shaped quickly once they come out of the oven. Loosen them with a metal spatula and immediately shape them around a pencil or wooden spoon handle—for cigarettes—or over a rolling pin—for tuiles. If they become too crisp to roll, warm them for a short time in the oven.

Almond petits fours pose no such technical problems. The basic mixture, made of ground almonds and sugar, is mixed with just enough egg whites so that it can be piped into varying small shapes. They are cooked until brown (but not dry), and while hot they must be brushed with a glaze of sugar and milk to make them moist and shiny.

The charming Rothschilds, made of a basic mixture of almond Swiss meringue with flour added, are piped into little sticks. Chopped almonds are sprinkled over them before baking, and after baking, their bottoms are spread with chocolate. If the base is piped into rounds rather than sticks and not coated with chocolate, they become *éponges*.

Don't let yourself be distracted by the range of petits fours made by a professional pâtissier. He, poor man, must please his customers with a good spread and must sell all, fresh or stale, if he is to make a profit. You can rival him any day with two or three kinds of simple petits fours fresh from the oven—or even just one. I well remember a dinner in a nondescript restaurant in the main square of an equally nondescript town. Appetizers and main courses were without distinction. But printed on the dessert menu was a single word—tuiles. When they came, they were fresh, crisp, see-through thin, and the size of a real-life Provençal tile. For once the word perfection was appropriate.

FOR SUCCESSFUL PETITS FOURS SECS

1. When adding egg whites to a butter and sugar mixture, whisk them in gradually so the mixture does not separate.

2. Petits fours must all be the same size, so spoon or pipe exactly equal amounts of batter onto the baking sheet.

3. Petits fours should not be too large—professionals count about 12–15 g (about ½ ounce) for each one.

4. Petits fours that spread during baking must be spaced well apart.

5. Oven heat may not be even with the result that the petits fours do not all bake at the same speed. Some may need to be taken from the oven before others.

PREPARING AHEAD

1. The basic mixture for most dry petits fours can be made ahead and kept for up to two hours, covered and refrigerated.

2. The petits fours batter can also be prepared, piped or spooned onto the baking sheet, and left ready for baking. They will keep without harm for up to two hours.

3. Petits fours are best eaten within a day or two of baking. However, if packed in an airtight container as soon as they are cool, most can be kept for up to a week. If they soften, heat in a 250°F (120°C) oven to crisp them.

Cigarettes Russes
(CIGARETTES RUSSES)

Roll these petits fours secs quickly while they are still warm. They are particularly good with sorbet.

> 5 ounces (150 g) butter
> 1 cup (135 g) powdered sugar, sifted
> 3 egg whites
> ⅔ cup (85 g) flour
> 1½ teaspoons heavy cream
> ½ teaspoon vanilla extract
>
> *pastry bag with ⅜-inch (1 cm) plain tip*

MAKES ABOUT 40 CIGARETTES.

Butter 2 or 3 baking sheets and heat the oven to 450°F (230°C).

Cream the butter and the sugar and gradually beat in half of the egg whites. Add 1 tablespoon of the flour and mix well. Gradually beat in the remaining egg whites. Stir in the remaining flour and then the heavy cream and vanilla and mix well. Scoop the mixture into the pastry bag and pipe mounds the size of walnuts well apart onto the prepared baking sheets.

Bang each baking sheet sharply on the table to flatten the mounds and then bake in the oven until light brown around the edges, 4–5 minutes. (NOTE: If overcooked, the cookies are hard to roll.) Loosen the cookies from the baking sheet with a metal spatula. Put one cookie upside down on the work surface, quickly roll it around a wooden spoon handle, and press down lightly on the seam. Remove the rolled cookie and leave on a rack to cool. Roll the remaining cookies as quickly as possible. If the cookies became too stiff to roll, put them back in the oven to soften for 1 minute.

Palets de Dames
(PALETS DE DAMES)

Palets, or quoits, are heavy iron discs used in a game, and these round light petits fours are "ladies' palets."

¼ **cup (35 g) currants or raisins**
6 tablespoons (95 g) butter
½ **cup (100 g) sugar**
2 egg whites, lightly beaten
½ **teaspoon vanilla extract**
¾ **cup (95 g) flour, sifted with a pinch of salt**

pastry bag with ⅜-inch (1 cm) tip

MAKES ABOUT 30 COOKIES.
 Butter 2 or 3 baking sheets and heat the oven to 400°F (200°C). Pour boiling water over the currants or raisins, let stand until plump, about 10 minutes, drain, and dry on paper towels.
 Cream the butter and the sugar until light and fluffy. Gradually beat in the egg whites. Stir in the vanilla and then fold in the flour. Scoop the mixture into the pastry bag and pipe 1-inch (2.5 cm) mounds well apart onto the prepared baking sheets. Put 2 or 3 currants or raisins on each mound.
 Bake the palets in the heated oven until the edges are golden but the centers still pale, 8–10 minutes. Transfer to a rack to cool.

Almond Tile Cookies
(TUILES AUX AMANDES)

These cookies are shaped while still warm around a rolling pin to resemble the curved tiles on traditional French roofs.

6 tablespoons (95 g) butter
⅔ **cup (90 g) powdered sugar, sifted**
1 teaspoon rum
2 egg whites
½ **cup (65 g) flour**
pinch of salt
1 cup (90 g) sliced almonds
½ **teaspoon vanilla extract**

MAKES ABOUT 20 COOKIES.
 Butter 2 or 3 baking sheets and set the oven at 400°F (200°C). Heat the butter over low heat until it is pourable but not completely melted.
 In a bowl mix together the powdered sugar, rum, egg whites, flour,

salt, almonds, and vanilla. Gently stir in the butter. Drop the mixture by teaspoonsful well apart onto the prepared baking sheets. Flatten each spoonful of batter with a fork dipped in cold water.

Bake the tuiles in the oven until the edges are browned, 6–8 minutes. Loosen the cookies from the baking sheet with a metal spatula and quickly shape them around a rolling pin or in a ring mold and leave until firm. If the cookies become too stiff to shape, put them back in the oven to soften for 1 minute.

Rothschilds
(ROTHSCHILDS)

These delectable little cookies end a dinner with a light touch.

1 cup (150 g) blanched whole almonds
¾ cup (150 g) sugar
2½ tablespoons (20 g) flour
5 egg whites
½ cup (70 g) chopped almonds
3 ounces (90 g) semisweet chocolate, chopped

pastry bag with ½-inch (1.25 cm) plain tip

MAKES ABOUT 30 COOKIES.

Butter and flour 2 or 3 baking sheets. Set the oven at 250°F (120°C).

In a food processor or rotary cheese grater grind the almonds and all but 2 tablespoons (25 g) of the sugar to a powder. Mix with the flour. Beat the egg whites until stiff, preferably in a copper bowl. Add the remaining 2 tablespoons (25 g) sugar and beat until glossy, another 20 seconds. Gently fold the almond mixture into the egg whites. Scoop the batter into the pastry bag and pipe it in 2-inch (5 cm) fingers well apart onto the baking sheets. Sprinkle with the chopped almonds and rap the baking sheets lightly on the table to remove any excess almonds. Bake in the oven until the cookies are crisp and lightly browned and the almonds are toasted.

Transfer to a rack to cool. Melt the chocolate in a water bath, spread a little on the flat side of each cookie, and leave upside down until the chocolate is set.

Almond Petits Fours
(PETITS FOURS AUX AMANDES)

Almond petits fours differ little from macaroons, though they are smaller and have a shiny sugar glaze. Pipe them into whatever small shape you like and top with the candied fruit of your choice.

> **1⅓ cups (200 g) blanched whole almonds**
> **¾ cup (150 g) sugar**
> **2 egg whites, beaten until frothy**
> **½ teaspoon vanilla extract OR ¼ teaspoon almond extract**
> **candied orange peel, cherries, or angelica (for decoration)**

For the glaze:
> **1 tablespoon powdered sugar**
> **2 tablespoons milk or water**

> ***pastry bag with large star tip***

MAKES ABOUT 20 COOKIES.

Butter a baking sheet and set the oven at 350°F (175°C).

Grind the almonds in a rotary cheese grater or a food processor and mix them with the sugar. Stir in enough egg white to make a mixture that is soft enough to pipe but still holds its shape. Beat in the vanilla or almond extract. Scoop the mixture into the pastry bag and pipe rosettes, zigzags, or knots on the prepared baking sheet. Decorate each with a piece of candied fruit and bake in the oven until the petits fours are just beginning to brown, 15–20 minutes. Gently heat the sugar in the milk or water until dissolved. Brush the sugar syrup over the cookies while they are still hot and transfer to a rack to cool.

Piping out Almond Petits Fours

Confiserie

OF ALL THE BRANCHES of French cooking, *confiserie*, or candymaking, is one of the most ancient. In medieval times, crystallized fruits and candies such as *bonbons au gingembre, dragées au musc,* and *massepains* were sold by apothecaries, sugar being so expensive it was considered a precious medicine. By the end of the eighteenth century, the making of marzipan, nougat, praline, and their cousins had been refined to an art, often devoted to the construction of elaborate edible *pièces montées* in the shape of Gothic *folies* or Chinese pavillions several feet high. A hundred years later, however, pastry chefs began to neglect the architecture in favor of individual bonbons—little almond pralines or fresh fruits dipped in sugar glaze or in fondant icing—the better to titillate the beauties of the Belle Époque. So durable is the charm of these small multi-colored candies that they have scarcely changed since then.

Confiserie is based on a single ingredient—sugar. Its cooking calls for meticulous accuracy and a talent for decoration. Equipment is simple enough. Pans must be heavy and of a material that spreads heat evenly—the traditional *poêlon* for sugar work is made of solid unlined copper. A sugar thermometer is important, preferably protected in a metal sheath so it cannot touch the base of the pan and register a distorted temperature. (A fat thermometer can be used instead, providing temperatures are clearly marked.) The sugar itself must be pure. Lump sugar is preferred because it is less contaminated with dust and other extraneous matter, and powdered sugar is never used since it contains cornstarch.

Sugar and water are combined in a pan and dissolved over gentle heat. Then over high heat the serious boiling begins. As water evaporates, the syrup becomes even more concentrated, exhibiting different properties at each stage of the cooking. Nowadays, each stage can be gauged with a thermometer, but an experienced *confiseur* follows the old way, using his eyes to judge the speed of breaking bubbles and his fingers to test the consistency of a ball of syrup. This last is done by dipping the middle finger and thumb into cold water, then into the boiling syrup, and immediately back into the cold water—the clinging syrup is rolled off finger and thumb under water. It's all a bit frightening the first time you see it, and many students prefer to use the method pictured on p. 294.

When pliable, at 239°F (115°C), the syrup is at the soft-ball stage, right for fondant icing and butter cream. Ten degrees hotter, at the hard-ball stage, it is ready for Italian meringue. Eight more (even one or two degrees are important) and the syrup is brittle but still slightly sticky at the soft-crack stage. Much hotter at the hard-crack stage of 295°F (146°C), the syrup glazes fruits and pastries, makes spun sugar, and can be shaped into roses or long ribbons of sugar that are an art in themselves. Last of all comes caramel, when the syrup changes rapidly from translucent gold to deep chestnut brown.

It sounds so easy, and indeed it is if you follow the rules. Sugar syrup must never be stirred during boiling, or it will crystallize. Sugar crystals that condense on the sides of the pan must be washed down with a brush dipped in water so they do not burn and discolor the syrup. When testing, lift the pan from the heat so the syrup does not cook further, and watch temperature constantly—it changes fast, particularly at later stages. A syrup that does cook too far can be diluted with water and brought back, but there is always a danger it may crystallize.

I well remember the first time I attempted caramel. Like most novices, I had unerringly picked the trickiest recipe in the cookbook at hand—a floating island. I was thirteen at the time. "Boil syrup until golden," it said. I stirred madly to make the sugar dissolve, and of course it did the opposite, crystallizing twice before showing faint signs of color at the edges of the pan. Hardly had the required golden caramel developed before thick black smoke was pouring from the pan. My mother, a conscientious housewife, spent days trying to clean that pan, but though *un*burned caramel dissolves easily enough in warm water, her efforts were unavailing.

Dark caramel makes an easy sauce or a flavoring for desserts such as crème caramel (p. 109). Paler sweeter caramel is used in nougatine for which blanched chopped almonds are stirred into the hot caramel, and then the mixture is rolled while still warm and cut into shapes for decorating cakes. And crisp little praline candies on the lines of peanut brittle can be made by leaving whole caramel-coated nuts to solidify in little heaps.

Simpler still is marzipan, or almond paste. Candies made of almond paste are shaped and colored in lifelike facsimiles of fruits, or sandwiched with prunes, candied fruit, or nuts. These *fruits déguisés* can be simply dipped into sugar syrup and then rolled in sugar, or they can be glazed with a crisp sugar coating. The flavor of the almond paste itself is best when made at home with almonds that have just been ground.

Fondant is an odd man out of the preparations involving sugar syrup because it is actually made, though not used, more often by amateurs than by professionals. When made at home, the syrup is cooked as usual to the required temperature and then allowed to cool until just warm to the touch. At this point, it is a transparent pliable mass. It is worked vigorously with a scraper or wooden spoon, which forces crystallization so that quite suddenly a stiff opaque ball is formed. Finally the fondant is worked, in the fingers bit by bit, to a smooth white paste. Understandably, given the work involved, pastry chefs prefer to buy fondant commercially by the bucket, and it is identical in taste to homemade (after all, fondant is only sugar and water).

Caramel, praline, almond paste, fondant, sugar glaze—cooked sugar covers a wide field. Even more varied are the candies made from it, so with a minimum of equipment, from just a few ingredients can appear an enticing platter of multicolored candies, bedecked with their paper cases. Besides a talent for decoration, it helps for a *confiseur* to have a steady hand, as pastry chef Albert Jorant proved one day at La Varenne. He was constructing a *pièce montée*, a three-foot windmill of pastry and sugar, and one of the sails broke. There was a gasp from the audience, but the chef remained unperturbed. Dipping the broken edges of candy in sugar syrup cooked to the hard-crack, he neatly stuck them together again. Sugar syrup also makes excellent glue.

 FOR SUCCESSFUL CONFISERIE

1. **Choose a pan that will hold the quantity of syrup comfortably. Syrup boils over if you use too small a pan; in too large a pan, it will cook too fast to measure accurately.**

2. **To prevent graining, add an acid such as cream of tartar, lemon juice, or vinegar. The addition of corn syrup not only inhibits graining but also makes cooked syrup less brittle when set.**

3. **Boil syrup as rapidly as possible but do not turn the flame up so high that it licks the sides of the pan or the syrup will cook unevenly.**

4. **Skim syrup during boiling, if necessary, so it remains clear.**

PREPARING AHEAD

Some candies, such as caramelized almonds, can be made ahead of time. Many have a sugar coating that does not hold well but include ingredients, such as fondant and almond paste, that can be made well in advance of serving.

COOKED SUGAR

STAGE	TEMPERATURE	TEST	USE
syrup	214°F (101°C)		soaking savarin and babas moistening génoise making sherbet
soft-ball	239°F (115°C)	can form into soft ball	fondant butter cream
hard-ball	248°F (120°C)	forms firm pliable ball	Italian meringue
soft-crack	257°F (125°C)	brittle but sticks to teeth	almond paste
hard-crack	295°F (146°C)	very brittle and doesn't stick to teeth	glazed fruits glazed pastry angel's hair pulled sugar
caramel	329-338°F (165-170°C)	light to deep golden brown	sauces crème caramel praline

FONDANT

1. Follow the instructions for making fondant exactly. If the syrup is not cooked to quite the soft-ball stage, it will not set properly; if cooked too much, it will be granular. If the fondant is worked before it has cooled to tepid, it will not set, and if left to cool too long, it will never be quite smooth.

2. **The least touch of grease will ruin fondant.**

3. **Choose a dry day for making fondant; it doesn't set well in humid weather.**

4. **The consistency of finished fondant can vary from stiff to hard. It must always be softened with water or another liquid.**

5. **Fondant is heated before use just to tepid. Do not overheat, or it will lose its gloss.**

Glazed Fruits
(FRUITS GLACÉS)

A delicious accompaniment to after-dinner coffee, glazed fruits are a luxury because they keep only a few hours before their crisp sugar coating dissolves.

12 pieces of fruit (grapes, cherries, strawberries), with stems left on

For the coating:
1 cup (200 g) sugar
½ cup (125 ml) water
pinch of cream of tartar, dissolved in 1 tablespoon water OR ½ teaspoon lemon juice or vinegar

sugar thermometer—optional

paper candy cases

MAKES 12 GLAZED FRUITS.

Wash the fruit and dry thoroughly on paper towels. The fruit must be very dry and the skins unbroken. Oil a baking sheet.

For the syrup: In a small heavy-bottomed pan dissolve the sugar in the water over low heat. Add the dissolved cream of tartar or lemon juice or vinegar, bring the syrup to a boil, and boil steadily to the hard-crack stage (295°F or 146°C on a sugar thermometer) or very slightly beyond it to a very pale caramel. Take the pan from the heat and dip the base into warm water to stop the cooking. Dip each piece of fruit, either by the stem or speared on a fork, into the syrup. Let the excess syrup drip back into the pan, put the fruit on the prepared baking sheet, and leave until cold and set. The fruits can be dipped up to 3 hours ahead and kept in a cool dry place.

Serve the glazed fruit in paper cases.

Frosted Fruits
(FRUITS GLACÉS AU FONDANT)

The glossy appearance and soft texture of fondant, so often used for icing pastries, make it ideal for dipping fruits and candies, too.

1 cup (250 ml) fondant (p. 324)
12 pieces of fruit (grapes, cherries, strawberries) with
**   stems left on**
powdered sugar (for sprinkling)
2 teaspoons kirsch

paper candy cases

MAKES 12 FROSTED FRUITS.

Make the fondant and leave to mellow. This can be done far ahead of time. Wash the fruit and dry thoroughly on paper towels. The fruit must be very dry and the skins unbroken. Sprinkle a baking sheet with a heavy coating of powdered sugar.

Soften the fondant in a water bath. Add the kirsch and heat to tepid. Add warm water, if necessary, so the fondant will just coat the back of a spoon. Dip each piece of fruit by its stem into the fondant and let the fondant drip back into the pan. The coating should be thin enough so the color of the fruit can be distinguished through the fondant. Put the frosted fruits on the prepared baking sheet and leave until cold and set. The fruit can be dipped up to 5–6 hours ahead and kept, uncovered, in a dry place or in the refrigerator.

Serve the frosted fruits in paper cases.

Frosting strawberries with fondant icing. They are set on a tray heavily sprinkled with powdered sugar.

Fondant
(FONDANT)

Food coloring and flavorings can be added to this sweet coating, as specified in individual recipes.

> **2 cups (400 g) sugar**
> **1 cup (250 ml) water**
> **2 tablespoons corn syrup or glucose OR big pinch of cream of tartar dissolved in 2 tablespoons water OR 1 teaspoon lemon juice or vinegar**

For flavoring—optional:
> **1 teaspoon vanilla extract OR ¼ teaspoon almond or mint extract**

sugar thermometer—optional

MAKES 2 CUPS (500 ml) FONDANT.

In a heavy-bottomed pan gently heat the sugar and water until the sugar is dissolved. Add corn syrup, glucose, dissolved cream of tartar, lemon juice, or vinegar. Bring to a boil and boil steadily to the soft-ball stage (239°F or 115°C on a sugar thermometer). Immediately take the pan from the heat and dip the base into warm water to stop the cooking. Stir in flavoring if used and then hold the pan about 2 feet (60 cm) above a dampened tray and pour the fondant slowly into it. Sprinkle with a little water to prevent the formation of a crust. Leave to cool.

When no longer warm put the mixture on a cool surface, preferably marble. Slide a sugar scraper or wooden spoon along one side of the mass of fondant and pull the far end back toward the middle. Do the same on the other side. Continue working the fondant vigorously with a sugar scraper, pulling the ends to the center until it becomes white and creamy. It will do this suddenly and become too stiff to continue working in the same way. Alternatively, work the fondant in an electric mixer with a dough hook.

If the fondant gets very hard and seems impossible to work, place a bowl over it for a few minutes, and the fondant will soften so it can be worked further. Work a piece of the fondant at a time with the fingers until smooth. Pack into an airtight container and let stand at least 1 hour and preferably 2–3 days to mellow. Fondant can be kept in an airtight container for several months.

Almond Paste Candies
(FRUITS DÉGUISÉS)

Fruits déguisés means disguised fruits and refers to all the fanciful candies made with almond paste and dried or candied fruits or nuts.

½ cup (435 g) almond paste (p. 327)
flavoring, coloring, and fruit or nuts according to
**   individual variation**
powdered sugar (for sprinkling)

For the coating:
1 cup (200 g) sugar
½ cup (125 ml) water
pinch of cream of tartar, dissolved in 1 tablespoon
**   water OR ½ teaspoon lemon juice or vinegar**

sugar thermometer—optional

paper candy cases—optional

MAKES 12 CANDIES.

Soften the almond paste by working it with the hands. Add the flavoring and coloring of the individual variation and knead on a work surface sprinkled with powdered sugar until the color is evenly distributed. Roll the paste to a smooth rope about 1 inch (2.5 cm) in diameter. Cut into ¾–1 inch (2–2.5 cm) pieces and shape according to the individual variation. The candies can be dipped immediately, or they can wait up to a day. The drier they are before dipping, the longer the coating will remain crisp.

Almond paste, colored pink, is rolled and cut for Orange Candies.

The top half of each almond paste candy is dipped in sugar syrup. On the baking sheet, from left to right: Orange Candy, Abu-Kir, Stuffed Prunes, Coffee-Walnut Candies.

For the coating: In a small heavy-bottomed pan dissolve the sugar in the water over low heat. Add the dissolved cream of tartar or lemon juice or vinegar, bring the syrup to a boil, and boil steadily to the hard-crack stage (295°F or 146°C on a sugar thermometer) or slightly beyond it to a very pale caramel. Take the pan from the heat and dip the base into warm water to stop the cooking.

Coat the top half of each candy in the cooked sugar by sticking a knife in the base of the candy to hold it, dipping it into the coating, and then pushing it off onto a slightly oiled baking sheet with another knife or other utensil, not your fingers. Leave to cool. If the almond paste was very dry before coating, the candies will keep, uncovered and in a dry place, for 8–12 hours.

Serve in paper cases or use to decorate cakes or other desserts.

Variations

STUFFED PRUNES *(Pruneaux Déguisés):*

12 prunes

Make a slit in each prune and remove the pit. Roll plain almond paste into ovals and put one in each prune. Some of the almond paste should stick out of the prune; press it against the wires of a rack to form a pattern of diagonal lines in the paste.

ORANGE CANDIES *(Bonbons à l'Orange):*

2 teaspoons Grand Marnier
few drops red food coloring
candied peel from 1 orange

large plain piping tip

Flavor the almond paste with Grand Marnier and color it pink. Using the piping tip, cut 24 rounds from the candied peel. Roll the almond paste into cylinders the same diameter as the orange peel rounds, put a round of candied peel on each end of the cylinders, and roll them again until smooth.

ABU-KIR *(Abu-Kir):*

2 teaspoons kirsch
few drops green food coloring
12 blanched whole almonds

Flavor the almond paste with kirsch and color it light green. Roll the almond paste into ovals. Cut a slit in each oval and insert a blanched almond so a crescent of almond shows above the almond paste.

COFFEE-WALNUT CANDIES *(Bonbons au Café et aux Noix):*

**½ teaspoon instant coffee, dissolved in 1 tablespoon
　　hot water
24 walnut halves**

Add just enough of the dissolved coffee to the almond paste to turn it the color of café au lait. Roll the paste into smooth balls. Press half a walnut into either side of each ball.

Almond Paste
(PÂTE D'AMANDE)

Almond paste is a basic ingredient in candy making and cake decorating. Chefs often buy it in bulk, but your own will be even better than ready-made.

**4 cups (600 g) blanched whole almonds
5 cups (1 kg) sugar
2 cups (500 ml) water**

sugar thermometer—optional

MAKES ABOUT 4 CUPS (1.75 kg) ALMOND PASTE.

In a food processor grind 1 cup (125 g) of the almonds and 2 tablespoons of the sugar to a powder. Continue in batches until all the almonds are ground.

In a heavy-bottomed pan dissolve the remaining sugar in the water over low heat. Bring to a boil and boil steadily until the sugar reaches the light-crack stage (257°F or 125°C on a sugar thermometer). Take the pan from the heat and dip the base into warm water to stop the cooking.

Slowly pour the hot syrup over the almond mixture, stirring constantly with a wooden spoon. Leave to cool. Press into a ball and wrap tightly. Almond paste can be kept, refrigerated, for several months.

Caramelized Almonds
(AMANDES CARAMELISÉES)

Ground caramelized almonds are a favorite French flavoring. In this recipe, whole ones are formed into bite-size pieces to be served as an accompaniment to ice cream or with after-dinner coffee.

**¾ cup (110 g) unblanched whole almonds
1 cup (200 g) sugar**

paper candy cases

MAKES 12–15 CARAMELIZED ALMOND CANDIES.

Oil a baking sheet. Put the almonds and sugar in a heavy-bottomed pan and heat gently until the sugar starts to melt. Continue cooking until the sugar is a medium brown caramel and the almonds pop, showing they are cooked. Dip the base of the pan in warm water to stop the cooking. Drop the mixture by teaspoonsful onto the prepared baking sheet. Leave until cold and crisp and then transfer the nuts to an airtight container, layering them with waxed paper. They can be kept for a week or more.

Serve the candies in paper cases.

Caramelized Almonds: Almonds are cooked in sugar syrup and spooned in small clumps onto a baking sheet to cool and crisp.

THE
FRENCH
TOUCH

SOUPE BRETONNE
One of the many versions of Breton cotriade, this soup is among the richest, made
of both firm-fleshed white fish and oily fish, sorrel, mussels, and heavy cream. The heart-
shaped croûtons are fried in a mixture of butter and oil.

Soups

ENGLISH VOCABULARY is inadequate to describe the French family of soups. In French, *soupe* is only a small part of the story, referring to a hearty vegetable mixture, which with the addition of meat or fish often develops into a kind of stew as in a Breton *cotriade*, or fish soup. At the other end of the scale come the consommés (see Chapter 11), delicate shimmering liquids whose brilliance delights the eye at the opening of a formal meal. In between are the purée soups, crèmes, veloutés, and potages that are the standard start to a traditional dinner.

They are standard with good reason. Without filling, they prepare the appetite and the palate for what's to come. Grimod de la Reynière, writing at the turn of the nineteenth century, likened the role of soups to that of the overture to an opera: ". . . they must be devised in such a manner as to set the tone of the whole banquet." Certainly the range of soups offers plenty of choice. Most popular are the purées of vegetables—green vegetables such as lettuce, root vegetables such as carrots, dried vegetables and even nuts mixed with stock, milk, or just their own cooking liquid. I've had a delicious soup based on artichokes mixed with hazelnuts, and a chestnut soup made by simmering fresh chestnuts in milk before puréeing them is one of the very best.

Potatoes or rice are usually added to thicken purée soups, unless a starchy vegetable is the base of the soup, and they give flavor as well as texture. The crèmes and veloutés, on the other hand, are always based on a butter and flour roux. The two are differentiated only by their final enrichments: crèmes, naturally enough, receive cream, but a vital ingredient of the classic veloutés, helping to earn them their name "velvety," is a liaison of cream and egg yolks, which thickens as well as enriches the soup just before serving. Strictly speaking a potage, though the term is often applied rather loosely to almost any soup, is a combination of classic possibilities—either a blend of two completely prepared soups, such as a purée of watercress mixed with a chicken velouté, or a mixture of ideas, such as a purée of carrot thickened as usual with potato or rice but finished as a velouté with cream and egg yolks.

Splendidly rich and satisfying, these soups are currently out of fashion, for they run counter to the new movement toward lighter, flourless cooking and minimal use of starchy vegetables. But whenever a velouté soup appears on the La Varenne table, to the murmurs of student appreciation, Chef Chambrette and I wink at each other. Cooks who insist on sticking strictly to nouvelle cuisine don't know what they're missing.

Just recently, avant-garde chefs have been exploring fruit soups—a field hitherto dominated by the Scandinavians. A few tart fruit combinations appear on nouvelle menus as first courses, but most are intended for dessert, like fresh peach soup or a soup of four fruits flavored with mint. They certainly make a change, but fruit soups recall the nursery too much for my taste.

One type of soup survives all the vagaries of fashion, and I'm not surprised—the shellfish bisque. The cooking principles for bisque have remained unchanged for two hundred years: the shellfish (lobster, shrimp, crab, or crayfish) is sautéed in its shell in butter with a *mirepoix* of vegetables. After brief cooking in cognac and wine, stock is added and the shellfish is simmered until tender. The meat is then extracted from the shells and puréed with the stock and vegetables. The soup is thickened with rice, making it a type of purée soup. Nothing goes to waste, for the shells are pounded with fresh butter and then strained to make shellfish butter, which is stirred into the bisque just before serving. A good bisque will vary from rose to a deep rust-red depending on the type of shellfish. It should be full-bodied from the amount of shellfish used and thick without being heavy. No wonder a fine bisque is rare—it demands expensive ingredients and a master hand.

And indeed in all soups the freshness of ingredients is important. What travesties have been committed in a soup pot with the good intention of using up leftovers. *"Mange ta soupe, chérie,"* still echoes in my ears from the year I lived with a couple and their six small children, who, poor things, were served a watery vegetable concoction five nights out of seven (meat in the evening being considered bad for infant digestion). Coming, as it does on adult tables, at the opening of a meal, a soup must sharpen, not dull, the appetite. And it should raise rather than dash expectations.

FOR SUCCESSFUL SOUPS

1. For a first course, allow at least ¾ cup (185 ml) soup per person and about double that for a main course soup.

2. Don't hestitate to improve virtually any soup as a French chef would, with generous measures of cream and butter stirred in at the last moment.

3. Fortified wines like Madeira and sherry should be added just before serving so they do not evaporate.

4. Croûtons are the most popular accompaniment to soups. When fried in butter, croûtons have a better flavor but do not stay crisp as long as when fried in oil. A mixture of the two is a good compromise. So they remain crisp, croûtons are never mixed into the soup, but passed in a separate bowl for guests to help themselves.

PREPARING AHEAD

1. Many soups can be cooked and puréed ahead of time and reheated just before serving. However, an egg yolk and cream liaison must be added at the last minute. Cream, fresh herbs, and butter also are best added when the soup is reheated so the flavors are fresh.

2. Vegetable, meat, and poultry soups can be stored, covered and refrigerated, up to two days. Shellfish bisques should be kept no more than one day.

3. Roux-thickened soups freeze well. Potato and rice-thickened mixtures tend to separate on thawing but can usually be reemulsified in the blender.

4. Croûtons for garnishing soup can be prepared ahead and reheated in a 250°F (120°C) oven.

Purée Crécy
(PURÉE CRÉCY)

Some say the name for this soup comes from the town of Crécy in the Ile de France region, known for its sweet and tender carrots, and others prefer the explanation that carrot soup was all the poor people in a different Crécy in the north of France had left to eat after the bloody battle of 1346 destroyed their town.

    4 tablespoons (60 g) butter
    5–6 medium carrots, chopped
    1 medium onion, chopped
    salt
    pinch of sugar
    4–4½ cups (1–1.10 L) beef (p. 118) or chicken stock
        (p. 115)
    5 tablespoons (65 g) rice

For the croûtons:
    3 tablespoons oil
    3 tablespoons (45 g) butter
    4 slices firm white bread with crusts removed, diced

SERVES 4–6.

    In a heavy-bottomed pan melt 2 tablespoons (30 g) of the butter and add the carrots, onion, salt, and sugar. Cover and cook over low heat until the butter is absorbed and the vegetables begin to soften, 5–7 minutes. Add 4 cups (1 L) of the stock and the rice, bring to a boil, cover, and then simmer until the rice is tender, 25–30 minutes. Purée the soup in a blender or food processor or work it through a sieve. Return it to the pan, bring just to a boil, and add more stock, if necessary, to make the soup the consistency of thin cream. The soup can be prepared ahead to this point and kept, covered and refrigerated, for up to 2 days.

    For the croûtons: Heat the oil in a frying pan, add the butter, and when it is hot, fry the diced bread until golden brown. Drain on paper towels.

    To finish: Bring the soup just to a boil, take from the heat, and stir in the remaining 2 tablespoons (30 g) butter, a small piece at a time. Taste for seasoning and add salt if needed.

    Ladle the soup into bowls and serve. Pass the croûtons separately.

Cream of Lettuce Soup
(CRÈME DE LAITUE)

Be sure to use a flavorful lettuce, such as romaine, for this soup.

    2 pounds (1 kg) leaf lettuce
    3 tablespoons (45 g) butter
    salt and pepper
    pinch of sugar
    béchamel made with 4–4½ cups (1–1.10 L) milk, a slice
        of onion, 1 bay leaf, 6 peppercorns, salt and pepper,
        nutmeg, 4 tablespoons (60 g) butter, and ¼ cup (30 g)
        flour
    ½ cup (125 ml) heavy cream

For the croûtons:
   3 tablespoons oil
   3 tablespoons (45 g) butter
   4 slices firm white bread with crust removed, diced

SERVES 4–6.

Remove any withered leaves and wash the lettuce thoroughly. Blanch the lettuce by placing in a large quantity of boiling salted water and bringing just back to a boil. Drain, refresh under cold running water, remove tough bases, and squeeze excess liquid from the leaves. Cut the lettuce into strips.

In a heavy-bottomed pan melt the butter, add the lettuce strips, salt, pepper, and sugar, and cook over medium heat, stirring often, until the lettuce is fairly dry, about 5 minutes. Make the béchamel with 4 cups (1 L) milk, add the lettuce, and simmer, stirring occasionally, about 20 minutes. Purée the soup in a blender or food processor. Return the soup to the pan, heat just to a boil, and, if necessary, add enough of the extra ½ cup (125 ml) milk to make the soup the consistency of thin cream. The soup can be prepared ahead to this point and kept, covered and refrigerated, for up to 2 days.

For the croûtons: Heat the oil in a frying pan, add the butter, and when it is hot, fry the diced bread until golden brown. Drain on paper towels.

To finish: Add the cream to the soup and bring just to a boil. Taste for seasoning and adjust if necessary.

Ladle the soup into bowls and serve. Pass the croûtons separately.

Parsley Velouté
(VELOUTÉ DE PERSIL)

Parsley, used so much as a garnish, is neglected as a flavoring. For this soup, it is the main ingredient.

   thin velouté (p. 193) made with 4–4½ cups (1–1.10 L)
       chicken stock, 4 tablespoons (60 g) butter, ¼ cup (30
       g) flour, and salt and pepper
   2 cups (125 g) chopped parsley
   3 egg yolks
   ½ cup (125 ml) heavy cream
   salt and pepper
   2 tablespoons (30 g) butter

SERVES 4–6.

Make the velouté with 4 cups (1 L) of the stock, add the parsley, and simmer 10 minutes. Purée in a blender or food processor or work it through a sieve. Add the extra ½ cup (125 ml) chicken stock, if necessary, to make the velouté the consistency of thin cream. The soup can be kept at this point, covered and refrigerated, for up to 2 days.

To finish: Bring the soup back to a boil. Mix the egg yolks and ½ cup (125 ml) of the heavy cream in a bowl, stir in a little of the hot soup, and then stir this mixture back into the remaining soup. Heat gently, stirring, until the soup thickens slightly. (NOTE: Do not boil or it will curdle.) Taste for seasoning and adjust, if necessary. Take the soup from the heat and stir in the butter, a small piece at a time.

Ladle the soup into bowls and serve.

Potage Olga
(POTAGE OLGA)

Potato and onion soup is common in France, but this version with the flavor of raw mushrooms and the addition of egg yolks and cream is unusual.

3 tablespoons (45 g) butter
1 large onion, chopped
1 large potato, thinly sliced
1 quart (1 L) milk
salt and pepper
bay leaf
¼ pound (125 g) mushrooms
12–18 watercress leaves (for garnish)
2 egg yolks
½ cup (125 ml) heavy cream

SERVES 4–6.

Melt the butter in a heavy-bottomed saucepan over medium heat, add the onion, and sauté until soft but not brown, about 7–10 minutes. Add the potato slices and press a piece of foil on top of them. Cover with a lid and cook over low heat, stirring occasionally, until the potato slices are very soft, about 20 minutes. Stir in the milk, salt and pepper, and bay leaf, bring to a boil, and simmer for 10 minutes. (NOTE: Don't let the soup boil hard, or it may separate.)

Discard the bay leaf and purée the soup in a blender or food processor or work it through a sieve. The soup can be prepared ahead to this point and kept, covered and refrigerated, for up to 2 days.

To finish: Purée the mushrooms and keep covered to prevent discoloration. Blanch the watercress leaves in boiling water for 1 minute and refresh with cold water. Bring the soup just to a boil. Mix the egg yolks with the cream, stir in a little of the hot soup, and then stir this mixture into the remaining soup. Heat gently, stirring, until the soup thickens slightly. (NOTE: Do not boil or it will curdle.) Strain the soup through a fine sieve and then add the mushroom purée. Taste for seasoning and adjust if necessary.

Ladle the soup into bowls and float the watercress leaves on the surface.

Cover the potato and onion with foil and then with a lid to cook them in butter with no liquid added.

Lobster Bisque
(BISQUE DE HOMARD)

This classic bisque recipe can be applied to other shellfish besides lobster, such as shrimp or crab.

1¼–1½ pound (625–750 g) lobster
6 tablespoons (95 g) butter
1 small carrot, chopped
1 small onion, chopped
1 bouquet garni (p. 118)
½ cup (125 ml) white wine
2 tablespoons brandy
5 cups (1.25 L) veal stock (p. 116)
2 tablespoons (25 g) rice
salt and pepper
pinch of cayenne pepper
2 tablespoons sherry or Madeira
3 tablespoons heavy cream

For the croûtons:
3 tablespoons oil
3 tablespoons (45 g) butter
4 slices firm white bread with crusts removed, diced

large mortar and pestle

SERVES 4–6.

To prepare the lobster: Lay it flat on a board, right side up, with the head facing to the right and tail to the left. Cover the tail with a towel, hold the lobster firmly behind the head with your left hand, and with the point of a sharp knife, pierce down to the board through the cross mark on the center of the head. The lobster is killed at once. Continue splitting the lobster body as far as the tail and then cut the tail from the body in one piece. Discard the head sac and intestinal tract. Scoop out the soft tomalley and any coral from the body of the lobster and reserve. Crack the claws.

Melt 2 tablespoons (30 g) of the butter in a large saucepan and add the carrot, onion, and bouquet garni. Cover and cook over low heat until the vegetables are soft, 7–10 minutes. Add the lobster and cook over high heat, stirring occasionally, until the shell begins to turn red. Add the wine and brandy and boil until reduced by one third. Moisten with 1 cup (250 ml) of the stock and simmer 10 minutes. Leave to cool slightly. Lift out the lobster, extract the meat, and reserve the shells. Return the lobster meat to the wine and vegetable mixture and add the remaining stock, rice, and salt and pepper and cayenne. Cover and simmer 15–20 minutes.

Pound the lobster shells with the remaining 4 tablespoons (60 g) of the butter in a large mortar with a pestle, breaking them up as much as possible. This can also be done in a food mill if you eliminate the hardest claw shells. Then work the mixture in a sieve to extract the lobster butter.

Discard the bouquet garni and purée the soup in a blender or a food processor or force it through a sieve. The bisque can be prepared up to a day ahead.

For the croûtons: Heat the oil in a frying pan, add the butter, and when it is hot, fry the diced bread until golden brown. Drain on paper towels.

To finish: Bring the soup just to a boil, add the sherry or Madeira and cream and simmer 2 minutes. Take the soup from the heat and stir in the lobster butter, a small piece at a time. Taste for seasoning and adjust if necessary.

Ladle the soup into bowls and serve. Pass the croûtons separately.

Position of the knife to kill the lobster instantly

Most of the lobster shell can be crushed in a food mill.

Autumn Soup
(SOUPE D'AUTOMNE)

Antonin Carême, the nineteenth-century French chef best known for his decorative pièces montées, also developed several hundred recipes for soup, including soupe d'automne.

> **white part of 2 small leeks**
> **¼ head romaine lettuce**
> **1 quart (1 L) chicken (p. 115) or veal stock (p. 116)**
> **leaves of 1 celery heart, chopped**
> **½ cup (75 g) uncooked green peas**
> **pinch of sugar**
> **salt and pepper**

SERVES 4–6.

Wash and drain the leeks and lettuce and cut them into julienne strips. Bring the stock to a boil and add the leek and lettuce strips, chopped celery leaves, peas, sugar, and salt and pepper. Simmer, uncovered, until the vegetables are tender, 15–20 minutes. Taste the soup for seasoning and add more salt and pepper if needed. The soup can be prepared up to 2 days ahead.

To serve, reheat the soup, if necessary, and ladle into bowls.

Preparation of Carême's Soupe d'Automne

Brittany Fish Soup
(SOUPE BRETONNE)

You can substitute other fish for the mackerel and whiting in this hearty fish soup; just be sure to use one fat fish and one lean variety. The soup is a meal in itself.

> **1 quart (1 L) mussels**
> **1 pound (500 g) mackerel**
> **1 pound (500 g) whiting**
> **fish stock (p. 115) made with 1 sliced onion, 1 tablespoon (15 g) butter, the heads and bones of the whiting, 1 quart (1 L) water, 10 peppercorns, and a bouquet garni (p. 118)**
> **½ pound (250 g) fresh sorrel OR 4 ounces (125 ml) canned sorrel**
> **2–4 tablespoons (30–60 g) butter**
> **3 onions, chopped**
> **4 small potatoes**
> **½ cup (125 ml) white wine**
> **¾ cup (185 ml) heavy cream**
> **salt and pepper**

For the croûtons:
> **12 slices firm white bread**
> **6 tablespoons oil**
> **6 tablespoons (95 g) butter**

SERVES 4–6.

Clean the mussels well. Cut the fish into chunks and use the heads and tails of the whiting to make the fish stock. If using fresh sorrel, pull off the stems, wash the leaves, and cook them in 2 tablespoons (30 g) of the butter until very soft, about 15 minutes. Drain canned sorrel.

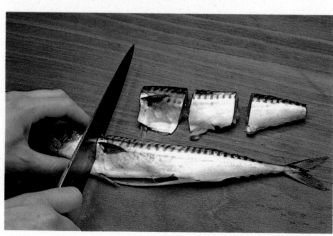

The cleaned fish are cut into chunks; discard the head and tail of the mackerel.

For the croûtons: From each slice of bread, cut a heart shape. Heat the oil in a sauté pan, add the butter, and when it is hot, fry the bread cutouts on each side until golden brown. Drain on paper towels.

Heat 2 tablespoons (30 g) of the butter in a large saucepan, add the chopped onions and cook slowly until soft but not brown, 7–10 minutes. Cut the potatoes in half and then into thin slices. Add the fish stock and potatoes to the pan and simmer for 5 minutes.

Add the wine and the pieces of fish and continue simmering until the fish is just barely done, about 5 minutes. Add the sorrel, the mussels, and the cream, and simmer until the mussels open. Taste for seasoning and adjust if necessary.

Serve the soup and pass the croûtons separately.

Salads

IN THE OLD DAYS, salads were not thought of as being typically French. In France *raw* (*cru*) tends to be equated with *crude*—the horror of any well-trained chef, and until a few years ago, salads suffered benign neglect. The South of France was an exception; there one could rely on a cornucopia of vegetable salads, both fresh and cooked. On the whole, however, *salade* meant green salad tossed in vinaigrette and served after the main course to brace the digestion for the onslaught of cheese and dessert.

Now all is changed, thanks to nouvelle cuisine. Young chefs give pride of place to their first course salads, with names like *salade folle, salade fantaisie, salade volcan*—that are as fanciful as the mixture of ingredients. Among the three-star chefs, Michel Guérard combines smoked salmon and sturgeon with a julienne of vegetables, avocado, and fresh ginger. Roger Vergé mixes wild mushrooms and quail with a vinaigrette of olive oil. The Troisgros brothers toss freshly sautéed foie gras and spinach leaves in a light version of mayonnaise. Perhaps the most imitated conceit is Jean Delaveyne's creation of fois gras, truffle, crayfish, and artichoke bottoms in vinaigrette, now proffered in restaurants the length and breadth of France from Provence to Picardy.

The temperature—hot, cold, or tepid at which a salad is served—is now up to the chef; hot and cold ingredients are even mixed on the same plate. Recently in a leading Paris restaurant, I had a salad of warm sweetbreads and cold oranges, which, despite my misgivings, proved to be delicious. But in trying these different ideas, chefs are conscious that the old rules were not invented without reason. Color, texture, and flavor are still the three criteria by which a salad (or any dish) is ultimately judged.

Contrast of color has always been an outstanding attribute of a good salad, as witness the two standbys of vegetable macédoine

SALADE DE TOMATES FARCIES AUX GOUJONETTES DE POISSON
The fish and tomato are dressed with a light herbed mayonnaise, the
green beans with a vinaigrette, and shrimp are the final garnish.

POIREAUX VINAIGRETTE (center)
A French household classic, with a mustard-flavored vinaigrette,
garnished with the yolks and whites of hard-boiled eggs

(multicolored dice of carrot, green peas, green beans, and turnip) and rice salad, with its cheerful potpourri of tomato, carrot, and green and red peppers against a snowy background. Now eye-catching salads often take an Oriental turn with meticulous arrangements of ingredients, sliced, diced, or cut in julienne and set off by sprigs of a carefully selected herb.

The French have tended to be rather less careful about the textures of their salads than their appearance, but the current fashion for new combinations of ingredients is helping here. Soft sweetbreads or chicken livers are combined with crisp greens, for example, and more use is being made of croûtons and nuts to add contrasting texture.

The remaining characteristic of a good salad, flavor, depends on two elements: the ingredients and the dressing that binds them. Bind is perhaps the wrong word, for nowadays lighter and lighter dressings are favored, and mayonnaise is less used than heretofore. Attention is thus focused on the type of oil or vinegar, and there is great play on nut oils, olive oil, and on sherry and fruit vinegars. The dressings must be suited to the ingredients they marry: strong flavors like those of meats, root vegetables, and peppery watercress can take a piquant sauce; whereas chicken, fish, and the more delicate vegetables need lighter seasoning. Almost as important are the little touches that give a salad character—the herbs, chopped shallots, the spoon of caviar, and the ever-present truffle, whose popularity never wanes despite its astronomic price.

The cardinal principles of color, texture, and flavor apply equally to the simplest salad of all—the green salad. The La Varenne chefs and I will never agree on one thing that affects texture. While they leave greens at room temperature, I think an hour or two in the refrigerator crisps them without affecting the flavor. And, to my dismay, they insist on leaving even the largest lettuce leaves whole, for cramming into one's mouth only at the peril of makeup and clothes. For their part, they regard my habit of tearing leaves into handy-sized pieces as equally uncouth.

On the question of dressing, thank goodness, we are united. A good dressing for greens, as for any salad, is one that brings out the flavor of the ingredients it accompanies without overwhelming them. It is unobtrusive without being bland and clings to salad leaves without being heavy. Certainly vinaigrette causes more discussion at La Varenne than almost anything else. Each day we use the same oil, vinegar, and seasonings (mustard, salt, pepper, sometimes a little garlic) and one member of the lettuce family or another; yet each day the salad is different, the personal creation of the student who made it. Nothing shows more clearly the difference in individual taste.

Mixing the salad greens with the dressing must be done just before serving. At La Varenne the student responsible for the green salad jumps up from the table while everyone is finishing the main course, adds the vinaigrette to the leaves, and tosses them well. Since the leaves wilt slightly as they absorb the dressing (the French call this reaction *fatiguer*—to tire), the salad is served at once because the leaves would become unpleasantly soggy within the hour.

Perhaps the most satisfying salads are neither old nor new and abide by only the most general rules. They are what I call household salads—the kind Chef Chambrette concocts for Saturday lunch at the cooking school when he wants to find a tidy refrigerator on Monday morning. There are certain recognized combinations like *salade parisienne* (beef in vinaigrette, often with potatoes) and *salade normande* (potatoes, with celery, ham, and a cream dressing), but most have a handful of this, pinch of that, and above all, a generous helping of imagination.

FOR SUCCESSFUL SALADS

1. Make sure all raw ingredients are thoroughly washed—nothing is worse than a gritty salad.

2. Taste constantly, particularly if changing the proportions of ingredients or using unfamiliar oil or vinegar.

3. Whenever possible, toss a salad with the dressing; this coats the salad more evenly than simply spooning the dressing over it.

4. To keep the serving bowl clean, toss the salad separately in a large bowl.

Lettuce must not only be thoroughly washed but also perfectly dried. For generations, French housewives have briskly shaken lettuce in a salad basket outside the kitchen door or patted every leaf dry in a towel. The modern salad spinner is a labor-saving device that deserves a gastronomique prize.

PREPARING AHEAD

1. All salads spoil more quickly when mixed with dressing. Prepare ingredients and dressing separately and mix them just before serving.

2. Salads dressed with vinaigrette can keep for twelve hours or so if the ingredients are robust, such as cold meat. However, the more delicate the ingredients, the shorter the time they can be kept already dressed.

3. Salads made ahead should be kept and served at room temperature.

VINAIGRETTE

1. The oil for a vinaigrette can be peanut (agreeably light), olive (rich and unmistakable in flavor), walnut (if you like walnuts), corn, sunflower, soybean (innocuous), or a novelty such as grape-seed oil.

2. The vinegar can be made from wine (red or white), sherry or Champagne (very fashionable), cider (low acidity), or fruits such as raspberry or cherry (for special effects). For a Mediterranean flavor, substitute lemon juice for the vinegar.

3. The dressing can be flavored with shallots, garlic (reserve this for strong-flavored ingredients), or fresh herbs. Salt and freshly ground black pepper are indispensable, and chefs usually include a teaspoon of mustard to help emulsify the mixture.

4. The standard proportion for vinaigrette is one part vinegar to three parts oil, but this can vary, depending on the kind of oil and type of vinegar used, the ingredients they are to dress, and the preference of the cook.

MAYONNAISE

1. Have all ingredients at room temperature or even lukewarm.

2. Use a balloon whisk for beating in the oil.

3. The bowl should have a small base so each stroke of the whisk reaches a large part of the mixture.

4. Do not add the oil too quickly, particularly at the beginning of mixing, or the mayonnaise may separate.

5. If too much oil is added, the mayonnaise will become very stiff and finally will separate. On the other hand, if not enough oil is added, the mayonnaise will be thin and will taste of raw egg. The egg is primarily a binding agent, and its flavor should not overpower that of the oil.

6. **If the mayonnaise does separate, there are several ways to save it. In a warm bowl whisk the curdled mixture drop by drop into any of the following:**

> **a. a few drops of warm water**
> **b. a few drops of vinegar**
> **c. a little mustard**
> **d. another egg yolk**

7. **Chefs do not advise chilling mayonnaise because the oil can congeal and separate from the sauce. However, if kept in the least cold spot of the refrigerator and allowed to return to room temperature before it is stirred, it usually survives.**

Zucchini Salad
(SALADE DE COURGETTES)

The inspiration for this salad comes from Maestro Martino, who was cook to the Renaissance cardinal Ludovico Trevisan, known because of his extravagance as the Lucullan cardinal. Martino was very keen on vegetable recipes— a clear break with the past when vegetables were the food of the poor.

> **1 pound (500 g) small zucchini**
> **¼ cup olive oil**
> **2 shallots, finely chopped**
> **salt and pepper**
> **½ teaspoon sugar**
> **1 tablespoon chopped basil or other fresh herb**
> **2 tablespoons white wine vinegar**

SERVES 4.

Wash the zucchini and cut them into thin slices. In a frying pan heat the oil. Add the shallots and zucchini and cook over low heat, stirring occasionally, for 5 minutes. Add the rest of the ingredients and continue cooking until the zucchini are just tender but not brown, about 5 more minutes. Taste for seasoning and adjust if necessary.

Transfer to a salad bowl or individual plates and serve at room temperature or chilled. The salad can be kept a day, covered and refrigerated.

Leeks Vinaigrette
(POIREAUX VINAIGRETTE)

Lightness, fresh flavor, and low price make leeks vinaigrette one of the most popular first courses in France, both at home and in restaurants.

> **1½ pounds (750 g) leeks**
> **½ cup (125 ml) vinaigrette (below)**
> **2 medium shallots, very finely chopped**
> **1 tablespoon chopped parsley**
> **2 hard-boiled eggs**

SERVES 4.

Trim the leeks so they are about 5 inches (13 cm) long, split them twice lengthwise down to but not through the white bulb, and wash thoroughly. Cook in boiling salted water until tender, 8–12 minutes. Drain thoroughly. The leeks can be cooked 6–8 hours ahead and kept covered, at room temperature.

Make the vinaigrette and add the shallots and parsley. Chop or sieve the egg whites and yolks separately. Arrange the leeks crosswise on a platter, spoon the vinaigrette over them, and put the egg whites in a row down the green ends of the leeks and the yolks along the white bulbs. Serve at room temperature.

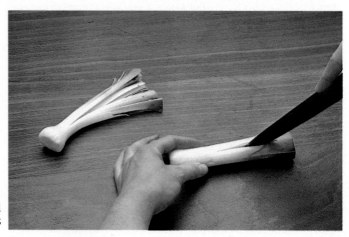

Slitting leeks so that all the sand can be washed out

Vinaigrette
(VINAIGRETTE)

Four men, say the French, are needed for a good vinaigrette: a spendthrift for the oil, a miser for the vinegar, a wise man for the salt, and a madman for the pepper.

2 tablespoons white wine vinegar
salt and pepper
1 teaspoon Dijon mustard
6 tablespoons oil

MAKES ½ CUP (125 ml) VINAIGRETTE.

Whisk the vinegar with salt and pepper and the mustard to make a smooth paste. Whisk in the oil, little by little, so that a thick emulsion is formed. The dressing may separate on standing; whisk to reemulsify.

Green Salad with Chicken Livers
(SALADE AUX FOIES DE VOLAILLE)

This salad, suitable for any tough-leaved greens, is served lukewarm as a first course.

1 head of escarole or curly endive OR 1 pound (500 g)
   dandelion leaves
½ cup (125 ml) vinaigrette (p. 348)
2 tablespoons oil
8 chicken livers
salt and pepper
2 tablespoons wine vinegar

SERVES 4.

Trim and wash the greens, dry thoroughly, and put in a bowl. Make the vinaigrette and a short time before serving toss the greens with the vinaigrette.

Just before serving, heat the oil in a frying pan until very hot. Season the livers with salt and pepper, add to the hot oil, and sauté over very high heat 1–2 minutes on each side until well browned on the outside but still pink inside. Remove with a slotted spoon, slice, and put on the greens. Discard any fat remaining in the pan and add the vinegar. Bring to a boil, scraping up any bits clinging to the pan with a wooden spoon, pour the hot vinegar over the salad, and mix well. Transfer to individual plates and serve immediately.

Artichoke Bottoms Filled with Vegetable Macédoine
(SALADE DE FONDS D'ARTICHAUTS FARCIS À LA MACÉDOINE)

The carrots, turnips, and beans in a macédoine should be cut into small even-sized cubes, all the same size as the peas.

> **1½ lemons**
> **4 large artichokes**
> **1 tablespoon chopped chervil or parsley**

For the macédoine:
> **1 medium carrot, cut into ⅜-inch (1 cm) dice**
> **1 medium turnip, cut into ⅜-inch (1 cm) dice**
> **½ cup shelled peas**
> **½ cup green beans, cut in ⅜-inch (1 cm) lengths**
> **⅓–½ cup (80–125 ml) mayonnaise (p. 351)**
> **salt and pepper**

SERVES 4.

Bring a large pan of water to a boil. Add salt and squeeze in the juice of ½ lemon. Add the juice of another ½ lemon to a bowl of cold water. Break off the stem from the first artichoke. Using a very sharp knife and holding it against the side of the artichoke, cut off all the large bottom leaves, leaving a soft cone of small leaves in the center. Trim this cone level with the top of the artichoke base. Rub the base well with a lemon half to prevent discoloration. Trim the base to an even round shape, slightly flattened on the bottom, and bevel the top edge. Rub again with cut lemon and drop into the bowl of cold lemon water. When all are prepared, drain them, drop them into the boiling water, and simmer until tender, 15–20 minutes. Drain and scoop out the choke with a teaspoon and set aside to cool.

Preparing artichoke bases: Break off the stem.

Cut off all the large bottom leaves, leaving a cone of the smaller center leaves.

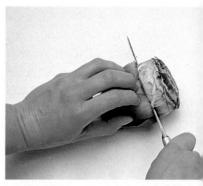

Cut off the cone of leaves at the top of the artichoke base.

Trim the base to an even round shape and bevel the top edge.

After cooking, remove the choke with a teaspoon.

For the macédoine: Put the chopped carrot and turnip in a pan of cold salted water. Cover, boil until just tender, 10–12 minutes, and drain. Drop the peas and green beans into a pan of boiling salted water and cook until just tender, 5–8 minutes. Drain, rinse in cold water, and drain thoroughly. Let the vegetables cool slightly. Make the mayonnaise. While the vegetables are still warm, toss them with the mayonnaise. Taste for seasoning, adjust if necessary, and set aside to cool.

When all the vegetables are cool, fill each artichoke base with macédoine, mounding the vegetables well. Arrange on a platter or on individual plates, sprinkle with the chopped chervil or parsley, and serve.

Mayonnaise
(MAYONNAISE)

La Varenne chefs usually add mustard to the egg yolks before beating in the oil because it not only adds flavor but also helps to emulsify the sauce.

1 egg yolk
salt and white pepper
2–3 teaspoons white wine vinegar or lemon juice
¼ teaspoon Dijon mustard, or to taste—optional
¾ cup (185 ml) oil

MAKES ABOUT ¾ CUP (185 ml) MAYONNAISE.

Using a whisk or an electric beater, beat the egg yolk in a small bowl with a little salt and pepper, 2 teaspoons of the vinegar or lemon juice, and the mustard until thick. Add the oil drop by drop, whisking constantly. When 2 tablespoons of the oil have been added, the mixture should be very thick. The remaining oil can be added a little more quickly, either 1 tablespoon at a time, thoroughly beating between each addition until it is absorbed, or in a thin steady stream.

When all the oil has been added, stir in the remaining vinegar or lemon juice to taste and more mustard and salt and pepper as needed. If necessary, thin the mayonnaise with a little warm water. Mayonnaise is best eaten within a few hours and never refrigerated. But if it is stored in the refrigerator, it can be kept up to 3 days. To avoid separation, bring it to room temperature before stirring.

Stuffed Tomato Salad with Fish Goujonettes
(SALADE DE TOMATES FARCIES AUX GOUJONETTES DE POISSON)

This first-course salad is typical of nouvelle cuisine: bright colors, an offbeat combination of flavors, and a careful arrangement of the various elements.

> **4 large tomatoes**
> **12–16 large shrimps, cooked and peeled but with the heads and tails left on**
> **2 flounder or other white fish fillets (about 10 ounces or 300 g)**
> **12 lettuce leaves**
> **1 teaspoon chopped chervil or parsley**
> **1 teaspoon chopped tarragon**

For the green bean salad:
> **¼ cup (60 ml) vinaigrette (p. 348)**
> **½ pound (250 g) green beans**

For the mayonnaise dressing:
> **mayonnaise (p. 351) made with 1 egg yolk, salt and pepper, 1 tablespoon lemon juice, ¼ teaspoon mustard, ¼ cup (60 ml) vegetable oil, and ½ cup (125 ml) olive oil**
> **2 tablespoons grapefruit juice**
> **1 tablespoon tomato ketchup**
> **1 teaspoon chopped chervil or parsley**
> **1 teaspoon chopped tarragon**

SERVES 4.

Cut the top off each tomato about a quarter of the way down and remove the seeds with a teaspoon. Sprinkle the shells with salt, turn upside down, and leave to drain.

For the green bean salad: Make the vinaigrette. Cook the green beans in a large pan of boiling salted water until barely tender, 5–7 minutes. Drain, refresh under cold water, and drain thoroughly. Toss the beans in the vinaigrette, taste for seasoning, and adjust if necessary.

For the mayonnaise dressing: Make the mayonnaise. Stir in the grapefruit juice, ketchup, chervil or parsley, and tarragon. Taste for seasoning and adjust if necessary.

Cut the fish fillets in ½-inch (1.25 cm) diagonal strips and poach them in simmering salted water just until the flesh can be pierced easily, 2–3 minutes. The strips should still be quite firm so they won't break when mixed with the dressing. Drain on paper towels and leave to cool. When cool, gently toss the strips of fish in the mayonnaise dressing.

To assemble: Place the strips of fish standing up inside the tomatoes and sprinkle with the chopped chervil or parsley and tarragon. Arrange the lettuce leaves on individual plates, put a stuffed tomato in the center of each, and garnish with the shrimps. Arrange the green bean salad in a wreath around each tomato and serve.

Beef Salad Parisienne
(SALADE DE BOEUF À LA PARISIENNE)

Traditionally, this hearty salad is made with the leftovers of a pot-au-feu. Any braised beef will do, and it can even be made with leftover roast beef.

1½ pounds (750 g) potatoes
¾ cup (185 ml) vinaigrette (p. 348)
2 shallots, finely chopped
2 tablespoons chopped parsley
1½ tablespoons chopped capers
1½ tablespoons chopped gherkins
1 clove garlic, very finely chopped
**1½ pounds (750 g) braised beef, cut in ⅜-inch (1 cm)
  slices**
3 hard-boiled eggs, quartered
3 medium tomatoes, peeled and quartered

SERVES 4.

Put the potatoes, unpeeled, in cold salted water, cover, and bring to a boil. Simmer until just tender, 15–20 minutes, and drain. Make the vinaigrette, stir in the shallots, parsley, capers, gherkins, and garlic. Peel the potatoes while still warm and cut them in ⅜-inch (1 cm) slices. Arrange the potato and beef slices in layers in a salad bowl, spooning a little of the vinaigrette mixture over each layer. Cover and refrigerate at least 2 hours and up to 12 hours so the flavors mellow.

A short time before serving, arrange the eggs and tomatoes around the edge.

First Course
Vegetables

ON A SUMMER DAY at Paris's famous market on the rue Mouffetard, it's the vegetables that steal the show. The first really red and juicy tomatoes flirt with huge globe-shaped Breton artichokes, while burgundy-colored eggplants, feather-leaved bulbs of fennel, and glossy red and green peppers play the chorus. There are small zucchini and baby carrots in the wings and leeks, fresh garlic, and four or five varieties of lettuce to act as understudies. Stretching from the Mediterranean to the Channel, France has a profusion of vegetables matched by no other European country, and the French treat these riches with respect. Each region has specialties based on the local produce. Dried beans are as evocative of Brittany as cabbage is of Picardy and wild mushrooms of the Alps. In cooking parlance, *lyonnaise* means with onions and *à l'alsacienne* denotes sauerkraut.

Provence is the luckiest region of all. Its bountiful and lengthy growing season helped create dishes like stuffed peppers, ratatouille, and pissaladière (p. 267), which have traveled throughout France along with the vegetables that Provence supplies to the rest of the country. Eggplants, tomatoes, onions, garlic, peppers—these all take kindly to the slow long cooking that fosters the melting texture and full flavor of such regional dishes.

Now this traditional repertoire is widening further. New menus offer more and more vegetable dishes as first courses rather than confining them to their conventional role as accompaniments to the main course. In classic haute cuisine, vegetables are served as a separate course only occasionally, for instance in the spring when

354

tiny new peas would be cooked with baby onions and lettuce and served on their own. Even when there is a vegetable course, however, it is generally tucked into the progression of a many-course meal rather than being elevated to the position of one of the three basic courses that form even a simple French dinner—appetizer, main course, and dessert.

In the new cuisine's first-course vegetable dishes, unusual combinations or treatments are featured, such as warm cucumbers filled with mushrooms. Asparagus is served in thin feuilletés with a butter sauce. Another idea is based on the deep pies called *tourtes:* the nouvelle cuisine version substitutes vegetables for the meat or fish and cabbage leaves for the pastry.

Vegetable tarts continue to be popular—with a few changes of course. Traditional tarts are baked in a pie-pastry shell and often include starchy vegetables such as potatoes, or the filling might be thickened with rice as in our zucchini tart, or bound with a sauce. Nouvelle cuisine chefs, who eschew starch insofar as is possible, wouldn't touch a grain of rice and opt instead for light vegetables and, in the tomato tart recipe in this chapter for instance, an egg-and-cream quiche mixture rather than any flour-thickened sauce to bind the vegetables together. Instead of pie pastry, puff pastry is used—the one pastry that has the wholehearted endorsement of the nouvelle movement, presumably because the proportion of flour to butter is lower in it than in any other pastry.

It is apparent that a definable nouvelle cuisine style is developing in vegetable cookery as in sauces. Innovative chefs are looking for lightness and color and for ingredients that cook quickly. Vegetables meet these criteria admirably. In clear contrast to traditional vegetable cooking, the nouvelle cuisine way with vegetables stresses light cooking—the vegetables should be crisp, though not to the extent of tasting raw or feeling tough. Prime candidates for this treatment are spinach, carrots, and green beans, any vegetable that is brightly colored.

Not everyone likes the new vegetable cookery, finding that flavors are not developed to their best advantage—a fully cooked string bean, after all, has more flavor than an undercooked one. Certainly the new style will never oust old favorites like stuffed peppers. And, the very existence of two schools of thought is but further evidence of the care lavished by the French on their vegetables, which are probably the finest in the world.

FOR SUCCESSFUL FIRST-COURSE VEGETABLES

1. When cooking different vegetables together, choose vegetables that are cooked for similar lengths of time, or vegetables such as tomatoes that can be cooked for varying lengths of time without coming to harm. Alternatively, partially cook tougher vegetables before adding more tender ones.

2. Cut the various vegetables in a mixed vegetable dish to the same size so they will cook at the same rate.

3. If substituting one vegetable for another, be sure the two have similar textures and cooking times.

4. Vegetables must be thoroughly drained before using in a dish that will be cooked further because they will continue to exude liquid when cooked again.

PREPARING AHEAD

1. Many mixed vegetable dishes can be made up to two days ahead; their flavor will mellow and improve. If serving them cold, allow to return to room temperature; if serving hot, cover and reheat in a 350°F (175°C) oven.

2. Vegetable dishes that include bread or pastry should not be prepared more than six hours ahead and are at their best eaten immediately.

3. Due to their delicate texture, vegetable dishes do not freeze well.

Cucumbers with Duxelles and Tomato Stuffing
(CONCOMBRES FARCIS À LA DUXELLES ET AUX TOMATES)

The name duxelles comes from the Marquis d'Uxelles, patron of the Renaissance chef Pierre de la Varenne. This classic mixture of mushrooms, shallots, and parsley has survived the shift to nouvelle cuisine and is still used in many vegetable, fish, and meat dishes.

    2 medium tomatoes, peeled and seeded
    salt and pepper
    2 pounds (1 kg) cucumbers
    1 egg, beaten to mix

For the duxelles:
>**2 tablespoons (30 g) butter**
>**1 shallot, finely chopped**
>**⅓ pound (150 g) mushrooms, finely chopped**
>**salt and pepper**
>**1 tablespoon chopped parsley**

For the sauce:
>**2 cups (500 ml) heavy cream**
>**1 tablespoon chopped parsley**
>**1 tablespoon snipped dill**
>**1 tablespoon chopped chives**
>**salt and pepper**

SERVES 4.

Cut the tomato flesh into very small dice. Sprinkle with 2 teaspoons salt and leave to drain in a colander for at least half an hour. Pat dry with paper towels.

For the duxelles: Heat the butter in a frying pan, add the shallot, and cook until it is soft but not brown. Add the mushrooms, salt and pepper, and cook over high heat, stirring, until all the moisture has evaporated, 5–7 minutes. Stir in the chopped parsley and set aside to cool.

Peel the cucumbers lengthwise in strips, leaving about ⅔ of the peeling on. Cut the cucumbers into 4-inch (10 cm) lengths, halve each section lengthwise, and scoop out the center with a melon baller or small spoon to make a boat shape. Blanch the cucumbers in boiling salted water for 4 minutes. Drain, refresh under cold water, and leave to drain thoroughly.

Heat the oven to 375°F (190°C) and butter a shallow baking dish. Toss the tomatoes with the duxelles and stir in the egg. Taste the mixture for

Mushrooms are sliced and then very finely chopped for a duxelles.

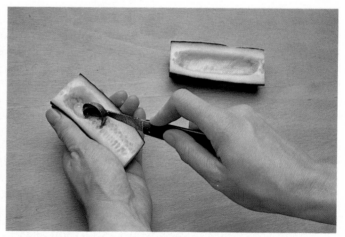

Making the cucumber boats. Because part of the skin is left on, buy unwaxed cucumbers, preferably the long "English" cucumbers that are now in American markets.

seasoning, adjust if necessary, and pack it into the cucumbers. Put the cucumbers in the prepared baking dish and bake in the heated oven until warm, about 10 minutes.

For the sauce: Boil the cream in a heavy saucepan over high heat until reduced to 1 cup (250 ml). Stir in the herbs and season to taste.

To serve, spoon the sauce onto medium-size individual plates and set the stuffed cucumbers on top.

Green Vegetable Torte
(TOURTE AUX LÉGUMES VERTS)

The vegetables used in this torte can be varied according to season. Add or subtract as you like, but keep the sturdy cabbage leaves to hold it all together.

> **1 medium head white cabbage**
> **1 pound (500 g) leeks**
> **salt and pepper**
> **½ pound (250 g) green beans, cut in 1-inch (2.5 cm) lengths**
> **2 tablespoons (30 g) butter**
> **⅓ pound (150 g) mushrooms, sliced**

For the custard mixture:
> **2 eggs**
> **2 egg yolks**
> **½ cup (125 ml) milk**
> **1½ cups (375 ml) heavy cream**
> **salt and pepper**
> **nutmeg**

> **9-inch (23 cm) round baking dish or deep cake pan**

SERVES 6.

Separate the cabbage leaves and remove the large ribs. Cook the leaves in boiling salted water until tender, 7–8 minutes. Drain, refresh under cold water, and drain again. Pat dry on paper towels. Trim the leeks, cutting off most of the green tops, split each twice lengthwise down to but not through the white bulb, and wash. Sprinkle with salt and steam over boiling salted water until just tender, 15–20 minutes. Refresh under cold water, drain, and pat dry on paper towels. Cook the beans in boiling salted water until just tender, 7–10 minutes. Drain, refresh under cold water, drain again, and pat dry on paper towels. Heat the butter in a frying pan and when it is hot add the mushrooms and salt and pepper. Sauté over high heat, tossing often, until tender and lightly browned, about 5 minutes. All the vegetables can be cooked up to a day ahead and kept, covered, in the refrigerator.

For the custard mixture: Beat the eggs, egg yolks, milk, and cream until smooth. Season well with salt and pepper and nutmeg.

Heat the oven to 350°F (175°C). Butter the pan generously and line the bottom and sides with cabbage leaves, letting them drape over the rim of the pan. Chop the remaining leaves. Layer the vegetables into the lined pan beginning with the mushrooms, then adding the leeks, green beans, and finally the chopped cabbage. Season each layer with salt and pepper. Pour in enough of the custard mixture to cover the vegetables. Fold the draped leaves over the filling, cover with foil, and bake in the heated oven until the torte is set, 1½–2 hours.

Let sit for a few moments and then turn out onto a serving plate. Serve hot or at room temperature.

Zucchini Tart Provençale
(TART AUX COURGETTES À LA PROVENÇALE)

This tart can be made with other squash in season or even with pumpkin.

> pie pastry (p. 254) made with 1½ cups (195 g) flour, 6
>   tablespoons (95 g) butter, 1 egg yolk, ½ teaspoon
>   salt, 4–5 tablespoons water
> 2 medium zucchini (about ¾ pound or 350 g)
> ¼ cup (50 g) rice
> 3 tablespoons oil
> ½ onion, finely chopped
> 1 small clove garlic, very finely chopped
> 2½ ounces or about ¾ cup (75 g) grated Gruyère
>   cheese
> 1 egg
> salt and pepper

> *9-inch (23 cm) tart pan*

SERVES 6.

Make the pie pastry. Butter the tart pan. Roll the pastry on a floured surface to a sheet ³⁄₁₆ inch (4.5 mm) thick, line the pan with the dough, and chill until firm, at least 15 minutes. The tart shell can be shaped up to 3 days ahead.

Heat the oven to 400°F (200°C). Prick the base of the shell with a fork, line the dough with aluminum foil, and fill with dried beans or rice. Bake in the heated oven until the pastry is set and beginning to brown, 12–15 minutes.

Remove the foil and beans or rice, return the tart to the oven, and continue baking until crisp, 5–7 minutes.

Slice the zucchini, drop in boiling salted water, and cook until very tender, about 10 minutes. Drain thoroughly. Cook the rice in boiling salted water until just tender, about 15 minutes, and drain. Heat 1 tablespoon of the oil in a saucepan, add the chopped onion, and cook slowly, stirring, until soft but not brown, about 7–10 minutes. Add the garlic and cook another minute. In a bowl mash the zucchini with a fork. Add the rice, onion, garlic, ½ cup (50 g) grated cheese, egg, and salt and pepper to taste. Spread in the baked pie shell. Sprinkle with the remaining cheese and oil. Bake in the heated oven until the filling is set and the top is light brown, 25–30 minutes.

Tomato Tart
(TARTE À LA TOMATE)

Puff-pastry trimmings are perfect to use for this tart shell since the pastry does not need to rise very much.

> **puff pastry (p. 237) made with ½ pound (250 g) butter, 1⅓ cups (175 g) all-purpose flour, ⅔ cup (80 g) cake flour, 1 teaspoon salt, 1 teaspoon lemon juice, ½–¾ cup (125–185 ml) water OR ½ pound (250 g) puff-pastry trimmings**
> **3 pounds (1.5 kg) firm tomatoes, peeled, seeded, and roughly chopped**
> **salt and pepper**
> **3 eggs**
> **1 cup (250 ml) heavy cream**
> **3 ounces or about 1 cup (90 g) grated Gruyère cheese**
> **2 tablespoons (45 g) butter**
>
> *9-inch (23 cm) tart pan*

SERVES 6.

If you make fresh puff pastry, cut it in half before the final rolling and shaping. You will need only ½ pound (250 g) for this recipe. The rest can be refrigerated or frozen. Butter the tart pan. Roll the fresh pastry or pastry trimmings on a floured surface to a sheet ¼ inch (6 mm) thick, line the pan with the dough, and chill until firm, at least 15 minutes. Sprinkle 2 tablespoons (30 g) salt over the prepared tomatoes, toss to mix, and leave in a colander to drain for 30 minutes. Pat dry with paper towels. Set the oven at 425°F (220°C). Beat the eggs with the cream and grated cheese. Season to taste with salt and pepper.

Spread the tomatoes in the bottom of the tart shell. Pour the custard and cheese mixture into the shell and dot with the butter. Bake in the heated oven until the pastry begins to brown, about 15 minutes, then lower the heat to 375°F (190°C), and bake until the custard is brown, about an hour. Leave to cool in the pan for at least 30 minutes. Serve warm or at room temperature.

Stuffed Peppers Niçoise
(POIVRONS FARCIS À LA NIÇOISE)

Stuffed peppers can be served right out of the oven or cooled, as a first course or as an accompaniment to roast lamb or baked fish.

4 medium red or green peppers
2 tablespoons olive oil

For the stuffing:
1 cup (200 g) rice
¼ cup (60 ml) olive oil
1 medium onion, chopped
½ cup (100 g) black olives, pitted and coarsely
  chopped
2 tablespoons capers
1 can (45 g) anchovy fillets, soaked in a little milk for
  20–30 minutes, drained, and chopped
2 teaspoons thyme
1 teaspoon rosemary
juice of 1 lemon, or to taste
pepper

SERVES 4.

For the stuffing: Cook the rice in boiling salted water until just tender, about 15 minutes, and drain. Heat 1 tablespoon of the oil in a frying pan, add the chopped onion, and cook slowly, until soft but not brown, 7–10 minutes. Mix the onions with the rice, the remaining oil, and the rest of the ingredients. Taste for seasoning and add more pepper if needed.

Set the oven at 350°F (175°C). Cut the peppers in half lengthwise and discard the cores and seeds. Oil a shallow baking dish with 2 tablespoons olive oil. Pile the stuffing into the peppers, mounding it well. Put the peppers in the prepared baking dish and cover loosely with foil. The peppers can be prepared up to 8 hours ahead and kept, covered and refrigerated.

Bake the stuffed peppers in the heated oven until they are very tender, about an hour. Baste occasionally and add more oil to the dish if it becomes dry.

Arrange the peppers on a platter or on individual plates. Serve hot, warm, or at room temperature.

Eggs

Larousse Gastronomique, which lists more than 400 egg recipes, still does not cover all the possibilities for variations of egg dishes. What with scrambling, soft-boiling, hard-boiling, poaching, cooking them *en cocotte*, *sur le plat*, and in omelets, the permutations are almost endless, especially since eggs blend accommodatingly with most other flavors—with onions and béchamel sauce in *oeufs boulangère*, with peppers and tomatoes in *omelette espagnole*, with everything from lobster (in *eggs à l'américaine*) to Brussels sprouts (in eggs *à la bruxelloise*).

An egg not only takes well to such theatrical makeup, but requires it to look attractive for serving. A coating of sauce gives a cosmetic touch to the pallid surface of poached, mollet, or hard-boiled eggs. Eggs lend themselves to all sauces—white, cheese, velouté, butter, and even brown. One of the most popular dishes of the moment is *oeufs en meurette*, a traditional Burgundian recipe with red-wine brown sauce.

Omelets can be topped with a spoonful of whatever flavoring is inside, plus a ribbon of sauce around the dish if you like, and scrambled eggs can be garnished in the same way. But a good thing should not be carried too far. The La Varenne chefs constantly admonish, "It should be scrambled eggs with peas, not peas with scrambled eggs!"

The serving dish itself forms the decoration for eggs *en cocotte* and eggs *sur le plat*, and I am always tempted to buy the pretty French flowered ramekins and appetizer dishes designed for cooking eggs. Scrambled eggs benefit from some kind of container besides the plate, preferably an edible one, as do poached eggs and oeufs mollets. A pastry tartlet shell or a fried or toasted croûton of bread is good because the crisp texture is a counterpoint to the soft egg. Lighter alternatives are a bed of vegetables such as spinach,

OEUFS EN COCOTTE (top left)
Eggs in individual ramekins can be set on a bed of the garnish of your choice, such as bacon, ham, sausage, chicken livers, or vegetables, finely diced.

OEUFS POCHÉS SKABELEFF (top right)
Individual shells of pâte brisée hold poached eggs on a bed of chopped shrimp, coated with a tomato-flavored mayonnaise and garnished with strips of smoked salmon.

OMELETTE AUX FINES HERBES (bottom left)
Fresh chives, tarragon, and chervil are the classic flavorings of a plain French omelet.

OMELETTE ESPAGNOLE (bottom right)
An "omelette plate" seasoned with onion, green pepper, tomatoes, and garlic, cooked on both sides, and cut in wedges for serving

mushroom purée (duxelles) or sliced tomatoes, and artichoke bottoms are perhaps the most luxurious container of all. Never serve an omelet or scrambled eggs on a hot plate, say the experts, for once they reach their climax in the pan any further heat will destroy the perfection. This is not a faux pas likely to be committed in our house, where there seems to be a constant battle to have enough hot plates.

As to what color of eggs to buy, it makes no difference. In France, brown eggs are more prevalent than white. In America, the opposite is true. Fashion seems to have shifted from favoring the purity of white to the country look of brown. In point of fact, the color of the shell has no bearing on the taste of the egg inside.

The number of eggs usually served per person varies very much depending on the way they are cooked. One egg is the usual serving if the egg is poached or mollet and a garnish is added, such as the hollandaise, croûton, and slice of ham called for in eggs Bénédict, or in the generous coating of gelée in eggs in aspic. The portion may, of course, be doubled if the eggs are served as a main course rather than an appetizer. Although one egg is usual for eggs en cocotte or boiled eggs, anything less than two eggs sur le plat looks a bit stingy.

For an omelet, two eggs per person is a minimum, and three is not too many. Scrambled eggs never seem to go far. They should be creamy, never cooked enough to hold their shape, so one scrambled egg on a plate looks like just a little blob of sauce, and three eggs per person is the normal allowance, even when served as an appetizer to be followed by a meat course as they so often are in France.

In the old days, the freshness of eggs caused a lot of concern. Nineteenth-century cookbooks list elaborate ways to "candle" eggs, illuminating the air pocket (the larger the pocket, the longer the egg has been evaporating through its porous shell). Or an egg was immersed in a twelve percent solution of salt water to see if it would sink in proof of its freshness. Nowadays there is little need to fuss. Eggs are all of more or less the same age by the time they reach the kitchen: not fresh from the chicken, you can be sure. They can be stored in nitrogen for months without changing state, and whatever one may think of this practice, it does ensure a supply of eggs at a relatively stable price.

A bad egg is all too unmistakable and is nearly always due to a crack in the shell (sometimes almost invisible). Prudent cooks examine egg shells and then break eggs individually into a cup before adding them to anything else. But practice and precept are not always the same. I remember when I was training in London some twenty years ago, my teacher, a starch-bosomed martinet if ever there was one, ignored her own rules and broke twenty eggs directly into a bowl. The nineteenth was bad. I could barely suppress a snicker at the time, but it was a lesson I have never forgotten.

Egg yolks that are left over form a crust in the open air within three hours, and even when tightly covered, they tend to dry overnight. So if I have spare yolks, I moisten them by adding a spoonful or two of water and then cover them tightly. Luckily, most kitchens have a surfeit of whites rather than yolks; they keep very well for up to three weeks in the refrigerator, or they can be frozen. Egg whites are one of the few foods that La Varenne chefs advocate freezing—they say whites beat up better after being frozen.

Eggs are versatile, they're quick to prepare, and they're good as lunch, snack, appetizer, or supper. Still I doubt if many cooks would go as far as Ali-Bab, whose cookbook dating from the 1930's suggests this Symphony of Eggs: "Chop two hard-boiled eggs. Poach six eggs and keep warm. Make an omelet from four eggs. Before folding it, sprinkle it with the chopped hard-boiled eggs and set the poached eggs on top. Fold the omelet and serve with tomato or cream sauce." Egg-centric to say the least.

FOR SUCCESSFUL EGG DISHES

1. Eggs start cooking at the relatively low temperature of 160°F (70°C), and they cook quickly—an omelet takes one to two minutes, and a poached egg three to four minutes. Twenty seconds can make the difference between eggs being done and being overcooked.

2. Eggs scorch easily, and high heat toughens them. In many dishes, the egg is cooked in its shell or in a container that protects it from direct heat. When eggs are in contact with the heat, as when they are fried, scrambled, or cooked in an omelet, the heat must be very carefully watched.

3. Eggs are often seasoned with white pepper because specks of black pepper are considered unattractive.

PREPARING AHEAD

1. Eggs can be poached several days ahead and kept in a bowl of cold water in the refrigerator. To reheat, immerse them in hot water, around 150°F (65°C), for three to four minutes and then drain and pat dry on paper towels.

2. Eggs can also be cooked "mollet" or boiled and kept at room temperature for up to one day. If chilled they become tough. Peeled eggs can be kept in a bowl of cold water, but it is best to peel them when needed.

3. Scrambled eggs will hold for a few minutes if undercooked somewhat and kept warm in a water bath (see Chapter 8).

4. Omelets and eggs en cocotte cannot be made ahead unless, for flat omelets for instance, they are to be eaten at room temperature. Most garnish ingredients for omelets and eggs en cocotte can be prepared in advance.

EGGS AND SALT

1. Salt has an important effect on eggs: it breaks down the whites so they become liquid. This is useful when egg whites and yolks are beaten to mix. More often, however, the liquefying effect should be avoided by adding salt at the last minute.

2. An omelet or scrambled eggs will be watery if the eggs are mixed with the salt more than a minute or two before cooking.

3. The effect of adding salt to water for poached eggs is disastrous—the salt breaks down the egg white, which detaches itself in strings from the yolk. An effective addition to poaching water for eggs is vinegar, which has the effect of sealing the egg white.

4. Salt sprinkled on eggs sur le plat or eggs en cocotte before cooking gives an undesirable spotted effect when the egg is cooked.

OMELET PANS

1. One of the keys to success in making omelets is a good pan. It can be made of aluminum or iron. The base must be heavy to distribute the heat evenly, and the sides fairly high, curved, and gently sloped so the omelet can be rolled easily. The handle is also angled to make rolling easier.

2. The size of the pan can vary from about 7 inches (18 cm) for making a two- to three-egg omelet for one to 10–11 inches (25–28 cm) for an eight-egg omelet for three or four. A 9-inch (23 cm) pan is right for a four- to five-egg omelet for two.

3. Omelet pans should be "seasoned" before use: Wash the pan well (without abrasives), dry, and pour in a ½-inch (1.25 cm) layer of oil and coarse salt. Leave for twelve hours and then heat gently until the oil is very hot and almost smoking. Pour off the oil and salt and wipe dry.

Eggs sur le Plat
(OEUFS SUR LE PLAT)

Traditionally, eggs sur le plat are cooked and served in the special shallow, white, heatproof dishes with two little handles, but they can be made in any shallow baking dish.

8 eggs

4 individual shallow baking dishes

SERVES 4.

Set the oven at 375°F (190°C) and butter the baking dishes. Break 2 eggs into each prepared dish. Cover the dishes with a lid or foil and bake in the heated oven until the whites are just set but the yolks are still soft, 8–10 minutes. The eggs will continue cooking in the heat of the dish. Serve them at once and season at the table.

Soft-boiled, Mollet, and Hard-boiled Eggs
(OEUFS À LA COQUE, MOLLETS, ET DURS)

To help prevent cracking, let the eggs come to room temperature before plunging them into the boiling water.

4 eggs

SERVES 4.

In a saucepan bring enough water to a boil to cover the eggs generously. Using a slotted spoon, lower the eggs into the water. Bring back to a boil and begin counting the cooking time. For soft-boiled eggs, allow 4-4½ minutes; for mollet, allow 5–6 minutes; for hard-boiled, 10–12 minutes.

When served plain, soft-boiled eggs are usually presented in the shell. To peel mollet or hard-boiled eggs, tap them gently all over and peel away the skin with the cracked shell. Be especially careful with mollet eggs because the yolk is soft. If the egg is difficult to peel, hold it under running water. Season the cooked eggs at table.

Hard-boiled Eggs Boulangère
(OEUFS DURS BOULANGÈRE)

These eggs are served the way a baker's wife, or boulangère, might prepare them—in crusty loaves of bread.

> **béchamel sauce (p. 192) made with 1 cup (250 ml) milk, 1 slice of onion, 1 bay leaf, 6 peppercorns, salt and pepper, and nutmeg**
> **2 tablespoons (30 g) butter**
> **2 medium onions, thinly sliced**
> **salt and pepper**
> **6 hard-boiled eggs (p. 367)**
> **4 French rolls**
> **1 ounce or ⅓ cup (30 g) grated Gruyère cheese**
> **2 tablespoons chopped parsley**

SERVES 4.

Make the béchamel sauce. Melt the butter in a heavy-bottomed pan, add the onions and salt and pepper, and press a piece of buttered foil or waxed paper on top. Cover with a lid and cook gently until very tender but not brown, 7–10 minutes. Mix the onions into the sauce. This mixture can be prepared ahead.

Set the oven at 400°F (200°C). Peel the eggs and cut 2 of them in half lengthwise. Scoop the yolks from the 2 halved eggs, push them through a sieve into a small bowl, and reserve. Coarsely chop the 2 egg whites with the rest of the eggs and combine with the béchamel and onions. Split the rolls in half lengthwise and remove most of the soft inside, leaving the crusty shell. Fill the shells with the egg mixture and sprinkle them with the grated cheese.

Set the filled shells on a baking sheet and bake in the oven until hot and brown, 15–20 minutes. Sprinkle the chopped parsley and the sieved yolks over the eggs and serve immediately.

Poached Eggs
(OEUFS POCHÉS)

Poaching eggs involves two cooking temperatures: a rolling boil when the eggs are added to the water and then just below a simmer to complete the cooking.

> **3 tablespoons vinegar**
> **4 eggs**

SERVES 4.

Fill a sauté pan or shallow saucepan two-thirds full of water, add the vinegar, and bring to a rolling boil. Hold an egg close to the water and break it into a bubbling patch. The bubbling water twirls the egg so the white sets around the yolk. Repeat with the remaining eggs. Turn down the heat so the water just almost simmers and poach the eggs until the white is set but the yolk still soft, 3–4 minutes. Test each egg by lifting it out with a slotted spoon and gently touching it.

Neaten the eggs by trimming any strings of cooked egg white, taking care not to break the yolk. Drain on paper towels. Season the poached eggs at the table. If preparing the eggs ahead, transfer cooked eggs immediately to a bowl of cold water to stop the cooking.

Hold each egg close to a bubbling patch of boiling water and drop it in. Then turn the heat down so the water barely simmers. Never add salt to the water.

The eggs will be done in 3–4 minutes; lift them out of the water to test that the whites are done but the yolks are still soft.

Poached Eggs Skabeleff
(OEUFS POCHÉS SKABELEFF)

The Russian name Skabeleff refers to the smoked salmon, which is an important ingredient in the garnish.

> pie pastry (p. 254) made with 1 cup (130 g) flour, 4
>   tablespoons (60 g) butter, 1 egg yolk, ¼ teaspoon
>   salt, and 3–4 tablespoons water
> ⅓ pound (150 g) shrimps, cooked, peeled, and coarsely
>   chopped
> 4 poached eggs (p. 368)
> 1 thin slice (about 2 ounces or 60 g) smoked salmon,
>   cut in thin strips

For the anchovy and tomato mayonnaises:
> **mayonnaise (p. 351) made with 1 egg yolk, salt and
> pepper, 1 teaspoon vinegar or lemon juice, ¼
> teaspoon Dijon mustard, and ¾ cup (185 ml) oil**
> **1 teaspoon anchovy paste**
> **2 teaspoons tomato paste**

> **four 4-inch (10 cm) tartlet pans**

SERVES 4.

Make the pie pastry. Butter the tartlet pans. Roll out the dough on a floured surface to a sheet ³⁄₁₆ inch (5 mm) thick, line the pans with the dough, and chill until firm, at least 15 minutes. The shells can be shaped up to 3 days ahead.

Set the oven at 400°F (200°C). Line the tartlet shells with rounds of waxed paper or aluminum foil and fill with dried beans or rice, or put a smaller tartlet pan inside each. Put the tartlets on a baking sheet and bake in the heated oven until the pastry is set and lightly browned, 8–10 minutes. Remove the paper and beans or the smaller tartlet pans and return the shells to the oven until crisp and brown, 5–7 minutes. Allow to cool slightly, then remove the pastry shells from the pans, and transfer to a rack to cool completely.

For the anchovy and tomato mayonnaises: Make the mayonnaise and mix half of it with the anchovy paste. To the rest of the mayonnaise, add the tomato paste. Thin the tomato mayonnaise with warm water, if necessary, so it is of coating consistency.

Mix the chopped shrimps into the anchovy mayonnaise. Poach the eggs and transfer to a bowl of cold water.

To finish: Spread the shrimp mixture in the tartlet shells. Pat the eggs dry with paper towels, put one in each tartlet shell, and coat the eggs with the tomato mayonnaise. Top with the strips of smoked salmon.

Scrambled Eggs
(OEUFS BROUILLÉS)

The slower scrambled eggs are cooked, the better. Old cookbooks say a dozen eggs should take thirty minutes.

> **12 eggs**
> **salt and pepper**
> **6 ounces (180 g) butter**

SERVES 4.

Beat the eggs with salt and pepper until thoroughly mixed and frothy. Melt the butter in a heavy-bottomed saucepan, add the eggs, and stir constantly over low heat with a wooden spoon until the mixture begins to thicken. Continue cooking over very low heat, scraping the cooked egg from the bottom and sides of the pan. (NOTE: The eggs mustn't lump. If they threaten to thicken too quickly, remove from the heat and let cool a little before continuing to cook.) When the eggs are saucelike with small bits of coagulated egg suspended in the creamy mixture, transfer to plates and serve immediately.

Scrambled Eggs Magda
(OEUFS BROUILLÉS MAGDA)

If you have plenty of time, try cooking the eggs in a water bath—this delicate cooking will make creamy and delicious scrambled eggs.

12 scrambled eggs (p. 370)
1½ ounces or about ½ cup (45 g) grated Gruyère
   cheese
2 teaspoons Dijon mustard
2 teaspoons chopped chives
2 teaspoons chopped parsley

For the croûtons:
3 tablespoons oil
3 tablespoons (45 g) butter
4 slices firm white bread with crusts removed, cut in
   half diagonally

SERVES 4.

For the croûtons: Heat the oil in a frying pan, add the butter, and when hot, fry the pieces of bread on each side until golden brown. Drain on paper towels and keep warm.

Make the scrambled eggs. When they are almost cooked, add the grated cheese and stir until it melts into the eggs. Remove from the heat and stir in the mustard, chopped chives, and parsley.

Transfer the eggs to a platter or individual plates, arrange the croûtons around them, and serve at once.

Eggs en Cocotte
(OEUFS EN COCOTTE)

Bacon, ham, sausages, chicken livers, and vegetables are a few of the possible garnishes for eggs en cocotte. Cook any choice of garnish, cut it into very small cubes, and put the dice in the ramekins before breaking the eggs into them.

> **2 tablespoons butter**
> **salt and pepper**
> **4 eggs**
> **2 tablespoons heavy cream**
>
> ***4 ramekins***

SERVES 4.

Set the oven at 375°F (190°C). Prepare a water bath (Chapter 8). In each ramekin put ½ tablespoon butter and salt and pepper. Heat the ramekins in the prepared water bath on top of the stove until the butter has melted and then break an egg into each one. Top each egg with ½ tablespoon of cream. Transfer the eggs to the heated oven and bake until the whites are almost set, 5–6 minutes—the eggs will continue cooking in the heat of the ramekins. When served, the whites should be just set and the yolks soft.

Omelet
(OMELETTE)

It is said that to be considered an expert, a chef must make omelets every day for three years. The four- to five-egg omelet given here is the easiest size to handle.

> **4–5 eggs**
> **salt and pepper**
> **2 tablespoons (30 g) butter**
>
> ***9-inch (23 cm) omelet pan***

SERVES 2.

Beat the eggs with salt and pepper until mixed. Melt the butter in the omelet pan over medium heat. When it foams, let it subside, then pour the eggs into the pan. Stir them briskly with the flat of a fork until they start to thicken. Then quickly but carefully pull the egg that is cooking at the sides of the pan towards the center, tipping the pan to pour uncooked egg to the sides. Continue until the edge is set and then leave to cook for 10–15 seconds to brown the bottom slightly. Do not wait for the top to set. When folded, the omelet should still be moist and creamy in the center.

To fold the omelet: Hold the pan handle in one hand, tip the pan away from you, and either give the handle a sharp rap with the other hand so the edge of the omelet flips over or, with the help of the fork, fold over the side of the omelet near the handle. Half roll, half slide the omelet into the serving dish so it lands folded in three. Neaten the omelet with a fork, if necessary, and serve.

Stir the omelet with the flat of a fork, pull cooked egg from the sides to the center, and tip the pan to move uncooked egg to the sides.

When all the edges are set but the center is still soft, tip the pan away from you and give the handle a sharp rap so that the near edge flips over and away from you.

Slide the omelet almost out of the pan and then roll it all the way out by turning the pan over so that the omelet lands folded in three on the plate.

Omelet with Fines Herbes
(OMELETTE AUX FINES HERBES)

An omelet with fines herbes, only one of the countless variations, is a classic that remains among the most popular.

1 omelet (p. 372) made with the addition of 2 teaspoons chopped chives, 2 teaspoons chopped chervil, and 2 teaspoons chopped tarragon

SERVES 2.

Make the omelet, beating the chopped chives, chervil, and tarragon with the eggs before cooking.

Flat Omelet
(OMELETTE PLATE)

Unlike a classic omelet, a flat omelet should be cooked until relatively firm.

4–5 eggs
salt and pepper
2 tablespoons (30 g) butter

9-inch (23 cm) omelet pan

SERVES 2.

Beat the eggs with salt and pepper until mixed. Melt the butter in the omelet pan over medium heat and, when foaming, add the beaten eggs. Stir them briskly with the flat of a fork until the mixture is almost as thick as scrambled eggs. Leave the omelet to cook until well browned on the bottom and almost firm on top, 15–20 seconds. Take from the heat, set a heatproof plate over the top of the pan, and invert the pan to turn out the omelet. Slide it back into the pan, brown the other side, and slide onto a serving plate. Serve hot or at room temperature.

Spanish Omelet
(OMELETTE ESPAGNOLE)

This omelet is served cut in wedges and is delicious served at room temperature as a snack or hors d'oeuvre.

> **4–5 eggs**
> **salt and pepper**
> **2 tablespoons (30 g) butter**

For the vegetable mixture:
> **2 tablespoons oil**
> **1 slice of onion**
> **½ green pepper, cored, seeded, and cut in strips**
> **2 tomatoes, peeled, seeded, and coarsely chopped**
> **1 clove garlic, finely chopped**
> **salt and pepper**

> ***9-inch (23 cm) omelet pan***

SERVES 2.

For the vegetable mixture: Heat the oil and add the onion, green pepper, tomatoes, garlic, and salt and pepper. Cook, stirring, until the vegetables are soft but not brown, 7–10 minutes.

Make a flat omelet (p. 374) stirring the vegetable mixture into the beaten eggs before cooking.

CROQUETTES DE GRUYÈRE (**front**)
Cheese croquettes, garnished with deep-fried parsley, to be served as a first course

SABLÉS AU FROMAGE
Rich and crisp, these cheese "cookies" are good with cocktails and can be made up to a week ahead.

Cheese

As far as I am concerned, cheese is a compelling reason for living in France. As a child it was cheese, not chocolate, that I would snatch when my mother's back was turned. Unlike most youthful passions, my love for it has continued; to me French cheeses are a constant diversion, a matter for research and pleasurable experiment.

What I'm talking about is not cooking with cheese but eating plain unadorned cheese as it comes from the *fromagerie*, with at most a hunk of bread and perhaps a piece of fruit. For home meals, we always include a cheese course, as do most French families. Perhaps this is why the French don't cook with cheese to any great extent. Those French recipes, primarily appetizers, that do feature cheese as the dominant ingredient are much easier to fit into an American menu than a French one.

In cooking, cheese plays two roles: it can take the lead in dishes like cheese croquettes or cheese ramekins, or it can play second fiddle, adding flavor, richness (cheese can contain up to seventy percent butterfat), or a golden topping to other ingredients. Its use in sauces, over gratins, and in quiches is well known. The favorite general-purpose cheese in France is Gruyère, a name used generically to include not only Gruyère but also Emmenthal, and the French Beaufort and Comté (both well-aged and nutty).

Runner-up to Gruyère is Parmesan. The French are not hesitant to recognize the special qualities of this piquant salty cheese from Italy. In cooking, Parmesan is unique: aged two years until very hard, it is so dry that it cannot cook into strings. (Even the best Gruyère has the distressing habit of cooking to rubber bands if heated too fast or for too long.)

Few other cheeses appear in the classic repertoire—Brie croquettes are acceptable, as are Muenster canapés, and Roquefort quiche. (Roquefort salad dressing, however, is an American invention, unknown in France.) Nouvelle cuisine chefs are a bit more adventuresome, using such ideas as Roquefort sauce for meat. Still, avant-garde chefs don't exploit cheese to nearly the extent that they do fruit and vegetables.

If classic cuisine makes scant use of the possibilities of cheese and nouvelle chefs little more, the story is very different in regional cooking. Almost every little country town boasts its own cheese, and local cooks put it to great use in the kitchen. In the provinces are the delectable lesser known cheeses like Cantal (rather like Cheddar), *mimolette* (resembling a Dutch cheese), and *ardi gastna* (a sharp, dry Pyrenean cheese).

Hard cheeses appear not just in classic gratins and quiches, but also in recipes like fondue (popular in the French Alps), and the Auvergnat *aligot*, a potato purée beaten over the heat with grated Cantal cheese. Cantal is also added to bread dough, and some authorities even claim that in Brie the local cheese was used in the same way, hence the name brioche.

All over France, local cheeses are used to make toasted croûtes—open-faced or two-slice sandwiches often including mushrooms or bacon with sliced cheese or a cheese sauce. *Croque-monsieur*, with Gruyère cheese and ham, is the national snack; *croûte comtoise* has Comté cheese and bacon; *croûte normande* calls for Camembert; and a host of croûtes use the creamy *tomme* cheeses, some soft, some firmer and piquant. Many of the monastery cheeses, such as St.-Paulin and Port-Salut, are good in croûtes, or in quiches. Cheese is a standard addition to soup, not just grated over the surface, but often browned to form a crisp topping or sliced and layered with toast in the soup bowl.

Most adaptable of all are the multitude of fresh cheeses made from cows', goats', or sheeps' milk. With a sprinkling of sugar, they are eaten with fruit; with a dash of garlic and a dose of chopped herbs, they make a savory spread (on the lines of *boursin à l'ail*). They are a filling for crêpes and the basis of cheesecakes, which crop up in several regions. Most French cheesecakes are cooked in pastry shells, and resemble a close-textured cake rather than the rich, dense American type. Nor are they very sweet. Some are flavored with raisins or lemon juice, and one version from Poitou called a *torteau* (crab) is almost spherical with a jet black crust.

Most important when cooking with cheese is an open mind. *Maître fromager* Pierre Androuet lists a variety of dishes that can be made with almost any cheese at all, taking the title of whatever kind happens to be used. He includes canapés, croûtes, croquettes, fritters, tarts and quiches, soufflés and scrambled eggs. A little ingenuity can lead to canapés Brillat-Savarin (a triple cream-cheese), croûte de Coulommiers, croquettes de Brocciu (a Corsican cheese), beignets de bleu d'Auvergne, quiche au Maroilles (a strong cheese from northern France), a soufflé or oeufs brouillés mimolette, and literally hundreds more.

FOR SUCCESSFUL CHEESE DISHES

1. When seasoning a dish to which cheese will be added, remember that most cheeses are somewhat salty.
2. For gratins and other broiled dishes, do not use a high-fat cheese, because this type separates when exposed to high heat.
3. Finely grated cheese melts more quickly and therefore is less likely to overcook into strings.
4. Add grated cheese, especially any Swiss type, to a hot mixture off the heat so it doesn't get stringy.

PREPARING AHEAD

1. Cheese must breathe and is best wrapped in waxed paper rather than foil or plastic wrap.
2. Most cheeses should be stored at 46–50°F (5–10°C)—the temperature of the refrigerator vegetable drawer.
3. Mixtures containing cheese should not be reheated over direct heat; use a water bath or, better still, add cheese after reheating.
4. Dishes with a high proportion of cheese such as toasted croûtes or fondue become rubbery when reheated. This is accentuated by freezing.

Cheese Sablés
(SABLÉS AU FROMAGE)

Cheese sablés could also be made with aged Cheddar cheese. In any variation, they make a good hors d'oeuvre with cocktails.

¾–1 cup (95–130 g) flour
salt and pepper
pinch of cayenne pepper
6 tablespoons (95 g) butter

3 ounces or about 1 cup (90 g) grated Parmesan or
    Gruyère cheese
1 egg, beaten to mix with salt
¼ cup (35 g) coarsely chopped walnuts OR 2 ounces or
    about ½ cup (60 g) grated Parmesan or Gruyère
    cheese (for sprinkling)

MAKES ABOUT 30 SABLÉS.

Sift ¾ cup (95 g) of the flour onto a work surface with salt and pepper and cayenne pepper. Add the butter and rub it in with the fingertips until the mixture resembles fine crumbs. Add the cheese and press the dough together. It should be soft but not sticky. If it is too moist, add more flour. Knead on a lightly floured surface, pushing it away with the heel of the hand and pulling it up with the fingers until it is as pliable as putty. Chill the dough for at least 30 minutes. It can be kept, refrigerated, at this point for up to 3 days, or it can be frozen.

Roll out the dough to a rectangle ¼ inch (6 mm) thick. Cut the rectangle into 2½-inch (6 cm) squares and cut each square into 2 triangles. Brush the dough with beaten egg and sprinkle with chopped walnuts or grated cheese. Set the sablés, leaving a little space between them, on a buttered baking sheet and refrigerate at least 15 minutes before baking. Set the oven at 375°F (190°C). Bake in the heated oven until golden brown, 15–18 minutes. Leave to cool for 5 minutes on the baking sheet and then transfer to a rack to cool completely. The sablés can be stored for up to a week in an airtight container, or they can be frozen.

Gruyère Croquettes
(CROQUETTES DE GRUYÈRE)

These croquettes can be shaped in rounds as described in this recipe or in the traditional cork shape: Roll the mixture into a rope on a floured surface and cut it in 1-inch (2.5 cm) lengths. If there is no time to chill the mixture overnight, this method of shaping is easier.

béchamel sauce (p. 192) made with 1½ cups (375 ml)
    milk, 1 slice of onion, 1 bay leaf, 6 peppercorns, salt
    and white pepper, 4 tablespoons (60 g) butter, and ⅓
    cup (45 g) flour
3 egg yolks
8 ounces or about 2½ cups (250 g) grated Gruyère
    cheese

1 teaspoon Dijon mustard
salt and pepper
nutmeg
¼ cup (30 g) flour, seasoned with salt and pepper
1 egg, beaten to mix with 1 tablespoon water and 1
   tablespoon oil
1 cup (100 g) dry bread crumbs
parsley (for garnish)
deep fat for frying

1½-inch (4 cm) plain pastry cutter

MAKES ABOUT 30 CROQUETTES.

Make the béchamel sauce, add the egg yolks, and simmer, stirring constantly, until smooth and thick, about 2 minutes. Take from the heat, stir in the cheese, mustard, salt and pepper, and nutmeg to taste. Pour a ½-inch (1.25 cm) layer of the mixture into a buttered pan and chill overnight.

To cut out the croquettes, warm the tray over low heat to melt the butter and loosen the mixture and then stamp out rounds of the cheese mixture with the cutter. Coat them with seasoned flour, brush them with the beaten egg, and coat with bread crumbs. The croquettes can be prepared 1 day ahead and refrigerated, uncovered, or they can be frozen.

To finish: Wash the parsley and dry thoroughly. Heat the fat to 350°F (175°C) on a fat thermometer. Fry the croquettes, a few at a time, until golden brown, 4–5 minutes. Drain them on paper towels and keep them in a 350°F (180°C) oven with the door ajar while frying the rest of the croquettes.

Let the fat used to cook the croquettes cool slightly and then toss in the parsley. Stand back because the fat will sputter. When the sputtering stops, after about 30 seconds, lift out the parsley and drain it on paper towels.

Arrange the croquettes, overlapping, on a serving dish or individual plates, garnish with the fried parsley, and serve.

**The cheese croquette mixture
can be cut into flat rounds
or rolled and cut into the more
usual "cork" shape.**

Cheese Turnovers
(CHAUSSONS AU FROMAGE)

Puff-pastry turnovers can be filled with almost any well-flavored cheese. Here Camembert cut in cubes is used, but another soft cheese like Brie or a hard cheese like Gruyère, grated and mixed with cream cheese, could be substituted.

> **puff pastry (p. 237) made with ½ pound (250 g) butter, 1⅓ cups (175 g) all-purpose flour, ⅔ cup (80 g) cake flour, 1 teaspoon lemon juice, ½–¾ cup (125–185 ml) cold water**
> **14 ounces (425 g) Camembert (about 1½ Camembert cheeses)**
> **1 egg**
> **1 egg yolk**
> **salt**
> **nutmeg**
> **pinch of paprika**
> **1 tablespoon cognac**
> **1 egg, beaten to mix with salt**
>
> *2½–3 inch (6–7.5 cm) fluted pastry cutter*

MAKES ABOUT 2 DOZEN TURNOVERS.

Make the puff pastry. Remove and discard the rind from the Camembert and chop the cheese. Mix together the chopped Camembert, egg, egg yolk, salt, nutmeg, paprika, and cognac.

Sprinkle a baking sheet with water. Roll out the pastry about ¼ inch (6 mm) thick and use the cutter to stamp out rounds. In the center of each round put a teaspoon of filling. Brush the border of each turnover with beaten egg, fold the dough over, and press the edges together to seal. Arrange the turnovers on the prepared baking sheet. Chill at least 15 minutes. They can be prepared to this point up to a day ahead and kept, refrigerated, or they can be frozen.

Heat the oven to 425°F (220°C). Brush the tops of the pastries with beaten egg and make decorative slits with the point of a knife to allow steam to escape. Bake the turnovers in the heated oven 8 minutes. Lower the heat to 375°F (190°C) and bake until puffed and brown, 12–15 minutes. Serve hot, warm, or at room temperature.

Cheese Ramekins
(RAMEQUINS AU FROMAGE)

The croûton base provides just the right contrast in texture for these creamy ramekins.

2 eggs
12 ounces (350 ml) heavy cream
3½ ounces or about 1 cup (100 g) Gruyère cheese, grated
salt and pepper
2 ounces (60 g) cooked ham, cut in thin strips

For the croûtons:
4 slices firm white bread
3 tablespoons oil
3 tablespoons (45 g) butter

four ½-cup (125 ml) ramekins or individual soufflé dishes

SERVES 4.

Beat the eggs until smooth, stir in the cream and cheese, and season to taste. You can prepare the ramekins 6–8 hours ahead to this point; keep the cheese mixture in the refrigerator.

For the croûtons: Cut a round a little larger than the ramekins from each slice of bread. Heat the oil in a frying pan, add the butter, and when it is hot, fry the bread rounds until golden brown. Drain on paper towels.

To finish: Set the oven at 375°F (190°C). Prepare a water bath (see Chapter 8). Butter the ramekins and arrange a few strips of ham in the bottom of each one. Stir the cheese mixture and pour it into the ramekins. Set them in the water bath and bring to a simmer on top of the stove. Transfer to the heated oven and bake until the tops are golden and firm to the touch, 15–20 minutes. Reheat the croûtons in the oven during the last 5 minutes of the cooking time. Remove the ramekins from the water bath and leave to stand for 1 minute.

Run a knife around the edge of each ramekin and turn out onto a croûton. Set each on an individual plate and serve.

After running a knife around the edge of the ramekin, center the crisp croûton over it, and then turn it out onto the serving plate.

Roquefort Napoleon
(MILLE-FEUILLE AU ROQUEFORT)

This is the smallest amount of puff pastry that can be handled easily. If serving fewer people, make the same quantity of pastry, but use only half of it for this recipe and refrigerate or freeze the rest for future use.

> puff pastry (p. 237) made with ½ pound (250 g) butter, 1⅓ cups (175 g) all-purpose flour, ⅔ cup (80 g) cake flour, 1 teaspoon salt, 1 teaspoon lemon juice, ½–¾ cup (125–185 ml) cold water
> béchamel sauce (p. 192) made with 2 cups (500 ml) milk, 1 slice of onion, 1 bay leaf, 12 peppercorns, salt and white pepper, nutmeg, 4 tablespoons (60 g) butter, ⅓ cup (45 g) flour
> 5 ounces (150 g) Roquefort cheese
> 5 egg whites

SERVES 6–8.

Make the puff pastry. Set the oven at 425°F (220°C).

Roll out the prepared dough into as thin a sheet as possible. It should be a large rectangle about 10 inches (25 cm) wide and 14 inches (35.5 cm) long. Sprinkle a baking sheet with water, lay the dough on top, prick it all over with a fork, and chill 10–15 minutes. Bake in the heated oven until brown, 10–15 minutes. Loosen the pastry with a metal spatula, turn it over, and bake 5 minutes longer to crisp the underside. Trim the pastry to a neat rectangle. Crush the trimmings and reserve them for another use. Cut the puff-pastry rectangle into 3 equal strips, each about 3 inches (7.5 cm) wide. The pastry can be prepared several hours ahead of time.

Reheat the pastry, if necessary, in a 250°F (120°C) oven. Make the béchamel sauce. Crumble the Roquefort cheese and, off the heat, add it to the sauce, stirring until melted. Beat the egg whites until stiff. Bring the sauce just to a boil and whisk in the beaten egg whites. Remove from the heat, taste for seasoning, and adjust if necessary.

Sandwich the layers of pastry with about ⅔ of the filling, and then spread the remaining filling on the sides and top.

Cut the Napolean into slices with a serrated knife and serve.

Baby Chickens en Cocotte with Cheese
(COQUELETS EN COCOTTE AU FROMAGE)

When baby chickens are not available, Cornish game hens or two 2–2½-pound (1–1.25 kg) chickens can be substituted. Cook the larger chickens for thirty minutes and then cut them in half for serving.

4 baby chickens
3 tablespoons (45 g) butter
salt and pepper
pared zest of 2 lemons
½ cup (125 ml) chicken stock (p. 115)
½ cup (125 ml) heavy cream
1 teaspoon arrowroot mixed to a paste with
  1 tablespoon water
1 ounce or about ¼ cup (30 g) grated Parmesan cheese
1 tablespoon chopped parsley

trussing needle and string

SERVES 4.

If using the oven, set it at 375°F (190°C). Truss the chickens (see p. 26). In a heavy-bottomed pan large enough for all the chickens melt the butter over medium heat and brown the chickens on all sides. Sprinkle with salt and pepper, add the lemon zest, and cover. Cook over low heat on top of the stove or in the heated oven, turning the chickens occasionally, until they are tender, 20–25 minutes.

Transfer the birds to a platter, remove the trussing string, and keep the chickens warm. Add the stock to the pan and bring to a boil, stirring to dissolve the pan juices. Boil until well reduced, about 5 minutes, and strain into a saucepan. Add the cream and bring just to a boil. Whisk in enough of the arrowroot paste so the sauce thickens slightly. Take from the heat and stir in the Parmesan cheese. Taste for seasoning and adjust if necessary.

Serve the chickens on a platter or set one chicken on each plate. Spoon the sauce over each chicken, sprinkle with parsley, and serve.

Goat Cheeses in Oil
(FROMAGES DE CHÈVRE À L'HUILE)

In Provence, olive oil and local herbs are used to preserve and add flavor to small goats' milk cheeses. After the cheese has been eaten, the flavorful oil can be used for salad dressings.

> **8 small round goats' milk cheeses (each about 2½**
> **ounces or 75 g)**
> **1 teaspoon cracked peppercorns**
> **8 small sprigs dried thyme**
> **2 teaspoons rosemary needles (unground)**
> **2–2½ cups (500–625 ml) olive oil**

> ***1-quart (1 L) jar***

Arrange the cheeses in the jar. Add the peppercorns, thyme, and rosemary and then pour enough oil over the cheeses to cover them completely. Cover and keep in a cool place for at least 2 weeks and up to 2 months before serving.

Goats' cheeses (chèvres) have become both popular and available in the United States. They are delicious "cured" in olive oil and herbs.

Brioche Cheesecake
(GÂTEAU BRIOCHÉ AU FROMAGE)

This unusual cream cheesecake is baked in brioche dough rather than pie pastry.

> **brioche dough (p. 265) made with 2 cups (260 g) flour, 1¼ teaspoons salt, 1 tablespoon (15 g) sugar, ½ package (⅛ ounce or 3.5 g) dry OR ½ cake (about ⅓ ounce or 10 g) compressed yeast, 1 tablespoon lukewarm water, 3–4 eggs, and ¼ pound (125 g) unsalted butter**
> **¼ pound (125 g) butter**
> **1 pound (500 ml) cream cheese**
> **4 eggs**
> **4 egg yolks**
> **¼ cup (35 g) potato starch or cornstarch**
> **⅔ cup (135 g) sugar**
> **grated zest of 2 lemons**
> **2 tablespoons of lemon juice**
>
> ***9-inch (23 cm) springform pan OR 10–11 inch- (25–28 cm) layer pan***

SERVES 8.

Make the brioche dough, letting it rise according to instructions, and chill so it will be easier to roll out.

To make the cheese filling, melt the butter and leave to cool. In a large bowl whisk together the cream cheese, eggs, egg yolks, starch, sugar, lemon zest, and lemon juice. Stir in the cooled melted butter.

Butter the springform or layer pan. Roll out the dough to a round about ¼ inch (6 mm) thick and line the base and sides of the pan. Add the cheese mixture—it should fill the pan about ¾ full. Leave to rise 15–20 minutes. Set the oven at 350°F (175°C). Bake in the heated oven until the filling is set, 50–60 minutes. Leave to cool in the pan and serve the cake at room temperature.

PAINS D'ÉPINARDS (left)
Spinach leaves enclose a spinach-and-custard filling. The "pains" are served with
a fresh tomato sauce.

COURGETTES AU GRATIN (right)
Sliced zucchini are baked in a custard sauce with a topping of grated Gruyère.

PURÉES DE LÉGUMES (front)
A tricolor of nouvelle cuisine purées—pumpkin, cauliflower, and Brussels sprout

Vegetable Accompaniments

UNTIL THE Renaissance, vegetables were regarded as food for the poor—the penance prescribed for monks when they undertook a particularly rigorous fast. Only in the fifteenth century did the Italians begin to consider vegetables as primary ingredients in their own right, not just as useful additives for flavoring meat or poultry. From then date many of our vegetable molds and gratins. When leadership in cooking passed from Italy to France in the seventeenth century, the French acquired the Italian appreciation of vegetables as accompaniments to main dishes and as colorful garnishes.

I personally think that plain boiled vegetables, tossed in butter just before serving, are extraordinarily hard to beat. Above-the-ground (green) vegetables should be quickly cooked in quantities of boiling salted water. Then they are drained and rinsed with cold water ("refreshed") to stop their cooking and set the color. Under-the-ground (root) vegetables are cooked beginning with cold water and simmered gently so they do not break up.

Boiling vegetables, then tossing them in butter, is just the beginning of the story. After boiling, both green and root vegetables can be puréed in a food processor or, more traditionally, by working through a food mill. Either way, the purée is reheated in butter, seasoned, often with spices like nutmeg, and enriched with cream. Enough butter and cream should be added so the consistency is soft and fluffy, never sticky. Milk can also be used to thin the purée. When very diluted, the vegetable purée becomes a soup. Purées of fresh green peas, split peas, beans, lentils, tomatoes, carrots, chestnuts, and spinach date back for centuries, and some of these purées such as lentil and mushroom were also used for thickening sauces—cooks seemed undeterred by the work involved in pushing vegetables through a drum sieve.

In classic cuisine, purées of vegetables with a low starch content, such as celeriac or green beans are bound with béchamel sauce or combined with a small amount of high-carbohydrate vegetable such as potato. Favorite combinations are green beans with dried flageolet beans, onions with potato, artichoke with flageolets, and mushrooms with potato. Nouvelle cuisine purées often exclude these additions, and at the moment the simpler purées are *le grand chic*.

Another traditional vegetable dish that has been adapted by young chefs is vegetable loaves, or *pains*. The vegetables are puréed or cut in pieces and then bound with eggs and white sauce or often with bread crumbs (hence the name *pains*). The mixture is seasoned, poured into individual molds, and baked in a water bath until set. For serving, the loaves are turned out and set like little castles around meat, or passed separately with their own sauce. The fashionable vegetable terrines are really no more than *pains* combining several different vegetables in multicolored layers like Neapolitan ice cream.

One good old-fashioned dish you can give me any day is a vegetable gratin. I cannot resist chunks of well-cooked vegetables with a rich sauce and a golden topping of cheese or bread crumbs. The sauce may be béchamel, mornay, or for starchy vegetables simply heavy cream.

Not all vegetables lend themselves to braising, but those that do are excellent cooked in that way. Chestnuts, which can be treated as vegetables (see p. 44), hearts of celery, cabbage, lettuce, all can be braised in the classic manner on a mirepoix of vegetables moistened with stock. When cooked, the vegetables are drained and a sauce is made with the cooking liquid. Some vegetables can be sautéed directly in butter without previous cooking, notably tomatoes, zucchini, and eggplant. A few, such as cauliflower, broccoli, and carrots can be blanched, then dipped in batter, and deep fried, and mushrooms and eggplant can be deep fried without blanching.

The choice of cooking method for vegetables often depends on the season—the younger and fresher the vegetables, the better they are when simply boiled and tossed in butter. But whatever is served—fresh green beans, perfectly cooked to a brilliant green, homely gratin, or a pretty-pretty group of contrasting purées nestling on a plate, the modern dinner is far from the medieval feast. A meal without some kind of vegetable would be strange indeed.

FOR SUCCESSFUL VEGETABLE ACCOMPANIMENTS

1. Use plenty of water for cooking green vegetables; a small quantity of water would take longer to come back to a boil after the vegetables were added, and they would cook more slowly.

2. Vegetables for purées should be cooked longer than usual so they are relatively soft.

3. Be sure that vegetables are thoroughly drained before adding them to a mixture for a gratin or vegetable mold. Even when well drained, vegetables will produce liquid during further cooking.

4. Make gratins in a shallow baking dish so that each serving has plenty of browned topping. In a shallow dish, vegetables also cook more quickly, so the vegetables give off less liquid.

PREPARING AHEAD

1. Although some fresh flavor is lost, green vegetables can be cooked up to two hours in advance. Do not keep them hot, but just before serving, reheat them in butter without cooking them further.

2. Root vegetables can be kept hot in a warm place for up to thirty minutes. They can also be prepared ahead and reheated as for green vegetables.

3. Vegetable purées can be kept hot for up to an hour in a water bath, though they lose some of their aroma. Unless they contain potato, they can be made up to three days ahead and kept in the refrigerator.

4. Vegetable molds won't be quite as fresh-tasting if made ahead, but they can be cooked in advance and kept in the refrigerator. They should be reheated in their molds in a water bath. Vegetable molds can also be served at room temperature.

Braised Lettuce
(LAITUES BRAISÉES)

This versatile accompaniment can be varied to complement the main dish by using the most suitable stock—chicken, veal, or beef.

> **4 medium heads leaf lettuce**
> **2 ounces (60 g) bacon, sliced**
> **2 medium shallots, chopped**

> **1 carrot, chopped**
> **1 cup stock (pp. 112–118)**
> **salt and pepper**
> **1 tablespoon chopped parsley**

SERVES 4.

Trim the tough base from each head of lettuce and wash the heads. Blanch them in boiling salted water for 5 minutes, drain, refresh under cold running water, and drain again. Cut each head in half lengthwise and gently squeeze out excess water. Fold the halves crosswise to form neat triangles.

Heat the oven to 350°F (175°C) and butter a flameproof baking dish generously. Put the bacon slices in the baking dish, scatter the chopped shallots and carrots over them, and top with the lettuce. Pour the stock over the lettuce, sprinkle with salt and pepper, and cover the dish first with buttered aluminum foil and then with the lid. Bring to a boil on top of the stove and then braise in the heated oven until very tender, 45–55 minutes. The lettuce can be made ahead to this point and kept, covered and refrigerated, up to 3 days. Reheat gently on top of the stove or in a 350°F (175°C) oven.

Lift the lettuce from the cooking liquid, pressing gently to extract some of the liquid, and arrange on a serving platter with whatever meat it is to accompany or on individual plates. Keep warm. Strain the cooking liquid into a heavy-bottomed saucepan and boil over high heat to reduce to a syrupy glaze. Spoon the reduced liquid over the lettuce and sprinkle with parsley.

Cauliflower Purée
(PURÉE DE CHOUFLEUR)

Cauliflower makes a surprisingly delicate-tasting purée.

> **1 medium cauliflower (2 pounds or 1 kg)**
> **2 tablespoons (30 g) butter**
> **salt and pepper**
> **nutmeg**
> **1–2 tablespoons heavy cream**

SERVES 4.

Divide the cauliflower into flowerets. Cook them in boiling salted water until tender, 10–12 minutes. Drain very thoroughly. Purée the cauliflower in a food processor or work it through a vegetable mill. The purée can be prepared ahead to this point and kept, covered and refrigerated, up to 3 days.

Melt the butter in a saucepan, add the purée, and season with salt and pepper and a grating of nutmeg. Cook over medium heat, stirring, until it is very hot and excess moisture has evaporated. Stir in enough of the cream so the purée is just soft enough to fall from a spoon. Taste for seasoning and adjust if necessary.

Transfer the purée to a serving dish or to individual plates, mark the top in waves with a knife if you like, and serve as soon as possible.

Pumpkin Purée
(PURÉE DE POTIRON)

Not only for pies and jack-o'-lanterns, pumpkin is delicious in this guise.

**2 pounds (1 kg) pumpkin
1 tablespoon (15 g) butter
salt and pepper
nutmeg
2–4 tablespoons heavy cream**

SERVES 4.

Remove the seeds from the pumpkin, peel it, and cut the flesh into pieces. Cook in boiling salted water to cover until tender, about 20 minutes. Drain very thoroughly. Purée the pumpkin in a food processor, push it through a sieve, work through a vegetable mill, or simply mash it. The purée can be prepared ahead to this point and kept, covered and refrigerated, up to 3 days.

Melt the butter in a saucepan, add the purée, and season with salt and pepper and nutmeg. Cook over medium heat, stirring, until it is very hot and excess moisture has evaporated. Stir in enough of the cream so the purée is just soft enough to fall from a spoon. Taste for seasoning and adjust if necessary.

Transfer the purée to a serving dish or to individual plates, mark the top in waves with a knife if you like, and serve as soon as possible.

Brussels Sprouts Purée
(PURÉE DE CHOUX DE BRUXELLES)

It's attractive to serve two or three purées of different colors. Brussels sprouts and pumpkin would make a good combination.

> **2 pounds (1 kg) Brussels sprouts**
> **6 tablespoons (95 g) butter**
> **salt and pepper**
> **nutmeg**
> **juice of ½ lemon**
> **1–2 tablespoons heavy cream**

SERVES 4.

Trim the stems from the Brussels sprouts and remove any discolored outer leaves. Blanch the Brussels sprouts by boiling in a large quantity of water for 2 minutes. Drain and refresh under cold running water. (NOTE: Blanching will make the flavor less assertive.) Cook in boiling salted water until quite tender, about 15 minutes. Drain very thoroughly. Purée the Brussels sprouts in a food processor or work them through a vegetable mill. The purée can be prepared ahead to this point and kept, covered and refrigerated, up to 3 days.

Melt the butter in a saucepan, add the purée, and season with salt and pepper and a grating of nutmeg. Cook over medium heat, stirring, until very hot. Stir in the lemon juice and enough of the cream so the purée is just soft enough to fall from a spoon. Taste for seasoning and adjust if necessary.

Transfer the purée to a serving dish or to individual plates, mark the top in waves with a knife if you like, and serve as soon as possible.

Zucchini Gratin
(COURGETTES AU GRATIN)

This is a quick and simple form of vegetable gratin, made with a custard mixture rather than the more usual béchamel sauce.

> **1 pound (500 g) zucchini**
> **1 ounce or about ⅓ cup (30 g) grated Gruyère cheese**

For the custard mixture:
> **2 eggs**
> **1 cup (250 ml) heavy cream**
> **salt and pepper**

SERVES 4.

     Set the oven at 400°F (200°C). Cut the zucchini in ½-inch (1.25 cm) diagonal slices. Blanch in boiling salted water for 3 minutes and drain thoroughly. Spread the slices in a shallow baking dish. The zucchini can be blanched up to 6 hours ahead of time.

     For the custard mixture: Beat the eggs with the cream and season to taste.

     Pour the custard over the zucchini and sprinkle with the cheese. Bake in the hot oven until the custard is just set and the top is brown, 10–15 minutes.

Provençal Tomatoes
(TOMATES PROVENÇALE)

When tomatoes are at their best, this useful recipe makes an ideal accompaniment to lamb, chicken, or steaks.

> **4 medium tomatoes**
> **salt and pepper**
> **2 tablespoons olive oil**
> **2 cloves garlic, finely chopped**
> **2 tablespoons chopped parsley**
> **3 tablespoons fresh bread crumbs**

SERVES 4.

     Set the oven at 400°F (200°C) and oil a baking dish or roasting pan generously. Cut the tomatoes in half. Cut out and discard the cores. Sprinkle the halves with salt and pepper. Put the tomatoes in the prepared baking dish or pan, cut side up, and sprinkle with 1 tablespoon of the oil. Bake in the hot oven for 10 minutes. Mix the garlic, parsley, and bread crumbs together and sprinkle the tomatoes with this mixture and then with the remaining tablespoon of oil. Return to the oven for 3 minutes and then brown the tops quickly in the broiler. Serve hot or warm.

Spinach Molds
(PAINS D'ÉPINARDS)

These spinach molds with tomato sauce are good with roast chicken or almost any kind of meat—veal, pork, lamb, or beef.

1 recipe tomato sauce (p. 397)
1½ pounds (750 g) spinach
1½ cups (375 ml) milk
¼ cup (35 g) fresh bread crumbs
3 tablespoons (45 g) butter
2 eggs, beaten to mix
1 egg yolk
salt and pepper
nutmeg

4 dariole molds or custard cups

SERVES 4.

Make the tomato sauce. This can be done well ahead of time if you like.

Remove the stems from the spinach, wash it well, and blanch about 16 large leaves in a large quantity of boiling salted water for 1 minute. Remove from the water with a slotted spoon and spread out carefully on paper towels. Put the remaining spinach in the boiling water, return to a boil, and cook until tender, 2–3 minutes. Drain and refresh under cold running water. Squeeze the cooked spinach by the handful to remove most of the water and then chop it.

Heat the oven to 350°F (175°C) and prepare a water bath (see Chapter 8). Butter the molds and line them with the blanched spinach leaves, letting them hang over the rims of the molds. Heat the milk in a small saucepan, add the bread crumbs, and set aside. Melt the butter in a saucepan, add the

Squeeze the water from the cooked spinach that will be used in the filling.

Lining the darioles molds with the blanched spinach leaves

chopped spinach, and cook over moderately high heat, stirring, until all excess moisture has evaporated. Remove from the heat and add the milk and bread crumbs, the beaten eggs, and egg yolk. Season to taste with salt and pepper and a grating of nutmeg.

Spoon the spinach mixture carefully into the lined molds, fold the overhanging leaves over the filling, and cover with buttered aluminum foil. The molds can be prepared up to 6 hours ahead and kept in the refrigerator.

Put the molds in the water bath and bring the water to a simmer on top of the stove. Transfer to the hot oven and bake until the molds are set, 20–25 minutes. Heat the tomato sauce if necessary.

Turn out the molds onto a platter and spoon some of the sauce around them. Serve the remaining sauce separately.

Tomato Sauce
(SAUCE TOMATE)

This basic sauce has a multitude of uses from accompanying vegetable dishes to coating fish. It can also be served with eggs, chicken, and meat.

1 tablespoon (15 g) butter
1 small onion, chopped
1 tablespoon flour
¾ cup (185 ml) white veal (p. 116) or chicken stock (p.
    115) or stock mixed with juice from canned tomatoes
1 pound (500 g) fresh tomatoes, quartered, OR ¾ pound
    (350 g) canned tomatoes, drained and chopped
1 small clove garlic, finely chopped
1 bouquet garni (p. 118)
¼ teaspoon sugar
salt and pepper

MAKES ABOUT 1¼ CUPS (310 ml) SAUCE.

In a saucepan melt the butter and cook the onion slowly until soft and lightly browned, 7–10 minutes. Stir in the flour and cook until foaming, 1–2 minutes. Remove from the heat, pour in the stock, and bring to a boil, stirring. Add the tomatoes, garlic, bouquet garni, sugar, and salt and pepper. Simmer uncovered, stirring occasionally, until the tomatoes are very soft and the sauce is slightly thick, 45–50 minutes for fresh tomatoes and 30–40 minutes for canned.

Work the sauce through a sieve, taste for seasoning, and adjust if necessary. It can be kept, covered and refrigerated, for up to 3 days, or it can be frozen.

Potatoes

GIVEN THE POPULARITY of the potato throughout the western world, it is hard to believe the suspicion they aroused in the sixteenth century when they were brought back to Europe from the Americas. Scottish Presbyterians objected because potatoes were not mentioned in the Bible, while the Dutch called them the "ill-starred root," believing them to be a slow poison. In both France and Germany, it took a century or two, punctuated by famine, to force acceptance of the suspect root. King Frederick William of Prussia took the direct approach to encouraging adoption, threatening to lop off the ears and nose of anyone who refused to plant potatoes. However, Louis XVI of France was more subtle: acting on the advice of an eccentric scientist, Antoine Auguste Parmentier, he placed his fields of potatoes at Versailles under armed guard and bedecked his queen, Marie-Antoinette, with their flowers. Titillated by this novelty, Louis' courtiers turned from wearing potato flowers to eating the roots.

Once launched, the career of the potato could hardly falter. Not only will it grow in almost any climate, but it adapts itself obligingly to just about every method of cooking. Oldest and simplest is to bake the potato in hot ashes or in their modern equivalent, the oven. The crisp skin and soft crumbly interior of a good baked potato are hard to beat (a foil wrap is nonsensical because it traps too much steam). In France, however, boiled potatoes are preferred as the background for rich sauces and stews.

I have to admit a long-standing aversion to boiled potatoes, dating from my youth in an English boarding school where potatoes appeared inexorably at lunch and supper seven days a week. And what potatoes! They were pocked with unpeeled eyes and mottled with gray-green bruises on the outside, soggy with water on the inside, and altogether inedible. So-called mashed potatoes were scarcely better—squashed to a sullen gray pulp, their rough appearance betraying the presence of innumerable lumps. It was only when I went to cooking school that I learned that mashed potatoes needn't be like this. We dried our *pommes purées* over heat to remove all trace of water and then beat them with hot milk and quantities of butter until they turned fluffy and creamy white due, the chef said, to the starch expanding over the heat.

I was never confident of his scientific background, but the starch in potatoes is important. Sometimes it is needed to glue dishes together, as in *soubriques* (grated potato pancakes). In recipes for which potatoes are sliced and then baked in liquid, like those for many potato gratins, starch helps to thicken the dish. However, when potatoes are deep fried, starch reduces crispness, so they should be sliced and then soaked in water to remove as much starch as possible.

As happens so often in cooking, one dish leads to another. Boiled potatoes become potato salad, for instance, or they may be sliced and dressed with parsley-flavored butter for *pommes maître d'hôtel* (p. 402). Potato purée becomes a whole family of dishes, best of which, I think, is potatoes dauphine (p. 71)—puréed potatoes mixed with half their volume of choux pastry and then deep fried to wonderful crisp balls.

After boiling, sautéing is the cooking method most often used at home for potatoes. Sautéed potatoes are a weakness of mine, and of M. Chambrette, the head chef of La Varenne—hash browns were one of his gastronomic discoveries during a recent visit to the United States. I quite often catch him making a snack on the sneak, nonchalantly tossing sautéed potatoes with a flick of the wrist as if the outsize frying pan weighed only a few ounces. He continues cooking the potatoes much longer than one would have expected, until the edges are deep golden brown and semitransparent. That way, I've learned, the potatoes stay crisp twice as long.

Other versions of sautéed potatoes include delectably crisp potato pancakes made with puréed potatoes or grated raw potato. The classic sautéed potatoes are made with parboiled or raw potatoes, cut and then fried in a small amount of fat so they toast to a crusty brown. *Pommes fondantes* are potatoes sautéed in butter in a covered pan so they cook in their own steam until "melting" (hence their name).

There are many different varieties of potato as well as ways to cook them. On a trip to the Andes, I saw green, purple, and pink ones, and extraordinary giant orange potatoes. However, in western cooking only a few kinds are used (sweet potatoes and yams belong to a different plant family). Basically they fall into two categories: those with firm almost waxy flesh and the soft floury potatoes. New potatoes are waxy while mature potatoes are more or less floury depending on the variety (Idahos are one of the best examples of fine floury potatoes). Waxy potatoes are good for boiling because they hold their shape; more mature potatoes are better for sautéeing and deep frying.

Forced to choose my favorite way to cook potatoes, I would probably opt for deep frying since there are so many variations, from the ubiquitous French fry through half a dozen more esoteric sizes of potato sticks (see p. 66) to chips, latticed gaufrettes, and the ambitious *pommes soufflées*. When cut to exactly the right thickness, small rectangles of potato can be induced to *soufflé* beguilingly like little balloons. The secret is to fry the potatoes first at a low temperature until soft and then to plunge them into scorching fat. They are sealed instantly on the outside, and the steam that forms as the heat penetrates to the center of the potato puffs the surfaces in a most satisfactory manner. Soufflé potatoes were discovered, runs the story, when King Louis Philippe of France opened a new stretch of railway. The train didn't start on time, the king was late for the lunch waiting at the other end of the track, and the chef was distraught. Suddenly the whistle was heard. The frantic chef plunged his already-cooked limp potatoes into hot fat to reheat them, and *voilà—pommes soufflées*.

 FOR SUCCESSFUL POTATO DISHES

1. Store potatoes in a paper bag in a cool palce around 55°F (15°C). When too warm, potatoes wither and the eyes sprout; when too cold, they turn black and acquire a sweet taste; when exposed to light, the flesh develops a green tinge and a musty flavor.

2. So that boiled potatoes will cook evenly, start them in cold water in a covered pan. Bring to a boil to begin the cooking, but then reduce the heat and simmer the potatoes so the outside of the potato doesn't fall apart by the time the center is done.

3. Potatoes have more flavor when cooked in their skins. Boiled potatoes also hold their shape better when cooked unpeeled.

4. Do not overcook boiled potatoes or they will be soggy; they should be just tender when pierced with a pointed knife. Cook potatoes to be puréed one to two minutes longer. Drain boiled potatoes as soon as tender so they won't become waterlogged.

5. For good flavor and crispness, sauté potatoes in a combination of oil and butter.

6. When deep frying, add just as many potatoes to the pan as will fit comfortably. If too many are introduced to the fat at once, the temperature will be lowered and the potatoes will be flabby rather than crisp.

PREPARING AHEAD

1. Potatoes can be peeled up to twenty-four hours before using. To avoid discoloration, keep them in cold water.

2. When starch should be removed, for example, for deep-fried potatoes, the potatoes can be cut in appropriate shapes and soaked in cold water at least one or up to twelve hours. Drain and dry thoroughly before using.

3. A cold potato is uninteresting gastronomically. However, you can partially cook many potato recipes several hours ahead of time and keep them at room temperature until ready to proceed.

Potato and Celery Salad
(SALADE DE POMMES DE TERRE ET DE CÉLERI)

For best flavor, the potatoes are dressed while still warm and are never chilled. If you must refrigerate a potato salad, allow it to come to room temperature before serving.

> 1½ pounds new potatoes
> vinaigrette (p. 348) made with 2 tablespoons vinegar,
>   salt and pepper, 2 teaspoons Dijon mustard, and 6
>   tablespoons oil
> 3 tablespoons white wine
> mayonnaise (p. 351) made with 1 egg yolk, salt and
>   pepper, 1 tablespoon vinegar, ¼ teaspoon mustard,
>   and ¾ cup (185 ml) oil
> 6 stalks celery, with leaves
> 1 tablespoon chopped tarragon
> 1 tablespoon chopped chervil or parsley
> salt and pepper

SERVES 4.

Put the potatoes, unpeeled, in cold salted water to cover and bring to a boil. Reduce the heat and simmer until the point of a knife pierces them easily, 15–20 minutes. Make the vinaigrette. Drain the potatoes as soon as they are tender. Peel and slice them into ¼-inch (6 mm) slices while still warm. Pour the wine over the potato slices and mix gently. Add the vinaigrette and mix carefully again. Make the mayonnaise. The salad can be made to this point 2–3 hours ahead, covered, and left at room temperature.

To finish: Cut the celery stalks into thin diagonal slices and reserve the leaves. Add the celery to the potatoes with the mayonnaise, tarragon, and chervil or parsley. Mix carefully, taste the salad for seasoning, and adjust if necessary.

Transfer to a serving bowl and decorate the edge with the celery leaves.

Maître d'Hôtel Potatoes
(POMMES MAÎTRE D'HÔTEL)

Here is yet another use for versatile maître d'hôtel butter. It makes a simple yet delicious dish from plain boiled potatoes, one that is very handy to know.

2 pounds potatoes
maître d'hôtel butter (p. 51) made with 2 teaspoons
  chopped parsley, 1 teaspoon lemon juice, 4
  tablespoons (60 g) butter, and salt and pepper

SERVES 4.

Cut the potatoes into halves, put them, unpeeled, in cold salted water to cover, and bring to a boil. Reduce the heat and simmer until the point of a knife pierces them easily, 15–20 minutes. Make the maître d'hôtel butter and leave at room temperature. Drain the potatoes as soon as they are tender, peel, and cut them in ⅜-inch (1 cm) slices.

Arrange the warm potatoes overlapping in a shallow dish, dot with the butter, and serve. (NOTE: The potatoes should be hot enough to melt the butter, but if not, heat the dish for a few moments in a 300°F [150°C] oven.)

Concièrge Potatoes
(POMMES DE TERRE CONCIÈRGE)

Some of the best simple cooking in Paris used to be done in the loges of the concièrges, and our head chef, Fernand Chambrette, names his favorite potatoes in honor of the traditional French concièrge.

2 pounds (1 kg) potatoes, peeled
4 tablespoons oil
4 tablespoons (60 g) butter
salt and pepper
1 tablespoon chopped parsley

SERVES 4.

Cut the potatoes into thin even slices. Wash them under cold running water to rid them of excess starch. Drain thoroughly and dry with paper towels.

Heat the oil in a large frying pan, add the butter, and when it is hot, sauté the potatoes over high heat until one side begins to brown. Toss them and sprinkle with salt and pepper. Cook the potatoes over medium-high heat, tossing occasionally, until they are tender and the edges are golden brown and crisp, 20–25 minutes. Taste for seasoning and adjust if necessary. Toss with the chopped parsley and serve.

Soubrique Potatoes
(POMMES SOUBRIQUES)

In the old days, soubriques were cooked on the hot bricks (briques) of the fireplace. Now they are usually sautéed in a frying pan.

2 pounds (1 kg) potatoes, peeled
3 tablespoons (15 g) flour
salt and pepper
nutmeg
3 tablespoons (15 g) grated Gruyère cheese
1 egg, beaten to mix
4 tablespoons oil
4 tablespoons (60 g) butter

SERVES 4.

Grate the potatoes onto a dish towel or piece of cheesecloth and squeeze to remove any excess liquid. Combine them in a bowl with the flour, salt and pepper, a grating of nutmeg, and cheese. Stir in the egg.

Heat half the oil in a frying pan, add half the butter, and when it is hot, drop in tablespoonfuls of the potato mixture to make 3-inch (7.5 cm) pancakes. Sauté them quickly until golden brown, 2–3 minutes a side, and drain on paper towels. Keep warm in a 350°F (175°C) oven with the door ajar. Heat the remaining oil and butter, fry the rest of the potato mixture in the same way, and serve as soon as possible.

Fondante Potatoes
(POMMES FONDANTES)

These potatoes are "turned" (cut into smooth ovals) and can be served at the most elegant repast.

> **2 pounds (1 kg) potatoes, peeled**
> **¼ pound (125 g) butter**
> **salt and pepper**
> **1 tablespoon chopped parsley**

SERVES 4.

Cut the potatoes in quarters and trim the edges to form the quarters into smooth ovals. In a sauté pan melt the butter and add the potatoes—they should fit in one layer. Cover tightly and cook over high heat until the potatoes are tender, 15–20 minutes, shaking the pan occasionally to turn the potatoes; they cook in their own steam and will brown without burning. Sprinkle with salt and pepper.

Transfer the potatoes to a serving bowl or to individual plates, sprinkle with chopped parsley, and serve.

Soufflé Potatoes
(POMMES DE TERRE SOUFFLÉES)

The keys to success in making these potatoes are the thickness of the slices and the temperature of the fat. If some of the slices don't puff, they're still very good to eat.

> **2 pounds (1 kg) medium potatoes, peeled**
> **deep fat for frying**
> **salt**

SERVES 4.

Cut the potatoes into 1½- × 3-inch (4 × 7.5 cm) blocks and round the corners. Cut them in even ⅛-inch (3 mm) slices, using a mandoline cutter if possible. Soak the slices in ice water at least 15 minutes. Dry very well before frying. Heat the fat to 350° F (175°C on a deep-fry thermometer). Fry the potatoes, stirring constantly, until tender and just beginning to brown, 6–8 minutes, and remove with a slotted spoon. The potatoes can be prepared to this point 2–3 hours ahead.

A short time before serving, heat the fat to 380°F (195°C). Add a few slices of deep-fried potato—they will puff almost at once. Fry them, stirring, until crisp and brown, 1–2 minutes. Drain the potatoes on paper towels and keep hot in a 350°F (175°C) oven with the door ajar while frying the rest.

Sprinkle the soufflé potatoes with salt and serve at once.

First cut the potatoes into even blocks and round off the corners.

Next, cut the blocks into ⅛-inch slices with a mandoline and leave them to soak in cold water.

The second frying in very hot fat will make the slices puff and brown.

NOUILLES À L'ITALIENNE
The French tend to give Italian names to their pasta dishes, here noodles simply dressed
with butter and Parmesan. A special variation is the mixture of plain, red, and green noodles.

Pasta

LEGEND HAS IT that Marco Polo brought pasta back from one of his trips to the Orient. Utter nonsense! The Roman Apicius, who lived at the time of Christ, gives a recipe for fried pasta strips with pepper and honey; and in 1279, a decade or more before Marco Polo's return from his travels, a chest of macaroni was listed as part of a Genoese inheritance. Through the centuries what is basically flour and water dough has been transformed into an ever more fantastic number of patterns and shapes. Flamboyant sauces have been added, and the union of pasta and Parmesan cheese has been sanctified. However, it was not until the mid-nineteenth century, with the invention of the extrusion machine for mass production, that pasta became an everyday staple food rather than a feast-day treat.

French cooks have never approached the Italian virtuosity with pasta; not surprisingly, many French pasta dishes bear Italian names—*nouilles à l'italienne* (with Parmesan cheese and butter), *à la napolitaine* (with beef stewed in red wine and tomatoes, grated cheese, and butter), and *à la sicilienne* (with grated cheese, butter, and puréed chicken liver). But the French have their own ways with pasta as well.

The Alsace region is famous for homemade noodles rich with egg yolks. These are often topped with toasted bread crumbs and butter. Sometimes cream and a few drops of vinegar are added to the noodles, with a winter touch of wild mushrooms and, for the well-heeled, diced foie gras. In Languedoc, macaroni is prepared with eggplant, tomatoes, and garlic, and it is no surprise that ravioli and cannelloni have spread along the Riviera from Italy to Provence. (For cognoscenti, by the way, there's even a spaghetti museum near Imperia not far from Genoa.)

The Corsicans fill their ravioli with a mixture of fresh sheeps' cheese, mint, fennel, and lettuce. More orthodox ideas include pasta shells with onions, à la lyonnaise, and a delicious Provençal cannelloni filled with fresh sardines and spinach, coated with white sauce and sprinkled with cheese.

Pasta is at its best when freshly made. However, the freshest of bought pasta rarely compares with that made at home. Ingredients for the dough are minimal: flour, salt, eggs, and a spoonful or two of oil to make the mixture easier to handle. The finished dough—made by the universal method of sifting the flour on a board and then adding the liquid ingredients to a well in the center—should be supple and moist. Don't be afraid of working pasta dough well—it should be a good deal more elastic than pie-pastry dough, and I like to pick it up and slap it on the table with a rhythm that works wonders on frayed nerves. If the dough tends to stick, work in a little flour, but never let it get dry or it will crack during rolling. The right consistency is aptly described in an old Alsatian recipe that calls for mixing one egg per person in a bowl and then beating in flour by spoonfuls until the dough is "too stiff to beat."

It is the rolling that takes time and skill. I have seen a little old Italian chef, who trained under Escoffier, make and roll dough by hand to wafer thinness in under twenty minutes, but he was a master. He used quantities of flour, shifted the dough, and turned it from one side to another constantly and, by sheer muscle power and a heavy rolling pin, reduced the elastic ball of dough to a vast sheet the texture of velvet. Then, sprinkling with yet more flour, he loosely folded the sheet and cut it across in strips to make perfect even noodles.

For less intrepid cooks like me, it helps to leave the dough for an hour or so (covered with an overturned bowl to prevent drying) so that it loses some of its elasticity before rolling is attempted. A pasta machine, which works on the principle of a laundry wringer, simplifies the task still further. The dough is passed several times through the machine, each time with the rollers closer together, until the pasta emerges in a ribbon of the required thickness—that is, as thin as possible.

Whether homemade or store-bought, and of whatever form, pasta is cooked in the same way. It should be immersed in large quantities of boiling liquid—at least 2 quarts (2 L) for ½ pound (250 g) pasta. Almost all pasta is cooked in salted water—allow 2 teaspoons (10 g) salt per quart (liter), but when you have it, stock will add flavor and richness. Always simmer pasta, do not boil it, and stir it several times during cooking to separate the strands. Timing depends on the type and size of the pasta, and dried pasta takes longer to cook than fresh. Very fine and fresh homemade noodles are often done when just brought back to a boil, whereas commercial noodles can take ten minutes or more. The only reliable test for cooking pasta is to taste it; it should still be resilient to the bite yet not taste of uncooked flour. The Italian phrase *al dente* perfectly sums up the correct texture—chewy to the teeth.

Although regional pasta specialties have long been popular in their own territories, it is only with the advent of *nouvelle cuisine* that pasta has come to elegant menus. The nouvelle chefs belie their preference for lightness by doting on noodles and serving them in combination with all manner of new ingredients—with fish, butter sauce, and fresh herbs; with strips of boned chicken breast, reduced cream, and slivers of fresh ginger; with wild game and fruit.

Serving possibilities are so many, and the flavor of pasta itself is so unobtrusive that it is hard to imagine anyone disliking it. On the contrary, pasta is addictive. When he was consul in Alexandria, Ferdinand de Lesseps would regale the plump son of the Egyptian viceroy with secret feasts of macaroni. When the son became viceroy in his turn, he permitted De Lesseps to try out his engineering talents on Egyptian soil. The Suez Canal, the eventual result, can therefore be said to be based on macaroni. . . .

FOR SUCCESSFUL PASTA

1. Always roll the dough to a thin sheet; thick pasta is heavy when cooked.

2. When rolling by hand, be sure the sheet of dough is of even thickness so that the cut pasta cooks at the same speed.

3. A firm dough is needed for rolling pasta by machine so it does not stick. Flour the dough thoroughly before passing it through the machine the first time and sprinkle the machine rollers lightly with flour between each rolling.

4. When cutting noodles by hand, leave the sheet of dough to dry first for thirty minutes so it does not stick to itself when folded. If time is short, dust the dough liberally with flour before folding.

5. A tablespoon of cooking oil added to simmering pasta prevents it from sticking together and helps keep the water from boiling over.

6. An onion studded with cloves and a clove or two of peeled garlic will add flavor to the cooking water.

7. Slightly undercook pasta that is to be cooked further with other ingredients.

8. Serve pasta on heated plates.

PREPARING AHEAD

1. Fresh pasta dough can be made ahead, rolled, and cut into noodles. These can then be left to dry and stored in the refrigerator for up to one week.

2. Pasta can be frozen and kept up to six months. However, the longer it is kept, the drier and more like bought pasta it will become. Do not defrost before cooking.

3. To keep pasta hot for up to fifteen minutes, return the drained pasta to a saucepan and cover with hot water; drain just before serving.

Fresh Pasta
(PÂTES FRAÎCHES)

To avoid drying the dough, and the attendant difficulty in rolling, choose a draft-free place to roll out the pasta dough.

> **2 cups (260 g) flour**
> **1 teaspoon salt**
> **1 tablespoon oil**
> **2 eggs, beaten to mix**
> **1–2 tablespoons water**

SERVES 4.

Sift the flour onto a work surface and make a well in the center. Beat the salt, oil, eggs, and water together with a fork and pour into the well. Gradually draw in the flour, working the dough lightly between the fingers so it forms large crumbs. If some dry crumbs remain that don't stick together to form large ones, sprinkle up to another tablespoon of water over the dough. Press the dough together into a ball. It should be soft but not sticky. Knead the dough on a floured surface until very smooth and elastic, about 10 minutes. Cover with an inverted bowl and leave to rest for about an hour.

Divide the dough in half and roll out each piece on a floured surface to as thin a sheet as possible, or, if using a pasta machine, crank the dough through the rollers. Leave the sheets to dry for about 30 minutes, preferably over a broom handle or wooden laundry rack so air will reach both sides. To cut the dough into noodles by hand, fold each sheet of dough loosely and cut crosswise into the desired widths. Alternatively, cut the dough in a pasta machine. The noodles can be cooked immediately or left to dry for an hour or two. They will keep for up to 1 week if left to dry several hours, wrapped in plastic, and refrigerated. They can also be frozen.

To cook the noodles: Bring a large pan of boiling salted water to a boil. Add the noodles, bring the water back to a boil and then simmer, stirring occasionally, until just tender, about 3 minutes, and drain.

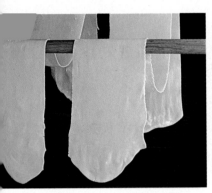  

Hang freshly rolled sheets of pasta to dry in such a way that air can reach both sides.

Fold the sheets loosely to cut them with a knife . . .

. . . or cut them in the pasta machine, which can be set for a variety of widths.

Green Pasta
(PÂTES VERTES)

The spinach used to color the pasta green adds liquid to the dough, so water is omitted.

> **fresh pasta (p. 410) made with ½ pound (250 g) spinach, 2 cups (260 g) flour, 1 teaspoon salt, 1 tablespoon oil, and 2 eggs**

SERVES 4.

Remove the stems from the spinach and wash it well. Put the spinach in a large pan of boiling water, return to a boil, and cook until tender, 2–3 minutes. Drain and refresh under cold running water. Squeeze the spinach by the handful to remove most of the water. Purée the spinach in a food processor or work it through a food mill. Put the purée in a small saucepan and cook over moderately high heat until fairly dry, 2–3 minutes.

Make the pasta, beating the spinach with the egg mixture.

Red Pasta
(PÂTES ROUGES)

Tomato paste colors pasta an appealing red but does not noticeably alter its taste. Both green and red pasta are used more for color contrast than for additional flavor.

> **fresh pasta (p. 410) made with 2 cups (260 g) flour, 1 teaspoon salt, 1 tablespoon oil, 2 eggs, 1–2 teaspoons water, and 2½ tablespoons tomato paste**

SERVES 4.

Make the pasta, beating the tomato paste with the egg mixture.

Noodles à l'Italienne
(NOUILLES À L'ITALIENNE)

Multicolored noodles, set off by the simple butter and cheese sauce, make this an unusual dish.

> **½ recipe fresh pasta (p. 410)**
> **½ recipe green pasta (p. 411)**
> **½ recipe red pasta (above)**
> **¼ pound (125 g) butter, softened**
> **3 ounces or ¾ cup (90 g) grated Parmesan cheese**
> **salt and pepper**

SERVES 6.

Make the fresh, green, and red pastas. Toss them together with the butter, half the cheese, and salt and pepper to taste. Transfer to a serving platter or individual plates and sprinkle the remaining cheese over the noodles.

Red Noodles with Goat Cheese and Chives
(PÂTES FRAÎCHES AU FROMAGE DE CHÈVRE ET À LA CIBOULETTE)

This is a nouvelle cuisine-inspired dish, colorful with red pasta and green chives and tangy with the new chefs' favorite cheese—chèvre.

1 recipe red pasta (p. 412)
¾ cup (185 ml) heavy cream
4 tablespoons (60 g) butter, softened
¼ pound (125 g) goats' cheese, crumbled
2 tablespoons chopped chives
salt and pepper
1 egg yolk

SERVES 4.

Make the red pasta. Warm the cream in a small saucepan. Toss the noodles with the butter, add the cream, and mix over low heat. Add the cheese, chives, and salt and pepper to taste and heat just until the cheese melts. Remove from the heat, add the egg yolk, toss well, and serve immediately.

Sole Fillets with Fresh Pasta and Shrimps
(FILETS DE SOLE AUX PÂTES FRAÎCHES ET AUX CREVETTES)

The sheer luxury of this dish makes sole seem especially appropriate, but other fish could be used, and another shellfish could be substituted for the shrimp.

1 recipe green pasta (p. 411)
2 tablespoons (30 g) butter
½ carrot, thinly sliced
¼ onion, chopped
½ pound (250 g) unpeeled shrimps
2 tablespoons cognac
1½ cups (375 ml) heavy cream
salt and pepper
4 sole fillets (about 1 pound or 500 g)
hollandaise sauce (p. 201) made with ¼ pound (125 g)
    butter, 2 tablespoons water, 2 egg yolks, salt and
    pepper, and the juice of ½ lemon

SERVES 4.

Make the green pasta and cut it into noodles.

Melt the butter in a heavy-bottomed pan, add the carrot and onion, and cook over low heat, stirring often, until soft but not brown, 7–10 minutes. Add the shrimp and sauté until the shells turn red, about 5 minutes. Add the cognac, ignite it, and let flame 4–5 seconds. Douse the flames with half the cream, stir in salt and pepper, and simmer for 10 minutes. Remove the shrimp and peel them, reserving the shells. Pound the heads and shells in a mortar with a pestle or work them in a food mill. Return the shells to the cooking liquid and simmer for 10 minutes. Strain the liquid into a small saucepan and boil, if necessary, to thicken slightly. The shrimp can be cooked and the shrimp cream made up to a day ahead and kept, covered, in the refrigerator.

Set the oven at 400°F (200°C) and butter a baking dish. Fold the fish fillets in half crosswise, put them in the prepared dish, and pour the remaining cream over the fish. Make the hollandaise sauce and keep warm in a water bath. Cook the sole in the heated oven until the fillets can be pierced easily with a fork, about 10 minutes. Meanwhile cook the green noodles. Lift the fillets out of the cooking liquid. Pour the liquid into a small heavy-bottomed pan, add the shrimp cream, and boil until thick enough to coat a spoon. Remove from the heat, whisk in the hollandaise sauce, and stir in the shrimp. Taste for seasoning and adjust if necessary.

To serve, arrange beds of pasta on heated plates, top each bed of noodles with a fish fillet, and spoon sauce and shrimps over all.

Young Wild Rabbit with Ginger and Noodles
(LAPEREAU AU GINGEMBRE ET AUX PÂTES FRAÎCHES)

The pear and ginger in this recipe complement game particularly well, but the dish is very good made with domestic rabbit.

- 1 recipe fresh pasta (p. 410)
- 4½ pound (2 kg) rabbit
- 4 tablespoons oil
- 1 onion, diced
- 1 carrot, diced
- 2 shallots, diced
- 2 teaspoons coriander seeds
- 2 teaspoons thyme
- 1 bouquet garni (p. 118)
- 2 teaspoons peppercorns, crushed

salt and pepper
2 cups (500 ml) white veal (p. 116) or chicken stock
  (p. 115)
½ cup (125 ml) red wine
2 tablespoons (30 g) butter, clarified
2 tablespoons olive oil
parsley, separated into small sprigs (for garnish)

For the pear garnish:
  1 large pear
  ½ lemon
  1½ cups red wine

For the sweetened ginger:
  1½-inch (4 cm) piece of fresh ginger
  ¼ cup (50 g) sugar
  1 cup (250 ml) water

SERVES 4.

Make the fresh pasta and cut it into noodles.

For the pear garnish: Peel the pear and rub it with the cut lemon so it won't darken. Quarter and core the pear, put it in a small saucepan, and pour in the red wine. Poach over low heat until just tender, 10–15 minutes. Cover and leave to cool in the wine. The pear can be cooked ahead of time and kept, covered and refrigerated, for 1 day.

For the sweetened ginger: Peel the ginger and cut the flesh in very fine julienne strips. Blanch by putting in a pan of cold water, bringing to a boil, and then draining. In a small saucepan heat the sugar and water together over low heat until dissolved. Bring to a boil, remove from the heat, and add the ginger. Leave to cool. The ginger can be kept, covered and refrigerated, for 1 day.

Cut up the rabbit (see p. 41), leaving the back all in one piece. Bone the rabbit pieces, reserving the bones: Carefully remove the strip of meat from each side of the backbone. There will be 2 long pieces. Bone each leg by slitting the meat down to the bone and then scraping the flesh away from the bone all the way around until meat and bone are separated. (See Chapter 7 for additional information on boning.)

Heat 2 tablespoons of the oil in a heavy pan and add the bones. Brown them over high heat. Add the onion, carrot, and shallots and cook over medium heat until lightly browned, 7–10 minutes. Add 1 cup (250 ml) of the wine in which the pears were poached, the coriander, thyme, bouquet garni, crushed peppercorns, a little salt, and the stock. Simmer uncovered, skimming occasionally, for 1 hour. Strain into a shallow pan and boil until reduced to 1 cup (250 ml).

Reserve the back meat and cut the rest in thick diagonal strips. Heat the remaining 2 tablespoons of oil in a heavy-bottomed saucepan over high heat until very hot. Add the rabbit strips and brown on all sides. Lower the heat, sprinkle salt and pepper over the rabbit pieces, cover, and gently cook for 5 minutes. Add the ½ cup (125 ml) red wine, bring to a boil, and then simmer for 5 minutes. Add the reduced stock made from the bones. Remove the ginger from its syrup and add it to the pan. Cover and continue to simmer until the rabbit pieces are nearly tender, about 15 minutes. Uncover and simmer until tender, about 5 minutes. Taste for seasoning and adjust if necessary.

In a sauté pan heat the clarified butter, add the strips of back meat, sprinkle with salt and pepper, and brown lightly. Cover and cook over low heat until tender, about 10 minutes longer.

Cook the pasta and toss with the olive oil. Reheat the pear in its remaining wine.

To serve, cut the pear in diagonal slices and arrange 4 or 5 pieces overlapping on one side of each plate. Cut the back meat in diagonal slices and arrange them down the opposite sides of the plates. Put the noodles in the center of each plate and spoon the rabbit strips in the sauce over them. Decorate with the parsley sprigs and serve.

Nuts

As a child I hated nuts. There was something about their crunchiness, their earthy taste, that set my teeth on edge, and I fancied I could detect the smallest particle of nut in any dish. I was in my teens before I realized what I was missing. Enlightenment began with macaroons, and from there I progressed rapidly to almond cakes and—dare I breathe the name—peanut butter. At last the chestnut filling in the Christmas turkey no longer elicited a moue of distaste but tempted me to a second helping.

But the full impact of nuts in cooking did not burst upon me until I came to France. Who else would have thought of putting pistachios into a terrine or making a velouté soup garnished with chicken quenelles and hazelnuts? I became aware of the subtleties of white praline, made with ground blanched almonds and sugar syrup, and dark praline made with unblanched almonds and caramelized sugar—the difference between the two being rather like that between white and black pepper. White praline is used almost exclusively to decorate the chewy nut-based meringue gâteaux of which the French are so fond, but dark praline is a universal flavoring for the pastry and butter creams, for ice cream, and custards, nearly as useful as coffee and chocolate.

In the nut family, almonds surely rank first as far as the French cook is concerned. Almond-meringue-based dacquoise (p. 295), almond petits fours (p. 317), macaroons, gâteau Alcazar with its almond-flavored filling, all are staples of the modern *pâtissier*'s repertoire. And medieval cooks appreciated almonds even more. Their cultivation in Europe was encouraged by the Arabs, who loved marzipan, nougat, and other nutty sweetmeats. In the fourteenth century, Taillevent, cook to King Charles VI of France, bound sauces with ground almonds and, of course, used them as the principal ingredient in blancmange (white food), a symbol of purity. Blancmange could be made of any white mixture, not necessarily sweet; it was often based on chicken or veal combined with ground almonds.

The French, with some inspiration from the Italians, also exploit chestnuts to the full. These nuts contain more starch and less oil than most and so can be cooked differently. They are the only nut that is treated like a vegetable, and at La Varenne, Chef Chambrette has a special way of glazing chestnuts (p. 44) to a lustrous brown for serving with turkey, goose, and especially game. Chestnuts are often simmered and puréed to accompany meat dishes or to make soup or desserts like petits Monts Blancs (p. 297) and pavé aux marrons (p. 423).

Of the other common nuts, pistachios are valued in cooking mainly for their color. For a truly brilliant green, you should shell them and then boil them in water for a few moments before peeling off the inner skin. They are used for decorating pastries and provide a vivid note when mixed in a terrine (see p. 157), stuffing for galantine, or the new "sausages" of shellfish. Hazelnuts are used ground in cakes and pastries and whole for decoration. Walnuts can double for hazelnuts in baking, but they are usually not browned because this can make them bitter. They are best, I think, in first-course vegetable salads, to which the nuts add texture, and walnut oil can be used in the dressing. Such combinations are typical of the nouvelle cuisine.

This oil content of nuts is important in cooking. Nuts with a good deal of oil like almonds, peanuts, hazelnuts, and walnuts must be ground carefully and handled lightly during mixing if the oil is not to separate and make the mixture heavy. Peanut oil, light and with a high scorching point, is excellent for deep frying and as a neutral element in salad dressings. The use of walnut oil is a matter of taste—its flavor is pronounced, and, delicious though it may be in dressings, a little goes a long way.

Because of their oil content, nuts easily turn rancid—and with a rancid mixture, nothing can be done. Nuts should therefore always be stored in an airtight container, preferably at a low temperature. They should also be chopped or ground just before using since once cut, they deteriorate rapidly. Nuts keep much better in their shells and freeze excellently.

Nut trees, and the recipes that go with them, are very much a matter of the local soil and climate. Almond trees withstand frost; chestnut trees can be found in most places, but plump chestnuts worth the peeling come mainly from central France, Italy, and Spain. Although hazelnuts grow all over Europe, we have dozens of the bushes in our garden in Normandy that never seem to produce a nut, and walnut trees can be equally cantankerous, as expressed in this now unpopular old saying, "A woman, a dog, and a walnut tree, the more you beat 'em, the better they be."

FOR SUCCESSFUL NUT DISHES

1. Almonds and pistachios are blanched in boiling water for 1 minute before peeling. Take a blanched nut between your thumb and index finger, press firmly, and the nut will pop from the skin.

2. Chestnuts are blanched before shelling and peeling. Take them from the hot water one by one while peeling and reheat them if they become hard to peel as they cool.

3. Hazelnuts are toasted until the skins crack and start to peel. Let the nuts cool slightly and then rub off the skins with a cloth.

4. Walnuts are somewhat troublesome to peel and are usually left as is.

5. Nuts are best ground by hand with a rotary cheese grater because this method does not bring out their oil. However, they can be ground in small quantities in a food processor provided they are not worked too long; if flour or sugar is to be added to the ground nuts, you can make the addition while the nuts are in the machine so as to keep them as dry as possible.

PREPARING AHEAD

1. Nuts can be peeled and kept in an airtight container for several weeks. Be sure they are very dry before storing.

2. Nuts can be toasted and kept tightly covered.

3. Store ground nuts in an airtight container and keep them for as short a time as possible.

4. Because of the high oil content, mixtures containing nuts mellow on keeping. Nut cakes, cookies, and pastries should be stored in an airtight container. They freeze well.

5. If nut pastry softens on standing, reheat it in a low oven to dry it; it will become crisp as it cools.

Salade Muguette
(SALADE MUGUETTE)

Once rare, salads combining fruit, vegetables, and nuts are now very much the rage in France.

   1 celery heart
   1 medium head of curly endive
   vinaigrette (p. 348) made with 1 tablespoon vinegar,
       salt and pepper, ½ teaspoon Dijon mustard, and 3
       tablespoons oil
   2 tablespoons heavy cream
   2 apples
   4 medium tomatoes, peeled, seeded, and chopped
   ¾ cup (90 g) walnuts, chopped
   salt and pepper

SERVES 4.

Cut the celery heart in julienne strips and soak for 1–2 hours in ice water to crisp. Trim the greens, discarding all the tough deep-green outer leaves, wash, and dry well.

Make the vinaigrette in a large bowl and whisk in the cream so the dressing thickens slightly. Wash the apples but do not peel. Quarter, core, and slice them and toss with the vinaigrette to prevent discoloration. Drain the celery, pat dry on paper towels, and add to the apples in the bowl along with the tomato and walnut pieces. Toss and season to taste. Arrange the greens around the edge of a salad bowl and mound the salad in the center. It can be kept, covered and refrigerated, for up to 2 hours.

Hungarian Nut Cake
(GÂTEAU HONGROIS AUX NOIX)

This rich mixture, scarcely a cake at all, is baked in a water bath to ensure that it will cook slowly and evenly.

   ¾ cup (95 g) hazelnuts
   1¾ cups (210 g) walnuts
   3½ ounces (105 g) semisweet chocolate
   5 eggs, separated
   ½ cup (100 g) sugar

   7-inch (18 cm) kugelhopf mold or bundt pan

SERVES 8.

Toast the hazelnuts in a 350°F (175°C) oven until the skins crack and start to peel. Let the nuts cool slightly and then rub off the skins with a cloth. Grind the hazelnuts and the walnuts in a rotary cheese grater or a food processor. Reduce the oven heat to 300°F (150°C), butter the mold generously, and prepare a water bath (see Chapter 8).

Melt the chocolate in a water bath and set aside. Beat the egg yolks with all but 2 tablespoons of the sugar until light. Stir in the ground walnuts and hazelnuts and melted chocolate and mix well. Beat the egg whites until stiff, adding the remaining sugar, and beat until glossy, about 20 seconds longer. Stir a quarter of the egg whites into the nut mixture and then fold this mixture into the remaining egg whites. Pour the batter into the prepared mold, set in the water bath, and bring to a simmer on top of the stove. Transfer to the heated oven and bake until a skewer inserted in the middle of the cake comes out clean, about 1½ hours. Allow the cake to cool thoroughly before turning it out of the mold.

Hazelnut Cake with Pineapple
(GÂTEAU DE NOISETTES AUX ANANAS)

This is a luscious concoction of hazelnut pastry, sandwiched with Chantilly cream and pineapple and topped with a cream-fruit-pastry pinwheel.

Chantilly cream (p. 285) made with 1½ cups (375 ml)
heavy cream, 1 tablespoon sugar, and 1 teaspoon
vanilla extract
1 large pineapple, peeled, sliced, and cored

For the pastry:
2 cups (260 g) hazelnuts
1¼ cups (160 g) flour
½ teaspoon salt
⅔ cup (135 g) sugar
¼ pound (125 g) butter, softened
1 egg yolk

pastry bag with medium star tip

SERVES 8.

For the pastry: Toast the hazelnuts in a 350°F (175°C) oven until the skins crack and begin to peel. Let the nuts cool slightly and then rub off the skins with a cloth. Grind the nuts in a rotary cheese grater or a food processor. Sift the flour with the salt onto a work surface and add the ground nuts and sugar. Make a well in the center of the flour mixture, add the softened butter and the egg yolk, and work them to a paste with the fingertips. Gradually draw in the flour, working the dough between the fingers until it forms large crumbs. When well mixed, press the dough into a ball, wrap, and chill until firm, about 1 hour.

Heat the oven to 375°F (190°C). Divide the dough into 3 equal portions and roll out each portion to an 8-inch (20 cm) round. Transfer the rounds very carefully to baking sheets and bake in the heated oven until golden brown, 10–12 minutes. While the rounds are still warm, trim them neatly with a knife, using a plate or pan lid as a guide. Cut one round into 8 equal wedges using a long serrated knife. Transfer the pastry to racks to cool. It can be kept up to 5 days in an airtight container, or it can be frozen.

Make the Chantilly cream. Cut 3 of the pineapple slices into thirds and set aside 8 of the thirds. Set one round of pastry on a serving plate. Spread it with ⅙ of the Chantilly cream and top with the remaining sliced pineapple. Cover with another ⅙ of the cream, set the second round of pastry on top, and spread another ⅙ of the cream on top. Spoon the remaining cream into the pastry bag and pipe 8 decorative lines from the edge of the round to the center, thus dividing the round into 8 equal sections. Press each wedge of pastry into the cream at an angle so it rests on a line of cream. Set one of the reserved pieces of pineapple on each of the 8 pastry wedges. Finish the cake with a rosette of cream in the middle and chill until served.

Peeling toasted hazelnuts by rubbing them in a cloth

One round of the hazelnut pastry is cut into eight wedges.

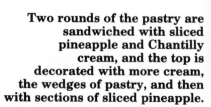

Two rounds of the pastry are sandwiched with sliced pineapple and Chantilly cream, and the top is decorated with more cream, the wedges of pastry, and then with sections of sliced pineapple.

Chestnut Paving Stone
(PAVÉ AUX MARRONS)

The name of this dessert refers to its appearance, which resembles that of the wooden blocks which used to line the streets of Paris.

> **2 pounds (1 kg) fresh chestnuts or 1½ pounds (750 g)**
>   **canned unsweetened whole chestnuts or chestnut**
>   **purée**
> **1 vanilla bean OR 1 teaspoon vanilla extract**
> **½ pound (250 g) semisweet chocolate, chopped**
> **½ cup (125 ml) water**
> **6 ounces (180 g) butter**
> **1 cup (200 g) sugar**
> **2 tablespoons brandy**
>
> ***9- × 5- × 3-inch (23 × 13 × 7.5 cm) loaf pan***

SERVES 8.

Lightly oil the loaf pan, line the base with waxed paper, and oil the paper.

To peel the chestnuts: Prick the shell of each nut with a knife. Put the nuts in a pan of cold water, bring to a boil, and then take from the heat and peel while still hot. Remove both outer and inner skin.

Put the peeled nuts in a saucepan with the vanilla bean, if using, and enough water to cover. Cover the pan and simmer until the nuts are tender, 25–30 minutes. Canned nuts needn't be cooked. Remove the vanilla bean, drain the nuts, and purée in a food processor or work through a food mill.

Melt the chocolate in the ½ cup (125 ml) water over low heat. Let it cool. Cream the butter and beat in the sugar until smooth and light. Stir in the cooled chocolate and then the chestnut purée, brandy, and vanilla extract, if using, and mix until smooth. Pack the mixture into the prepared pan, cover, and chill overnight. The pavé can be kept, refrigerated, for up to a week, or it can be frozen.

To serve, turn the pavé out onto a platter and mark the top in a lattice pattern with the back of a knife.

Choux Pralinés
(CHOUX PRALINÉS)

Classic butter cream flavored with praline makes a meltingly rich filling for these petits fours.

⅔ cup (90 g) chopped almonds
choux pastry (p. 225) made with 1 cup (130 g) flour, 1
  cup (250 ml) water, ¾ teaspoon salt, ¼ pound (125 g)
  butter, 4–5 eggs
1 egg, beaten to mix with salt
powdered sugar (for dusting)

For the filling:
butter cream (p. 282) made with 3 egg yolks, ½ cup
  (100 g) sugar, ¼ cup (60 ml) water, 6 ounces (180 g)
  butter
⅓ cup (100 g) praline (p. 425)

pastry bag with ⅜-inch (1 cm) plain tip

MAKES ABOUT 4 DOZEN CHOUX.

For the filling: Make the butter cream and praline and combine. This mixture can be made ahead and kept, covered and refrigerated, for up to a week.

Toast the chopped almonds in a 350°F (175°C) oven until golden brown. Heat the oven to 400°F (200°C) and lightly butter 2 baking sheets. Make the choux dough, spoon it into the pastry bag, and pipe ¾-inch (2 cm) mounds well apart onto the prepared baking sheets or, alternatively, shape the choux with two spoons. Brush with the beaten egg, score lightly with the tines of a fork, and sprinkle with the browned almonds. Bake in the heated oven until the puffs are firm and brown, 20–25 minutes. While they are still warm, make a hole in the bottom of each puff with the pastry tip to let the steam escape.

Scoop the butter cream into the pastry bag and pipe butter cream into each puff. Dust the tops with powdered sugar. Serve these petits fours within 2 hours of making them.

Praline
(PRALINE)

Since praline keeps so well, it is an extremely convenient flavoring to keep on hand. You'll find you use it for everything from a spectacular soufflé to a simple ice-cream topping.

⅓ cup (50 g) unblanched whole almonds
¼ cup (50 g) sugar

MAKES ⅓ CUP (100 g) PRALINE.

Oil a marble slab or a baking sheet. Combine the almonds and sugar in a heavy-bottomed pan. Stir over low heat until the sugar melts. Continue cooking slowly until the sugar turns a golden brown and the almonds pop. Pour the mixture onto the prepared marble slab or baking sheet and leave until cool and crisp. Grind to a powder, a little at a time, in a rotary cheese grater or a food processor. The praline can be kept for several weeks in an airtight container.

Orange Almond Balls
(BOULES À L'ORANGE)

Turn these into boules au citron by using candied lemon peel if you prefer. The boules are very much like macaroons but are easier to make.

1¾ cups (260 g) blanched whole almonds
1¼ cups (250 g) granulated sugar
1 cup (125 g) candied orange peel, chopped
2–3 egg whites, lightly beaten
1 egg white, lightly beaten (to finish)
powdered sugar (for dusting)

MAKES ABOUT 45 BOULES.

Oil a baking sheet lightly and line it with parchment paper. Set the oven at 400°F (200°C). Grind the almonds with the granulated sugar in a food processor. With the machine still on, gradually add the candied peel and then enough egg white so the mixture is moist enough to shape but not sticky. Turn the mixture out onto a work surface dusted with powdered sugar and roll into a ball. Divide the ball in two and roll each half into a cylinder about an inch (2.5 cm) in diameter. Cut the cylinders into 1-inch (2.5 cm) pieces and roll each piece into a ball. Roll the balls in the 1 lightly beaten egg white and then in powdered sugar and put them on the prepared baking sheet.

Bake in the heated oven until they crack on top but are still soft inside, 10–12 minutes. Remove them from the paper and transfer to a wire rack to cool. If it is difficult to remove the boules from the paper, lift one end of the paper slightly and pour a glass of water under the paper onto the baking sheet. The hot baking sheet will cause steam to form, making it easy to remove the boules after a few minutes. The boules can be stored for 1–2 weeks in an airtight container, but they tend to harden with time.

Index